CAMBODIA VOTES

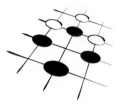

Governance in Asia

Series Editor: Tak-Wing Ngo, Professor of Political Science, University of Macau
(twngo@umac.mo)

Most Asian countries have experienced radical social transformation in the past decades. Some have undergone democratization yet are still plagued by problems of political instability, official malfeasance and weak administration. Others have embraced market liberalization but are threatened by rampant rent seeking and business capture. Without exception, they all face the challenge of effective governance. This book series explores how Asian societies and markets are governed in the rapidly changing world and explores the problem of governance from an Asian perspective. It also encourages studies sensitive to the autochthony and hybridity of Asian history and development, which locate the issue of governance within specific meanings of rule and order, structures of political authority and mobilization of institutional resources distinctive to the Asian context. The series aims to publish timely and well-researched books that will have the cumulative effect of developing theories of governance pertinent to Asian realities.

Also published in this series

Politicized Society: The Long Shadow of Taiwan's One-Party Legacy, by Mikael Mattlin

Negotiating Autonomy in Greater China: Hong Kong and Its Sovereign Before and After 1997, edited by Ray Yep

Governing Civil Service Pay in China, by Alfred M. Wu

China's Contested Internet, edited by Guobin Yang

NIAS Press is the autonomous publishing arm of NIAS – Nordic Institute of Asian Studies, a research institute located at the University of Copenhagen. NIAS is partially funded by the governments of Denmark, Finland, Iceland, Norway and Sweden via the Nordic Council of Ministers, and works to encourage and support Asian studies in the Nordic countries. In so doing, NIAS has been publishing books since 1969, with more than two hundred titles produced in the past few years.

UNIVERSITY OF COPENHAGEN

Nordic Council of Ministers

CAMBODIA VOTES

Democracy, Authority and
International Support for Elections
1993–2013

Michael Sullivan

*Cambodia Votes: Democracy, Authority and
International Support for Elections 1993–2013*
Michael Sullivan

Nordic Institute of Asian Studies
Governance in Asia series, no. 5

First published in 2016 by NIAS Press
NIAS – Nordic Institute of Asian Studies
Øster Farimagsgade 5, 1353 Copenhagen K, Denmark
Tel: +45 3532 9503 • Fax: +45 3532 9549
E-mail: books@nias.ku.dk • Online: www.niaspress.dk

A CIP catalogue record for this book is available from the British Library

ISBN: 978-87-7694-186-4 (hbk)
ISBN: 978-87-7694-187-1 (pbk)

Typesetting by Lene Jakobsen
Printed and bound in Great Britain by
Marston Book Services Limited, Oxfordshire

Cover image: Cambodian Prime Minister Hun Sen casts his ballot
at a polling station in Kandal province, Cambodia, on 28 July 2013
during the country's fifth national assembly elections (photo: Khem
Sovannara, with permission EPA/Scanpix).

Contents

Foreword

As the Executive Director of Cambodia's largest election monitoring organization, the Committee for Free and Fair elections (COMFREL), it gives me great pleasure to contribute to this timely and detailed study of Cambodia's elections for the two decades after the historic United Nations-organized and -managed elections in 1993. Michael Sullivan's book provides an in-depth analysis, rich in detail, of how electoral politics in Cambodia has evolved since 1993, culminating in the dramatic parliamentary elections in 2013. Some western scholars sometimes view elections in Cambodia as one-time events. This book's chronological narrative clearly shows that this is not the case here. To date, Cambodia's elections, both local and national, have been connected events in the overall evolution of the country's political-economic system. In this regard Sullivan's study is a unique study on the subject.

In the last two decades, organizations like my own have been working hard to establish elections as instruments that can be relied upon to deliver results and outcomes deemed acceptable enough for all players in the game. Given the high political and economic stakes, this continues to be an extremely difficult, frustrating and dangerous enterprise. Powerful political forces within the dominant Cambodian People's Party (CPP) have consistently and unremittingly manipulated the electoral process to ensure the outcomes they desire. Manipulation over the years has included a variety of strategies involving lethal force, intimidation, coercion, threats, bribery, use of state resources, control of media, and administrative and bureaucratic malfeasance.

And yet despite these circumstances we and others like us, who want to see a freer and fairer system of electoral politics, continue to do what we can. We survive and have made steady progress in disseminating the message to larger numbers of people in order to bring about positive social and political change. Like Cambodia's organized political opposition parties we survive because we keep the system credible enough to satisfy the needs and interests of Cambodia's international partners and donors. Michael Sullivan's book does an excellent job of explaining how international assistance with elections has simultaneously reinforced the position of both authoritarian elements within the state and those political and non-state actors who challenge the status quo through elections. This has given rise to a situation that can be best described by what some scholars of elections have termed electoral authoritarianism. Simply put, under these conditions opposition parties get to compete in elections, supported and observed by international actors, that seem competitive enough but they can never really win because of authoritarian manipulation and meddling.

The book is timely because the closely contested results of the 2013 national elections sent shockwaves throughout the ranks of the CPP when that party lost 22 seats in the national assembly. This suggested the CPP's grip on controlling electoral outcomes might be loosening. Emboldened by the results, the main opposition party Cambodian National Rescue Party (CNRP) pushed the government to enact electoral reform in time for the crucial 2017 local and 2018 national elections. Cautiously, a civil society grouping calling itself the Electoral Reform Alliance (ERA) did what it could to ensure the best possible outcomes of the reform process. When the reforms came, we found that some were positive while others fell short of expectations. On the positive side there was bi-partisan agreements on a re-structured National Election Committee (NEC) and reform of the voter registration process. But worryingly there are lingering concerns that the new NEC will not be able to fully execute its duties and responsibilities independently and without fear. Of greater concern was the breakdown of an apparent rapprochement between the Prime Minister, Hun Sen, and president of the CNRP, Sam Rainsy, not long after the reforms were enacted. What followed was an all too familiar round of repression involving violence and legal harassment of CNRP officials.

The latest round of repression took many by surprise, coming as it did before the electoral cycle got started proper. But as Sullivan's study suggests, the CPP was probably facing the greatest electoral threat in 2018 to its positions of power than at any other time since before the 1998 elections. Thus, discussion in Phnom Penh and elsewhere about how a possible transfer of power in 2018 might be managed was rife, fuelling tension among the political elite on both sides. By the end of 2015, the CNRP president was again in self-imposed exile overseas and his party's leadership faced further repression and harassment in Phnom Penh. In time-honoured fashion, blatant attempts by the CPP to discredit, marginalize and break up the CNRP was an obvious indication that a peaceful transfer of power in 2018 was a remote possibility.

Be that as it may, over the course of two decades, electoral politics have evolved to a point where in 2013 they posed a serious threat to the entrenched power of the CPP. As the book makes clear, there is a younger generation of Cambodians who appear less fearful in exercising civil and political rights and participating in democratic processes like elections. Cambodia's youth, equipped with electronic mobile devices and with access to the Internet and social media, may well determine future electoral outcomes. How the CPP responds to future election challenges remains to be seen. Suffice it to say here, elections and electoral competition will be at the forefront of the struggle between authoritarians controlling the state and political and civil forces challenging their power.

The book is very much relevant to the work of my organization and others engaged with elections in Cambodia. It also provides international actors and agencies with a comprehensive account of international assistance and engagement with Cambodia's elections over the last twenty years. In this regard, *Cambodia Votes: Democracy, Authority and International Support for Elections 1993–2013* is long overdue and a welcome addition to the literature on contemporary Cambodian politics and international relations. It is an indispensible reference book for practitioners, theorists, activists and students engaged in elections everywhere.

Koul Panha, Executive Director of the Committee for Free and Fair Elections in Cambodia (COMFREL), September 2016

Acknowledgments

Many people contributed to making this book a reality. Some of the early chapters evolved out of a PhD dissertation at the University of London's School of Oriental and African Studies (SOAS) supervised by Steve Heder. Access to Steve's UNTAC archive and other research materials was invaluable. Special thanks go to Steve for pushing me toward the analysis of Cambodian elections. His generosity and support over the last decade has been extraordinary and greatly appreciated. I would also like to thank Brad Adams for access to documents from his archival materials. Initial fieldwork research was made possible by a studentship from the Economic and Social Research Council (ESRC) in the UK. I would like to thank John Vijghen for the valuable use of office space in Cambodia. Other research opportunities would not have been possible without the help and resources provided by staff from the Committee for Free and Fair Elections in Cambodia, especially from Executive Director Koul Panha, Kim Chhorn, Neang Sovann, Vong Sotheara and Phat Sopheak. Tem Pharath and Chheang Sophanna deserve thanks for their infinite patience and good humour during frequent fieldwork trips away from home. For work on early versions of the manuscript, I would like to thank Richard Crasta and Suzanne Freilich both of whom provided editorial advice and made corrections.

No worthwhile work is possible without the love and support of friends and family. Sasha Constable was the first to make me welcome when I began my five-year stint in Siem Reap province and has been supportive ever since. Thanks go to Rafael Winer for his contribution to the book's title. In Phnom Penh, Michael Powell has long suffered my frequent rants about Cambodian electoral politics and was extremely supportive during the review process. Our frequent motorcycle trips to the far corners of Kampong Cham province are sorely missed. Since 2008 Michael Hodgson and I have shared many other motorcycle adventures all over Cambodia witnessing first-hand the dramatic socio-economic and environmental changes the country has been undergoing since 2002. His witty and intelligent analysis is a welcome antidote to some of the more egregious political realities and frustrations encountered by foreigners choosing to live and work in Cambodia. Lee-Anne Pitcaithly's exuberance and advice on all matters is pretty hard to match. Finally, none of this could have been possible without the unstinting love and support of my mother Eileen.

Glossary

khum	commune, the third-level administrative division in Cambodia, a sub-unit of the district
krama	traditional Khmer scarf
phum	village, a sub-unit of the commune
phumpheak	zone, more often used in military contexts
sarong	traditional Khmer skirt (also sampot)
youn	Vietnamese

Abbreviations and Acronyms

ADB	Asian Development Bank
ADHOC	Cambodian Human Rights and Development Association
ANFREL	Asian Network for Free Elections
ASEAN	Association of Southeast Asian Nations
BLDP	Buddhist Liberal Democratic Party
CC	Constitutional Council
CCHR	Cambodian Center for Human Rights
CDC	Commune Development Committee
CEC	Communal Election Committee
CDRI	Cambodian Development Resource Institute
CFF	Cambodian Freedom Fighters
CG	Consultative Group (of donors)
CGDK	Coalition Government of Democratic Kampuchea
CIHR	Cambodian Institute for Human Rights
CIVPOL	UNTAC civilian police
CLEC	Community Legal Education Center
CNRP	Cambodian National Rescue Party
COFFEL	Coalition for Free and Fair Elections
COMFREL	Committee for Free and Fair Elections
CPAF	Cambodian People's Armed Forces
CPP	Cambodian People's Party
CSD	Center for Social Development
DES	district election supervisors
DK	Democratic Kampuchea (Khmer Rouge)

EAD	UN Electoral Assistance Division
EAS	Elections Assistance Secretariat
ECCEU	Election Complaints, Compliance and Enforcement Unit
ELC	Economic Land Concession
EMO	electoral monitoring organization
ESU	UNDP Electoral Support Unit
EU	European Union
EUEOM	European Union Election Observer Mission
FEMA	Fair Election Monitoring Alliance (Bangladesh)
FOC	'Friends of Cambodia' group
F'pec	Front Uni National pour un Cambodge Indépendant, Neutre, Pacifique et Cooperatif
FTUWKC	Free Trade Union Workers of the Kingdom of Cambodia
FUNSK	United Front for the Salvation of Kampuchea
FUNCINPEC	See F'pec
GMS	Greater Mekong Sub-Region
HDI	Human Development Index
HRP	Human Rights Party
HRW	Human Rights Watch
ICTR	International Criminal Tribunal for Rwanda
ICTY	International Criminal Tribunal for the former Yugoslavia
IFES	International Foundation for Electoral Systems (US-based)
IRI	International Republican Institute
JIMs	Jakarta Informal Meetings
JIOG	Joint International Observer Group
KAF	Konrad Adenauer Foundation
KID	Khmer Institute of Democracy
KNP	Khmer Nation Party

KPNLF	Khmer People's National Liberation Front
KPRP	Kampuchean People's Revolutionary Party
KWVC	Khmer Women's Voice Center
LEMNA	Law on the Election of Members to the National Assembly
LICADHO	Cambodian League for the Promotion and Defense of Human Rights
LMAP	Land Mapping and Administration Project
LTO	Long Term Observers
MoI	Ministry of the Interior
NADK	National Army of Democratic Kampuchea
NAMFREL	National Citizens' Movement for Free and Fair Elections (Philippines)
NDI	National Democratic Institute for International Affairs
NEC	National Election Committee
NECC	National Election Computer System
NGO	non-governmental organization
NGOCC	NGO Coordinating Committee
NICFEC	Neutral Independent Committee for Free and Fair Elections in Cambodia
NPE	'neutral political environment'
NPGC	National Provisional Government of Cambodia
NRP	Norodom Ranariddh Party
NSP	National Solidarity Party
NUF	National United Front
NVCR	National Voice of Cambodia Radio
PDK	Party of Democratic Kampuchea (Khmer Rouge)
PEC	Provincial Election Committee
PGNSNSC	Provisional Government of National Solidarity and National Salvation of Cambodia
PIB	NEC Public Information Bureau

PPA	Paris Peace Agreements
PRK	People's Republic of Kampuchea
PWG	party working group
RCAF	Royal Cambodian Armed Forces
RFA	Radio Free Asia
RGC	Royal Government of Cambodia
SCM	Supreme Council of the Magistracy
SGRC	UN Secretary-General's Representative in Cambodia
SNC	Supreme National Council
SoC	State of Cambodia
SRSG	Special Representative of the Secretary-General of the United Nations
SRP	Sam Rainsy's Party
TAF	The Asia Foundation
UNAMIC	United Nations Advance Mission in Cambodia
UCD	Union of Cambodian Democrats
UN	United Nations
UNDP	United Nations Development Programme
UNDPA	United Nations Department for Political Affairs
UNEAS	see EAS
UNOHCHRC	United Nations Office of the High Commissioner for Human Rights in Cambodia
UNOSGRC	Office of the UN Secretary-General's Representative in Cambodia
UNTAC	United Nations Transitional Authority in Cambodia
USAID	US Agency for International Development
VDC	Village Development Committee
VIN	Voter Information Notice
VOA	Voice of America
VOCE	Volunteers of the Cambodian Elections
VRA	voter registration audit

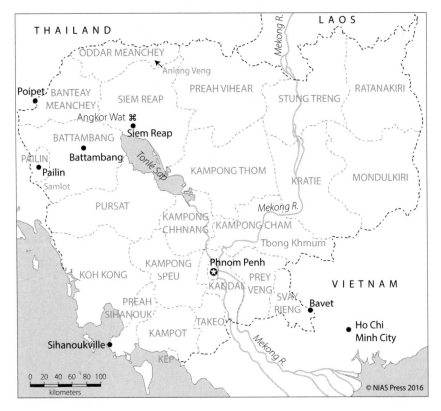

Map of Cambodia

Note: In 2014 Tbong Khmum district in Kompung Cham province became its own province.

Introduction

On 23 May 1993, millions of Cambodians turned out to vote in elections they hoped would end years of armed conflict and allow desperately needed international aid for reconstruction and development to flow into the crippled country. The elections were unique. Never before had national elections in a sovereign state been conceived, planned and organized by foreigners to the extent they had been in Cambodia. They were the culmination of an unprecedented and complex international operation known by the acronym UNTAC, the United Nations Transitional Authority in Cambodia. Irrespective of its successes and failures, UNTAC's impact on Cambodia's political and socio-economic development has been undeniably profound. As a result, a fusion of national and international dynamics and interests has produced a relatively stable but hotly contested political economic system. Political stability and economic transformation have been uncertain and disproportionate frequently punctuated by statesponsored violence and repression of new social and political forces unleashed in the UNTAC period, embodying alternative ideas about the country's future development.

At the centre of this struggle between opposing forces is the question of the conduct and integrity of elections. Elections are the principal and formal mechanisms that help regulate and contain this struggle. Electoral politics evolved out of the UNTAC operation. The 1993 constitution promulgated after the elections in 1993 provided for periodic democratic multi-party elections. However, it said nothing about how these elections would be organized and conducted. As an independent and sovereign state after the transitional period, Cambodia was unable to organize and conduct elections without further significant international technical and financial support. International assistance for Cambodia's elections in the period after UNTAC contributed to what was already becoming a battle for control over the form and conduct of the electoral

1

system between authoritarian enclaves within the state and competing political and social forces.

This book seeks to understand and explain the impact the 1993 UNTAC elections had on the subsequent development of electoral politics in Cambodia up to and including polls in 2013. There are two principal reasons why this is important. Firstly, the Cambodian experience is unique in the fields of political transitions and electoral studies. International involvement and control of the transitional elections process was unparalleled in the early 1990s. Continued international technical and financial assistance for electoral development and engagement after UNTAC is a key variable in understanding the ensuing struggle for control over the processes and the outcomes of elections. Furthermore, new social and political forces that emerged from the UNTAC operation became significant players in the evolution of electoral politics. Secondly, the Cambodian experience provides new insights into the inconsistencies and contradictions inherent in international support for multi-party democratic elections in conflict prone states. At the same time, the Cambodia case demonstrates that elections do hold out possibilities for meaningful social and political change despite manipulation and constraints placed upon them by authoritarian tendencies within the state apparatus.

Beginning with UNTAC in 1993, the book argues that internationally supported elections have been the central site in a struggle between opposing political and civil forces for access to and control of the Cambodian state. In the two decades since UNTAC, authoritarians within the Cambodian People's Party (CPP) led by Prime Minister Hun Sen have, through manipulation and force, successfully controlled and managed electoral politics to maintain power. In an internationalized local environment characterized by aid dependency and foreign direct investment elections have provided opportunities for alternative political and civil society forces to gain footholds and challenge the status quo.

In this time, Cambodia has held four more sets of parliamentary and three sets of local or commune council elections. With the exception of the 2012 local and 2013 parliamentary elections, all of these took place with significant international technical and financial support. Twenty years on, for the first time in 2013, there were clear signs that the CPP's control might be faltering as the main opposition force, the Cambodian

National Rescue Party (CNRP), made impressive gains in National Assembly elections, setting in motion the longest post-election political standoff in Cambodian political history. These impressive results, like those in 1993 and 1998, took almost everybody by surprise, especially considering the stranglehold Hun Sen and the CPP seemed to have on electoral politics. Elections, even those dominated by the power and money of the CPP, are meaningful, displaying the political, economic, social and cultural changes that had been underway in the country since UNTAC.

What follows is not just a story about Cambodia. The narrative also includes an account of international engagement and with support for Cambodian elections. In his address to UNTAC personnel just before the elections, Boutros Boutros-Ghali, the then Secretary General of the United Nations, summed up the importance of the elections when he said that it is 'not just the future of Cambodia that hangs in the balance', but the 'nature and scope of future United Nations mandates and operations all over the world'.[1] As such, they were much more than a convenient instrument for resolving a particularly troublesome Southeast Asian conflict at the end of the Cold War. With the arrival of UNTAC, Cambodia became a crucible within which post-Cold War international ideas about democracy, democratization and development were fused with the stark political and social realities of a country desperately struggling to come to terms with the devastation caused by its recent violent past. From the outset, the dramatic outcome of the UNTAC elections laid bare glaring differences between post-Cold War western, liberal democratic idealism and the expediency of establishing what US President George H. W. Bush referred to in his 1991 state of the union address as a 'new world order'.[2]

Boutros Boutros-Ghali and George H. W. Bush may possibly have had different interpretations about how a new world order would be established, but there was international consensus at the time that multi-party democratic elections were an indispensable part of the process. Almost

1. UNTAC Information Education Division, July 1993. Document in author's possession.
2. See for example State of the Union Address, George H. W. Bush, 29 January 1991, in http://www2.hn.psu.edu/faculty/jmanis/poldocs/uspressu/SUaddress GHWBush.pdf, p. 12.

two years later, UNTAC would play a central role in show-casing its establishment. Under the new order, the number of states seeking western aid and legitimacy through UN and internationally assisted elections grew dramatically. However, as the 1990s wore on, less than democratic electoral outcomes in places like Cambodia and elsewhere in the post-communist and developing worlds suggested that the peace, freedom and security espoused by western leaders in 1991 were far from being realized on the ground.

A decade later on 11 September 2001, terrorist attacks on the World Trade Center buildings in New York turned the world on its head. Any possibility of an expanded role for the UN as envisaged by the Secretary General in 1993 faded fast as the US and its allies prepared for war. The then US president, and son of G. H. W. Bush, George W. Bush and his allies presided over the neo-conservative response to the attacks with a 'War on Terror'. The devastating consequences of internationally led war in Afghanistan and the illegal invasion of Iraq by western allies caused irreversible damage to the US's reputation as defenders of global democracy and human rights. Widely reported human rights abuses at the US' Guantanamo Bay detention camps in Cuba and grotesque abuses perpetrated by US military personnel at Abu Ghraib prison in Iraq were some of the most vivid illustrations of renewed accusations of double standards seriously challenging the democratic and moral underpinnings of the new order.

International Support for Elections in the 1990s

The Cambodian experience provides fertile ground for a detailed examination of the impact international support for elections had for the trajectory of national political development. UNTAC's elections were a product of geopolitical expediency at the end of the Cold War. Subsequent international support after UNTAC also had a major bearing on the development of electoral politics throughout the 1990s and into the 21st century. Events in the 1990s, followed by the consequences of the 9/11 terror attacks, had a profound effect on the meanings attached to internationally supported elections in places like Cambodia which had undergone a political transition.

Debates among both theoreticians and practitioners of international democracy promotion focused on the mixed political outcomes of elections. At the heart of the debate was a question of timing or sequencing of transitional and post-conflict elections. That is to say, what ought to come first in countries making some form of political transition with little or no experience of democratic politics, and in the absence of the kinds of socio-economic pre-conditions often associated with the development of democracy elsewhere? On this side of the debate there were concerns that 'first time' or transitional elections, introduced into particular configurations of social and political conflict like those found in Cambodia, could actually hinder the development of genuine democratic politics. Transitional elections are therefore unlikely to lead to a fully-fledged democracy in societies with weak states, weak civil societies and where judiciaries are ineffective or there is an absence of the rule of law.[3]

India (handwritten marginalia)

This viewpoint asserts that international democracy promotion policies ought to focus on building and supporting viable and strong states and civil societies, and help ensure that civil and political rights and the rule of law are present before considering international assistance for these types of elections. On the other hand, opponents of this view maintain that international attention and resources ought to stay focused on elections. Underpinning this perspective is the idea that a focus on elections need not come at the expense of other aspects of the democratization process, such as the strengthening of states, support for civil societies, and the rule of law. This is because, 'elections open the window to a broader understanding of what is happening' in terms of social and political development in countries that underwent political transition in the early 1990s.[4]

This idea of elections as windows to a broader understanding of social and political change is a central theme that runs through this book. Much of the criticism levelled at international assistance for elections in places like Cambodia in the early 1990s was that, as quintessentially western liberal constructs, elections represented a minimalist conception of what democracy is, or ought to be. A questioning of Schumpeterian

---

3. O. V. Cranenburgh, International Policies to Promote African Democratization in Jean Grugel (ed.), *Democracy without Borders: Transnationalization and Conditionality in New Democracies*, Cambridge: Polity Press, 1999.

4. Elizabeth Spiro Clark, 'Why Elections Matter', *The Washington Quarterly*, Summer 2000.

and 'polyarchic' conceptualizations of democracy by scholars in this period thus had significant implications for the meanings attached to elections, not only in the west, but elsewhere in the post-communist and developing worlds. Consider the idea, for example, that 'to equate democracy with electoral competition for public office, or multi-partyism ... is to elevate a means into an end, to confuse an instrument with its purpose.'[5] Implicit in this statement is the question of what happens to democratic development, that is, democratization, in between electoral events. While this is no doubt an important question to be asked of the established western liberal democracies, it takes on a different meaning when raised in places like Cambodia where, in order to hold an election, an entire electoral infrastructure had to be built from scratch with an enormous amount of international financial and technical assistance.

In these circumstances, the creation and institutionalization of electoral systems and politics has fundamental and far-reaching implications, not only for national, social and political development, but also for a country's relations with international partners. Just as democracy in the west cannot simply be equated with electoral competition for public office or multi-partyism, elections such as those held in Cambodia in 1993 cannot be seen solely in western minimalist procedural terms, or as a means to a particular end. In instances where there was no electoral infrastructure and limited experience of multi-party democratic politics, the creation and institutionalization of the means, elections, becomes an end in themselves. The scale and reach of such a task is enormous, hugely complex and uncertain. It involves not only the operationalization of practical and logistical tasks associated with the mechanics of voting, but also the drafting and promulgation of a raft of election related legislation, and the formation of administration units to handle a multitude of associated tasks at national and local levels. At a more

---

5. See Joseph Schumpeter's frequently cited minimalist definition of democracy as 'that institutional arrangement for arriving at political decisions in which individuals acquire the power to decide by means of a competitive struggle for the people's vote', in J. A. Schumpeter, *Capitalism, Socialism, and Democracy*, London: Unwin University Books, p. 269. See Robert Dahl's institutions of 'polyarchy', which include a mix of representative government and citizen's right to information, expression, association and participation. See Robert Dahl, *Democracy and its Critics*, New Haven: Yale University Press, 1989 and. David Beetham, *Democracy and Human Rights*, Cambridge: Polity Press, 2000, p. 3.

fundamental level, where there were none before, political parties need to be formed, as do civil and media groups and organizations to help transform a population previously under the control of a one-party state system into an electorate capable of making an informed political choice in safety on polling day. Without the necessary state structures and technical and financial resources available, all of this must be achieved with the intrusive presence of large groups of foreigners.

International Assistance for Elections

Debates about international assistance for elections and other aspects of democratization comprise a set of assumptions about the promotion of liberal governance in so-called developing countries. Sequencing or timing of elections may actually be irrelevant in situations where established national power holders have no real interest in governing their countries along liberal democratic lines. In these circumstances, they may view elections as nothing more than a necessary condition for ensuring much needed international aid and legitimacy rather than a means to consolidate or further any process of democratization. Indeed, multi-party democratic elections actually threaten existing and entrenched authoritarian power structures within the state and society more generally. Elections are therefore mechanisms to be controlled and manipulated to guarantee the most favourable outcomes for authoritarian enclaves within the state, while ensuring international legitimacy and aid.

International assistance for elections is often requested by liberal-minded members of the regime. Assistance is offered based upon an assumption that the host country's government is committed to establishing democratic procedures and norms in the long term. Depending upon specific donor interests, flawed elections are tolerated to the extent that those interests can be realized. Continued assistance thus relies upon judgements about a government's commitment to democratization and the extent to which donors deem flawed elections acceptable enough based on subjective historical and cultural interpretations and conditions. In this way, internationally assisted elections are supposed to become part of a broader liberal governance agenda of reforms to be carried out by governments over time. However, in places like Cambodia, donor assistance for elections after UNTAC instead became an integral part of the democratic façade, promoted and maintained by authoritarian enclaves within the state, making it difficult to separate out the two.

By the mid-2000s, scholars of political transitions had developed the concept of 'electoral authoritarianism' to describe regimes that 'play the game of multi-party elections' but 'violate the liberal-democratic principles of freedom and fairness so profoundly and systematically as to render them instruments of authoritarian rule rather than 'instruments of democracy'.[6] Elections of this type are described as 'broadly inclusive' and 'minimally competitive' insofar as they are held under universal suffrage, and opposition parties, while denied outright victories, are allowed to win votes and seats. These elections are open in the sense that opposition parties are not subject to 'massive repression but may experience repressive treatment in selective and intermittent ways'.[7] Because of the severe and widespread extent to which these elections are subject to authoritarian manipulation, they can 'hardly qualify as democratic'.[8]

Manipulation by dominant authoritarian forces can take various forms. Legislation, rules and regulations governing elections can be 'discriminatory', placing obstacles in the way of, or preventing political parties, their supporters and candidates from competing on a level playing field. Civil and political rights of voters, opposition party activists, members and candidates are curtailed or denied. Restrictions are imposed on access to 'media and campaign finance'. Through coercion or corruption, opposition party members leave the opposition camp 'or votes and seats are simply redistributed through electoral fraud'.[9] To this list could be added an overall abuse of state resources and state personnel in the service of the authoritarians. Election commissions are exposed to influence and control, rendering them partial and untrustworthy. State officials at all levels of the administration, the police, the military and the security services engage in discriminatory practices, distribution of largesse through patronage and vote buying. Voters and opposition members, activists and candidates are subjected to physical

---

6. A. Schedler, *Electoral Authoritarianism: The Dynamics of Unfree Competition*, Boulder: Lynne Reinner, 2006, p. 3.

7. Ibid.

8. Ibid.

9. Ibid.

coercion, intimidation through arbitrary arrest and detention by state officials, and in severe cases murder.

All of the above manipulations have been persistent features of Cambodia's elections during and after UNTAC. International assistance for elections after UNTAC departed the country complicated national political development further. In the mid-1990s, the post-UNTAC coalition government, comprising two co-Prime Ministers, received direct technical and financial electoral support from multilateral agencies like the UN and foreign donor governments. This contributed to political party conflicts as the struggle began for control over the creation of the machinery and institutional rules of elections, especially the National Election Committee (NEC). Additionally, international NGO support for emergent civil groups with vested interests in the development of elections such as election monitoring, democracy promotion and human rights groups created a third dimension in the struggle to engage, educate and protect voter civil and political rights, and reform the system as it evolved.

The Cambodian experience with elections from 1993 to 2013 illustrates how the 'power of elections', tainted by violence, intimidation, repression, exclusion, discrimination and fraud can bring to the surface contradictions and inconsistencies in the international and national political game.[10] For this reason, international and national attempts to stabilize authoritarian rule in Cambodia through flawed elections post-UNTAC has only been partially successful. The necessary survival of credible opposition political parties and civil groups struggling to reform the electoral system has kept open the lid on a democratic impulse. Consequently, elections have been and will continue to be key sites of struggle and conflict among opposing political and civil groups for more political–economic accountability and transparency, and better governance from those laying alternative claims to state power.

So far, there has been no attempt in the existing literature to analyse Cambodia's elections since 1993 in a systematic fashion. There is a tendency to treat these elections in isolation from others, as distinct events. This book takes a different approach. It asserts that electoral politics is still evolving. Electoral politics in the period under review had not yet evolved to the point where all groups involved accepted outcomes as le-

---

10. Ibid., p 12.

gitimate. On the contrary each election event from 1993 to 2013 was part of this evolutionary process. In this sense, they are analysed as episodes in a continuous struggle to establish elections as instruments that can relied upon to deliver results and outcomes deemed acceptable enough for all players in the game. The following chapters are thus organized chronologically. A chronological approach makes it easier for the reader to follow what at times can be a difficult and complex narrative.

They offer a detailed account of each phase of the struggle for elite control over the election process and its outcomes. Chapter one describes conditions under which the 1993 UNTAC elections took place. At the beginning of 1979, Cambodia was at the centre of the Third Indochina War, which began not long after a large Vietnamese army invaded the country at the end of December 1978 and forced out the incumbent Communist Democratic Kampuchea (DK) regime, popularly referred to as the Khmer Rouge. The DK regime was led by Saloth Sar, known to the world as the notorious Pol Pot. The Cambodian Communists had seized control of the country after overthrowing a government led by the US-backed republican general Lon Nol in 1975. Lon Nol was a central figure in a bloodless coup that ousted Cambodia's enigmatic former King, Prince Norodom Sihanouk in 1970. Hand-picked by French colonialists, Sihanouk ruled the country as monarch from 1941. In 1955 he abdicated the throne officially to enter national politics, which he succeeded in dominating until his overthrow in the 1970 coup. The Vietnamese remained in Cambodia until 1989. Not long after their withdrawal peace agreements were signed in Paris in 1991, formally bringing the civil war to an end and initiating a period of uncertain recovery.

By the time of the first deployment of UNTAC in 1992, Cambodia had suffered over twenty years of violent unrest and armed conflict. The policies and actions of Sihanouk, Lon Nol, the Cambodian Communists, the United States and Vietnam turned out to be cataclysmic, tearing the small nation apart. During their short term in power the Khmer Rouge leadership was responsible for inhumane living and working conditions and the eventual murder and deaths of as many as two million people. After 1979, foreign opposition to the continued presence of the Vietnamese in Cambodia only made matters worse for the general population, if indeed things could be any worse. When the time came to seek a peaceful political resolution to the conflict, relations between warring Cambodian parties were bitter to the point that none could trust the other to organize free and fair elections, ultimately resulting in international intervention. By any standards, the organization and management of elections by outsiders under such circumstances was going to be a task of monumental proportions.

Chapter two deals with the uniqueness of the UNTAC elections. It seems fairly obvious that the organization of elections by foreigners in these exceptional conditions 'is fundamentally different from those organized under normal circumstances'.[11] The chapter examines these fundamental differences and the meanings elections had in the context of the resolution of the conflict. The main purpose of the elections was to transfer power to a democratically elected government that had national and international legitimacy, and was capable and willing to get on with the job of re-building Cambodia in partnership with foreign donors. There was also a broader assumption, or at least in some quarters there was hope, that elections would be the first step in the democratization process. Yet the distribution of political power in the newly-elected coalition government did not reflect the election results, placing a huge question mark over their legitimacy. The coalition was ultimately weak and unwieldy, having as it did two prime ministers who would attempt to share power equally. This outcome clearly demonstrated how elections could be used for a variety of purposes, some of which are not necessarily democratic.

This first set of elections should have established what scholars of elections have referred to as 'the ground rules for subsequent national-level politics'.[12] While this was to a large extent the case in Cambodia, they also had significant implications for the subsequent conduct of local electoral politics. UNTAC's efforts to prise the incumbent party away from the state apparatus were successful enough to allow elections to be held in a relatively 'neutral political environment'. In spite of the incumbent party's frequent violent resistance to UNTAC's efforts, UN personnel were able to penetrate rural areas and disseminate information about the vote, democracy and human rights more generally. Chapter

11. Krisna Kumar (ed.), *Postconflict Elections, Democratization and International Assistance*, Boulder: Lynne Reinner, 1998.

12. Robert Taylor (ed.), *The Politics of Elections in Southeast Asia*, Washington D.C.: Woodrow Wilson Center Press and Cambridge University Press, 1996, p. 7.

two looks in detail at the processes by which UNTAC achieved this objective from the perspective of the meanings attached to the elections by all national and international groups.

Rejection of the election results by the Cambodia People's Party (CPP) pressured the winners of the election, the Front Uni National pour un Cambodge Indépendante, Neutre, Pacifique et Cooperatif, (FUNCINPEC, hereafter F'pec), and the United Nations into acquiescing to CPP demands for a 50-50 share of power in the new government. In terms of the legitimacy of the elections, this was far from ideal. The alternative, a threat by the CPP to return to armed conflict if their demands were not met, was at the time totally unacceptable to almost all Cambodians and the UN. Withdrawal of the Khmer Rouge from the election process in 1992 and their continued armed resistance from their strongholds on the Thai–Cambodia border was no doubt a major factor in the deliberations over the power-sharing arrangement. Although not ideal, there was at least an expectation that the new coalition government might put differences aside to tackle this and other problems facing the country.

To that end, a constitution was finally promulgated in October 1993. It stated that Cambodia would follow a liberal democratic system underpinned by pluralism, and provided for periodic and genuine elections. It did not state how these elections were to take place or under what conditions. With the UNTAC structures dismantled, full sovereignty had been handed back to the Cambodian state. Hence a new election infrastructure had to be built, again from scratch. Without technical know-how and financial resources the new government sought international assistance from the United Nations and other international agencies. Chapter three explores how the government approached the UN with its plans to hold local and national elections. It examines the role and impact that lengthy and destabilizing election preparations had on the already deteriorating relationship between the co-prime ministers in the early to mid-1990s. In addition, the chapter considers the important ways in which opposition groups and civil organizations engaged in a struggle over the process and conduct of the preparations. It suggests that plans for local elections, followed directly by parliamentary elections, meant that the vital question of who controlled the process, and the nature and extent of international involvement, was again a central site of conflict.

The reality of potential large-scale violence in rural areas led to the postponement of local elections originally initially scheduled for 1997. Plans for national elections in 1998 nonetheless continued, albeit at a glacial pace, in the context of the worsening relations between Ranariddh and Hun Sen. By the beginning of 1997 they had almost ground to a halt. The CPP and Hun Sen were facing a considerable electoral challenge from a coalition of opposition groups calling themselves the National United Front (NUF). The prospect of another CPP defeat was very real. The situation on the ground was further complicated by efforts of both prime ministers to court dissident elements of the remaining Khmer Rouge willing to defect to the government. Matters finally came to a head in July when armed forces loyal to Hun Sen attempted to disarm F'pec forces in and around the capital. The confrontation resulted in three days of fierce fighting in Phnom Penh and the ultimate defeat of F'pec military units.

Hun Sen's military action fundamentally altered the political landscape. Ranariddh and other opposition leaders of the NUF fled the country in fear for their lives. As many as 100 or more senior F'pec officials were summarily executed in the bloody aftermath of the fighting. The July 1997 events were to have a profound impact on the role and meaning attached to the 1998 elections for all national and international groups. Chapter four examines this role and these meanings in the light of these events. It suggests that in the aftermath of the July fighting Hun Sen and the CPP were in a pre-eminent position to exercise a considerable amount of control over the election process, a position largely denied them by UNTAC in 1993. Before the 1992–93 election process the CPP had little choice but to accept UNTAC. After July 1997 the UN and other international groups involved in the election preparations seemed compelled to recognize the dominance of Hun Sen and the CPP. Ironically, with almost all of the credible political opposition in self-imposed exile or dead, the deadlock that had prevented the preparations for the elections from moving forward was now broken. This had a powerful effect on international perceptions of domestic Cambodian politics. These perceptions in turn had an equally powerful political effect on how the 1998 elections were conducted and judged by international observers.

In a reversal of fortunes from 1993, the CPP emerged victorious in what were seriously flawed elections in 1998. However, under the system of proportional representation, no one party had a large enough majority to form a government alone. Opposition complaints that the elections were flawed were rejected by the election authorities, leading to a lengthy political standoff, demonstrations and counter demonstrations, which ultimately turned violent. In a similar fashion to the standoff in 1993, a deal was eventually struck between F'pec and the CPP. Another coalition government was formed, this time with Hun Sen as sole Prime Minister and Ranariddh the President of the National Assembly. In spite of the problems and controversies surrounding the conduct of these elections, and with the final dissolution of the remnants of the Khmer Rouge, by late 1998 Cambodia finally entered a period of relative peace and stability, but ultimately at the cost of the democratization process.

In the absence of any serious external threats, the beginning of 1999 saw real opportunities for the new coalition government, along with its international sponsors, to turn attention to Cambodia's most pressing socio-economic problems. Central to solving these problems was the implementation of longstanding legislation and reform programmes, especially an anti-corruption law and the reform of state institutions and public administration. A key element of the public administration reform program was the decentralization and deconcentration of political and financial powers to democratically elected commune councillors. Local elections postponed in 1997 would now be held in 2002 to establish commune councils. Chapter five deals with some of the main issues and events related to these elections and the role and meaning they had in the development of national political structures.

In the international language of development, commune elections were regarded as essential first steps in the expansion of existing multi-donor funded rural development programs for the alleviation of poverty through local processes of democratization. For the elections and decentralization to be meaningful, much depended on the performance of prevailing state institutions at the centre in Phnom Penh. This chapter suggests that the commune elections were thus yet another phase in the struggle between disparate national political and civil forces to pursue and protect their competing visions of Cambodia's future. They were intended to replace CPP-appointed commune chiefs, many of whom had been in office since 1979, with elected councillors in Cambodia's 1,621 communes. As such, they presented a considerable threat to CPP rural power structures developed throughout the 1980s and early 1990s.

International interests in stabilizing Cambodia's national political context allowed Hun Sen and the CPP to consolidate power through internationally sponsored elections that had little to do with the democratization of the system. With Hun Sen firmly in control at the centre, international donors and development organizations could utilize local elections to further their interests in both stabilizing local politics and pursuing development agendas like decentralization. For Hun Sen and the CPP, the elections provided further opportunities to re-consolidate power and control over rural administrative structures that potentially were under threat because of the polls. That said, although the events of the preceding two years had significantly reduced the political threat to the CPP's control of local power structures, internationally supported commune elections still provided opportunities for opposition political parties and civil society groups to organize and mobilize resources in the furtherance of their interests. Political implications were therefore uncertain and the prospect of further instability and violence was still very real.

At the same time, they provided an opportunity for the government and relevant international agencies, in particular the United Nations Development Programme (UNDP), to fulfil a 1996 commitment to holding local elections to mark the next phase in Cambodia's democratic development. Furthermore, they also provided opportunities for local democracy-promoting NGOs and election monitoring organizations to consolidate and develop their roles as independent intermediaries between opposition political parties, the state, and wider society. For the opposition political parties in particular, there were further opportunities to penetrate into the rural areas and build upon previous electoral successes. However, because of the inherent threats and opportunities the elections represented, legislative, institutional and political problems remained at the forefront of the preparations. What was to follow was a continuation of the protracted struggle between the CPP-dominated government and state, the opposition and NGOs over the form and conduct of the election process, all taking place under the glare of international scrutiny.

The 2002 local elections were to be followed by parliamentary elections the following year, each with significant international assistance. Chapter six describes the 2003 parliamentary elections process. The overwhelming CPP victory in the commune elections the previous year left opposition parties and civil organizations with less space in which to manoeuvre in preparation for the 2003 elections. CPP victories at the local level were achieved by the now familiar and persistent politically motivated violence, intimidation, coercion and partisan politics. National and international assessments of the commune elections suggested they were 'free', but not 'fair'. These assessments, emanating from non-governmental and international circles, again exposed the significant differences in interpretation attached to the role of elections in Cambodian politics by all groups. Once again, these differences were on display during the preparations for the 2003 polls. The political and social environment was beset with the same kind of problems encountered in the long pre-election period of 1998 and 2002. At the centre of the continuing struggle between government, the opposition and local and international NGOs was the impartiality of the NEC, and its provincial and commune equivalents.

In recommending the establishment of guidelines to help prevent abuses, donors like the European Union (EU) in particular simultaneously acknowledged that the government was both part of the problem and the solution. However, the political and economic implications of tackling these problems with the government head on was not something the UN or the EU were realistically prepared to countenance. Seemingly intractable political problems of an authoritarian nature were to be circumvented through the technical management of internationally proposed and supported governance reforms, including elections.

Implicit in this view is an acknowledgement that Cambodian elections simultaneously display both an inherent democratic impulse within the body politic and a yoke of a powerful entrenched authoritarian tendency within the state. From a management perspective, this is hugely problematic for foreign liberal governors and development professionals. Under these circumstances, the early stages of democratization in places like Cambodia can destabilize the status quo, making it difficult to 'do development'. By subsuming events like elections under the UNDP rubric of international development, technical and procedural improvements can be achieved, as the 2003 elections process demonstrated. Cultural and historical interpretations and misinterpretations can be deployed in an attempt to explain the democratic authoritarian dichotomy and the persistence of repeated patterns of malfeasance involving state officials and local authorities.

The 2003 elections ended in much the same way as in 1993 and 1998, with disputes over the preparation, conduct and outcome of the process. Again, no single party won enough seats to form a government alone. However, unlike 1993 and 1998, it would be almost a year before a new government formed. The political elite stalemate after the 2003 polls was much more than dissatisfaction with electoral procedures on the part of opposition groups. The origins of the latest impasse could be traced right back to the formation of the first coalition government in 1993. On this occasion, the opposition party leaders Sam Rainsy and Ranariddh formed the 'Alliance of Democrats' and flatly refused to form a coalition government with Hun Sen as Prime Minister. Chapter seven follows the events of that standoff until its final outcome with the formation of a new government in June 2004, again with Hun Sen as sole Prime Minister.

The manner in which Hun Sen outmanoeuvred his political opponents during the lengthy standoff after the 2003 elections left nobody in any doubt that his predominant position was, for the foreseeable future, unassailable. The question remained, what would these latest coalition arrangements mean for the future of Cambodian electoral politics? The 'Alliance of Democrats' had failed in their goal to remove or marginalize Hun Sen. F'pec was a now politically spent force. There was, however, still a sense that the Sam Rainsy Party could potentially pose an electoral threat to the CPP, if not in the rural areas then certainly in towns and cities. By the time of the 2007 commune and 2008 parliamentary elections, there would be a generation of young Cambodians of voting age that had no personal memories of the Khmer Rouge regime, and only vague memories of UNTAC. However, CPP intimidation and violence directed at opponents left the opposition in disarray, making CPP victories almost foregone conclusions. Moreover, the CPP was benefiting from a period of impressive economic growth and infrastructural development, producing unprecedented wealth among its patronage networks; wealth that was brought to bear in the service of elections.

Chapter eight examines the extent to which the 2008 elections had any real political meaning in the face of Hun Sen's seemingly indisputable power and control of national and local politics. Ironically, under these circumstances, internationally supported elections simultaneous-ly suppressed and provided opportunities for democratic participation. Paradoxically, a democratic culture and civic participation could be encouraged but only to the extent that it didn't threaten the prevailing political-economic interests of the regime. In partnership with the NEC, it was relatively easy therefore for the UNDP and donors to adjust and develop legal and technical aspects of elections, but as with other elements of the donor reform agenda it was politically unpropitious di-rectly to challenge the regime when electoral penal laws and regulations and codes of conduct were not implemented in practice.

Impressive pre-election displays of wealth and political power backed by frequent violent suppression of criticism and dissent are effective tools in laying the groundwork for elections proper. These alone, how-ever, are insufficient to ensure desired outcomes, requiring continued careful management of the various stages of the election process.

In general, and almost without exception, various observer groups stated that the elections marked some kind of 'progress', democratic and technical, but failed to reach unspecified international standards of free-dom and fairness. As in 2002 and 2003, the tendency was to measure progress by the reduction in serious violence and killings, and by tech-nically well-administered polling and counting phases. Nonetheless, unacceptable levels of political intimidation, violence and threats directed at political party activists together with serious administrative shortcomings persisted. National and international analysis of the ex-tent and impact of these problems depended upon the perceptions and interests of the particular organizations involved in producing reports.

This is not to say that internationally supported 'authoritarian elec-tions' are irrelevant beyond the one-party dominance of the state. On the contrary, during the electoral cycle, the whole of the 'political and social system is on display'. Mobilization of conspicuous wealth and state resources through party working groups to deliver votes in the countryside for the CPP exposed the façade of infrastructural projects that lacked long-term sustainable investment and the provision of adequate public services. Failure by authorities properly to investigate serious election-related crimes, including murder, reflected the general, chronic culture of impunity for perpetrators of political violence. The killings of the SRP-affiliated newspaper journalist Khim Sambo and his son, days before the 2008 elections, brought the total number of murders of journalists to twelve since 1993. An overall reduction in election-related murders and violence had not led to the eradication of widespread, localized intimidation, coercion and harassment of voters and opposition party activists by local CPP authorities. The reduction in serious incidents of violence accompanied by the disenfranchisement of hundreds of thousands of voters through administrative misconduct marked a new phase in the struggle between authorities, opposition political parties and electoral monitoring organizations (EMOs) over the form and conduct of electoral processes.

With financial and technical backing from a wide range of international donor organizations, EMOs, much like the SRP, survived in order to add legitimacy to a political system increasingly dominated by one party. As such, they had to tread a fine line between legitimate criticism of flawed elections and presenting a radical challenge to the dominance of the CPP. By charactering both the 2007 and 2008 elections as steps in 'strengthening democratic governance', while at the same time forensically analysing non-democratic aspects of the elections process, they expressed a belief in the value of elections as instruments for bringing about positive social and political change.

After another convincing CPP win in the 2012 commune elections, few would have predicted the outcome of the parliamentary elections the following year. The 2013 election results demonstrated the power of elections, dominated by the force, wealth and resources of one party, to cause unpredictable shifts within the body politic. Possibly because of past experiences, for the first time since UNTAC there was no direct foreign technical and financial engagement in the preparation of these elections. The ninth and final chapter outlines the background leading up to the 2013 parliamentary elections in an effort to explain the seemingly anomalous results. Resistance to and discontent with Hun Sen's brand of predatory governance had been building since before the 2008 elections. In the face of a grasping, abusive regime that responded to challenge and criticism with threats and violence, many Cambodians used the polls as the only means they had to register their dissatisfaction collectively and en masse.

Yet another post-election standoff after the 2013 polls seemed to suggest that despite the results it was business as usual. Post-election events followed similar patterns but with noticeable differences. Opposition forces rejected the results and staged peaceful mass protests calling for a thorough investigation into credible claims of electoral fraud. The CNRP parliamentarians-elect refused to take their seats in the National Assembly until their demands were met. There was a heavy, ominous police and military presence on the streets of Phnom Penh. Violence flared and several people were shot and killed by security forces that moved to end the protests which continued into January 2014. Unlike in the past the deadlock was broken in July 2014, not with horse-trading of political posts, but with an agreement between the CPP and the CNRP to reform the electoral system, including a restructuring of the NEC, in time for the scheduled 2017 local and 2018 national elections.

The apparent rapprochement was, however, short lived. In an obvious attempt to discredit, marginalize and weaken the opposition the CPP staged a systematic crackdown against the CNRP, using all too familiar methods including questionable judicial procedures, intimidation and outright violence. Amidst talk of a possible CNRP electoral victory in 2018, by the beginning of 2016 the CNRP president Sam Rainsy was once again in self-imposed exile in France facing prison if he returned to Cambodia. CNRP Vice-President Kem Sokha had been removed from his position as Vice-President of the National Assembly. While crack-downs on opposition are nothing new the timing came as a surprise. The CPP regardless of the lip service paid to electoral reform have made it clear from early on in the process that it will not tolerate electoral defeats in 2017 and 2018. The stage is set for the 2018 national polls that will be decisive in determining the future direction of Cambodian political development, perhaps for decades to come.

CHAPTER 1

The United Nations Elections

*T*he distinguished elections analyst Norman Palmer once wrote, 'elections have different meanings and play different roles in different political systems, and can be used as devices for a variety of purposes'.[1] Elections organized by the United Nations Transitional Authority in Cambodia (UNTAC) in 1993 certainly had different meanings for the disparate national and international groups involved in their conception and execution. The role they would play in the formation of a post-UNTAC political system would largely depend upon the interests and purposes these groups had in mind at the time. Norman Palmer's statement seems to hold true when the outcome of the UNTAC elections is considered. The distribution of political power within the government did not reflect the election results. A dramatic circumstance such as this clearly demonstrated that the UNTAC elections were used by a variety of actors for a variety of different purposes. To grasp the importance of this for Cambodia's subsequent political and electoral development, it is necessary to understand the kind of socio-economic and political conflicts into which elections were introduced.

On 23 October 1991 the four warring parties of the Cambodian conflict signed the Paris Peace Agreements (PPA).[2] The agreements were the end result of a lengthy and rancorous international search for a 'comprehensive political solution' to the war that began in the early 1980s. From these agreements UNTAC and its controversial mandate emerged and began to take shape. UNTAC's central goal was to organize

---

1. N.D. Palmer, *Elections and Political Development: The South Asia Experience.* London: C. Hurst and Company, 1975, p. 2.

2. The four warring parties: The incumbent Cambodian People's Party (CPP), led by the then prime minister Hun Sen; F'pec, led by the son of the former Cambodian King Sihanouk; the Khmer People's National Liberation Front, KPNLF, led by a former Sihanouk era Prime Minister Son Sann; and the Party of Democratic Kampuchea, PDK, also known as the Khmer Rouge, led by Pol Pot.

and manage multi-party democratic elections within a tight time-frame. Elections were also to take place in what was termed, somewhat ambiguously, a 'neutral political environment' (NPE). According to the agreements, Cambodian administrative agencies, bodies and offices which could directly influence the outcome of the elections were to be placed under direct United Nations supervision. The agreements also stated that UNTAC needed to exercise such control as was necessary to ensure the strict neutrality of the bodies responsible for them.[3]

The issue of necessary control went straight to the heart of the problem about exercising power that had previously hindered the search for a comprehensive political solution leading up to the 1991 agreements. In an apparent effort to resolve this problem in September 1990 a Supreme National Council (SNC) was created as the ultimate legal authority in Cambodia, comprising representatives from all warring factions, and chaired by former King Norodom Sihanouk. The SNC was expected to delegate to UNTAC all powers necessary for it to implement the agreements. It was the job of UNTAC's Civil Administration component to ensure that no party had a decisive advantage over another. This would prove to be especially difficult to do when it came to dealings with the incumbent State of Cambodia (SoC). The SoC, formerly known as the People's Republic of Kampuchea (PRK), was formed under the auspices of the Vietnamese after their military intervention ousted the Khmer Rouge regime in late 1978. With extensive Vietnamese administrative and military support, the PRK had effective control over the majority of Cambodian territory and its population. After ten years of incumbency as a single party/state entity, the SoC was thus better placed than the others to protect and further its interests in open electoral competition, but only if it could effectively neutralize the influence of UNTAC.

Indeed, one of the most damning criticisms levelled at UNTAC by some foreign commentators was UNTAC's inability fully control the SoC's 'existing administrative structures' as it was mandated to do.[4]

3. Agreement on a Comprehensive Political Settlement of the Cambodian Conflict. Part 1. Article 6.

4. It is perhaps worth noting at this point that the UNTAC 'shadow governor' of Cambodia's North West province, Siem Reap, Dr Benny Widyono concluded that the UN Secretariat 'never intended UNTAC to exercise full control over SoC, which would have required tens of thousands of staff. His conclusion was based on comments made by Hedi Annabi, a senior UN official who had participated

While this was true to greater and lesser degrees, analysis of the election and the results suggests that UNTAC was nonetheless able to lift the lid on the one party state system enough to allow the electorate to make a reasonably informed choice. However, UNTAC's inability or unwillingness to enforce respect for the election results highlighted the harsh political and socio-economic realities it had to contend with. Those realities were the outcome of events and actions that evolved after the Vietnamese military intervention and the ensuing conflict in the 1980s, ultimately leading to an international search for a political solution.

Cambodia Post-Vietnamese Intervention

In practical terms, the Vietnamese invasion of Cambodia polarized the international response and ultimately pushed the already devastated country back into civil war. On one side, China, the United States and some countries of the Association of Southeast Asian Nations (ASEAN) sought the removal of the Vietnamese and the dismantling of the PRK regime. Seen from this perspective, the Vietnamese action was judged to be an act of aggression. On the other side, the Vietnamese were supported by the Soviet Union and its allies, who recognized the legitimacy of the Vietnamese-installed PRK regime. The long-term presence of a large Vietnamese army in Cambodia was unacceptable to the Chinese, the Americans and the non-communist members of ASEAN, not to mention the vast majority of Cambodians. As a consequence, and after heated debate, the United Nations voted to retain Democratic Kampuchea's seat in the UN General Assembly. Moral outrage and international condemnation of the vote especially in the western media did nothing to alter the outcome. The Khmer Rouge regime responsible

---

in a fact-finding mission in Cambodia in April–May 1990. Annabi, according to Widyono, had argued in 1993 that 'It was never intended for the United Nations to have been mandated to practically take over the administration of Cambodia. This is not the case. It has never been considered and is obviously not possible.' B. Widyono, *Dancing in Shadows: Sihanouk, The Khmer Rouge, and The United Nations in Cambodia.* For other critical accounts of the UNTAC operation see: M. W. Doyle, *UN Peacekeeping in Cambodia: UNTAC's Civil Mandate*; T. Findlay, *The Legacy and Lessons of UNTAC*; J. Heininger, *Peacekeeping in Transition: The United Nations in Cambodia*; and D. W. Roberts, *Political Transition in Cambodia 1991–99: Power, Elitism and Democracy.*

for the deaths of so many Cambodians would continue to be recognized as the legitimate leader of what was left of Cambodia and its population.

The internationalization of the situation had dramatic implications for events inside Cambodia. Chinese aid, with the tacit support of the US and its allies, was channelled through Thai ports, breathing new life into what was left of the Khmer Rouge. From camps on the Thai–Cambodian border, Khmer Rouge military, known as the National Army of Democratic Kampuchea (NADK), were thus able to conduct armed resistance against the PRK and the Vietnamese. Elsewhere, international support was given to other armed groups that coalesced around two non-communist resistance movements, the Khmer People's National Liberation Front (KPNLF), formed in 1979 by a former Prime Minister Son Sann, and Prince Sihanouk's F'pec. In an effort to somehow legitimize continued western and Chinese support for the Khmer Rouge, all groups were pressured to join together as the Coalition Government of Democratic Kampuchea (CGDK). In 1982, the coalition was thus recognized as Cambodia's legitimate representative at the United Nations by those who were working to remove the PRK and the Vietnamese.

Meanwhile, a wretched Cambodian population had to confront the abject desolation caused by years of war, and the cataclysmic consequences of the policies of the outgoing regime. In this context the task facing Cambodia's new leadership from 1979 onwards was indeed monumental. That leadership was drawn from members of a group of Khmer Rouge dissident cadres assembled by the Vietnamese prior to the invasion. From this group – known as the United Front for the Salvation of Kampuchea, FUNSK – the Kampuchean People's Revolutionary Party was formed to preside over a new state system. Three members of the Front emerged as central players in the establishment of the PRK, which was ostensibly organized along Vietnamese communist bureaucratic lines.[5] They would go on to play lead roles in the new dramas beginning to unfold. The Front's president was Heng Samrin, a former Khmer Rouge military officer who had escaped to Vietnam, avoiding Pol Pot's purges in 1978. Second was Chea Sim, minister of the interior for the new regime, a former Khmer Rouge Eastern Zone district chief who had

---

5. For a detailed account of the evolution of the PRK regime, see Margaret Slocombe, *The People's Republic of Kampuchea 1979–1989*, Silkworm Books, 2003, pp. 37–125.

also escaped the purges by fleeing to Vietnam in the same year. Third, Hun Sen, another Khmer Rouge military officer from the Eastern Zone who had fled earlier in 1977, and had become PRK foreign minister, and later prime minister.

Much has already been written about the situation facing the PRK leadership in the first few years after they were installed by the Vietnamese. The extent of the destruction and human cost facing them, for example, was succinctly summed up by an Oxfam UK aid worker who was in Cambodia in the 1980s as follows:

> The Heng Samrin government inherited a country whose infrastructure had been destroyed. Of 450 doctors before 1975, only 45 remained in the country in 1979. The rest had been murdered or had escaped abroad. Of the 20,000 teachers in the early 1970s, only 7,000 remained. Very few trained administrators survived, so those who found jobs in the Heng Samrin government were generally very young and inexperienced and often rejected by their friends as 'working for the Vietnamese'. The fishing industry was hampered by a lack of boats and nets ... The country by 1979 had no currency, no markets, no financial institutions and virtually no industry. There was no public transport system; no trains ran and the roads were damaged and unrepaired. There was no postal system, no telephones and virtually no electricity, clean water, sanitation or education.

The immediate impact on ordinary Cambodians was profoundly disturbing, as she goes on to write:

> Freed from the slavery of the Pol Pot years, people criss-crossed the country in attempts to return to Phnom Penh and to their homes and villages, and to seek out the remnants of their families. Many found their homes in ruins or disrepair, and many small towns and cities had become ghost towns. As the Khmer Rouge retreated, they took a quarter of the rice harvest and destroyed any draught animals they could not take with them – other animals died en route. The chaos of Summer 1979 prevented normal planting and so the 1979/80 harvest was only one third of the usual output. Once more the country was threatened by famine as the hungry 'road people' wandered in search of their old lives and sought to begin again.[6]

---

6. Eva Mysliwiec, *Punishing the Poor: The International Isolation of Kampuchea*, Oxford, Oxfam, 1987: pp. 10–11. See also Evan Gottesman, *Cambodia After the Khmer Rouge: Inside the Politics of Nation Building*, Silkworm Books, 2003.

Fortunately, an expected famine was averted with the help of a massive international emergency relief operation that lasted from 1979 until the end of 1981, although food self-sufficiency and shortages remained serious concerns. The general situation was made worse by the developing armed insurgency against the PRK and the Vietnamese. Also, because of the continued presence of the Vietnamese, Cambodia was controversially denied desperately needed aid for development by western powers.[7]

The Transformation of the PRK

Insurgency, food insecurity, and the denial of aid for reconstruction and development through the UN system, had a profound impact on the PRK leadership. Besides the obvious security threats posed by continued armed conflict, the leadership was fearful of insurgent groups winning support from ordinary Cambodians beyond their bases on the Thai border. Various policies to prevent this happening either generated resentment among the general population or failed outright. Attempts by the PRK army to recruit volunteers to fight alongside Vietnamese units against the insurgency, for example, proved to be extremely unpopular, leading to the introduction of conscription. Resistance to conscription was met with harsh punishment. Construction of a huge defensive project known as the K5, comprising fortifications that would stretch the length of the Thai–Cambodian border to prevent incursions from insurgents, resulted in the deaths of thousands of civilian labourers working in atrocious conditions. *Krom Samaki,* or solidarity groups organized to implement agricultural collectivization policies also proved to be unpopular, and by the mid-1980s had more or less stopped working.[8] Measures like these combined to make it extremely difficult for the emergent party-state to realise its stated goal of advancing any kind of socialism.

In such dire economic conditions, the majority of people came to rely more upon free market activities rather than a weak state dependent upon the Vietnamese. The opening up of borders with Thailand and Vietnam, initially for the delivery of emergency aid, encouraged petty trade, black markets and smuggling that was difficult to control from the centre. So too were the commercial networks, composed mainly of Sino-Khmers

---

7. For a full discussion of the controversy see Mysliwiec, *Punishing the Poor,* chap 5.

8. Gottesman, *Cambodia After the Khmer Rouge,* pp. 226–73.

and ethnic Chinese, which again began to flourish in the re-populated rural centres. Attempts by state cadres to centralize control of cross border trade, including smuggling, and suppress urban commerce was in the long run ineffective. Ideologically indifferent, local authorities tended to collude with local merchants and Khmer, Vietnamese and Thai military personnel in profiting from these activities, especially in the trade of natural resources such as rice, fish, timber, rubber and precious stones. Similarly, state policies aimed at curtailing the activities of Chinese and Sino-Khmer merchants were not generally supported by many officials in the cities and towns who benefited directly from them.[9]

The Rise of Hun Sen

The unpopularity of the new regime's socialist oriented policies, the growing insurgency, and the lurch towards petty trade and free market activities had by the early 1980s placed a considerable strain on the party leadership. In turn, these conditions had a major impact on the regime's relations with its Vietnamese patrons. Fault lines within the party were typically ideological and ran between the veteran Khmer Viet Minh cadres, who had received extensive revolutionary training in Vietnam in the 1950s and 60s – men such as Pen Sovann and Chan Si – and some of the more pragmatic Khmer Rouge East Zone cadres like Chea Sim and Hun Sen. Pen Sovann, in spite of his revolutionary training by the Vietnamese, or even perhaps because of it, was particularly strident in asserting the independence of the Cambodian revolution and resisted Vietnamese dominance. His appointment as prime minister during the party's fourth congress in 1981 was, however, short-lived. Isolated from his more pragmatic colleagues, his anti-Vietnamese behaviour soon led to his removal and arrest by the Vietnamese. He was taken to Hanoi where he spent the next ten years in prison. Chan Si, another Hanoi-trained veteran, replaced Sovann as prime minister in December 1981. His tenure like that of Sovann's was also short-lived. He died four years later in 1984.

Pen Sovann's arrest and incarceration followed by Chan Si's untimely death cleared the political path for Hun Sen, who replaced Chan Si as prime minister in 1985. Within the space of less than ten years, Hun Sen had risen from the relatively low ranks of the Khmer Rouge military to

---

9.   Ibid.

become one of the central figures in the unfolding geopolitical drama of the late 1980s. Beginning in 1979 as minister for foreign affairs at the age of twenty-six, with no previous experience, Hun Sen had quickly built a reputation among the Vietnamese as a 'loyal', quick learning, articulate and effective diplomat. Also, like his comrade and former minister of the interior, Chea Sim – and unlike his more ideological comrade Heng Samrin – Hun Sen was well tuned to the political economic realities inside and outside of Cambodia, and was in a position to capitalize on them. As chairman of the Council of Ministers, he began to build his own personal patron–client networks, favouring overseas-educated, non-ideological, technocratic individuals seemingly better equipped to deal with the complex challenges the country faced. Add to this the continued pervasive influence of Chea Sim's own personal patronage system within the security apparatus and among provincial and local officials, which he had developed during his time at the ministry of the interior, it was easy to understand how he and Hun Sen emerged as the two most powerful men in Cambodia in the mid-1980s.[10]

Because of his experience at the ministry of foreign affairs, and his nuanced understanding of the regime's international predicament, it would be Hun Sen, and not Chea Sim, who would lead the PRK in the negotiations for a political settlement of the military conflict. As the geopolitical situation intensified after 1985, his bureaucratic skills and pragmatism proved invaluable for his party's survival. His reformist attitudes towards the role of the state in markets and the private sector also seemed to be in keeping with Vietnam's pragmatic adjustments to its own economic and political problems. In order to strengthen his and the party's position during those negotiations he had to ensure he had enough influence and control over free market activities to be able to maintain and develop loyal networks of patronage, if, as seemed increasingly likely, he would have to face his opponents in open electoral competition. Moreover, for someone as close to the Vietnamese as Hun Sen was, the introduction in 1986 of the *Doi Moi* economic reforms in Vietnam, combined with Gorbachev's perestroika and glasnost reforms in the Soviet Union, were a clear indication that the PRK might have to consider going it alone.

The political and economic consequences of a complete Vietnamese withdrawal were fully understood by Hun Sen. Control of economic

---

10. Gottesman, *Cambodia After the Khmer Rouge*, p. xxii.

activity was vital if the political game through elections was to be won. Indeed, as some analysts have persuasively argued, by 1989 the PRK had survived because it had tolerated state cadres' involvement in free market activities. For example one analyst cites Hun Sen in June 1989 talking about elections:

> Exerts pressures on our policies and forces us to go the path [of economic reform and national reconciliation] so that [workers] don't lose their personal benefits from the state and they will follow us politically. If we don't resolve this problem in time, then when there is an election, the [resistance] will come and take houses and land and campaign against us incessantly. [People] will understand that if they vote for [the resistance parties, those parties] will give them rights over the houses and land they used to possess. Will lose in the countryside and the city.[11]

Resolving the problem of maintaining political loyalty through reforms and national reconciliation was not a straightforward proposition for Hun Sen and the PRK. To a great extent, these policies were driven by the exigencies of external events and the international orientation of the Cambodian conflict. By the time Hun Sen had assumed office as prime minister, the military situation on the ground was more or less deadlocked. As the decade wore on, the willingness to seek a political solution to the conflict by those international powers that had been providing military assistance to the various warring groups on both sides meant a decisive military victory by either side was unlikely. Introducing multi-party democratic and competitive elections as a means to settle the conflict was deeply problematic for the PRK. The enfranchisement of a war-weary population disenchanted with socialist experimentation posed a considerable political threat to a numerically small, weak, unpopular and ideologically moribund party that had ridden to power on the back of a Vietnamese military invasion force. Matters were made worse when, in the late 1980s, the Vietnamese prepared for their eventual withdrawal as Soviet-bloc aid for their adventure in Cambodia began to dry up.[12] For the party, maintaining political loyalty among state cadres and their dependents was always going to be a tough proposition; now

---

11. Taken from Minutes 91, Cabinet, Council of Ministers, June 1989, pp. 2–5 (Doc. 6-71), cited in Gottesman, *Cambodia after the Khmer Rouge*, p. 282

12. According to Evan Gottesman, 'By the end of 1989, Cambodia had lost some hundred million rubles in commercial credit and a long list of imports, including

more than ever the party needed to exercise maximum control if it was to survive.

In their efforts to counter these threats and adjust to exogenous economic shocks, Hun Sen and the party leadership initiated a transformation of the state, beginning by officially discarding socialist ideology in April 1989. To symbolize the event and appeal to voters ahead of the elections they changed the name of the regime from the PRK to the State of Cambodia. The leadership's role in the process of national reconciliation was couched in the language of national development and liberation from, and defence against, the return of the genocidal Khmer Rouge. At the same time, a series of liberalizing economic reforms were introduced that had the practical effect of formalizing state involvement in the private sector. Reforms, as well as reflecting a general trend among impoverished, cash strapped Soviet client states, exacerbated the problem of corruption and strengthened mutually dependent networks of patronage, power and privilege established by the leadership to preserve and protect political loyalty and support among state cadres.

A further upsurge in economic activity ensued as a result of the privatization of land, the pursuit of investment and trade, and the sale and leasing of state industries and property. This proved extremely profitable for many state power holders in the ministries, and strengthened the networks at all levels. In the countryside, local officials and military personnel had even greater independence and control over revenues and resources. In an environment of increasing impoverishment, they were engaging in profitable entrepreneurial activities with foreign companies and businessmen as demand for Cambodia's natural resources such as land, fish, timber and rubber increased with the opening up of local economies. In Phnom Penh, the privatization of state enterprises and the sale or leasing of state property, particularly to foreign business interests, greatly enriched individuals within the party and government ministries. Like their counterparts in the cities, state employees and local officials in the countryside were permitted to supplement their paltry incomes through private enterprise. They used their positions within the state apparatus to profit from low-level extortion and bribery.

---

construction materials and parts, vehicles, pharmaceuticals, chemicals, and most important, fuel.' Gottesman, *Cambodia after the Khmer Rouge*, p. 316.

Such activities clearly had serious implications for the development of state institutions capable of effectively dealing with the socio-economic problems facing the country. The granting of greater autonomy by the party leadership to local and provincial authorities had, as one analyst succinctly puts it, perpetuated:

> A system in which local positions were valued according to their revenue generating potential, while higher level officials wielded power in accordance with their ability to distribute those positions. Authority was handed down, money was passed upward. It was a system that maintained unproductive levels of employment, exacerbated absenteeism, and encouraged pilfering of state resources.

It was congenitally and endemically corrupt, allowing politically and economically well connected individuals to operate with impunity provided political loyalty to the regime was maintained. But it was a system constructed and driven by the necessity to protect and prepare the leadership for the challenges ahead, as the analysis continued:

> Hun Sen and like-minded leaders were creating a kind of state capitalism in which officials were apt to consider the resources at their disposal – land, factory parts, timber, vehicles, soldiers – as assets to be exploited for profit. For Hun Sen and much of the rest of the leadership, a permissive system of this sort was the key to consolidating power. It created networks of happy officials whose loyalty the regime could count on, even after the Vietnamese withdrew and Sihanouk returned.[13]

The Importance of Elections

Given the circumstances under which elections would be held, having happy and loyal officials alone could not guarantee an electoral victory for the regime. Having total control over the electoral process, however, would. In light of the geopolitical climate, Hun Sen and the PRK were fully aware that they would have very little choice but to face the resistance groups in open electoral competition. They were also fully aware that powerful external forces were always going to play a pivotal role in determining the eventual outcome of the conflict. Indeed, it was the struggle over control of elections between all the Cambodian and international actors involved that defined the search for a comprehensive

---

13. Gottesman, *Cambodia after the Khmer Rouge*, p. 300

political solution to the conflict in the late 1980s. Central to that struggle was the problem of how political power would thus be distributed before elections could be held. Attempts made by Hun Sen and Sihanouk in 1987 and 1988 to circumvent the issue and arrive at a 'Cambodian' solution of sorts ultimately failed. These failed attempts were followed by a series of events known as the Jakarta Informal Meetings (JIMs), and other meetings elsewhere. Although bitter disagreements continued over power-sharing and the position of the Khmer Rouge in the process, these meetings at least succeeded in bringing all factions, including the Khmer Rouge, together.

In the end, it was the five permanent members of the United Nations Security Council or Perm-5 (China, Soviet Union, United States, United Kingdom, France) who in the summer of 1990 decided upon the 'framework for a comprehensive political settlement of the Cambodian conflict', without any representation from the Cambodians.[14] To settle the interim power-sharing question, the framework document proposed the establishment of the Supreme National Council (SNC) comprising thirteen members drawn from each of the warring factions, six from the SoC and two representatives from the Khmer Rouge, F'pec and the KPNLF. Although according to the framework document the SNC would serve as the 'unique legitimate body and source of authority' in Cambodia during a transition period, it would delegate all necessary powers to the United Nations Transitional Authority in Cambodia (UNTAC), who would take control of organizing and managing multi-party democratic elections.[15]

Because of the rapidly changing geopolitical situation all Cambodian factions had little choice but to accept the terms and conditions of the framework document. While the framework was far from ideal for all

---

14. For a more detailed description of the search for a comprehensive political solution to the conflict and the associated controversies, see Pierre Lizée, 'The Evolution of Great Power Involvement in Cambodia', in D. Werfel and B. Burton (eds), *Southeast Asia in the New World Order* (New York: St Martin's Press, 1996) and also David W. Roberts, *Political Transition in Cambodia 1991–2001: Power, Elitism and Democracy* (Richmond: Curzon, 2001).

15. According to Benny Widyono, the idea underpinning the framework document was initially put forward by Sihanouk and US congressman Stephen Solarz, and later 'officially proposed by the Australian Minister for Foreign Affairs, Gareth Evans. Widyono, *Dancing in Shadows*, p. 34.

concerned, especially those with the most to lose, namely Hun Sen and the SoC leadership, it was perhaps an early indication that Cambodia's political elite was conscious of the need to adapt to the changing nature of the conflict if their ultimate interests and objectives were to be met. In this sense, the elections would take on different meanings for the various national and international groups involved, and would play a significant role in determining the best strategies to protect and further those interests and objectives. In other words, implications for the configuration of the social and political conflict in Cambodia once elections were introduced were profound.

The leadership's pragmatic response to the failure of a more benign form of socialism and the development of patronage networks certainly strengthened Hun Sen's and the PRK's position in relation to their political opponents. However, this came at a cost. The distribution of benefits was thinly spread and disproportionate. Economic liberalization created adverse social effects, alienating many Cambodians who were either unable or unwilling to participate in and endorse the actions of the party and the state. The newly enriched state networks of patronage and privilege were, therefore, vulnerable to attack from those with alternative visions of Cambodia's future.

In many respects, it was these alternative and competing visions of Cambodia's future that presented UNTAC with its biggest challenge. The job of trying to make this happen was given to Yasushi Akashi, a Japanese national and former United Nations Under-Secretary-General for Disarmament, who was appointed to lead the operation. To say Akashi's and UNTAC's mandate was ambitious is seriously to understate the complexity of the situation they were facing. Nothing like UNTAC had been attempted before by the United Nations. The logistical and practical challenges of working in a country so thoroughly devastated by war were enormous. The political challenges were extraordinarily complex and highly dangerous. In order to create the neutral political environment stipulated in the agreements, UNTAC had to take control of the existing administrative structures of the SoC, as Article 6 of the peace agreements states:

> ... to ensure a neutral political environment conducive to free and fair general elections, administrative agencies, bodies and offices which could directly influence the outcome of the elections will be placed

under direct United Nations supervision and control. In that context, special attention will be given to foreign affairs, national defence, finance, public security and information. To reflect the importance of these subjects, UNTAC needs to exercise such control as is necessary to ensure the strict neutrality of the bodies responsible for them.[16]

In addition to this, UNTAC also had to repatriate hundreds of thousands of refugees, canton and disarm at least 70 per cent of all armed forces, and verify the withdrawal of all foreign military personnel. All of this had to be done in less than three years.

UNTAC: Meanings from Below and Above

UNTAC was divided into a number of operational components tasked with a specific area of control related to civil administration, civil police, military, repatriation and rehabilitation, information and education, human rights and elections. The overall operation was to take place in two distinct phases. Phase I began in November 1991 with the deployment in Phnom Penh of the United Nations Advance Mission in Cambodia (UNAMIC). Led by the French Brigadier General Jean Michel Loridon, his task was to oversee the implementation and maintenance of a cease-fire agreed upon after the signing of the agreements in Paris. Phase II, the demobilization of 70 per cent of all of the four factions' armed forces, was to take place in June 1992, and conclude just before the voter registration process for the elections in May 1993. Largely due to non-compliance by the Khmer Rouge, the demobilization and cantonment phase had to be abandoned, seriously jeopardizing the whole operation.[17]

Indeed, UNTAC has been analysed and criticized a great deal in a number of texts.[18] Given that such a complex and politically dangerous

---

16. 'Agreement on a Comprehensive Political Settlement of the Cambodian Conflict. Part 1. Article 6.'

17. For a detailed discussion of the demobilization issues, see Widyono, *Dancing in Shadows*, chap. 5.

18. For a detailed critique of the UNTAC operation, see David W. Roberts, *Political Transition in Cambodia 1991–2001*. See also J. Heininger, *Peacekeeping in Transition: The United Nations in Cambodia* (New York: Twentieth Century Fund Press, 1994), T. Findlay, *The Legacy and Lessons of UNTAC* (Oxford University Press, SIPRI Research Report, No 9, 1995), and M. W. Doyle, *UN Peacekeeping in Cambodia: UNTAC's Civil Mandate* (London & Boulder: Lynne Rienner).

and intrusive operation had never been attempted before, it was inevitable that problems would arise. A later than anticipated deployment in March 1992, five months after the signing of the peace agreements, the withdrawal of the Khmer Rouge, UNTAC's failure to demobilize armed forces, and, as shall be shown, its failure fully to control SoC administrative agencies, were without doubt major setbacks. And yet, despite this, and against all odds, UNTAC achieved its ultimate goal in organizing and holding reasonably free and fair elections in 1993; a remarkable achievement. It was remarkable insofar as UNTAC was able to create sufficient conditions within which it could reach a critical mass of ordinary Cambodians through its information and education channels, informing people not just about the mechanics of voting, but more importantly about the ideas underpinning the concept of the vote, including human rights. Probably for the first time since elections in 1946, Cambodians had the opportunity to make an informed choice and take some control over decisions, albeit temporarily, that would have an impact on their day-to-day lives.[19] What this meant in the long-term, however, would nonetheless be determined by the meanings attached to the elections by other more powerful national and international groups, and its ultimate outcome.

Meanings from Below

The presence of such a large and exotic United Nations operation in Cambodia at the end of the Cold War meant many different things to the many diverse national and international groups involved. For the vast majority of Cambodians, the prospect of elections in 1993 meant much more than a brief few minutes in a polling booth. The idea of elections, and what needed to be done in order to make them happen, brought more than a fair amount of optimism and hope. Shortly after the arrival of UNAMIC, Sihanouk's rapturous return to Phnom Penh after ten years of exile, riding in an open topped car from the airport, hand in upraised hand in a gesture of unity with Hun Sen, was a visible and potent display of that hope. With the United Nations actually on

---

19. For a concise summary of Cambodia's post-colonial elections, see Steve Heder, *Cambodian Elections in Historical Perspective*, in John Vijghen (ed.), *People and the 1998 National Elections in Cambodia: Their Voices, Roles and Impact on Democracy* (Phnom Penh: Experts for Community Research (ECR) No. 44, 2002).

Cambodian soil alongside Sihanouk and Hun Sen, Cambodians could be forgiven for thinking that elections would be the catalyst through which their lives were about to finally change for the better.

As intoxicating as these events of 1991 were for many people, there were also signs that seemed to confirm what others saw as the fragility of the peace agreements, foisted upon the Cambodian factions by powerful outside forces who had very little or no understanding of Cambodian social and political realities. The arrival in Phnom Penh of the Khmer Rouge leaders Khieu Samphan and Son Sen to take up their seats in the SNC was met with protests from angry crowds. The protests turned violent, and Khieu Samphan sustained a slight head wound in a scuffle, which was irreverently bound with a pair of 'Y' front underpants to stem the flow of blood. Both leaders left the city immediately, without taking up their positions in the council. There was some doubt as to whether or not the protests were orchestrated or a genuine and spontaneous outburst of anger against the Khmer Rouge. In any event, the protests were a good indication that the way ahead was far from straightforward.

Critics of the peace agreements felt that a big part of the problem was the imposition of western liberal democratic values via elections on a country with little or no experience of multiparty democracy.[20] Cambodia it was argued was just not ready for democracy as conceived by the designers of the peace agreements. After many years of international war and isolation it was probably the case that many Cambodians knew little about western notions of democracy and elections, however conceptualized. But there was evidence to show that people understood the political implications of the UN operation. Interviews conducted at the time in both urban and rural areas seemed to suggest that ordinary Cambodian voters had sophisticated understandings of the situation, and were very much aware of the notion of political choice afforded them by the elections. For example, before the UN's deployment, it was reported in 1992 that Cambodians knew the difference between the roles of UNAMIC and UNTAC, and were impatiently waiting for them to arrive. Interviewees were also impatient to know the date of the elections, but when asked, they 'refused to state their political prefer-

---

20. For a scathing critique of the inappropriateness of Western Liberal Democracy in Cambodia in the 1990s, see David W. Roberts, *Political Transition in Cambodia 1991–2001.*

ence', frequently explaining that there was an 'absence of real freedom of expression', and lack of information about the political parties and their agendas.[21]

Meanings from Above

Because of the bitterness, enmity and mistrust that existed between the four political factions, it was hardly surprising that potential Cambodian voters were reluctant openly to express their political views and preferences. While it was clear what the elections meant for the majority of people – an end to war and a chance to rebuild their lives in peace – the actual outcome was far from certain. UNTAC was a completely unknown force, and Cambodians could not be sure that it was capable of fulfilling its mandate. In many ways, the same was true for the leaders of the four factions. The UNTAC operation had different meanings for them, depending on what each had to gain or lose. Their perception of what they stood to lose would have a major determining effect in shaping their particular strategies and engagement with the UN.

For Sihanouk and the non-communist parties of the CGDK, as insurgents the elections meant they had a lot to gain. By contrast, for the incumbent Hun Sen and SoC leadership, elections meant their entrenched positions of power and privilege were under considerable threat. From the very outset, the formation of the SNC power-sharing mechanism had already compromised their incumbency and its attendant benefits. And yet, at the same time, as officeholders they did potentially at least enjoy certain decisive advantages *vis-à-vis* opponents. However, with the SoC's capacity to influence the outcome of the elections greatly reduced by the presence of UNTAC, they had no choice but to embrace the international intervention and make the most of the state resources available to them in implementing their electoral strategies.

Of all the combatants, the Khmer Rouge – known as the Party of Democratic Kampuchea, PDK, for the purposes of electoral competition – had the most to lose by participating in the elections. Indeed, the Khmer Rouge decision to participate in the process placed it in a curious and precarious position. On the one hand, as repugnant as its inclusion

21. See for example, Raoul M. Jenner, 'Cambodian Chronicles (II): The Very First Steps Towards a Very Fragile Peace' (Jodoigne, European Far Eastern Research Center, 1992), p. 3.

in the formation of the SNC was to some, as an equal member it was at first glance in a relatively strong political position. In addition, militarily, it was the strongest of the insurgent forces and controlled large areas of Cambodian territory. On the other hand, it had to consider the nature of its relationship with voters. The extent of its involvement in the election process would be determined by two principal factors. First, much of the PDK's capacity to influence the electoral outcome would depend on the ability of UNTAC to neutralize, as mandated, the SoC power structures. Increasingly isolated internationally – as their Chinese and American patrons distanced themselves from their erstwhile client – the Khmer Rouge could only rely on their own existing resources and UNTAC, if they were to stand a chance of regaining any political power. Secondly, with a warped sense of reality they would have to persuade a sufficient number of the electorate to vote for them, the vast majority of whom had suffered in unimaginable ways as a result of their policies between 1975 and 1978.

The United Nations also had a lot riding on the operation. Embedded within UNTAC's mandate were the ambitions of an organization seeking a more strident role in the new post-Cold War world order, seemingly underpinned by dominant western liberal democratic values. As far as the United Nations headquarters in New York were concerned, failure of UNTAC was not really an option if the UN's pre-eminent place in the new order was to be assured. An encrypted fax sent by Kofi Annan, (then head of the Department for Peace Keeping Operations) to the head of UNTAC, Akashi, almost a year after his arrival in March 1992, clearly illustrated the importance the UN attached to the success of the operation. The fax suggested that 'Cambodia should not be held to un-realistically high standards.'[22] It is not immediately apparent exactly what those unrealistically high standards were. Presumably, they referred to the principles laid out in the peace agreements, which placed great emphasis on the good faith of the signatories to fulfil their commitments and their obligations to abide by them.

Unfortunately for Akashi and UNTAC on the ground, those principles were seriously compromised from the very beginning. No doubt

---

22. Crypto Fax to: Akashi, UNTAC, Phnom Penh. From Annan, United Nations, New York, Number UNTAC-1157. Subject: *Preparations for Elections and Reporting.* CYP 189, March 1992, pp. 1–2.

having reflected upon their curious and precarious position, including the treatment of Khieu Samphan at the hands of an angry crowd in Phnom Penh, the Khmer Rouge adopted a strategy of non-compliance, seriously jeopardizing the whole operation before it had even got started. Problems began with the Khmer Rouge first breaking the cease-fire, and then refusing to allow UNTAC access to its administrative areas so that its military personnel could carry out the critical disarmament, demobilization and cantonment of armed forces it was obliged and had agreed to do in Paris.[23] The Khmer Rouge's refusal to comply effectively brought a halt to the demobilization and disarmament process. The consequences for the general security situation in the run up to the elections were dramatic. With large numbers of soldiers from all factions still under arms, the first key phase of the operation had ended disastrously, leaving the potential for large-scale armed conflict an ever-present possibility.

By June 1992, the Khmer Rouge's non-compliance with the agreements, continued intransigence and violence against ethnic Vietnamese and UNTAC personnel left the operation in a severe quandary. Given what was at stake, what would be the best course of action for the UN to take? In a report to the Security Council in July 1992, the UN Secretary General put forward two possible alternatives, 'to suspend the operation until all parties comply with the agreements', or to carry on, 'thus demonstrating the international community's determination to assist the Cambodian people despite the lack of cooperation from the PDK'.[24] The option of using armed force had been ruled out by Akashi and UNTAC's military commander Lieutenant General Sanderson. When pushed on the issue of using it against the Khmer Rouge, Akashi stressed

---

23. Just two months after his arrival in Cambodia, Akashi accompanied the Australian Commander of UNTAC's military component, General John Sanderson, and attempted to gain access to Khmer Rouge controlled territory in Battambang province. In what has become embarrassingly known as the 'Bamboo Pole Incident', after visiting the Khmer Rouge stronghold in the town of Pailin near the border with Thailand, Akashi and Sanderson stopped at a roadblock consisting of a single bamboo pole and were prevented from proceeding further into Khmer Rouge territory by young, unarmed Khmer Rouge soldiers. Later, the Khmer Rouge informed Akashi by letter that they would allow UNTAC personnel to access any of the areas under its control. For further details of the incident see Widyono, *Dancing in Shadows*, p. 77.

24. See n.23 above.

that UNTAC was a 'classic type of peacekeeping operation which was essentially based on the agreement and consent of the parties involved'. He argued that UNTAC was 'obliged to resort to diplomatic persuasion and negotiation and exercise patience in its dealings with all factions'.[25]

Some public commentary at the time characterized the notions of diplomatic persuasion, negotiation and patience as 'passive' and even 'timid'.[26] However, Akashi and UNTAC's position expressed a more general feeling among those in the international community engaged with the operation to push on, no matter what the cost. The timetable for implementation was tight and the operation was costing approximately 100 million dollars per month. Any further delays would be too costly in terms of time and money. In any event, any attempt to use military force against the PDK would in all likelihood destabilize the operation further, making it impossible for the elections to take place as scheduled. At the same time however, a patient diplomatic approach also ran the risk of allowing the PDK to further undermine the election preparations if their concerns were not met. Either way, the question was raised, to what lengths would the PDK go to derail the operation entirely, and how would UNTAC and the other factions respond to that eventuality?

SoC, CPP and UNTAC

To compete in the elections and appeal to voters once the UNTAC operation was underway, the SoC leadership changed the name of the Khmer People's Revolutionary Party to the less ideologically oriented Cambodian People's Party, CPP. For all intents and purposes, and in the interests of a neutral political environment, the CPP was supposed to be distinct from the SoC. The reality on the ground, however, consistently belied the Party's public pronouncements concerning its dealings with UNTAC. Just nine months after UNTAC's arrival, the newly appointed Party secretary, Chea Sim, outlined the SoC's and CPP's official position concerning the implementation of the agreements. In a speech broadcast on SoC radio in July 1992, he emphasized the importance both the SoC and CPP placed on cooperating with UNTAC in order to implement

---

25. UNTAC, Information/Education Division, *Summary of Press Conference by the Special Representative of the Secretary-General for Cambodia.* Mr Yasushi Akashi. Phnom Penh, 11 Jan. 1993.

26. Ibid.

the agreements 'quickly' and 'comprehensively'. He was careful in stating that the 'existing administrative structures' were not only in conformity with the peace agreements, 'but were also a determining factor in ensuring social stability', and any 'demands made against the agreement or attempts made to affect the social order would bring about serious consequences'.[27] In reality, however, UNTAC was the single biggest obstacle preventing the SoC from exercising enough control over the process to ensure an election victory for the CPP.

In order to overcome this obstacle, the SoC developed a strategy whereby it could plausibly defend its commitment to uphold the letter and spirit of the agreements, while at the same time use its existing administrative structures to undermine UNTAC attempts to take full control and establish a neutral political environment. Ever since the prospect of using elections as a mechanism for resolving the conflict had become a reality, Hun Sen had been conscious of the need to maintain the 'military and political situation', right up until the elections were to be held.[28] Put another way, outright non-compliance was not a realistic option unless they felt they had nothing to lose, but neither was full compliance if they were to stand any chance of winning come election time. The question remained, what was the best way to handle UNTAC and the opposition parties?

One of the biggest problems the CPP had to deal with, and for that matter the other political parties too, was control over the dissemination of information. UNTAC brought with it alternative sources of information and the means for getting the message about elections out to the majority of Cambodians, even in remote rural areas. A new vocabulary was introduced expressing ideas about democracy, voting, political participation, choice and human rights. To counteract the threats posed by possible alternatives to its incumbency, the CPP had to adapt existing SoC administrative structures and mobilize the resources and networks already at its disposal.

---

27. UNTAC Information/Education Division, *State of Cambodia News Broadcast Media. 22–29 July.* CPP Extraordinary Party Congress 27–29 July 1992. Full Digest.

28. Minutes 29, Cabinet, Council of Ministers, December 29, 1989 (doc 8-26), cited in Gottesman, *Cambodia After the Khmer Rouge*, p. 338.

CHAPTER 2

Electoral Strategies

U N Secretary General Boutros Boutros-Ghali's address to UNTAC personnel on the eve of the elections emphasized the importance of the operation by underscoring that the organization's role in future operations was at stake. Contained within UNTAC's mandate were the ambitions of an organization seeking a more active role in the new post-Cold War World Order. If a pre-eminent place in that order was to be assured, failure was not an option. Success or failure would, however, be determined to a greater or lesser degree by the response of senior officials at UN Headquarters in New York to events as they unfolded on the ground in Cambodia. Just how far the UN was prepared to go to uphold the lofty principles contained in the Paris Peace Accords remained to be seen. Unfortunately for Akashi and UNTAC, those principles were seriously compromised from the very beginning, setting in motion a series of events that would have profound implications for the future development of electoral politics in Cambodia.

The Khmer Rouge and UNTAC

The PDK had the most to lose from open electoral competition. It was hard to imagine that large numbers of the Cambodian electorate, when offered an informed choice, would vote for members of a regime that almost succeeded in wiping out a fifth of the population between 1975 and 1978. It was not inconceivable, however, that the PDK could achieve some electoral success through fear, intimidation, coercion and violence in areas under their control. After all, they had been resuscitated as a military and political force by those foreign powers seeking to remove Vietnamese forces from the country after 1979. Further, the PDK's inclusion as an equal member of the SNC meant that politically it also had influence over the operation as it was unfolding. Militarily and politically, it was still a formidable force to be reckoned with. And yet,

42

irrespective of any political advantages accrued from membership in the SNC, if the PDK was to compete in the elections in a meaningful way, they would have to figure out how to persuade voters to vote for them. By participating in the election process in accordance with the Paris Peace Agreements, they risked losing both military and political power.

Again, it is difficult to imagine that the Khmer Rouge leadership was not fully cognisant of the risks posed by participating in a 'free and fair' election. They nonetheless developed a political strategy *vis-à-vis* UNTAC, but one that did not necessarily envisage electoral success. Indeed, it was speculated that they may not have intended to run in the elections at all.[1] Rather, the intention was to survive and avoid complete elimination by looking beyond the transition, with the ultimate goal of regaining political power through the exploitation of a coalition government formed after the elections, a coalition government which, because of the nature of the parties involved, would be weak and ineffective. In the meantime, during the transition, they would use rhetoric and propaganda to promote the idea that they supported the PPAs and would cooperate, provided UNTAC fulfilled its mandate. If UNTAC was unable to do this, they would subvert the operation while shifting blame for any transgressions of the PPAs onto their opponents and UNTAC.

Such a strategy might have been adopted, but there were early signs that the PDK was refusing fully to cooperate with the UN. A number of violations of the accords were perpetrated by the National Army of Democratic Kampuchea during the deployment of the UN's advance mission between November 1991 and March 1992, including an attack on a UN helicopter.[2] Khmer Rouge intransigence intensified after UNTAC's deployment began in March 1992. The leadership justified its non-compliance by arguing that UNTAC was failing to fulfil its mandate, thereby, according to their interpretation, rendering the

1. David W. Roberts presents selected citations from the work of Khmer Rouge scholars Steve Heder and Christophe Peschoux to show that in early 1992 the Khmer Rouge were prepared to 'switch over from political struggle backed by military struggle ... to political struggle, and were also prevented from making preparations 'in all provinces', to 'receive the UN'. A possible US embassy source speculated sometime in late summer 1992 that 'by all accounts, the KR do not intend to try to win the 1993 elections. In fact, the KR may not even run.' Roberts, *Political Transition in Cambodia 1991–99*, Chap V, pp. 98–9.

2. See, for examples, T. Findlay, *The Legacy and Lessons of UNTAC*, p. 25.

agreements signed in Paris 'meaningless'. They claimed that there was no neutral political atmosphere in either Phnom Penh or the provinces, that UNTAC had not taken full control of the existing administrative agencies as it was supposed to do, and that the SoC remained in thrall to the 'Vietnamese aggressors'.[3] It was also claimed that UNTAC had not verified the withdrawal or removal of all 'foreign forces', and thus Vietnamese soldiers remained on Cambodian territory. Despite the Khmer Rouge's insistent claims to the contrary, UNTAC, after conducting extensive investigations, found no evidence to support their allegations. However, the distinction between Vietnamese 'forces' and Cambodia's sizeable ethnic and immigrant Vietnamese population became blurred. Although all of the factions made similar claims regarding the presence of the Vietnamese, it was the Khmer Rouge that singled out ethnic Vietnamese as legitimate targets for physical attack.

By June 1992, the Khmer Rouge's non-compliance with the agreements and its continued violence against ethnic Vietnamese and UNTAC personnel left the operation in a severe quandary. Refusal to allow UNTAC access to its administrative areas so its military personnel could carry out the critical disarmament, demobilization and cantonment of armed forces as it was obliged to, meant that large numbers of soldiers from all factions would remain under arms, with the potential for renewed armed conflict as an ever-present danger. The consequences of this for the general security situation in the run-up to the elections were dramatic. The following month, in a report to the Security Council, the UN Secretary General put forward two possible alternatives: 'to suspend the operation until all parties comply with the agreements' or to carry on, 'thus demonstrating the international community's determination to assist the Cambodian people despite the lack of cooperation from the PDK'.[4]

Given what was at stake, what would be the best course of action for the UN to take? At one point the possibility of using force to deal with Khmer Rouge intransigence was considered. This option was quickly ruled out by Akashi and UNTAC's military commander, Sanderson. When pushed on the issue, Akashi stressed that UNTAC was a 'classic

---

3.   UNTAC Information/Education Division, *Digest and Analysis of the Cambodian News Media. Part of Democratic Kampuchea*, 23 April 1992.

4.   See Chapter 1, n. 23.

type of peacekeeping operation … essentially based on the agreement and consent of the parties involved'. He argued that 'UNTAC was obliged to resort to diplomatic persuasion and negotiation and should exercise patience in its dealings with all factions'.[5]

However, Akashi and UNTAC's position expressed a more general feeling among those in the international community engaged with the operation to push on no matter what the cost. Any further delays would be too costly in terms of time and money. In any event, any attempt to use military force against the PDK would in all likelihood destabilize the operation further, making it impossible for the elections to take place as scheduled. At the same time, a patient diplomatic approach ran the risk of allowing the PDK further to undermine the election preparations if their concerns were not addressed. Either way, the question was raised as to what lengths the PDK would go to derail the operation entirely, and how UNTAC and the other factions would respond to that eventuality.

Though the UN and the international community had tried throughout the remainder of 1992 to persuade the PDK to fulfil its obligations, these efforts ultimately failed. Consequently in November, Phase II of the operation to canton, disarm and demilitarize the various armies was suspended. According to UN estimates, only one quarter of the 200,000 soldiers, and none from the NADK, had been cantoned and disarmed.[6] At the end of the month, the UN Security Council condemned the PDK for non-compliance and formally reaffirmed its determination to hold the elections no later than May 1993. The Council demanded that the PDK allow UNTAC full access to the areas under its control, and not disrupt the voter registration process which had begun in October, or the election preparations of the other political parties. The PDK and the NADK completely ignored these demands. By December, as the dry season got underway, the general security throughout the country worsened, spreading fear and insecurity among the Cambodian population.

Although the UN had left the door open for further negotiations, it was clear by March 1993 that the PDK would not fulfil any of its obligations under the terms of the agreements. Continued cease-fire

---

5. UNTAC, Information/Education Division: *Summary of Press Conference by the Special Representative of the Secretary-General for Cambodia.* Mr Yasushi Akashi. Phnom Penh, 11 Jan 1993.

6. http://www.un.org/en/peacekeeping/missions/past/untacbackgr2.html#three.

violations and artillery exchanges between the SoC's Cambodian People's Armed Forces (CPAF) and NADK had been intensifying since the end of 1992. Although casualties were few, the fighting forced many Cambodians to flee their homes. Incidents of detention and attacks against UNTAC also increased, causing serious injuries and fatalities. By far the most atrocious instance of NADK violence was the targeted attack of 10 March 1993 on ethnic Vietnamese fisher-folk living on the Chung Kneas floating village on the Tonle Sap Lake, in Siem Reap province. Thirty-three individuals, including women and children, were massacred, and a further thirty-four people were seriously injured. More massacres targeting ethnic Vietnamese followed in other provinces.[7]

UNTAC's responses to the massacres – and violence more generally – were shaped by adherence to the peacekeeping mandate and operational imperatives. UNTAC's mandate was limited to the traditional precept of UN peacekeeping missions: the avoidance of the direct use of force except in self-defence or 'defence of the mission'. For political and military reasons a direct confrontation with the Khmer Rouge was ruled out. As analysts noted, for UNTAC to switch from peacekeeping to peace enforcement would require a change in mandate, which would be politically unacceptable to some signatories of the PPAs, such as China and Japan. It was argued that without significant logistical and operational reinforcements, UNTAC was not capable of engaging in what could turn into a protracted guerrilla insurgency.[8] Moreover, attempting to organize elections was difficult enough already. An escalation in violence involving direct military engagement between the Khmer Rouge and UNTAC would make that task impossible. Elections were the central goal of the operation; not to hold them meant failure, something the UN and the signatories of the agreements were not prepared to countenance.

The question remained, just how much violence and instability could realistically be tolerated before the operation was compromised to a

---

7. For a detailed account of the plight of Cambodia's ethnic Vietnamese during UNTAC see Jay Jordens, 'Persecution of Cambodia's Ethnic Vietnamese During and Since the UNTAC Period', in Heder and Ledgerwood (eds), *Propaganda, Politics and Violence in Cambodia: Democratic Transition under United Nations Peacekeeping*. New York: M.E. Sharpe, 1996.

8. Findlay, *The Legacy and Lessons of UNTAC*, pp. 87–88.

point where elections could not be held? Earlier comments by the head of UN peacekeeping operations about not holding Cambodia to too high a standard was a clear indication that UN HQ New York felt that the elections should go ahead as planned. What this amounted to was an admission that the original expectations were, as the UN Secretary General put it in a later report in May, 'overly optimistic'. In other words, because of Cambodia's recent past, conditions were always going to be imperfect, and up to that point in time it was deemed that the levels of violence and instability were not enough to stop the elections from going ahead.[9] This was a huge gamble for the UN that would only pay off if NADK did not launch widespread attacks, and the large number of Cambodians who had registered to vote actually turned out on polling day.

That gamble became increasingly hazardous as the situation evolved in early April. First of all, Khieu Samphan formally announced the PDK's decision not to compete in the elections. This was followed just over a week later by the closing of the PDK's office in Phnom Penh on the grounds that it was no longer safe for the PDK representatives to remain in the capital. These moves only served to fuel rumours that the NADK were indeed planning armed assaults to stop the elections from happening. Although acts of violence, including the murders of several UNTAC personnel, reportedly involving the PDK, intensified during the campaign period, the all-out attacks expected at polling stations on election day did not materialize.

The elections provided the PDK with opportunities to further their interests. The success or not of the strategies they employed to exploit those opportunities would depend upon the extent to which they could manipulate and control the process. Attempts to do so through non-cooperation did not yield the outcomes the PDK would have liked. Instead, it toughened the resolve of the peace accords signatories to push on regardless of intransigence, violence and intimidation. Perhaps the biggest single impediment to the PDK's electoral strategies was the availability and dissemination of alternative sources of information and education provided by UNTAC. For good or ill, elections and electoral practices are inextricably bound up with information and idea flows. Despite the difficulties, or maybe because of them, UNTAC's electoral and human rights components and its information education division

---

9. UN, Fourth progress report of the Secretary-General, 3 May 1993, pp. 28–29.

succeeded in raising awareness of the operation's goals and objectives to a sufficient degree to provide Cambodian voters with alternative informed choices. This influx of new ideas and information, combined with the obvious desire for peace and stability, created a potent force for change among the Cambodian electorate that the PDK was unable to control militarily or politically.

SoC/CPP and UNTAC

The PDK's refusal to comply with the agreements and their persistent use of violence and intimidation fundamentally altered the terms upon which all groups participated in the electoral process. One of the principal justifications for the PDK's behaviour was UNTAC's inability to control the existing administrative structures of the incumbent SoC as it was mandated to do. As incumbents since the Vietnamese intervention in 1979, the SoC had had a great deal to lose by competing in multi-party elections organized and managed by external forces. The SoC leadership was fully aware of the dangers posed by the elections to their power bases. Speaking about the dangers of not reforming the party in 1989, Hun Sen told the Council of Ministers that if they didn't resolve the problem of how to adjust to the changing political circumstances 'come election time', they 'would lose in the countryside and the city'.[10] The problem for the SoC when it came to elections was that in its previous incarnation, the PRK, it was not 'genuinely popular'.[11] In much the same way as the Khmer Rouge, the SoC and its political party, the CPP, had to develop a strategy that would ensure electoral victory in the absence of complete control over the process.

UNTAC never fully succeeded in sufficiently supervising and controlling the civil administration of the SoC as it was expected to do. Post-UNTAC analysis posited a number of reasons for this, ranging from a lack of sufficient planning to, a lack of suitably qualified personnel, language difficulties and an overall lack of political will to confront the issues.[12] In retrospect, whatever the reasons, UNTAC personnel charged

---

10. Gottesman, *Cambodia After the Khmer Rouge*, p. 282

11. Slocombe, *The People's Republic of Kampuchea 1979–1989*, p. 262.

12. For a more detailed discussion, see Findlay, *The Legacy and Lessons of UNTAC*, pp. 137–38.

with the task of supervision and control would find it next to impossible to penetrate and disrupt the mutually beneficial networks of power and patronage created by the PRK in the 1980s. The failure of UNTAC adequately to implement the control and supervision aspect of the mandate is not to suggest the SoC had it all its own way. On the contrary, they may have been able to stymie UNTAC's attempts to control the administration, but they still had to circumvent the challenges posed by other elements of the operation such as education and awareness programs, and the presence and activities of the opposition parties, especially the PDK.

From the outset, part of the SoC's strategy was an attempt to manage public perception by portraying itself as a guardian of the peace agreements alongside UNTAC. At the CPP 'Extraordinary Party Congress' in July 1992, the party chairman Chea Sim laid out the SoC's official position, emphasizing the importance both the SoC and CPP placed on cooperating with UNTAC in order to implement the agreements quickly and comprehensively. He claimed that the existing administrative structures were not only in conformity with the peace agreement, 'but were also a determining factor in ensuring social stability', and any 'demands made against the agreement or attempts made to affect the social order would bring about serious consequences'.[13]

Chea Sim's remarks highlighted broader concerns among UNTAC personnel at the time that SoC propaganda was actually compromising its role as a neutral, non-partisan arbiter in the process. At first glance it seems reasonable that as a signatory of the agreements, the SoC would be committed to working with UNTAC to implement its mandate. It also seems fair that the SoC would be justified in condemning the actions of other parties if they refused to implement the agreements or were responsible for social unrest and instability. However, on closer inspection of subsequent print and broadcast media reports, it is apparent that the SoC attempted to use UNTAC as a political tool to manipulate public perception in the furtherance of its own agendas. It is clear that Chea Sim's comments were directed primarily towards the PDK, but the SoC would explicitly accuse opposition party members of working in

---

13. UNTAC Information/Education Division. *State of Cambodia News Broadcast Media.* 22–29 July. CPP Extraordinary Party Congress 27–29 July 1992. Full Digest.

collaboration with the PDK or being responsible for banditry or other criminal acts. By making pronouncements implying cooperation with UNTAC, the SoC gave the misleading impression that UNTAC was complicit in condemnations of the activities of the other parties.[14]

Publicly at least, the SoC maintained its official stance of cooperation with UNTAC to implement the agreements and create the neutral political environment. The reality on the ground, however, consistently belied the Party's public pronouncements. Notwithstanding official rhetoric, UNTAC represented a major obstacle in the way of the SoC CPP achieving an all-out electoral victory. In order to circumvent this, the SoC developed a strategy plausibly to defend its commitment to uphold the letter and spirit of the agreements. At the same time it could use existing administrative structures to undermine UNTAC attempts to take full control and establish a neutral political environment. When the prospect of using elections as a mechanism for resolving the conflict had become a reality, Hun Sen was conscious of the need to maintain the military and political situation right up until they were to be held.[15]

Outright non-compliance was not a realistic option. Neither was full compliance if they were to have any chance of winning come election time. The question facing the SoC leadership was how to maximize the inherent advantages of incumbency and get around the obstacles represented by UNTAC and the opposition parties. Part of the answer was to develop a strategy whereby SoC/CPP actions that contravened the agreements could be plausibly denied by claiming political and social instability, and that criminality was as a result of actions carried by PDK 'allies' within the opposition parties. At the same time, SoC propaganda would propagate the idea that they were the only entity capable of upholding the principles and integrity of the agreements and maintaining social order.

'Plausible deniability' proved difficult for the SoC to maintain. Towards the end of 1992, as the security situation deteriorated, UNTAC received numerous reports of an increase in politically motivated violence, intimidation and threats against political parties involving SoC officials,

---

14. Information/Education Division, Digest and Analysis of SoC Print Media, 6–23 February 1993. Full Report.

15. Minutes 29, Cabinet, Council of Ministers, December 29, 1989 (doc 8-26), cited in Gottesman, *Cambodia After the Khmer Rouge*, p. 338.

military, police and security forces. In response, Akashi issued a statement in November reaffirming UNTAC's commitment to the establishment of a neutral political environment. The statement urged all factions to take 'effective measures to stop all forms of intimidation, harassment or killing of the civilian population', and committed UNTAC to strengthening its 'supervision and control over all administrative agencies, bodies and offices which could directly influence the outcome of the elections'. It set forth priorities intended to protect a number of freedoms, including freedom of political party affiliation, adding that all Cambodians must feel free from harassment by the authorities, and no Cambodian party or group had any right to intimidate voters into changing their vote; every 'Cambodian must be free to form, join to work or campaign for, to support and vote for party of choice'. There must be freedom of action for political parties for their 'staffs [sic] to feel confident that they can operate freely and safely in accordance with the United Nations electoral law'.[16]

Although it was diplomatically worded to include all factions, it was clearly directed at the SoC leadership. The SoC's response to Akashi's statement a week later was equally diplomatic, but fell well short of any admission of culpability or a willingness to address the issues. In a letter to Akashi, the content of which was later broadcast on the SoC-controlled television station TVK, Hun Sen reiterated the SoC's commitment to the creation of a neutral political environment and the maintenance of law and security. The letter emphasized that not only has the SoC 'endeavoured' to cooperate with UNTAC in every way but has also opened 'all doors to political parties who have agreed to act in accordance with the statutes of the United Nations Electoral Law'. Hun Sen went on to add that the SoC alone should not be responsible for maintaining the neutral political environment when 'other factions desire to create unrest, insecurity and carry out political murders in order to place blame' on the SoC. Hun Sen stressed that it was not the policy of the SoC or to its 'advantage or intention to create an atmosphere' of violence and instability. He concluded by attempting to shift the blame to another faction or persons behind that faction who could have been in a position to gain some advantage, and 'expressed regret that UNTAC

---

16. 'Establishment of a Neutral Political Environment'. Statement by Mr. Akashi, Special Representative of the Secretary-General for Cambodia, 19 November 1992.

had not learned the lesson of how to conduct investigations with proper evidence before accusing the host faction'.[17]

In January 1993 UNTAC took up Hun Sen's apparent challenge to conduct investigations and gather evidence of SoC involvement in political violence and intimidation. UNTAC control teams were formed to carry out operations at the provisional and local levels in an effort to gather evidence. UNTAC personnel had figured out that the forces behind the upsurge in politically motivated violence might not necessarily be from the Phnom Penh offices of the SoC Ministries of Security and Interior, 'but most likely the Council of Ministers and the CPP'. This realization went a long way in helping to explain 'plausible deniability'. Senior SoC leaders could utilize the decentralized system built up in the 1980s and mobilize patron-client networks and familial and personal relationships to harass, intimidate and prevent the political activities of other parties without being implicated directly.

The control team operations were to be conducted under Article 4(a), Section B, Annex 1 of the Paris Peace Agreements, which granted unrestricted access to all administrative operations and information, and targeted provincial and district offices. Operations were to be conducted discreetly to maintain an element of surprise; the relevant authorities would not be warned in advance of the purpose of the team's visit, although appointments would be made. The team was made up of about 8-12 inter-component UNTAC international personnel: Civil Administration (Public Security and Defence), CIVPOL (UNTAC civilian police), Human Rights, Military and Information/Education. It was authorized and instructed through the 'mission order' and verbally to inform the provincial and district governors or other senior officials that unrestricted access was required to all administrative operations and information, including police and military records as well as judicial and financial information. Provincial and local officials were also requested 'to assist and provide follow-up in the resolution of incidents involving politically motivated intimidation and violence involving administration officials'.[18]

17. 'H.E. Hun Sen, Cambodia's Prime Minister and member of the Council of Ministers sent a letter to H.E. Yasushi Akashi, Special Representative of the Secretary-General of the United Nations and Chief of UNTAC'. 26 November 1992. Copy of unofficial translation of the letter in author's possession.

18. Ibid.

The team deployed in four provinces – Prey Veng, Takeo, Kampong Cham and Kandal – between February and April 1993. They succeeded in gathering a large volume of documentation consisting of official memorandums, circulars, instructions and minutes from meetings and police reports from the national, provincial and local levels. The documentation revealed a systematic and widespread SoC/CPP electoral strategy intended to prevent, suppress and disrupt the political activities of the other factions, and mobilize state resources and assets, including state employees, police, military and civil servants for CPP electioneering. This included the use of 'state funds, the "complete use" of SoC information apparatus for CPP campaigning activities, and plans to infiltrate UNTAC's electoral component by SoC employees'.[19] The use of state resources and assets for political purposes clearly violated the peace agreements.

To implement the strategy, clandestine groups known as 'reaction forces', *Kamlang protekam*, and 'A Groups' were formed. 'Reaction forces' were recruited by local SoC police to engage in attacks on political party members and offices. Documentary evidence from SoC offices in Prey Veng, Takeo and Kampong Cham provinces showed beyond reasonable doubt that the SoC was implementing a policy of organizing 'reaction forces all the way down to the village level, and indicates that they are probably responsible for most of the political violence against the legitimate activities' of the other political parties who were considered enemies and thus legitimate targets for intimidation and harassment. SoC and CPP involvement in these activities could be plausibly denied because these groups were not members of local authorities or security forces. Instead their activities were blamed on common criminals and disgruntled or outraged citizens 'acting on their own'. By contrast the 'A Groups' were formed to infiltrate political parties and engage in the disruption and subversion of structures and reputations through a variety of methods, including the creation of 'contradictions and splits'. Unlike the reaction forces, the A Groups comprised individuals of high standing, with influence among the ranks of the popular masses; some of these individuals received remuneration for their services.

---

19. UNTAC. Deputy Special Representative of the Secretary General. Profile: The Control Team. 16 April 1993.

In the areas which they operated the control teams did penetrate the heart of SoC/CPP power structures at the provincial and district levels – something UNTAC was unable to do before. This had two damaging effects. First, if continued, the control teams' activities threatened severely to disrupt or break those structures. This would send clear signals to opposition parties that UNTAC was after all capable, albeit temporarily, of neutralizing the political situation. A reduction in or elimination of opposition parties' fear of SoC/CPP intimidation and violence severely compromised the incumbents' chances of electoral success. Second, since the beginning of the operation, SoC/CPP had publicly stressed commitment to abiding by the terms of the agreements, unlike the PDK and their allies, the opposition parties. Clearly, evidence contained in the retrieved documents revealed the SoC/CPP had systematically set out to subvert the peace process it was publicly claiming to promote.

UNTAC's existing dilemma, however, was the elections. After the PDK's withdrawal, it could not afford a protracted standoff with SoC/CPP if the elections were to be held as scheduled. UNTAC's response to the discovery of the documents had to be carefully measured. At the same time, Hun Sen and the CPP leadership could not afford to 'over-react' to the obvious threat posed by the control team's activities if it wanted to secure a credible electoral victory. The interaction between UNTAC and the SoC/CPP leadership regarding the control teams set the tone for future dealings between Hun Sen and the UN. A meeting in March 1993 between UNTAC and the SoC/CPP authorities to discuss the matter illustrates the point. Akashi and the directors of Civil Administration and Security components met with Hun Sen and the governors of the provinces where most of the documents were discovered. Hun Sen was indignant, accusing the control teams of exceeding their mandate in what amounted to the conduct of a 'criminal search'. He went on to suggest that UNTAC 'was trying to destroy the peace agreement itself'. He asked the SRSG 'what would happen if [UNTAC] overstepped [their] rights and I decided not to participate in the elections'.[20] It was made quite clear that without the cooperation and

---

20. UNTAC Control Team transcript of a meeting between Hun Sen and SRSG Akashi, 25 March 1993. The meeting took place on Monday 22 March at the 'Council of Ministers', Phnom Penh.

patience of the SoC/CPP, UNTAC would not be able to implement the agreements and hold the elections.[21]

The SoC/CPP's attitude towards UNTAC was succinctly summed up in a Council of Ministers memo: 'What locates the point at which UNTAC dies is whether we co-operate with it or not.'[22] In a similar way to the PDK, the SoC/CPP leadership was acutely aware that the SRSG and UNTAC were under pressure to hold the elections within the required time frame and could not do so without the CPP. In sum the SoC/CPP strategy was Janus-faced. Publicly it was the guardian of the peace agreements. On the ground it used all means necessary to gain electoral advantage at the expense of the neutral political environment. Opposition parties, newly formed human rights organizations and the electorate were thus subjected to a systematic strategy of violence, intimidation and coercion. When confronted with the incriminating evidence, the SoC/CPP leadership used cover stories denying any involvement in these types of activities.

The 'Opposition', Sihanouk and UNTAC

Out of the twenty political parties that would contest the elections, F'pec, and to a lesser extent the Buddhist Liberal Democratic Party (BLDP), posed the biggest threat to the SoC/CPP's chances of an outright victory. Virtually all SoC/CPP-orchestrated political violence, intimidation, coercion and propaganda was directed at these parties, but mainly at F'pec. Both parties were created from the armed insurgent groups that fought the guerrilla war to remove the PRK and its Vietnamese patrons from Cambodia in the 1980s. Founded by Prince Sihanouk in 1981, F'pec relied upon promoting an idealized version of Sihanouk's rule in the 1950s and 60s, often romanticized as a period of peace, prosperity and development. The BLDP emerged from the Son Sann faction of the KPNLF, the third largest of the political movements formed to remove the PRK and the Vietnamese. As a former prime minister during the Sihanouk era, Son Sann had a reputation among his followers as being incorruptible amidst the corrupt excesses of the Sihanouk and subsequent Lon Nol regimes.

---

21. Ibid.

22. 'Secret Memorandum', Cabinet of the Council of Ministers (COM), No. 1909, 17 October 1992, Prey Veng Control Team Report. Appendix, p. 11.

Like F'pec, the BLDP was made up of former resistance veterans from the border camps and Khmers returning from overseas, many from the US, bringing with them republican-based political ideas that would be amalgamated with indigenous Buddhist principles, creating an unclear political platform.

To be able to participate in the elections in a meaningful way, F'pec faced the enormously difficult and dangerous task of building up party membership and grassroots power bases in areas outside of their control, areas run by the SoC/CPP authorities, police and military. These tasks may have been easier and less dangerous if UNTAC had succeeded in creating and maintaining a neutral political environment. But the reasons discussed above, UNTAC's inability to create such conditions allowed the SoC/CPP to organize and perpetrate hundreds of attacks on newly opened political party offices and party members.[23] In the face of outright hostility and violence, opposition parties, particularly F'pec, had to develop strategies that were as unobtrusive as possible to reach out and build the necessary support among voters.

In spite of the violence and intimidation directed at them, opposition parties managed successfully to open offices and carry out political activities across the country. Because of its connections to Sihanouk and greater access to resources F'pec was the most successful party, opening offices in almost every province and district. Organizationally, the party leadership divided the country into five zones or *phumpheak*. Each of these zones' activities was organized along political and military lines. As the party leader, Ranariddh, appointed provincial party leaders, and political councils were established to advise provisional and district offices. At the district level, offices were run by small committees of three members. Because F'pec as a political party had recruited a number of returnees from overseas, most of the political work and organization were conducted by individuals from the border camps and veterans from the guerrilla struggle in the 1980s. Party organizers also included local

23. Kate Frieson notes that 'UNTAC's investigations concluded that the SOC police and military were responsible for the death or injury of 96 FUNCINPEC and BLDP members from November 1992 to January 1993 and another 114 members of these parties between March and May 1993'. K. Frieson, 'The Politics of Getting out the Vote in Cambodia', in Heder and Ledgerwood (eds), *Propaganda, Politics and Violence in Cambodia: Democratic Transition under United Nations Peace-keeping,* p. 196.

activists and supporters who had been incarcerated by the SoC as political prisoners and then released under the terms of the peace agreements. In the absence of a neutral political atmosphere, the utilization of 'old networks' of local supporters and veterans from the resistance allowed F'pec to conduct a low profile strategy to protect its nascent party structures in the rural areas.[24]

By far the greatest electoral advantage F'pec had over other opposition parties and the incumbent SoC/CPP was its royalist credential. For centuries, Cambodian royalty had been venerated with semi-divine status, especially among Cambodia's majority rural population. As the former King, Sihanouk embodied a potent unifying force for peace and the resuscitation of a traditional past in a country ravaged by decades of war. The party leadership and activists exploited this advantage to the hilt among the electorate, claiming that a vote for F'pec was a vote for Sihanouk. In a similar vein, F'pec made political capital from the SoC/CPP's preparedness to continue to fight, to prevent the 'return of the Khmer Rouge'. F'pec's campaign rhetoric and propaganda tapped into the desperate need for an end to civil war and internecine conflict by promising a post-election government made up solely of Khmers, even if that meant including the Khmer Rouge, which was considered a price worth paying for peace.

The attitude of the opposition parties to UNTAC was mixed. Aside from general criticisms of the perceived and actual disrespectful and sometimes physically abusive behaviour of some UNTAC personnel towards Cambodians, the general feeling was one of frustration with UNTAC's inability to implement key aspects of its mandate as they had wished.[25] While UNTAC's presence was initially welcomed, its inability adequately to protect opposition parties from SoC/CPP attacks was a major source of consternation. Another major issue for the opposition was the Vietnamese question. In the early stages of the operation, all of the opposition groups severely criticized UNTAC's efforts to verify the

24. Ibid., p. 197

25. An UNTAC information/education division analysis of people's perception of UNTAC found 'a very serious erosion of public confidence in UNTAC'. Many Cambodians complained about UNTAC's reckless driving, chronic drunkenness and a total lack of respect for local laws and customs. Other complaints included UNTAC personnel frequently visiting brothels and flaunting their high salaries. Info/ed. Field Trip Report: Phnom Penh, 7–12 January 1993.

withdrawal of Vietnamese forces. Finally, satisfied that the Vietnamese military and other personnel had withdrawn, both F'pec and BLDP continued to focus on anti-Vietnamese in propaganda to secure votes.

Historical fear and mistrust of Vietnamese intentions in Cambodia, real and imagined, is deeply embedded in the Khmer collective consciousness, which harbours a largely unquestioned notion of a shared Khmer national identity. Like the PDK, F'pec and the BLDP effectively politicized these anxieties, propagating ideas that Cambodia's ethnic Vietnamese, many of whom had lived in the country for generations, were part of a broader conspiracy to 'destroy' the 'Khmer nation'. Only they, who had fought to remove the Vietnamese, could save the nation from total Vietnamese control. They claimed that, because the SoC and its CCP party had been installed as puppets by the Vietnamese, a vote for them was a vote for continued Vietnamese domination of Cambodian affairs. Although there was no direct evidence that either F'pec or BLDP were involved in the massacres of ethnic Vietnamese, they had little to say about the murders. However, their reliance on ethno-nationalist and anti-Vietnamese rhetoric and propaganda only served to heighten ethnic tensions.[26]

At the apex of Khmer nationalist discourse during UNTAC was the personality of Sihanouk. In order to take up his position as Chairman of the SNC, Sihanouk passed on the Presidency of F'pec to his son, Ranariddh. Sihanouk himself was no stranger to electoral politics, nor the violent repressive means needed to eliminate all opposition to ensure outright electoral victories. After abdicating the throne in March 1955, Sihanouk presided over four elections before his overthrow in the coup of 1970. In all four elections, all seats in the national assembly were held by the *Sangkum Reastr Niyum* (Popular Socialist Community), a political organization formed by Sihanouk to develop his vision of a paternalistic authoritarian system of governance and socio-economic development. Ostensibly, the *Sangkum* was intended as an organization for 'national unity' under the tutelage of Sihanouk. But as the four elections in 1955,

---

26. For an excellent and detailed discussion about ethno-nationalism in Cambodia see Penny Edwards, 'Imagining the other in Cambodian Nationalist Discourse Before and During the UNTAC Period', in Heder and Ledgerwood (eds), *Propaganda, Politics and Violence in Cambodia: Democratic Transition under United Nations Peace-keeping*, pp. 68–73.

1958, 1962 and 1966 demonstrated, any vocal dissent or alternative political organization outside of the *Sangkum* was systematically and brutally repressed or eliminated altogether.[27]

The Paris Peace Accords and the 1993 UNTAC elections circumscribed Sihanouk's room for political manoeuvre to some extent. In the late 1980s, Sihanouk's attempts to strike a deal with Hun Sen outside of the formal search for a political solution failed, largely due to international pressure. Sihanouk nonetheless attempted to exploit the election process once again in service of his own quixotic political agenda under the guise of national unity and reconciliation. To be sure, all parties, including UNTAC, recognized that Sihanouk had a central role to play in the furtherance of their own interests and agendas. None of this was lost on Sihanouk, who saw himself as the only Cambodian political figure who could 'reconcile and unify' the country and the various factions without excessive foreign interference. To that end, his interactions with the various factions and UNTAC typified past behaviour. He made frequent public statements in support of the SoC/CCP, comparing their achievements in the 80s with those of his *Sangkum* in the 50s and 60s. Other statements included plans for the formation of a provisional government of national reconciliation under his presidency, which were supported by the PDK, suggesting a political role for them after new elections had been organized under the provisional arrangements.[28] Sihanouk's initial cooperation with UNTAC gave way to severe criticism and threats to resign from the SNC because of UNTAC's failure to fulfil its mandate. This was followed by a complete about-turn as he resumed relations with Akashi and the SNC when the idea for holding presidential elections, either before or simultaneously with parliamentary elections, was floated. UNTAC had supported and encouraged the idea of holding presidential elections, with the expectation that Sihanouk would put

27. See for example S. Heder, 'Cambodian Elections in Historical Perspective', in J. L. Vijghen (ed.) *People and the 1998 National Elections in Cambodia: Their voices, roles and impact on democracy*. Experts for Community Research, Phnom Penh, 2002, pp. 1–4.

28. UNTAC Information/Education Division Analysis Reports 1/930 *'Criticisms of UNTAC by Hun Sen, Chakrapong, Sihanouk'*. January 1993.

forward his candidacy and win.[29] This idea was, however, later dropped by both the UN and Sihanouk.[30]

Sihanouk's national unity and reconciliation rhetoric, while attractive in one way or another to all parties, could only be exploited by Ranariddh and F'pec. The mutual enmity among the other parties meant they could hardly campaign for unity and reconciliation. F'pec, because of its organizational history and connections with Sihanouk, could. Indeed, because of problems in establishing party offices and the attendant SoC/CPP violence and intimidation faced by the opposition parties, the outcome of the elections for F'pec may have been very different were it not for its relationship with Sihanouk. F'pec was the most popular of the opposition parties, but its reputation and popularity were diminished by perceptions among Cambodians living in the camps under its control. People complained of harsh conditions in the camps, and the predatory behaviour of some F'pec leaders, who seemed to be more concerned with personal enrichment from the lucrative trade in natural resources than in ordinary people's welfare[31]. In terms of its internal organization, it had also suffered a number of splits as key military officers defected to the CPP after the arrival of Ranariddh. Notably, Ranariddh's half-brother, Prince Chakrapong, aggrieved at being usurped by him in the party hierarchy.[32] Nevertheless, in spite of these problems, F'pec, and Ranariddh's stated commitment to 'Sihanoukism', and the promise of peace, unity and national reconciliation, appealed to enough voters on election day to give it the edge over its opponents.[33]

---

29. UNTAC Information/Education Division. Digest and Analysis Report. '*Press Conference by the Special Representative of the Secretary – General for Cambodia, Mr. Yasushi Akashi.*' 11 January 1993.

30. Report of the Secretary-General on the Implementation of Security Council Resolution 792 (1992). S/25289, 13 February 1993, p. 8, VII. Electoral Matters, paragraph 33.

31. UNTAC Information/Education Division. Analysis Report. *Assessment of Popular Support for Political Parties.* 8 January 1993.

32. UNTAC Information/Education Division. Analysis Report. '*Defection of FUNCINPEC/ANKI Figures to SoC/CPP.*' 24 April 1993.

33. UNTAC Information/Education Division. Information Control Report. '*Interview with Norodom Ranariddh on FUNCINPEC Radio.*' 26 March 1993.

The Creation of an Elections Infrastructure

In the midst of all these political machinations, UNTAC succeeded in creating an elections infrastructure from scratch. The Electoral Component was responsible for designing and implementing the necessary systems for every phase of the elections process. In consultation with the SNC, a legal framework that included an electoral law, regulations to govern the electoral process and an electoral code of conduct was formulated. It was also involved in civic education and training, compliance and complaints as well as voter and political party registration. The Component had personnel in twenty-one provincial offices, and district election supervisors (DES) in approximately two hundred district offices around the country.

The electoral law to govern the process was submitted by UNTAC to the SNC for approval at the beginning of April 1992. A number of issues were raised by members of the SNC that delayed its promulgation until August. First of all, the PDK in particular objected to the enfranchisement of any individual over the age of eighteen born in Cambodia provided for by the Paris agreements. PDK and other parties were concerned that resident ethnic Vietnamese would be enfranchised. Both F'pec and the BLDP pushed for the inclusion of overseas Cambodians, including ethnic Khmers residing in Cambodia, but born in or with a parent born in, the Kampuchea Krom or 'Lower Kampuchea' region of Southern Vietnam. The final revised law did not disenfranchise ethnic-Vietnamese who had lived in Cambodia for several generations. However, only those individuals over the age of 18 born in Cambodia with one parent born in Cambodia, and all individuals over 18 who had one parent and one grandparent born in Cambodia, were eligible to vote.

One of UNTAC's biggest successes was the creation of an electorate with access and exposure to information beyond the propaganda of the various parties. The overall success or failure of the operation would be judged by the numbers of Cambodians who were able and willing not just to exercise the right to vote, but to do so in a way that was more than just a ritual 'for reasons of conformity or social pressures'.[34] Raising the consciousness and awareness of a population, the vast majority of whom had little or no knowledge of what democratic multi-party elections meant, was an incredibly difficult task within the available time frame.

34. Palmer, *Elections and Political Development*, p. 4.

This was made doubly difficult by political elites on all sides attempting to manipulate people's perceptions of the meanings and importance of the elections for their own political ends.

One of the Electoral Component's major tasks was voter registration. The process began in October 1992 and was extended to the end of January 1993 due to the large numbers of people who wanted to register. UNTAC district election supervisors and an estimated four thousand Khmer registration staff carried out the job of enrolling the population. By the end of the process, the Electoral Component had managed successfully to register 4.6 million potential voters, including individuals residing in PDK controlled areas where UNTAC had limited access. For the most part, the registration process proceeded without too many problems. However, UNTAC received numerous complaints from people that their registration cards had been confiscated by SoC officials and police, and in some cases had not been returned. When confronted by UNTAC personnel, SoC district officials claimed they were told they were acting on orders from the president of the provincial CPP headquarters to ascertain who had not registered. The process involved the collection of the cards and the recording of personal information at the village level, which was then passed on to the commune and districts levels and beyond. This practice not only contravened the electoral law but also created anxiety and confusion among people who were unclear why they had to effectively register twice. Based upon the findings of UNTAC investigations, what this amounted to was harassment and intimidation leading to a lack of confidence among the population about the secrecy of the vote.[35]

Reassuring people that their vote was secret and that they could vote according to their conscience was another challenge faced the Electoral Component. As well as the collection of voter registration cards, the CPP embarked on an ambitious recruitment drive to dramatically increase the number of party members, thereby 'consolidating and strengthening state control over local populations'. For this purpose local groups of party loyalists were formed into 'grassroots strengthening teams' tasked with assessing popular support for the CPP, assisting with voter

---

35. UNTAC Information/Education Division. Report on Political Intimidation in Battambang. 19 March 1993. See also Frieson, 'The Politics of Getting out the Vote in Cambodia', pp. 191–92.

registration and issuing new party membership cards. In practice, many ordinary Cambodians and state employees felt they had little choice but to accept the membership cards offered by the teams, fearing that refusal to do so could invite further trouble or lead to the loss of their jobs. As a result of these practices, there was widespread fear that local authorities would know who they had voted for.[36] People wanted to know whether being a member of one particular party meant they had to vote for it.

In an effort to answer this and other questions, and to combat the associated fear and intimidation, the Electoral Component launched a civic education campaign to instil confidence and trust in the secrecy of the vote. The campaign focused on three main themes: 'Why Elections?', 'How to Vote', and 'Democracy and Human Rights'. Cambodian and international staff from the Electoral Component organized civic education meetings and forums in local pagodas, giving people the opportunity to listen to presentations related to the three themes, ask questions and express concerns about any aspect of the elections process. The presentations and forums explained a variety of concepts including the importance of the right for people to choose government representatives, what a constitution is for, what type of government will follow the elections and how it is supposed to function. They explained the voting procedure step-by-step and convinced the audience that their vote would be secret. The importance of choice based upon accurate information about all of the parties and what they stood for was emphasized, as well as the importance of being able to question politicians about their programs and policies. Basic democratic and human rights were covered, including fundamental freedoms regarding personal security and safety, freedom from intimidation and violence, freedom of expression, movement, and association, and the right to run for office and join a political party.[37]

Because of the circumstances within which they were operating, the creation of an electoral infrastructure was never going to be straightforward. Its success would require the cooperation and willingness of the four parties and the Cambodian population. The redrafting of the

---

36. Ibid.

37. UNTAC Electoral Component. *Civic Education Training and Material*. 19 February 1993. See also 'Civic Education Sweeps Cambodia's Provinces', UNTAC Free Choice Electoral Component Newsletter, Issue No. 16, March 1993.

electoral law to accommodate the concerns of the PDK, F'pec and the BLDP regarding voter eligibility was managed fairly smoothly. Despite SoC/CPP interference, the registration process was a huge success. The enrolment of approximately 4.6 million Cambodians, even in a climate of fear and intimidation, was a good indication that the majority of Cambodians wanted to participate. Whether they turned out to vote or not and how they would vote remained to be seen. In this regard, the dissemination of information and the civic education campaign were of vital importance. It was probably true that in the time available, they were limited, but they did raise the consciousness and awareness of ordinary Cambodians enough to make reasonably informed political choices, even if those choices were qualified and limited. In any event, turnout would depend on the security situation and extent to which Cambodians were determined and brave enough to make it to the polling stations.

The Campaign

The formation of a multi-party political environment was yet another significant achievement of the UNTAC operation. Twenty political parties registered with the Electoral Component to compete in the elections. However, outside of the main four parties most of these were either a mix of offshoots from F'pec and the BLDP, or independent groups led by individuals returning from diaspora communities in the US, France and Australia. The independent groups lacked adequate resources or bases of popular support to make any real impact. The official campaign period ran as scheduled from 7 April until 19 May. In retrospect, it was perhaps unsurprising that the three principal contestants relied on fear-based nationalist tropes and memes in an effort to convince the electorate of the righteousness and legitimacy of their platforms. They could offer very little else beyond promise of protection from the 'enemies within', be they the Khmer Rouge and their 'allies' or the Vietnamese.

Hundreds of rallies were staged across the country, the majority of which were held in the electorally key rural areas. Due to the advantages of incumbency the CPP were able to stage more rallies and attract more people than the other parties. The SoC/CPP leaders based their campaign rhetoric on their role in the liberation of the nation from the Khmer Rouge. They emphasized past achievements since the liberation, focusing on development, security and the prevention of the return of the Khmer Rouge. F'pec and the BLDP were consistently portrayed as allies of the Khmer Rouge, and thus enemies of the nation. Essentially, the CPP claimed that a vote for the opposition was a vote for the Khmer Rouge.[38]

F'pec and BLDP campaign messages continued to utilize nationalistic rhetoric exploiting historical fear of Vietnamese expansion in Cambodia. The use of the pejorative term *youn* in the Khmer language to refer to the Vietnamese was frequently used at opposition rallies to exploit that fear. They reminded people that the SoC had been installed by the Vietnamese, and that it was they, F'pec or BLDP, who had fought to remove the Vietnamese. In response to CPP accusations that they were colluding with the PDK, the opposition capitalized on the fact that Hun Sen, Chea Sim and Heng Samrin were themselves former Khmer Rouge cadres installed by the Vietnamese. In stark contrast to the CPP's campaign approach, F'pec's message emphasized peaceful reconciliation. In keeping with Sihanouk's ideas of creating a government of national unity including elements of the Khmer Rouge, Ranariddh was offering a peaceful solution by harnessing his Sihanoukist credentials to the notion of reconciliation.

The atmosphere at the hundreds of political meetings and rallies held throughout the country during the campaign was for the most part peaceful. There were no reported incidents of overt intimidation or violence. This was surprising giving the vitriolic propaganda put out by all parties in print and broadcast media before the campaign got underway. Indeed, the struggle for control over the flow and dissemination of information is possibly one of the most emblematic and enduring features of the 1993 elections. UNTAC played a vital role in providing alternative sources of information. It was one of the responsibilities of UNTAC's Information/Education Division to engage in informing Cambodians about the purpose, goals and objectives of the Paris agreements and the United Nations operation. The Division worked closely with the electoral and human rights component in assisting in the production of educational radio and TV programmes and printed information such

---

38. See for example K. Frieson, 'The Cambodian Elections of 1993: A Case of Power to the People?', in R.H. Taylor (ed.), *The Politics of Elections in Southeast Asia*. Washington, D.C.: Woodrow Wilson Center Press and Cambridge University Press, 1996, p. 236.

as posters, leaflets and comic books, explaining the role and purpose of the various components. Hundreds of video cassettes showing dramas to explain electoral and human rights issues such as violence and intimidation were produced and sent to all UNTAC offices in the provinces.[39]

Access to print and broadcast media for electoral purposes by all political parties was essential if the elections were to be considered fair. The Information/Education Division was directly involved in the development of a media charter and the introduction of 'Media Guidelines for Cambodia'. The guidelines were produced in an effort to promote a safe and independent press free from state control and interference, and to prevent unacceptable propaganda inciting war or racial and religious hatred, intimidation and violence. UNTAC was successful in creating a safe environment for new media outlets to begin publishing, but failed to curb the negative propaganda of the SoC and PDK. In response to opposition party complaints about state control of radio and TV broadcasts, UNTAC successfully launched an 'information campaign' just before the official election campaign, allowing all parties 'equal access and equal time' in the form of short, five minute slots on UNTAC radio to make political statements.[40] UNTAC TV played interviews with political party leaders and video-taped roundtable discussions in the months before the campaign. UNTAC also negotiated with the SoC for 'fair access' to state-run media outlets, allowing information about the elections process to be broadcast on the state-owned TV station, TV Kampuchea during the campaign period.[41]

Polling and Results

Expected attacks on polling stations by the Khmer Rouge never materialized. UNTAC's military component had redeployed forces to provide added security for the electoral process. However, in the weeks before polling there were numerous violent incidents linked to the PDK, resulting in the deaths of UNTAC personnel. There were also small-scale but deadly cease-fire violations, including Khmer Rouge attacks on the town

---

39. UNTAC Free Choice Electoral Component Newsletter, *Interview with Tim Carney* (Director of UNTAC Education and Information Division). Issue No.16. 26 March 1993, pp. 13–14.

40. Ibid.

41. Ibid.

of Siem Reap and a civilian train, resulting in the killing and wounding of passengers. The heightened fear of an all-out Khmer Rouge military attack caused some within opposition parties and international circles to question the commitment to hold the elections at all costs. However, both international and domestic resolve to do so remained steadfast.[42]

The increase in violence and tension during the campaign period did nothing to deter Cambodians from turning out in their millions on the voting days of May 23-28. Indeed, it could be argued that it was precisely because of the persistence of conflict and violence that so many were brave and determined enough to make the journey to the polling stations. In the end, an estimated 89.5 per cent of the registered electorate turned out and voted. With the assistance of hundreds of United Nations volunteers and local Cambodian staff, including 1,000 international polling station officers, the polling and counting processes went relatively smoothly. With the exception of some minor incidents, the presence of UNTAC military personnel and civilian police at the polling stations ensured that voting and counting proceeded peacefully. They also ensured that ballot boxes were kept safe until they reached the counting stations.[43] The results showed that F'pec came out on top with 45.47 per cent of the votes cast, followed by 38.23 per cent for the CPP, 3.81 per cent for the BLDP, 1.37 per cent for Moulinaka, and an 11.12 per cent share among the other parties. Under the electoral system of proportional representation, F'pec had won 58 seats in the constituent assembly, CPP 51, BLDP 10 and Moulinaka only one seat.

UNTAC Elections, Success or Failure?

UNTAC achieved its primary goal of creating, organizing and supervising multi-party democratic elections in Cambodia. A huge gamble had paid

---

42. For a concise summary of events leading up to polling days, see Findlay, *The Legacy and Lessons of UNTAC*, pp. 76–82.

43. The SoC/CPP leadership claimed that ballot boxes had been interfered with, leading to allegations of fraud. There were incidents during transportation when the seals and padlocks on some of the boxes were broken and some ballots fell out. However, an investigation by UNTAC found that there was no evidence of fraud, and the integrity of the votes in the boxes concerned remained intact. See for example the report of the Inter-Parliamentary Union Delegation to observe the election in Cambodia, http://www.ipu.org/elcn-e/rptcamb.htm#Treatment.

off, or had it? On the one hand critics argued that UNTAC had failed to fulfil its mandate as laid out in the Paris Peace Agreements, thus rendering the elections virtually meaningless. It was argued that the elections process was hardly democratic, in the absence of a neutral political environment and the presence of unremitting political violence and intimidation. Furthermore, the distribution of power in the new coalition government did not reflect the election results. The Khmer Rouge was still at large with the capacity, albeit limited, to continue armed resistance. Critics concluded that any attempt to impose a western inspired liberal democratic solution was bound to fail in a country with a political elite culture that was antithetical to democracy. [44] From this perspective, internationally sponsored elections in places like Cambodia are relatively unimportant 'ephemeral' political experiments by outside forces.[45]

UNTAC was unable to take full control and supervise SoC administrative structures and create a completely neutral political environment as mandated. The PDK stated repeatedly that they signed the peace agreements with the understanding that UNTAC would completely dismantle SoC administrative structures. UNTAC's failure to do so justified – so they claimed – their non-cooperation and eventual withdrawal from the elections process. The abandonment of the disarming and cantonment phase of the operation as a consequence of the PDK's non-cooperation threw the operation into crisis. Any possibility there may have been of creating a political environment that was neutral and relatively peaceful was lost. Despite this and given what was at stake, the UN and the signatories remained determined to stay the course and hold the elections as planned. In the meantime, the SoC took full political advantage of the multiple cease-fire violations and the upsurge in violence and general insecurity to bolster their electoral strategy. By shifting the blame for violence onto the PDK and other criminal elements, the SoC leadership would plausibly deny any involvement. Overtly and covertly they mobilized the administration to coerce and intimidate large numbers of the population to become members of the CPP while SoC security forces, police and military organized the har-

---

44. For a critical account of the UNTAC operation, see D. W. Roberts, *Political Transition in Cambodia 1991–99*.

45. Elizabeth Spiro Clark, 'Why Elections Matter.' *The Washington Quarterly*, 23:3, Summer 2000, p. 30.

assment, repression and murder of political opposition. To be sure, the behaviour of the political elites and their supporters during this process was hardly democratic, but did this mean the elections were politically unimportant or undemocratic?

The dismantling of a repressive one-party state system by foreigners was always going to be a extremely difficult and dangerous task. Mutually dependent systems of powerful patron–client networks nurtured by the SoC leadership in the 1980s were too deeply entrenched to be taken apart by a UN peacekeeping operation in only eighteen months. Nonetheless, UNTAC was able to create conditions within which a multi-party political system could be established. To be sure, the leadership of the political parties formed out of the 1980s resistance groups, including Prince Sihanouk, were hardly archetypal democrats. Ranariddh and Sihanouk were no doubt fully committed to peaceful national reconciliation but only to the extent that they could exercise full control over the process in ways that would not necessarily be democratic. For good or ill, opposition groups were able to penetrate into SoC controlled areas and offer Cambodians an alternative to the SoC/CPP. This would not have happened at this time without elections.

The UNTAC elections were unique. Never before or since has an UN operation on the scale of UNTAC been mounted to create an elections infrastructure in a sovereign state from virtually nothing. The presence of a large contingent of foreign peacekeepers enabled those necessary conditions to take hold. Sources and flows of information and education were essential for the creation of those conditions. UNTAC's notable successes were the establishment of environments where print and broadcast media could operate relatively safely and securely, providing opportunities for ordinary Cambodians to inform and educate themselves about the elections and the principles underpinning them. However, it is hard to know the extent to which voters did actually vote according to their conscience rather than as a result of organized fear or obligation. One thing is certain, regardless of circumstances: the millions of Cambodians who turned out to vote recognized just how important the elections were to them.

A new coalition government finally emerged out of the post-election turmoil and a new constitution was promulgated. The new constitution stated that Cambodia would hold regular, democratic elections every five years. It had nothing to say about how those elections would be organized. The new Cambodian government had neither the technical nor financial resources to organise elections alone. As the following chapters will show, continued foreign assistance would play a significant role in the struggle for control of electoral politics.

CHAPTER 3

Elections and International Assistance Post-UNTAC

On 10 June, Yasushi Akashi officially announced to the SNC the results of the 1993 UNTAC elections in Cambodia. He stated that 'this phase of the elections process had been carried out in a free and fair manner' and 'fairly and accurately reflected the will of the Cambodian people and must be respected'. Later that day the 120 members of the constituent assembly were formally declared to be elected. On 15 June, the UN Security Council resolution 840 approved the election results and certified them as 'free and fair'. All parties except for the CPP accepted the results. The CPP claimed that massive irregularities had taken place and that UNTAC had displayed bias against the party throughout the elections process. They refused to accept the results and until these complaints had been satisfactorily resolved.

In June 1996, during a meeting with a senior representative from the United Nations Department of Political Affairs (UNDPA), Hun Sen went 'on a tirade against the UNTAC elections', reportedly describing them as 'the worst in Cambodia's history and one of the worst in the world'.[1] The final outcome of the UNTAC elections thus had profound consequences for the trajectory of the political system and electoral politics in Cambodia. The formation of a peculiar and unwieldy government with two prime ministers suggested that the way ahead was far from straight forward. There was nonetheless some hope of consolidating the democratic gains that had resurfaced with UNTAC. The new coalition government was acknowledged as legitimate, paving the way for Cambodia to re-integrate into regional and international markets

---

1. Report on Francesc Vendrell, Director of the United Nations Department of Political Affairs, Asia and the Pacific Division visit by to Cambodia: 10–13 June 1996. Outgoing Code Cable 1809. United Nations, HQS, New York, 26 June 1996, p. 3, Paragraph 6.

and allow desperately needed aid for reconstruction and development to enter the country.

The newly configured state and societal power structures, in the context of future elections, were deeply problematic for democratic development. The unusual two prime minister system was only intended as an interim arrangement, to be dissolved after the end of the first term of the new assembly, when a single prime minister would assume power following elections in 1998. When the new 'liberal democratic' constitution was promulgated in September 1993, it had very little say about how future elections were to be organised and conducted. Clearly, in the post-UNTAC period, as a sovereign independent nation it was Cambodia's state power holders who would be responsible for the organization of elections. The new government had neither the technical expertise nor the financial resources to organise further elections without external support.

As early as 1994, less than a year after the UNTAC elections, elements within the new government began to address the elections issue. In June 1996 the government formally approached the UN for technical and financial assistance for the local and parliamentary elections to be held in 1997 and 1998. UN support for commune elections was postponed due to the perceived potential for widespread violence. Plans for national elections went forward. Elections once again would be at the centre of a long drawn out struggle between competing political forces for control over the process. Although international involvement was not on the same scale as UNTAC, it was nonetheless a major factor in the developing struggle. In addition, new social forces that had emerged out of the UNTAC operation began to play an increasingly significant role in the evolution of electoral politics.

Post-UNTAC Political Developments

Under the proportional representation electoral system, neither F'pec nor the CPP had the necessary two thirds majority to form a government alone, even with the support of the other parties. Without an outright electoral victory, the SoC/CPP's monopoly on state power was compromised. Hun Sen and the CPP were facing the prospect of a marginalised position in any government formed by a legislative assembly once constitutional arrangements could be agreed upon. These arrangements posed a huge potential threat to the patron-client structures of power and privilege built up by the SoC/CPP leadership in the 1980s, especially in the provinces and rural areas where any future elections would be won or lost. This explains to a great extent Hun Sen's and the CPP's initial refusal to accept the election results and the transition of SoC power to a coalition government led by Ranariddh and F'pec.

The resulting political hiatus effectively dispelled the enormous sense of relief accompanying the relatively trouble free polls as a post-election political crisis developed. The Paris agreements did not include provisions for post-election political issues. As far as the peace agreements were concerned, it was the duty and responsibility of a legislative assembly to form a new government free from interference by outsiders. What happened in the interim period before the formation of the new government was nonetheless highly uncertain. Early indications suggested further instability and possibly armed conflict. On May 29 when it became apparent that the CPP would not get the majority they expected, its leadership protested against the broadcasting of the partial results by UNTAC radio. This was followed by complaints of numerous irregularities in an attempt to throw into question the validity of the election results.

Initial CPP complaints of UNTAC bias and election irregularities precipitated an intense period of closed door meetings and negotiations. In the days immediately following the first broadcasts of election results, senior SoC/CPP officials solicited the support of Sihanouk in mediating negotiations. After meeting with Chea Sim and Hun Sen on 3 June, Sihanouk took a decision to announce the formation of the 'National Government of Cambodia' with him as Chief of State, President of the Council of Ministers and Commandant of the armed forces and police. Ranariddh and Hun Sen would share power as co-prime ministers. Sihanouk's announcement was influenced by suggestions at the meeting that if a compromise could not be reached, there might have been an unpredictable, even violent, response from elements within the CPP. To make matters worse, the decision was taken without the approval of Ranariddh who had left for Thailand the previous day. Sihanouk seemed to be under the impression that in Ranariddh's absence he had his 'unconditional support'.[2] When it became clear that neither Ranariddh, UNTAC

2.   R.M. Jenner, 'Cambodian Chronicles: non-paper', p. 15.

and some members of the foreign diplomatic 'core group' supported the proposal, it was withdrawn the following day. [3]

Meanwhile, the SoC/CPP kept up the pressure to push for demands for an equal share of power. On June 4 in a letter to Akashi, SoC chairman Chea Sim requested that 'the election results be held in abeyance until an impartial panel can hold hearings and consider the large number of election disputes and irregularities'.[4] Akashi was unequivocal in his response and Chea Sim's request was denied. Akashi explained that the suggestion that UNTAC's professional electoral staff and other senior officials from member states who had travelled to Cambodia to take part in the administration of the election 'would seek or allow others to distort in any way the expression of the will of the Cambodian people' was 'unthinkable'. He went on to add that no 'credible evidence' has come to light to support the idea of fraud and irregularities that would call into question the integrity of the election results.[5]

In an attempt to discredit the process the SoC/CPP delayed the post-election formation of the legislative assembly. Under the circumstances, few people outside of the SoC/CPP felt the elections were anything other than an unimaginable success. The suggestion that they

---

3. The informal 'Core Group' comprised representatives from the five permanent members of the UN security council and members from Australia, Canada, Germany, India, Indonesia, Japan and Thailand. According to Benny Widyono, 'Apparently France, Japan, and Russia had supported the idea of an interim government while the United States, China, UK and Australia opposed it. See B. Widyono, *Dancing in Shadows*, pp. 124–26. According to Raoul Jenner, on the same day as Sihanouk's announcement, the US mission in Cambodia released a statement, referred to as a 'non-paper', which concluded that the US was '... opposed to the establishment of any interim government'. See R.M. Jenner, 'Let the Khmers decide on democracy', *The Nation*, Bangkok, 10 June 1993. The paper did however state that the US 'would be prepared to encourage political leaders to establish the broadest possible coalition among parties that took part in the election. However, we must make it clear that this should not in any way pre-empt the Constituent Assembly's promulgation of the new constitution which would detail the structure of the new government to be formed. To do so would be to undermine the entire electoral process and the transition to democracy begun so successfully with last week's elections.' Jenner, 'Cambodian Chronicles: non-paper', Annex 1, p. 20.

4. UN Special Representative Yasushi Akashi's letter of response to Chea Sim, President, Cambodia People's Party, 9 June 1993, Phnom Penh.

5. Ibid.

were somehow flawed was perceived as a direct attack on the professionalism and integrity of Akashi and UNTAC personnel. This was especially difficult for UNTAC to accept given the levels of political violence and intimidation directed at political parties involving SoC/CPP authorities and their supporters, and the climate of fear this engendered among the general population. In any event, UNTAC's chief electoral officer Professor Reginald Austin and his staff at the Election Complaints, Compliance and Enforcement Unit (ECCEU) thoroughly documented and investigated all CPP allegations of fraud, impartiality and irregularities, finding no evidence to support their claims.[6] In addition, as the political situation deteriorated, Akashi finally did agree to Chea Sim's request to set up an impartial panel to examine the alleged irregularities and UNTAC bias. An Electoral Advisory Committee was created, which also found no evidence to show that the alleged irregularities were deliberate acts.[7]

The botched attempt by SoC/CPP and Sihanouk to negotiate a compromise exacerbated rather than ameliorated the general atmosphere of insecurity and fear. CPP propaganda continued to attack UNTAC. In some provinces demonstrations were organised rejecting the election results, with protesters claiming the process had been unjust.[8] At the same time, on 10 June 32 CPP candidates for the constituent assembly supported an attempt to create a secession movement led by a breakaway faction of the SoC/CPP including SoC Deputy Prime Minister Prince Chakrapong and CPP General Sin Song. The stated intention of creating an autonomous zone of provinces east of the Mekong River

---

6. See R.H.F. Austin, UNTAC Interoffice Memorandum. 'CPP Electoral Complaints'. 21 June 1993. Phnom Penh. The CPP cited numerous irregularities ranging from the tampering of ballots after seals were broken on some boxes during their transportation, to blunt pencils. As a result of these alleged irregularities the CPP demanded recounts in the provinces of Battambang, Kompong Chhnang, Phnom Penh, and Prey Veng. Because of a lack of evidence, no re-counts were undertaken in any provinces.

7. Report of the Special Representative's Electoral Advisory Committee. 23 September 1993. Phnom Penh.

8. See, for example, UNTAC Information/Education Division *Notable Reports in the Cambodian Media. 23 May to 5 June 1993.* UNTAC Analysis/Assessment Unit. Information Education Division. 18 June 1993.

in protest over the elections resulted in outbreaks of violence, including attacks against F'pec and UNTAC personnel.

In much the same way as the involvement of SoC/CPP authorities in acts of political violence and intimidation could be plausibly denied during the run up to the elections, there was no definitive evidence to show that these events were part of a broader SoC/CPP strategy to destabilise the post-election political environment. Given what was at stake, it is hard to imagine that a party as internally disciplined as the CPP would not have a strategy in place to deal with an electoral defeat.[9] Either way, the combination of sustained anti-UNTAC propaganda, CPP refusal to accept the results and the idea of secession only served to increase the fear of a return to armed conflict.

SoC/CPP pressure ultimately paid off. A compromise was finally reached. Ranariddh was persuaded to accept the realities of the administrative, military and financial strength of the CPP and avert further bloodshed. For similar reasons, UNTAC and the members of the core diplomatic group originally opposed to the idea of an interim administration accepted the compromise. At its inaugural meeting on June 14 the constituent assembly agreed a resolution to form the 'National Provisional Government of Cambodia' (NPGC), which it later ratified on 1 July. Almost immediately, the so-called secession ended just as quickly as it had started. The CPP accepted the elections results and committees were formed to draft a new constitution. Promulgated in September it established a system of governance that was not that dissimilar to the one proposed by Sihanouk in June. Ranariddh and Hun Sen would serve as first and second prime ministers respectively. Almost all ministerial portfolios would be divided between F'pec and the CPP. Each ministry would have a co-minister from either party. There would also be lesser roles for other parties that won seats in the assembly. The NPGC was formally dissolved and the new Royal Government of Cambodia (RGC) was created. The major difference between the PNGC and the RGC was the role of Sihanouk. Under the new constitutional arrangements, Sihanouk once again became head of state as king; however, he would 'reign but not rule'.

---

9. For a full discussion of issues related to the 'secession', see D.W. Roberts, *Political Transition in Cambodia 1991–99*, pp. 109–15.

Post-UNTAC International Electoral Assistance

The UNTAC-managed elections conditioned the behaviour and determined the strategies of the warring political factions and international actors. Perhaps inevitably, no one group completely achieved what they wanted. Hun Sen and the CPP did not get the majority victory they had expected. However, through threats and intimidation they forced a compromise with Ranariddh and F'pec, allowing them to retain a significant amount of state control. For Sihanouk, a Cambodian solution of sorts was arrived at, but not without international interference and with only a symbolic role for himself. The PDK, although still not an insignificant threat, were more isolated than ever. UNTAC and the international and regional powers saw their objective in the formation of a new government met. Nonetheless, because of the circumstances under which it was formed serious questions remained about the capacity of the new government to function effectively. In particular, questions were asked about the politically inexperienced Ranariddh and his ability to work with the more politically experienced and astute Hun Sen. This uneasy political relationship was to be severely tested as the issue of elections and international support for them once again took centre stage.

Since the vast majority of Cambodians live in the countryside, the key to future electoral success lay in the rural areas. Administratively in Cambodia there are three principle tiers of organizations outside of the capital Phnom Penh; the province, the district and the sub-district or commune *khum*. Below the commune or *khum* is the village, *phum*. Commune and village chiefs were appointed by the Phnom Penh authorities in the 1980s. As early as August 1994 Sar Kheng, Minister of the Interior for the CPP, began making preparations for local elections to be held at the commune level, instructing his staff to draft a commune election law.[10] The reasons why the new government began tentative preparations for local elections at this time is not clear.[11] Presumably because of the new power-sharing arrangements, elements within the CPP felt it important to tackle what was potentially a volatile and destabilizing issue as early as possible before the constitutionally required parliamentary elections took place in 1998.

---

10. S. Peou, *Intervention and Change in Cambodia? Towards Democracy?* Silkworm Books, Chiang Mai; Institute of Southeast Asian Studies, Singapore, 2000, p. 219.

11. The idea for local elections was discussed during the UNTAC period.

While the RGC could draw upon the UNTAC experience, it none-theless had to create an electoral infrastructure that reflected political realities. For all intents and purposes, UNTAC had functioned as the central, impartial, independent electoral authority. In order to hold cred-ible elections in 1998 an independent election committee needed to be created alongside a legislative framework. This could not be realistically achieved without external support. Sar took the lead by soliciting for-eign support, initially from the German international NGO, the Konrad Adenauer Foundation (KAF), to discuss the subject of international assistance for Cambodia's elections. In late October 1995, the Ministry of the Interior (MoI) organised an international seminar on 'Electoral Systems and Administration' in collaboration with a number of interna-tional partners including KAF and the US based Asia Foundation. The seminar was attended by a mix of international electoral experts and consultants, some of Cambodia's fledging non-governmental organi-zations, bilateral donors, UN representatives and senior Cambodian political figures including the king and Ranariddh.[12]

At the end of the seminar, the RGC made a 'solid public commitment to a free and fair electoral process'. In his closing speech, Sar laid out eleven comprehensive principles for free and fair elections. Among them was a commitment to the establishment of an independent election commission and a state program of voter education, with priority given to rural areas. The principles also outlined a role for the state in providing political parties with financial support for campaigns. He added that if state resources are not available, then an independent organization should be created to 'openly supervise the financial income and expenditure of all parties'. Access to print and broadcast media must be made available to all parties on an equal basis during the campaign period. During the preparation for the elections 'all armed forces must be put under special assignment' to ensure order and security, and the election laws 'must include firm punishment for all election-related acts of violence'.[13]

---

12. United Nations Office of the High Commissioner for Human Rights in Cambodia, UNOHCHRC, Legal Assistance Unit Memorandum 'Election Seminar and Related Events', 1 November 1995.

13. UNOHCHRC. Copy of the speech delivered by HE. Sar Kheng, Acting Co-Prime Minister, Deputy Prime Minister, and Co-Minister of Interior in the closing cere-mony of the seminar on 'Election Systems and Preparations'. 25 October 1995.

A comprehensive set of principles discussed at a seminar in Phnom Penh was a far cry however from actually planning, organizing and executing elections again from virtually nothing. While international assistance was necessary, it was ultimately up to the state power-holders to ensure that the principles were adhered to. The notions of control, time and resources were again crucial factors. In December, in collaboration with a 'core group' of representatives from the diplomatic community and local and international NGOs, the MoI drew up a provisional but detailed action plan. The plan included the establishment of 'two parallel working groups', one comprising members of the government, the other members of the diplomatic community. The creation of an independent national election committee was an essential prerequisite not just for electoral matters but also as a focal point for coordination with the international donors. At the same time, coordination links with local and international NGOs were to be established. The initial timetable for implementing the myriad tasks included the promulgation of a commune election law by March 1996, an electoral administration to be in place by June at the latest, and voter registration to run from October–January 1997. The commune elections would take place in May or June.[14]

Prospects for International Electoral Support and Coalition Politics

Although the scale of international involvement was not at the same level as UNTAC, it was once again a decisive factor in conditioning the responses and behaviours of the main parties. The overall task of coordinating both domestic and international efforts in the preparation and organization of these elections was technically complex and politically highly sensitive. Before technical preparations could get fully underway and assistance could be offered, international donors had to be satisfied that underlying political conditions were conducive to the preparation and organization of elections. Moreover, for technical and financial reasons, it made sense to centralise activities through a single entity or organization to ensure effective coordination between the various Cambodian and international agencies involved. Given the

---

14. Elstra/OSS Core group meeting, 2 December 1995.

UNTAC experience, the UN seemed the natural choice. Just over a year after UNTAC's withdrawal, in December 1994 the UN had formally established a country office under the auspices of the United Nations Development Programme (UNDP) to assist the Cambodian government in solving socio-economic development problems. Earlier in the same year the UN Secretary-General appointed a special representative for political affairs, while the office of 'The United Nations Center for Human Rights' had already been operating in Cambodia since October 1993.

As the elections process developed UN involvement became a major source of tension. Matters were complicated further by the different mandates and priorities of the various UN offices present in Cambodia at the time. The UNDP for instance was chiefly concerned with economic and social issues, whereas the UN Human Rights Center was responsible for monitoring, protection and public reporting functions as they related to human rights as well as providing technical assistance and advice. Added to this was the role of the UN Electoral Assistance Division (EAD). Through the EAD the UN offered seven basic forms of assistance with elections, including 'the organization and conduct of elections (Cambodia 1992–3), supervision, verification, coordination and support for international observers, technical assistance and observation'.[15] This type of assistance became a major political problem, deepening the divisions between the two prime ministers, as did the role of the human rights office in the reporting of election-related violence and intimidation.

After UNTAC, the UN was acutely aware of the potential dangers and pitfalls involved in the organization and conduct of elections in a conflict-ridden state. Any further request for elections assistance in Cambodia would therefore be subject to rigorous needs assessment missions conducted by the UNDPA to examine first-hand the political, institutional and security conditions on the ground. Such missions required an assessment of the appropriateness, necessity and potential impact of UN assistance and whether or not the main contesting political parties and civil society representatives supported UN involvement.[16] Requests

---

15. UN General Assembly Document A/50/332. III. Electoral Assistance. Paragraph 43.

16. http://www.un.org/Depts/dpa/ead/ea_content/ea_types_of_assist.htm.

for assistance were coordinated by the relevant government authorities, the resident UNDP representative and the Under-Secretary-General for Political Affairs, also known as the focal point for the purposes of electoral assistance to sovereign states.[17] A formal request for assistance for two elections, the commune elections scheduled for 1997 followed by the 1998 national elections, was sent to the UNDP resident representative in early May 1996 by Co-Ministers of the Interior Sar and his F'pec counterpart You Hockry. In the meantime, the working relationship between the two prime ministers had begun to deteriorate dramatically.[18]

In the first year after the formation of the coalition government relations between the co-prime ministers were outwardly stable. Now that a modicum of political stability had been established, the RGC along with donors were faced with the enormous task of tackling Cambodia's dire socio-economic problems. As it was now an internationally recognised and legitimate sovereign state, huge amounts of foreign direct assistance to that end poured into the country. The nascent private sector had taken took root in the late 1980s also showed signs of booming as trade and foreign, private, direct investment took full advantage of the relatively stable political conditions. However, alongside the many benefits of foreign assistance for reconstruction, development and investment were new sets of technical and political problems to contend with. Technically and institutionally the new government was simply ill-prepared in terms of capacity and skills to effectively deal with the changing circumstances. The influx of aid and investment exacerbated corruption, providing further opportunities for politically well-connected individuals to enrich themselves at the expense of the national purse. These problems combined to create both internal and external dissent and criticism of

---

17. Ibid.

18. A letter dated 9 May from Co-Ministers of the Interior Sar Kheng (CPP) and You Hokry (F'pec) was sent to UNDP Resident Representative Paul Mathews requesting assistance for two elections: The *Khum* (commune) elections to be organized 'around the end of 1997, and 'the national election around May-June 1998'. The letter claimed that,' [a]t the end of March 1996, both Prime Ministers [Hun Sen and Ranariddh] provided an official mandate to the two Co-Ministers of Interior to organize these elections and contact all potential donors, countries and organizations to seek all kinds of technical assistance to prepare the two up-coming elections'. Unofficial translation. 17 May 1996. Phnom Penh.

the co-prime ministers' performance and behaviour, which in a short period of time led to renewed political instability.

Beginning in 1994, renewed fighting between the elected government's newly reconstituted Royal Cambodian Armed Forces (RCAF) and the Khmer Rouge broke out in the country's north-western provinces. The fighting came about after negotiations at the end of 1993, initially involving King Sihanouk and later Ranariddh, failed to reach a peace deal that would again leave open the possibility of a political role for elements of the Khmer Rouge leadership. Hun Sen and the CPP opposed such ideas on constitutional grounds. Further talks in Pyongyang, North Korea in May also broke down. The failure of these negotiations did little to quell speculation in CPP circles about royalist plots to subvert the coalition and the constitution by allowing Sihanouk more power to broker deals with the Khmer Rouge. In an interview with an international journalist a month later, Sihanouk criticized the RGC's inability to solve the country's problems. In direct response to Sihanouk, Hun Sen reportedly affirmed his commitment to the coalition and the constitution which did not include any kind of political role for the Khmer Rouge.[19] In any event, ideas about government positions for any Khmer Rouge leaders were finally laid to rest a few days after the coup when the National Assembly voted to outlaw the organization; nonetheless, the government continued with its earlier 1994 policy of encouraging defections within its ranks.

The following month on 2 July, 1994 a number of disgruntled senior CPP officials including Prince Chakrapong took part in what was termed by the government as 'an attempted coup'. Considered to be yet more political theatre than a serious attempt to overthrow the government, it nonetheless raised serious questions about the true motivations of the individuals involved. It was rumoured at the time that the move was part of a broader plot to isolate Hun Sen by elements associated with the CPP Party Chairman and Head of the National Assembly, Sim, and Deputy Prime Minister Sar, who were more sympathetic to royalist elements that favoured expanded powers for Sihanouk.[20].

---

19. Nate Thayer, 'Last Act: Sihanouk's Plan to Retake the Reins of Power', *Far Eastern Economic Review*, 23 June 1994.

20. For accounts of the 1994 'attempted coup' see B. Widyono, *Dancing in Shadows*, Chapter 10, 'A Mysterious Coup'.

Sam Rainsy and Critical Voices

The most vocal and significant critic of the two co-prime ministers at the time—especially in terms of the development of electoral politics—was the F'pec Minister of Finance Sam Rainsy. Born in Phnom Penh in the 1950s, Rainsy had spent most of his life in France where he had developed a career in business investment, finance and banking. His father, Sam Sary, was a former Sihanouk deputy prime minister, critical of Sihanouk's policies, who disappeared in the early 1960s. Rainsy was expelled from F'pec in 1994 and later controversially removed from the National Assembly. During his short tenure as Finance Minister, he introduced a number of budgetary and financial accountability reforms, earning a reputation inside and outside of Cambodia for his commitment to eradicating government corruption. He was particularly outspoken against both Ranariddh and Hun Sen, accusing them of professional and moral slackness, and presiding over what he described as 'a mafia state'. Not long after his expulsion from the National Assembly in 1995 he formed the Khmer Nation Party and would emerge as one of the central players in the unfolding political electoral drama.

Stifling of dissent within the coalition government was accompanied by a general increase in insecurity and fear. Journalists critical of government corruption and its links to foreign business interests were threatened with suppression or legal action. In several incidents in the period 1994–95, a number of journalists were murdered in circumstances that strongly suggested a political motive.[21] Although some arrests were made, no thorough police investigations were conducted, creating an atmosphere of impunity. After the events of 1994, social unrest—including demonstrations to protest against government corruption and support for Sihanouk's ideas of national reconciliation— further contributed to the sense of political instability.[22]

---

21. United Nations Secretary-General Representative Cambodia. 'Monthly Assessment Report for the month of March 1995'. UNSGRC1051. See also Human Rights Watch Report, *Cambodia at War*, 1 March 1995, available at http://www.refworld.org/cgi-in/texis/vtx/rwmain?page=publisher&publisher=HRW&type=&coi=KHM&docid=3ae6a7dd8&skip=0

22. Ibid.

Assessing Electoral Prospects

Preparations for elections were conducted against this background of renewed political instability. The UN had responded positively to the RGC's request in 1996 for assistance in coordinating technical assistance for local and national elections. Assistance however was to be given on a step-by-step basis to ensure the RGC adopted the necessary legislation and upheld the minimum guarantees for free and fair elections'.[23] UN assistance was not necessarily 'conditional', it was predicated on the establishment of a solid legal and administrative framework. As well as the creation of an independent and impartial electoral committee, a raft of laws needed to be enacted, including a general electoral law, laws to govern the actions of political parties, a law on nationality as well as the commune election law. Not long after the elections seminar in 1995, the Ministry of Interior had established a committee composed of F'pec and CPP officials to begin this process. Due to the general deterioration in the political atmosphere, however, by the beginning of 1996 very little progress had been made.

Lack of progress at the Ministry of Interior in drafting the electoral laws highlighted the broader problem of the politicization of administrative and institutional functions. The realities of power-sharing at the administrative and institutional levels were inextricably bound up with the struggle for control over authority and resources. The absorption of F'pec and BLDP officials into the existing administrative structures created new tensions and conflicts. State employees, civil servants, police and the military at all levels were resistant to any challenges from outside. More experienced and entrenched CPP loyalists were unwilling to relinquish any more power than was necessary. This had the practical and destabilizing effect of politicizing the day-to-day running of state institutions. Moreover, it placed an added strain on an already bloated administration as F'pec and to a lesser extent, BLDP party loyalists, were integrated into the system.

The system was particularly problematic for F'pec. In order for the party to consolidate its 1993 electoral successes, sufficient access to the state was of vital importance. Distribution of attendant benefits and rewards to party loyalists was essential if it was to ensure continued support. Nowhere was this more vital than in rural areas. With the

23. Correspondence between UNDPA and UNSGRC. CYP-32.

presence of a large peace-keeping force during UNTAC F'pec was able to successfully penetrate areas under SoC control and open hundreds of party offices. In spite of SoC/CPP-orchestrated intimidation and violence the party had managed to secure the largest percentage of the vote. In the absence of UN peacekeepers, repeating or improving on that success required disrupting CPP rural power structures.

Since the attempted coup in 1994, if not before, Hun Sen had intensified his efforts to strengthen his position within the CPP and among the security services, police and military. Ranariddh by contrast had drawn a lot of criticism from senior F'pec officials for his ineffectual leadership style and his apparent unwillingness to confront Hun Sen over power-sharing issues, particularly at the provincial and district levels. Senior party stalwarts felt that Ranariddh and the party had conceded enough to Hun Sen and the CPP. The resignation and subsequent arrest of F'pec Deputy Prime Minister and Foreign Minister Prince Sirivudh, King Sihanouk's half-brother, highlighted the level of growing disaffection within the party. Before and after his resignation at the end of 1994, Sirivudh had been at the forefront in challenging CPP control over rural administration. In November 1995, he was arrested for allegedly expressing in private to a number of individuals his desire to 'kill Hun Sen'. He was temporarily imprisoned before being released after the intervention of King Sihanouk. He subsequently left the country and went into self-imposed exile.[24] Not long after the Sirivudh 'affair' Ranariddh set about silencing his critics by taking a tougher stance against Hun Sen, resulting in the precipitation of a crisis that culminated in military action in July 1997.

At the end of January 1996, a relatively small group of F'pec officials still loyal to Ranariddh attended 'a closed-door seminar' in the south west province of Sihanoukville. The seminar was held to discuss F'pec and Ranariddh's weakened position within the coalition. Participants resolved to push the issue of power-sharing in the context of elections and strive for military balance with the CPP.[25] A public statement regarding F'pec's stance towards elections was issued after the seminar. Given its highly provocative nature the notion of military balance with the CPP was kept out of the public domain. It is reasonable to assume that after

24. See for example Widyono, *Dancing in Shadows*.

25. Ibid., pp. 213–14.

threats of military action by the militarily superior SoC/CPP, F'pec leaders would not wish to be in the same vulnerable position they were after the 1993 polls.

Two months later in March 1996, the fragile working relationship between Ranariddh and Hun Sen reached crisis point. Hun Sen was invited as a special guest to give a speech at the F'pec party conference, in what should have been a display of coalition unity. After Hun Sen's departure from the conference, Ranariddh addressed supporters describing himself and his ministers as 'puppets', and the partnership with the CPP as nothing more than a 'slogan'. He threatened to withdraw from the coalition if Hun Sen did not address the power-sharing issue. In addition to the threat to withdraw, Ranariddh suggested that F'pec might not wait until the 1998 elections to act; he could call for a vote to dissolve the National Assembly and hold elections before the end of the year. The speech was later broadcast on F'pec TV and radio.[26] Ranariddh's public comments were a significant departure from his previous position, precipitating the looming crisis between the coalition partners further.

UN Assessments

Ranariddh's outburst came less than three months before the arrival of a senior UNDPA official to assess the political conditions for UN assistance for the coordination of technical support for the elections. Prior to the UNDPA's arrival the United Nations Secretary-General's Representative in Cambodia (SGRC) was invited to a private meeting with Hun Sen in April at his fortified residence on the outskirts of Phnom Penh. The meeting was clearly intended to inform the foreign diplomatic community in Phnom Penh and the UN of Hun Sen's position after the challenge laid down by Ranariddh in March. During the meeting Hun Sen expressed the belief that Ranariddh had made 'grave political errors, unleashing "extremists" within his party and reaching a point of no return'. The threat of withdrawal from the coalition and call for a vote to dissolve the assembly would according to Hun Sen lack the necessary support from F'pec 'moderates' and factional elements from other political parties. He also claimed to have knowledge of F'pec's

---

26. Ibid., pp. 214–17.

plans to build military forces in preparation for the elections in 1997 and 1998, and threatened to arrest key F'pec ministers and military personnel whom he accused of procuring weapons for that purpose, and to use military force if necessary. Regarding the elections, he feared there was a royalist strategy involving the king and the Khmer Rouge to stand against him and the CPP. He was also totally opposed to any kind of international supervision of elections.[27]

Hun Sen's interpretation of events clearly showed the seriousness with which he took Ranariddh's threat of early elections. Technically, according to Article 78 of the 1993 constitution, elections could only be held within sixty days of the dissolution of the National Assembly. The assembly, however, could not be dissolved by the king before the end of its term 'except when the Royal government is twice deposed within a period of twelve months', and only then with a proposal from the Prime Minister and agreement from the President of the National Assembly.[28] Article 132 allowed for constitutional amendments but they would ultimately require a two thirds majority vote by the members of the assembly. Furthermore in terms of time, resources, and necessary international assistance, it was highly doubtful, if not impossible, to hold parliamentary elections before the end of 1996.

Ranariddh's interpretation of events, by contrast, was born out of his party's frustration with the re-consolidation of Hun Sen's power within the coalition after 1993. Although a F'pec electoral victory in 1996 was a real possibility, it was not a foregone conclusion. Without sufficient access to rural administrative structures, it would be difficult to prevent the CPP from adopting electoral tactics and deploying state resources to ensure votes as it had done in 1993, something of which senior F'pec officials were only too aware of. However, according to the account of the UN Secretary-General's Representative, Ranariddh seemed confident of a F'pec election victory regardless of power-sharing in the rural areas. This confidence seemed to stem from Ranariddh's belief that perceived moderates within the CPP like Sim and Sar, could keep Hun Sen's power in check. He denied Hun Sen's allegations concerning the build-up of armed forces, implying that he and F'pec already had sufficient forces

---

27. UNOSGRC 0311. Monthly Report for April 1996. *'From Paris to Takhmau by FAX.'* CPY 049.

28. See Findlay. (1995) Appendix. Constitution of the Kingdom of Cambodia.

of their own. The message he wanted to get across to the international community was that F'pec wanted a peaceful solution to the current crisis and that it should avoid talking about military force lest it give the other side a pretext to act. The threat to withdraw from the coalition was an attempt to alert his detractors that under the two-prime-minister arrangement, Hun Sen could not work alone, and his refusal to co-operate could effectively paralyse the government. As far as elections were concerned, Ranariddh wanted to see an extensive role given to international monitors.

The war of words channelled through the UN Representative's office in Cambodia by the two prime ministers provided the backdrop for the first visit of the Director of the Asia and Pacific Division of the UN Department of Political Affairs. The purpose of the visit was to assess the political situation and provide recommendations after the RGC's earlier request for technical assistance for the two elections. Between 10-13 June the director met with both prime ministers, as well as the F'pec Minister for Foreign Affairs, Ung Huot, Chairman of the National Assembly Sim, both Co-Ministers of the Interior Sar (CPP) and You Hockry (F), and the Vice-Chairman of the National Assembly and Chairman of the Human Rights Committee of the National Assembly Kem Sokha (BLDP). On the international side there were meetings with the UNDP Resident Coordinator, the Director of the Center for Human Rights, and staff, and a 'late night strategy meeting' with a core group of ambassadors from the US, the UK, Canada, Australia and the Chargé d'Affaires of France.

In his report back to the Under-Secretary for Political Affairs the director described Cambodia as 'a country of paradoxes'. On the one hand, it was noted that the party that had won the most votes in the UNTAC election 'lacks a coherent programme and has failed to establish a proper organization in the countryside'. On the other hand, the CPP 'retains the major levers of power and increasingly behaves as if in full control'. After audiences with the two prime ministers, he underlined the 'frayed' relations between the two, pointing out that Ranariddh 'feels increasingly marginalized by Hun Sen, whereas the Second Prime Minister believes the Prince is plotting with his father against him'. The idea of plots explains to some extent other observations about Hun Sen's actions and behaviour. In relation to the objection that Government officials and members of the National Assembly should not hold dual nationality, the UN director remarked that 'Hun Sen has a canny habit of staking a position that by itself seems reasonable' but when 'seen in the context of other actions, then one perceives a disturbing pattern'. Using the examples of the removal of Sam Rainsy from the National Assembly and the arrest of Prince Sirivudh, the report added that it is only 'when all these separate actions are considered together that a clear objective can be discerned'.[29] The clear objective was not stated in the report. However, in the context of other observations and impressions it was clear that Hun Sen's objective was to eliminate, co-opt, marginalise or destroy all opposition in order to advance his own political ambitions by winning the elections.

Regardless of disturbing patterns and Hun Sen's clear objectives, the UN's overall assessment of electoral assistance was for the most part favourable. The problem was the commune elections. As the report noted, because the draft election law gave control of the commune elections to the Ministry of the Interior and the commune chiefs, they would 'likely produce an overwhelming' and unbalanced CPP victory 'without opposition representation'. It later added that 'the risk of violence and foul play, particularly in the countryside, should not be underestimated'.[30] There was no enthusiasm among the diplomatic community at the time to fund commune elections on this basis. Indeed, the attitude of the Phnom Penh based diplomatic community was 'cautious bordering on apathy'. According to this view, Cambodia was no longer a key factor in a geopolitical power struggle, and there was a 'temptation' for policy makers in the international community 'to ignore or at least take a laid back attitude'. It was in their interests to promote stability, however, including Cambodia's early entry into the Association of Southeast Asian Nations, and the 'continuation of free market policies'. The deterioration in relations between the two prime ministers thus raised serious concerns among the Phnom Penh diplomatic community. The UN therefore recommended that they push the RGC to request assistance in monitoring and verification of the various stages of the elections

---

29. United Nations, HQS New York. Outgoing Code Cable CYP 029 P2/9. To: B. Widyono, SGRC, Phnom Penh. From: M. Goulding United Nations. Date: 26 June 1996. Number 1809. Subject Vendrell's Report. pp. 2–5.

30. Ibid., pp. 7–9.

process. Importantly, in light of the director's findings, 'the UN and do-nors insist that the election law provide for the establishment of a truly independent election commission.'[31]

Elections and Violence, Opposition, Civil Society

Deterioration in relations between the two prime ministers was ac-companied by a steady increase in politically motivated violence and intimidation against political parties. Beginning in September 1995, in two separate incidents on the eve of a party congress, hand grenades were thrown into the offices of the BLDP Son Sann faction and a pagoda where faction supporters were gathered. The attacks came after the BLDP had split into two factions in May, when the BLDP Vice President and Minister for Information Ieng Mouley attempted, unsuccessfully, to usurp party president Son Sann. The split in effect created two wings of the party, resulting in a legal battle for the right to use the party's name and logo before the elections in 1998. The motivations for the attacks were not clear and the perpetrators were never found. However, the Ieng Mouley faction later aligned itself with Hun Sen, suggesting a strong link to an apparent strategy to exploit fault lines within political groupings opposed to Hun Sen and the CPP; a strategy not that dissimilar from tactics employed by the CPP in the 1993 elections.

In terms of the evolution of electoral politics during this period, the attacks against the newly formed Khmer Nation Party (KNP) are the most significant. After his expulsion from F'pec and the National Assembly, Sam Rainsy created the KNP in December 1995. His anti-corruption, social justice stance successfully tapped into a well of discontent among urban social groups such as students, teachers, civil servants and an emergent organized labour force, primarily in the rapidly growing garment factory sector. He was the central figure in the establishment of the first labour union, the Free Trade Union Workers of the Kingdom of Cambodia (FTUWKC), which was involved in a number of demonstrations of garment workers in Phnom Penh asking for better pay and conditions in December 1996. Almost from its incep-tion, the party and its members were subjected to threats, intimidation and violence. After two attempts by members to divide the party, the

---

31. Ibid.

government refused to recognise Sam Rainsy's legal claim to the party's name and logo, leading him to later rename the organization Sam Rainsy's Party (SRP). Violence reached a deadly crescendo in March 1997 when several hand grenades were thrown into a public rally organized by the KNP, killing twenty people and injuring about 100. Among the injured was a US citizen employed by the International Republican Institute who had been working closely with the SRP. The involvement of one its citizens prompted an FBI investigation into the incident. To date the perpetrators have not been brought to justice. After extensive independent investigations, FBI evidence suggests the attack was organized by individuals close to the second prime minister Hun Sen.[32] In the second half of 1996, FUNCINPEC party offices and members were also subjected to numerous countrywide threats and intimidation.[33] The attack on the KNP rally however marked a dramatic turning point in the level of violence against political parties.

Election Preparations and NGOs

As the conflict among political elites intensified, preparations for the elections continued. A follow up meeting to the October 1995 elections conference was held in December. Attendees included an ad-hoc group of diplomats, development experts, UN personnel and international and local NGOs to address the question of international assistance for elections. The initial action plan produced after the conference envisaged an election-monitoring role for local groups of NGOs. A steadily growing number of non-state organizations filled the space that had been created after the signing of the Paris agreements, forming what was considered to be a post-UNTAC 'civil society' in Cambodia.[34] By the mid-1990s, the numbers of NGOs had increased significantly; some estimates had the number at about 164 by 1996. Many of these organizations were

---

32. http://www.hrw.org/news/2012/03/29/cambodia-15-years-no-justice-grenade-attack.

33. See for examples, UNCHRC, Note for the File: Harassment and Intimidation of Members of the FUNCINPEC Party. 27 June 1996.

34. For a theoretical discussion of the concept of 'civil society' in Cambodia, see C. Hughes, *The Political Economy of Cambodia's Transition*, Chapter 7.

engaged in socio-economic development issues and relied heavily on international sources for funding and training.[35]

Other organizations were overtly more political in their orientation, engaged in human rights and democracy promotion activities, election monitoring and voter education. Notable among this group were three election-monitoring groups or networks: the Committee for Free and Fair Elections (COMFREL), a coalition of three local NGOs that were involved in monitoring the 1993 elections, the Coalition for Free and Fair Elections (COFFEL) formed in 1995 from a group of about 125 local NGOs, and the Neutral Independent Committee for Free and Fair Elections in Cambodia (NICFEC), formed out of a group of 11 NGOs in the month before the 1998 elections. Prominent democracy promotion and human rights organizations included the Khmer Institute of Democracy (KID), the Center for Social Development (CSD), Cambodian Institute for Human Rights (CIHR), Cambodian Human Rights and Development Association (ADHOC) and the Cambodian League for the Promotion and Defense of Human Rights, like ADHOC known by its French acronym LICADHO.

Both LICADHO and COMFREL had some experience of elections during UNTAC. LICADHO in particular had conducted voter-education campaigns and monitoring of the pre-election political environment in 1993.[36] Generally, however, the majority of civil organizations were in their infancy with limited resources and experience. Also, given the nature of their activities, their relationship with the authorities was fraught and highly politicized. Provisions for independent civil election monitors were included in an early 1996 draft of the commune election law, demonstrating in principle government recognition of the need for non-partisan and independent domestic observers.[37] However, there was no formal NGO representation in the drafting of electoral legislation. With limited resources and an ambiguous relationship with the government, civil groups relied a great deal on the support of international donors and organizations. Indeed, the extent to which NGOs could meaningfully participate in the process would to a large degree depend on donors and other international agencies.

---

35. Ibid. p. 142.

36. http://www.licadho-cambodia.org/aboutus.php.

37. Chris Fontaine, 'Election Watchdogs gear up', *Phnom Penh Post*, No 15. July 1996.

From the outset, local election-monitoring networks and human rights organizations were directly involved with an array of international groups involved in the preparation process. Representatives from COMFREL and COFFEL met with the UN Under Secretary-General for Political Affairs during his visit to Cambodia at the end of August 1996. They impressed upon him the importance of NGO involvement in all aspects of the preparations and the worrying problem of security.[38] Shortly after the visit the UNDP organized elections-coordination meetings. These monthly meetings provided a regular forum for the election-monitoring networks and human rights organizations to interact with bilateral and multilateral donors and government representatives involved in the elections process.

Alongside these UNDP forums, international organizations like The Asia Foundation (TAF), the National Democratic Institute (NDI) and the German Konrad Adenhauer Foundation (KAF) provided additional sources of support and funding for local NGOs. Both TAF and the NDI assisted the election-monitoring networks with technical issues as well as providing funds for the start-up costs of voter-education programmes. KAF provided support to democracy promotion and human rights organizations like KID and CIHR in the production of election-related literature in the Khmer language concerning civic education programmes, democracy, human rights and rule of law. The Asia Foundation provided funds to the CSD for the analysis and reporting of electoral issues, and funds to CIHR for the training of provincial and local employees. With international support from the NDI, the election-monitoring networks forged links with other similar international and regional organizations like the Bangladeshi Fair Election Monitoring Alliance (FEMA), and the Philippine National Citizens' Movement for Free and Fair Elections (NAMFREL).

Like everything else related to elections—and political development more generally in post-UNTAC Cambodia—for NGOs engaged in the process, it was a case of learning as they went along. In the absence of a centralized and dedicated electoral authority, elections—and the roles of the various national and international groups—were once again evolving anew. Moreover, each group had specific interests and agendas that were

---

38. UNOSGRC, Cryptofax CPY 102. 'Preparations for the Elections'. 4 September 1996. Phnom Penh, p. 4.

not always compatible. NGOs involved in democracy-promotion and election-monitoring thus constituted a third element in the unfolding drama between the state—increasingly dominated by Hun Sen and the CPP—and other political parties. Drawing on the UNTAC experience, their interests lay not just in voter education but also in ensuring a level playing field for the conduct of election activities at every stage of the process. By necessity this involved both the prevention, where and when possible, of election-related irregularities, violence and intimidation. In the broadest sense, NGOs saw themselves as public representatives promoting informed participation and dialogue in political processes and developing democratic and human rights awareness.[39] As such they were subject to similar kinds of internal and external political pressures as the political parties. In an effort to mitigate the inevitable politicization of their activities and survive, it was imperative that they maintained and strengthened an independent, impartial, non-partisan position.

Such a position was not always easy to achieve, especially because many of the concerns they had were more often than not the same as those of the political parties. Like the opposition political parties, they were acutely aware of the difficulties they faced in working alongside CPP administrative structures outside of Phnom Penh. They were fully aware of the potential for widespread violence and intimidation during the commune elections. Local elections were seen by some NGO leaders as a 'test' to see if the government, local NGOs and international monitors could work together effectively before the national election in 1998.[40] Of particular concern was the partisan role of the commune chiefs in the country's 1,621 communes, almost all appointed by the PRK in the 1980s. Another pressing concern for the NGOs, as well as the other political groups, was the creation of the National Election Committee. They had a great interest in ensuring the independence and impartiality of the new body. There was a persistent society-wide belief that it would be virtually impossible to establish a truly politically independent commission capable of fairly adjudicating a highly volatile elections process. Furthermore, it was feared

---

39. For a description of the goals and objectives of Cambodian Electoral Observer coalitions see Hughes, C. (2000) *Strategies and Impact of Election Observer Coalitions in Cambodia*. ECR. Experts for Community Research. Report No 38. With assistance from Chhor Bonnaroath.

40. Chris Fontaine, 'Election Watchdogs gear up', *Phnom Penh Post*, No 15. July 1996.

that if the commission came under the control of the Ministry of Interior (MoI), which seemed likely at the time, then the freedom and fairness of the elections process would be undermined and compromised.

Elections Preparations Stalled

In terms of moving the elections process forward, NGOs, like the various international players, were constrained and frustrated by the vicissitudes of elite politics. A draft law to govern NGO conduct and behaviour in this regard was by February 1997 being considered by the Council of Ministers.[41] However, the failure of Hun Sen and Ranariddh to agree on substantive legislative and institutional issues continued to cause serious delays in the preparations. It was precisely because of the elections that the fragile coalition was edging towards a precipice. Apart from the role of the UN, there were a number of other major sources of conflict including: the various election laws, dual nationality of National Assembly members, the choice of the electoral system, and the creation of an institutional framework including the formation of the national election authority, the supreme council of the magistracy and a constitutional council.

As far as the UN was concerned, in spite of the delays both Hun Sen and Ranariddh were nonetheless committed to holding the two elections in 1997 and 1998. This was confirmed by the UN Assistant Secretary-General for Political Affairs after his visit to Cambodia at the end of August. Agreement between the two co-prime ministers on the extent of UN involvement was probably the biggest obstacle to progress at the time. Despite this and other legislative and institutional problems the UN representative was satisfied that there was 'a clear determination on behalf of the Cambodian authorities' to conduct the elections. At the same time, three international election experts working with the Ministry of Interior, two of whom had extensive experience with UNTAC's electoral component, recommended that the commune elections be postponed until early 1998.[42]

41. UNOSGRC, OO125. Crypto Fax CPY025. 'Minutes of meetings held during Mr. Vendrell's visit to Cambodia 23 February–26 February 1997', Part I. 4 March 1997. Phnom Penh.

42. Huw Watkin, 'Experts recommend local elections be postponed', *Phnom Penh Post*, No. 20, 6–19 September 1996. The three experts were Ron Gould from Canada,

Based upon the UN's first assessment report in June the UN representative's proclamation may have been overly optimistic. That report warned about disturbing patterns related to Hun Sen's treatment of opposition critics and the prospect of widespread fraud and violence. By the time of the UNDPA's second visit in February 1997, little had changed. Hun Sen remained committed to holding the commune elections in November or December but questioned why a sovereign state needed UN involvement in elections. Ranariddh agreed that neither election should be postponed, but still insisted that the UN monitor or observe the elections from start to finish. On almost all of the other issues they remained deeply divided.[43] Hun Sen and the CPP were insisting that the election laws include a provision that required all elected officials above the rank of commune chief to hold a single nationality. This was a major stumbling block preventing the passage of the commune election law at the time, as many F'pec officials held dual nationality, including Ranariddh. Justifiably fearing CPP control, Ranariddh insisted on two election control commissions instead of only one under the control of the Ministry of Interior. A National Election Committee could not be formed until the Constitutional Council had been appointed, which in turn could not happen until the judicial oversight body, the Supreme Council of Magistracy, had met. Again, because of the CPP-controlled judiciary, Ranariddh was insisting on the appointment of some of his party members to the council. As a constitutional requirement, the Constitutional Council would be the ultimate adjudicator in the resolution of serious election disputes and complaints.[44]

A breakthrough was finally achieved in March after the CPP Standing Committee agreed to no longer pursue the issue of dual nationality for officials standing in elections. Agreement was also reached on the electoral system of proportional representation and the creation of only one election commission. In what at the time was considered to be real progress, both parties jointly announced the intention to hold the

---

Michael Maley from Australia, and Theo Noel from the US-based International Foundation for Electoral Systems (IFES). It should also be noted that there was a small team of rotating French advisers working on voter registration issues.

43. UN Report UNOSGRC, OO125, Part II. Crypto Fax CPY025.

44. UNCHR, Legal Assistance Unit. Confidential Memorandum. Briefing note on the Preparation of Elections in Cambodia. 23 February 1997. Phnom Penh.

national elections in November 1998 and local elections as originally planned at the end of 1997.[45] Cross-party agreement on the timing of elections, however, did little to mask the continued underlying political tensions between the two prime ministers. In addition to the CPP 'concession' on dual nationality, F'pec officials further insisted on the safe return of Prince Sirivudh and the removal of Ieng Mouley, the leader of the breakaway faction of the BLDP, from his position as Minister for Information.[46] One month before the agreement about the election date was reached, fighting broke out between CPP and F'pec factions within the RCAF in Battambang province. The cause of the fighting was linked to joint efforts by the CPP and F'pec to negotiate defections with Khmer Rouge elements in the key areas of Samlot in the west and Anlong Veng in the north.[47] F'pec's s role in the negotiations with Khmer Rouge leaders in Anlong Veng was cited by Hun Sen as a justification for his military strike against F'pec in Phnom Penh in July.[48]

The closer the date for the elections the more unstable the political situation became, stalling preparations further. In April, a group of F'pec 'dissidents', led by Minister of State Ung Phan and Siem Reap governor Toan Chhay, broke away from the party, protesting against Ranariddh's ineffectual leadership. Ung Phan, who had defected from the CPP to F'pec in 1992, was known to be close to Hun Sen. He was directly involved in the arrest and detention of Prince Sirivudh. Publicly, Hun Sen supported the dissidents in the expectation that the CPP could rely on their support in the National Assembly.[49] The move by the dissidents effectively brought the assembly to a standstill as the CPP attempted to block F'pec efforts to remove them from their seats. After the physical and quasi-legal attacks against the BLDP and KNP, this latest episode involving F'pec seemed to confirm, if indeed confirmation was needed,

45. UNDP. Note to the File. *Elections Coordination Meeting of the 2ND April 1997. UNDP Service Center.* 10 April 1997. Phnom Penh.

46. Phnom Penh Post Staff, 'A Hint of Hope for Elections', *Phnom Penh Post*, April 1997.

47. Sok Pov, 'Factional Fighting Jolts the Northwest', *Phnom Penh Post*, March 1997.

48. For background information, see Jason Barber, 'Negotiations falter as heat goes on Ta Mok', *Phnom Penh Post*, April 1997.

49. Phnom Penh Post Staff, 'Funcinpec Renegade backed by Hun Sen', *Phnom Penh Post*, April 1997.

a deliberate and determined policy by Hun Sen and the CPP to weaken or eliminate any serious electoral competition.

Meanwhile, the political hoopla was proving to be a serious thorn in the side of the international community engaged in the elections preparations. In May, the UNDP resident representative urged the high level contact group of foreign diplomats in Phnom Penh to press the Co-Ministers of the Interior to pass all the necessary legislation as soon as possible to allow the technical preparations to proceed.[50] The deadlock continued into June. At the UNDP election coordination meeting on 6 June, attended by donor country ambassadors and senior Ministry of Interior officials, the prospect of denying further assistance for the elections was raised. It was suggested the RGC provide concrete 'benchmark' evidence of its commitment to holding the elections as planned before the Consultative Group (CG) of donors met in Paris in July to discuss aid contributions. It was generally felt that failure to do so could jeopardize not just aid for assistance for elections but also aid for other purposes.[51] On 26 June a spokesman for the Ministry of Interior and adviser to Sar Kheng informed the participants at the 7th UNDP election coordination meeting that the CPP and F'pec had now agreed to hold the general elections in May 1998, and that the CPP was ready to postpone the commune elections.[52] Eight days later, armed forces loyal to Hun Sen launched a *coup de force* against Ranariddh and F'pec fundamentally altering the political landscape upon which the elections would be contested and controlled.

***

Looking back, even before the official results of the UNTAC elections in 1993 were announced, the CPP knew they needed to exercise as much control over the post-election political environment as possible if the party was to win elections in 1998. The formation of a weak coalition government from within which they could exercise that control was

---

50. Copy of minutes of UNDP '5th and 6th Elections Coordination Meetings'. 11 May 1997.

51. United Nations Cambodia Office for Human Rights. Memorandum. Election Donor Meeting at UNDP, 5 June 1997.

52. UNDP Election Coordination Meeting. Note to the File. UNDP Service Centre. 26 June 1997. Phnom Penh.

the first step in the process. Provided Ranariddh and F'pec remained compliant the task was relatively straightforward. When preparations for commune elections began as early as 1994, the situation became more complex and uncertain. The 1995 elections seminar highlighted the need for international assistance. Opposition to Hun Sen and Ranariddh's crony-capitalist style of government was ruthlessly suppressed. Politically related violence against government critics, including political parties like the BLDP and Sam Rainsy's populist KNP, increased. When Ranariddh responded to his party's exhortations regarding power-sharing the coalition began to disintegrate. Various international groupings were, in the interests of post-UNTAC stability, willing to support the elections process, but UN assessments of the disturbing 'patterns of behaviour' demonstrated by Hun Sen predicted further instability and violence. International assistance included support for Cambodia's emerging NGO sector, adding another potentially destabilizing dimension to the elections process.

The formation of the NUF posed a considerable electoral challenge to Hun Sen and the CPP, seriously threatening an outright CPP victory. The resulting instability and fear of armed conflict intensified as both prime ministers sought the support of dissident elements within the Khmer Rouge, and the DK began to finally disintegrate. The prospect of the remaining elements of the Khmer Rouge aligning with the NUF was enough for Hun Sen to launch his attack in July. The military action may have fundamentally altered the political landscape in the CPP's favour, but an outright victory in the 1998 elections was not necessarily a foregone conclusion.

CHAPTER 4

Elections and the 1997 Coup

*T*he military coup orchestrated by Hun Sen on 2-7 July 1997 and its aftermath placed him and the CPP in a position to influence the outcome of the 1998 elections in ways they were unable to do in 1993. A terrifying public display of military force in the capital city, combined with the brutal extrajudicial murder of senior F'pec officials demonstrated unambiguously Hun Sen's political and military superiority.[1] With only nine months until the official start of the campaign period for the May elections, the only credible opposition to the CPP had fled the country in fear for their lives. In the days and weeks after the fighting, the main political party infrastructures were virtually destroyed in both urban and rural areas.[2] With the opposition in disarray and its leadership outside the country the CPP were able to better control the institutional and legislative preparations for the 1998 elections.

Control was not absolute. Elections had to be credible enough to ensure international legitimacy and the attendant benefits of aid and foreign direct investment. For these reasons, the government had little choice but to follow through on its commitment to hold the elections. Cancelling or postponing them, although constitutionally possible, was simply not a practicable option for the CPP and Hun Sen. For the sake of political stability and security, albeit at the expense of fairness and democracy, donors would insist they took place as scheduled. The opposition had been severely weakened, making an outright CPP victory possible in an election process that would satisfy the interests of some international donors. However, intense international scrutiny

---

1. The Cambodian Office of the United Nations Centre for Human Rights, Memorandum to the Royal Cambodian Government, 'Evidence of Summary Executions, Torture and Missing Persons Since 2–7 July 1997', 21 August 1997.

2. See for example, United Nations Report of the Secretary-General, 'Situation of Human Rights in Cambodia', A/52/489, 17 October 1997, pp. 39–56. Also Peou, *Intervention and Change in Cambodia?*, pp. 308–09.

of the process, combined with UN support for the safe return of the opposition and the involvement of national NGOs, meant the outcome was still nonetheless uncertain.

International Perceptions and the Coup

Reaction to the coup by various international groupings engaged with Cambodia was at best ambivalent. Hun Sen's military strike was seen by those who had been closely following events as the final act in a drama that had begun in March 1996. Neither the UN Secretary-General nor any Western or ASEAN powers referred to Hun Sen's military action as a *coup d'etat*. Some members of the international press and human rights organizations, including Thomas Hammarberg, the UN's Special Representative of the Secretary General for Human Rights in Cambodia, were unequivocal in their characterization of the events as a coup. Hun Sen strongly objected to the use of the term coup, claiming instead that Ranariddh 'had started movements toward military action'.[3] The creation by the CPP of an official narrative to justify military action in the form of a 'White Paper' was a key element in Hun Sen's attempts to shape international perceptions of the situation and influence official responses. The 'White Paper' presented a simplistic interpretation of the complexities of Cambodian elite politics since March 1996, in an effort to dominate and control that narrative of events. In the paper, Ranariddh and those loyal to him were accused by the CPP and Hun Sen of having 'embarked on a strategy of provocation' in an effort to destabilize the government. This strategy according to the content of the paper involved secret negotiations with the 'outlawed' Khmer Rouge in an effort to strengthen F'pec armed forces and win the support of political leaders for the NUF. It also accused F'pec and Ranariddh of illegally importing arms, and the infiltration of soldiers, 'many of whom were Khmer Rouge', into Phnom Penh, a move seen by Hun Sen and the CPP as 'virtually a declaration of war'.[4]

International responses to the claims made in the paper had to be considered in the context of what the Phnom Penh based international

---

3. 'Situation of Human Rights in Cambodia', A/52/489, 17 October 1997, pp. 39–56.

4. Peou, *Intervention and Change in Cambodia?*, pp. 298–99.

community understood about events leading up to the coup. Most foreign diplomats and analysts were fully aware that by mid-1996 both prime ministers were pursing separate political agendas in competing for the loyalties of breakaway Khmer Rouge factions, regardless of the 1994 law that prohibited 'deals' with DK leaders.[5] They were also aware that Hun Sen had been building up and consolidating his control over military and security forces since the 'attempted coup' in 1994. The UN Secretary General's Special Representative reported that Hun Sen was in possession of transcripts of the F'pec January 1996 'closed door' meeting, when Ranariddh allegedly gave the order for '"physical" forces to be organized for 1997 and 1998'. Hun Sen seemingly interpreted this situation as the unleashing of extremist forces within F'pec that could be traced back to Ranariddh. According to him, in two separate incidents, F'pec Secretary of State for the Interior Ho Sok and Senior General Nhek Bun Chhay had taken weapons to distribute to F'pec border police but had been intercepted. Hun Sen threatened to arrest the two officials and would caution Ranariddh against opposing him, adding that if he 'starts armed attacks he will destroy FUNCINPEC's machinery'.[6] Ho Sok was subsequently murdered shortly after being detained by Hun Sen's forces at the Ministry of Interior in the days after the coup. Nhek Bun Chhay survived the fighting and managed to escape to the Thai-Cambodia border in the north-west.

The organization of F'pec's '"physical" forces in preparation for 1997 and 1998' referred to in the UN Special Representative's report was a clear reference to commune and national elections. The CPP's biggest fear was a repeat of the UNTAC election results in 1998 which, according to the constitution, meant the leader of the party with a majority of seats would become sole Prime Minister. Even if F'pec had planned to use armed force, and there is no credible evidence that has come to

---

5.   UN Secretary General's Special representative: Monthly Report for January 1997. UNOSGRC 0069. CPY 014. See also S. Heder, 'Hun Sen and Genocide Trials in Cambodia', in J. Ledgerwood (ed.), *Cambodia Emerges from the Past: Eight Essays.* Southeast Asia Publications. Center for Southeast Asian Studies. Northern Illinois University, 2002, pp. 194–95.

6.   UNOSGRC0311. CPY 049. Secretary General's Special Representative. Monthly Report for April 1996. See also Brad Adams: http://www.hrw.org/news/2007/07/27/cambodia-july-1997-shock-and-aftermath.

light to show they had, Hun Sen was confident he would prevail.[7] This was again communicated to the UN Special Representative by Hun Sen, who stated that Ranariddh stood to lose if he engaged in armed conflict with the CPP, and 'he had the forces to do it'.[8] After the January 1996 meeting in Sihanoukville, F'pec issued a public statement in which it committed the party to upholding 'respect for the principles of the constitution and a free, fair and democratic general election with the presence of international observers'.[9] No two issues provoked Hun Sen more than the involvement of the international community and the role of the king in electoral politics. His contempt for the UNTAC elections was made clear to the UN in June 1996. He didn't trust Sihanouk, believing he was not neutral, and felt it was 'unfair that FUNCINPEC runs together with the king and CPP runs alone'.[10]

Elite Politics and the End of the Khmer Rouge

Foreign diplomats in Phnom Penh were also aware of the huge political capital to be gained by either prime minister in bringing about the final demise of the Khmer Rouge leadership. To that end, in late June 1997, two weeks before Hun Sen's military action, both prime ministers signed a letter sent to the UN seeking assistance for 'bringing to justice those persons responsible for genocide and crimes against humanity during the rule of the Khmer Rouge'.[11] In the same month, in an internal purge that could be traced back to the defection of the Ieng Sary group in August 1996, Pol Pot arranged the murder of the former DK defence minister Son Sen and his wife.[12] Both were arrested and killed for allegedly running a 'major spy network for Vietnam and Hun Sen'.[13] It was believed at the time that Hun Sen was conducting separate

7.   Post Staff, 'Kevin's views labeled "regrettable"', *Phnom Penh Post*, October 1997.

8.   UNOSGRCO311. P. 2

9.   Claudia Rizzi and Nick Lenaghan, 'F'pec "remembers the resistance" in congress date', *Phnom Penh Post*, January 1996.

10. UNOSGRC0311. P 8.

11. Hurley Scroggins, 'Moves to get Pol Pot in the dock', *Phnom Penh Post*, June 1997. See also Heder, 'Hun Sen and Genocide Trials in Cambodia', p. 197.

12. Heder, 'Hun Sen and Genocide Trials in Cambodia', pp. 195–97.

13. Nick Lenaghan, 'Hardliners Split as PMs Quarrel', *Phnom Penh Post*, June 1997.

negotiations with Son Sen.[14] In fear for his own life, Ta Mok, considered to be third in the Khmer Rouge hierarchy since 1978, and one of the DK regime's chief henchmen responsible for organizing much of the killing in 'zones' under his control, arrested Pol Pot. These internal purges and defections, culminating in Pol Pot's arrest, effectively marked the end of the Khmer Rouge as an insurgent movement with a clear and consistent political agenda. All that remained was a fractured organization of military commanders and political leaders seeking to preserve and protect as best they could the benefits accrued from the lucrative trade in natural resources in areas under their control, and maybe get immunity from prosecution in a possible future international tribunal.[15]

In terms of what both prime ministers could get from the disintegration of the Khmer Rouge, it was the political not the military dimensions that were decisive. Military analysts at the time felt the remaining Khmer Rouge forces were 'not critical to the balance of military power' between F'pec and the CPP.[16] Since 1995, many former Khmer Rouge soldiers had been incorporated into the RCAF, some of whom would serve in units loyal to both prime ministers. Hun Sen, for example, had successfully incorporated key Khmer Rouge defectors such as General Keo Pong and his troops into his military structure. Keo Pong would play a significant role in coordinating the attack on F'pec forces during the July coup. It was the political competition to co-opt and neutralize the remaining Khmer Rouge leaders that would eventually tip the balance of power leading to the July coup.

In July 1996, Hun Sen initiated negotiations with Khmer Rouge military commanders loyal to the former foreign minister, Ieng Sary, who was number three in the hierarchy in the Pailin and Phnom Malai areas of the north-west. To secure his defection and gain his political loyalty, Hun Sen offered Sary the 'political rights and other interests as other citizens without discrimination'.[17] After some initial resistance, Hun Sen

---

14. Ibid.

15. See for example the analysis of Khmer Rouge researchers and scholars like Steve Heder, in Michael Hayes, 'After Pol-Pot: the politics of survival', *Phnom Penh Post*, June 1997.

16. Ibid.

17. National Voice of Cambodia Radio (NVCR) 9 August, 1996, cited in Heder, 'Hun Sen and Genocide Trials in Cambodia', p. 196.

persuaded Ranariddh to sign a letter needed from both prime ministers to request a royal amnesty from the king.[18] The decree granting Sary a pardon and amnesty 'immunized him from punishment based on the conviction of the 1979 Revolutionary People's Court', when he and Pol Pot were convicted in absentia for crimes committed by the DK regime and sentenced to death, and the 1994 'Law Outlawing the Democratic Kampuchea Group' which excluded DK leaders from amnesty.[19] By signing the letter leading to Ieng Sary's immunity, both prime ministers completely ignored the letter of the 1994 law. Vigorously pursued at the time, Hun Sen compelled Ranariddh to sign the letter, arguing that an amnesty for Sary would expedite the end of the insurgency. However, Hun Sen pointed out that it would only hold provided Sary remained committed to ending hostilities toward the RGC; if at any time he resumed opposition, he would 'automatically become guilty again'.[20]

Similar amnesties for other DK era leaders, except Pol Pot and Ta Mok – who by August 1996 were calling themselves the Provisional Government of National Solidarity and National Salvation of Cambodia (PGNSNSC), nominally led by Khieu Samphan – were not ruled out by either prime minister or the king. Government attempts at negotiating with the PGNSNSC held in the areas around Anlong Veng in the north of the country continued throughout the first half of 1997. In February, a team of 11 government negotiators, mainly F'pec officials hoping to talk with Ta Mok, were attacked; several were killed and the remainder taken hostage. Pol Pot, having been informed of this, was initially supportive of a resumption of talks in May. However, disillusioned and fatigued with his leadership, senior Khmer Rouge negotiators sought to exclude Pol Pot, reasoning that they were more likely to have their interests met without him. Negotiations were thus continued in 'secret'. His exclusion from the negotiations and mistrust of his subordinates led to the semi-successful attempt to eliminate him in June, in an effort to stall the negotiations. His arrest and detention cleared the way for

---

18. UN Secretary General's Special Representative. 'Weekly Report 102 covering the period from 19 to 25 August 1996'. UNOSGRC0645. CPY 097.

19. http://www.khmerrough.com/pdf/FairTrialPrinciples160606.pdf. See also Heder, 'Hun Sen and Genocide Trials in Cambodia', pp. 195–96.

20. NVCR 16 September, 1996, cited in Heder, 'Hun Sen and Genocide Trials in Cambodia', p. 196.

Khieu Samphan to conclude the clandestine talks with F'pec officials, in particular General Nhek Bun Chhay.

At the time, accurate and detailed information was difficult to come by in Phnom Penh, fuelling numerous rumors and speculation among foreign diplomats and observers about the drama unfolding in Anlong Veng. An announcement by F'pec on 20 June that Pol Pot had been arrested and Khieu Samphan was 'prepared to surrender' was met with a good deal of scepticism. Earlier F'pec announcements concerning the possible exile of Pol Pot, Ta Mok and Son Sen went unsubstantiated, and the apparent deal collapsed when it was made clear that no country would accept them. If the latest claims were therefore true, F'pec stood to reap enormous political benefits before the elections, effectively upstaging the CPP. However, the problem for Ranariddh and F'pec was Ta Mok, and his willingness or not to hand over Pol Pot to the government in return for amnesty. Sihanouk had reiterated his refusal to grant Ta Mok and Pol Pot amnesties, making this unlikely. Nevertheless, with Pol Pot effectively neutralized and with Ta Mok's support, Khieu Samphan concluded negotiations with F'pec, which, if successful, would for all intents and purposes symbolize the final dissolution of the Khmer Rouge leadership.

The agreement between F'pec and the Khmer Rouge – now calling itself the National Solidarity Party (NSP), headed by Samphan – was reportedly scheduled to be signed at a ceremony at Preah Vihear temple on Sunday 6 July 1997.[21] Hun Sen's armed forces launched the coup that weekend, preventing the ceremony from taking place. His unilateral military action was the culmination of weeks of tension in Phnom Penh as the negotiations were taking place in Anlong Veng. Unable to solicit support from senior colleagues within the CPP to use armed force, he instead indicated his intention to arrest Ranariddh in late June in relation to the highly questionable charge of illegally importing arms. Senior CPP military officers alongside the likes of Sar and Sim had expressed scepticism about the use of force against F'pec. [22] The deal that was about to be struck was a step too far for Hun Sen. Before the

---

21. Nate Thayer, 'Secret talks led to final purge', *Phnom Penh Post*, August 1997.

22. UN Secretary General's Special Representative Monthly Report for May 1996. 'Ranariddh Responds'. 31 May 1996. UNOSGRC0397. CPY 064. See also Brad Adams, 'Cambodia July 1997: Shock and Aftermath. Blood Feud'.

fighting began on 5 July, Ranariddh received warning of the coup and his imminent arrest from some senior generals; he fled the country on 4 July.

Ranariddh and Hun Sen Miscalculate: the 'International Community' Response

In many respects, the events of July 1997 can be seen as the beginning of the end of a drama that began not in March 1996, but in the 80s when the PRK prepared for the reality of multi-party elections as means to resolve the conflict. Speaking about political reform in late 1989, Hun Sen told a visiting Laotian dignitary of the importance of maintaining 'the [current] political and military situation right up to the time of the elections'.[23] He was confident enough of an outright electoral victory in 1993 from which the CPP could dominate any coalition government. When that didn't happen, the CPP threats of renewed armed conflict were sufficient enough to challenge Ranariddh's electoral success. Provided he was unopposed, Hun Sen was content to steadily re-consolidate and strengthen his and the CPP's power to ensure the victory denied them in 1993 was achieved in 1998. In a June 1996 speech, referring to elections, Hun Sen told a group of predominately female employees, 'now it's [19] '96 close your eyes and open them, it's [19] '98... and [in] '98 we'll win, we'll definitely win, there's no letting a-UNTAC, a-foreigners [sic] to hold the ballot boxes this time'.[24]

A year later, the likelihood of an outright electoral victory for the CPP and Hun Sen in 1998 was far from guaranteed. The NUF together with the prospect of a significant international role in the elections posed a formidable challenge to the CPP. In addition, if Ranariddh and F'pec could take full credit for the surrender of what was left of the Khmer Rouge then a central and powerful electoral propaganda meme

---

Human Rights Watch, http://www.hrw.org/news/2007/07/27/cambodia-july-1997-shock-and-aftermath.

23. Minutes 29, Cabinet, Council of Ministers, 29 Dec. 1989 (8–26 Dec.), cited in Gottesman, *Cambodia After the Khmer Rouge*, p. 338.

24. Unofficial translation of the text of a speech given by second Prime Minister Hun Sen to employees of the Ministry of Public Works and Transport 29 June 1996. Reproduced by Post Staff, 'Hun Sen: Exhorting the Party', *Phnom Penh Post*, July 1996.

carrying the idea that CPP was the only party that could prevent the return of the Khmer Rouge and guarantee order and stability would be lost. This combination of factors made it unlikely that there would be an overwhelming CPP victory in the 1998 elections. As commentators from the CPP and the foreign diplomatic community pointed out after the coup, 'Hun Sen wants to go into the election with the certainty of a landslide' ... 'He wants to use democracy as his way to return to dictatorship,' [i]f he has taken such a risk [to attack Funcinpec], it is really because he was not sure of himself' ... '[h]e was not so sure that he would win the elections.'[25]

Politically, Ranariddh badly mishandled the negotiations with Khieu Samphan, seriously miscalculating Hun Sen's response and probably that of the foreign diplomatic community in Phnom Penh. By associating Khieu Sampan with the 14 principles of the NUF, Ranariddh gave Hun Sen the cause to justify his actions. The NUF promulgated 14 guiding principles, the second of which, *Free and Fair Elections*, supported 'the presence of national and international observers, before during and after the elections'. The third, *'Support for One Prime Minister'*, favoured no co-ministers. Although it didn't mention the Khmer Rouge by name, the fifth principle, *Defence for Human Rights and Fight Against Dictatorship*, stated the NUF 'will not allow the return of the genocidal regime'.[26] As commendable as these 'principles' might have been, instead of claiming what would have been an historic victory for the 'coalition government', Samphan and the NSP were portrayed as yet another possible member of the anti-Hun Sen NUF movement.

The fact that both prime ministers had since March 1996 adopted strategies designed to provoke the other into making damaging political mistakes in front of the international community was common knowledge among analysts and the Phnom Penh diplomatic community.[27] When matters came to a head in the manner they did, however, it seemed that both sides had miscalculated the international response.

25. Michael Hayes, 'Hun Sen moves as KR talks completed', *Phnom Penh Post*, July 1997.
26. 'The National United Front's Political Beliefs and Objectives', unpublished official document, cited in Peou, *Intervention and Change in Cambodia?*, pp. 295–97.
27. United Nations Secretary General's Special Representative reports 0311 CPY 049 April 1996, and 0397 CPY 064, May 1996.

Ranariddh's appeals to the international community to universally condemn Hun Sen's action as a *coup d'état* were for the most part dismissed
in foreign policy circles. Likewise, if Hun Sen expected the international
community to accept his version of events and legitimize the coup, he
was mistaken. As far as the foreign powers' interests in political stability
were concerned, the situation was not so straightforward. Irrespective
of the accusations made against Ranariddh in the CPP 'White Paper',
Hun Sen had removed by force a legitimately elected prime minister. To
ignore that would effectively negate the UNTAC elections, and undermine the democratic principles enshrined in the Paris Peace Accords.

At the same time, diplomats engaged with Cambodia's political
development since UNTAC regarded Ranariddh's leadership as ineffectual, and since March 1996 as destabilizing. By contrast, Hun Sen
was admired in international diplomatic circles for his pragmatism,
diligence and ability to command and control. The problem for foreign
diplomats and their superiors was that he was engaged in a systematic
effort to eliminate, marginalize and co-opt any opposition to him and
the CPP by any means necessary, including violence and intimidation.
While he may have had the right kind of leadership qualities required by
foreign powers to meet their interests of political stability and security
in Cambodia, his methods subverted and compromised the principles
of democracy and human rights. The situation was summed up in the
attitude of the then Australian ambassador who, in a secure embassy
communication cable leaked to the Australian press, reportedly alluded
to what he believed to be Hun Sen's commitment to good governance.
In an attempt to clarify his position in a subsequent interview with the
English language newspaper, *The Phnom Penh Post*, he acknowledged
that splits within the opposition parties and the murders of newspaper
editors and journalists, culminating in the 'atrocity' of the March 30
grenade attack on the peaceful KNP demonstration, 'were committed
by people close to Hun Sen'.[28]

While the Australian ambassador's personal views did not necessarily represent a consensus, there was no desire among foreign diplomats
to publicly hold Hun Sen to account for the behaviour of 'those close to
him'. Sixteen years later, the perpetrators of the atrocities committed in

28. Huw Watkin, 'Tony Kevin: Captives, Cables and Non-Coups', *Phnom Penh Post*,
     October 1997.

the lead-up to the coup and its aftermath have not been brought to justice. At the same time, as there was a need for political stability – even if that meant glossing over human rights abuses and the rule of law – there was also a need for the international community in Cambodia to at least be seen to be 'promoting liberal democratic values'.[29] As a result, elements within the international community were not prepared to directly legitimize Hun Sen's arrangements to replace Ranariddh as First Prime Minister with the former F'pec Foreign Minister Ung Huot in the weeks after the coup. In two separate votes on 6 August, the National Assembly lifted Ranariddh's parliamentary immunity, allowing his replacement as First Prime Minister. After his immunity was lifted, a military court issued two warrants for his arrest, accusing him of 'committing crimes against national security and illegally importing weapons from Sihanoukville'.[30] The procedures by which the National Assembly voted on these issues were not only unconstitutional but were conducted in a manner that caused some assembly members to feel intimidated into supporting Ung Huot.[31]

Meanwhile, as Hun Sen was building the case against Ranariddh inside Cambodia, Ranariddh, Sam Rainsy and other NUF opposition leaders formed the 'Union of Cambodian Democrats' in Bangkok (UCD), with the express purpose of bringing as much international attention to their plight as possible. They launched an international media campaign protesting against the formation of an illegal government in Phnom Penh, exhorting the signatories of the 1991 Paris agreements to intervene to put Cambodia back on a democratic path. Intervention involved the recognition of a caretaker government, a time frame and conditions for the conduct of the 1998 elections, and international guarantees for the safe return of the exiled leaders to participate in them.[32] UCD leaders were encouraged by the decision on 10 July to postpone Cambodia's

---

29. See also Hughes, *The Political Economy of Cambodia's Transition*, p. 105.

30. Mary Kay Magistad, 'Court builds Ranariddh's case', *Phnom Penh Post*, October 1997.

31. See for example Peou, *Intervention and Change in Cambodia?*, pp. 303–04.

32. Barbara Crossette, 'Cambodian leaders in Exile Seek International Monitoring of new elections', *New York Times*, September 28, 1997. See also Elizabeth Moorthy and Jason Barber, 'Exiles vow no return yet', *Phnom Penh Post*, August 1997, and Hughes, *The Political Economy of Cambodia's Transition*, p. 108.

entry into the regional grouping ASEAN because of Hun Sen's action. Attempts by ASEAN and Indonesian diplomats to mediate the crisis were rejected by Hun Sen when it became apparent that ASEAN still recognized Ranariddh as First Prime Minister and supported his return to participate in the elections.[33]

ASEAN's decision was regarded as a setback for Hun Sen.[34] It was clear that the tide of international opinion – especially in the context of the PPAs and UNTAC – worked against his attempts to legitimize a new government with dissident members of F'pec who remained in Phnom Penh. International focus was concentrated more on the return of the UCD leaders to participate in the elections than on the illegality of Hun Sen's actions and human rights abuses perpetrated by forces loyal to him. Responses from other countries were mixed, but most supported the holding of the elections in May 1998. The US and Germany appeared to take the strongest stance by suspending aid programmes. The US was particularly vocal in its condemnation of Hun Sen's action but stopped short of officially calling it a coup.[35]

Uncertain about what to do about the Cambodian situation, international donors looked to the United Nations. Cambodia's seat at the UN General Assembly was contested between two rival delegations. Before the General Assembly meeting in October, both the UCD and Ranariddh, and the Hun Sen–Ung Huot coalition in Phnom Penh sent delegations to New York. The UN Credentials Committee responsible for allocating seats to member states met in an effort to resolve the impasse. Unable to make a decision either way, the committee decided to leave Cambodia's seat vacant. The decision was made despite Sihanouk's official endorsement of the Hun Sen–Ung Huot arrangement.[36] The message was clear enough; the architects of the PPAs and the UNTAC

---

33. Post Staff and Reuters, 'Asean backs off as Hun Sen digs in', *Phnom Penh Post*, July 1997. See also Nick Lenaghan, 'Asean says 'No' – foreign aid put on ice', *Phnom Penh Post*, July 1997.

34. Ibid.

35. For a detailed account of the international response to the coup, see Peou, *Intervention and Change in Cambodia?*, pp. 398–96.

36. See for example, Post Staff and Reuters, 'King dangles abdication card', *Phnom Penh Post*, 29 August 1997. Also, Hurley Scroggins and Chea Sotheacheat, 'King returns, gives nod to Ung Huot', *Phnom Penh Post*, 26 September.

elections could not accept the removal of an elected prime minister by force. Due to political developments in the previous two years, they were also not prepared to universally condemn Hun Sen's action as a *coup d'état*. The 1998 elections, as far as the international community was concerned, had to go ahead as planned with Ranariddh's participation.

If Hun Sen was hoping for international endorsement for his case against Ranariddh, he clearly miscalculated.[37] Likewise, if Ranariddh was expecting a stronger, more unified international response to Hun Sen's coup then he was also mistaken. The single most important factor in the crisis for all national and international groups was the elections. There was never any real doubt that elections would have to take place sooner or later. Elections were thus factored into everyone's calculations. In this sense, Hun Sen probably correctly anticipated the international response and emerged the stronger for it. Before the coup he and the CPP were facing a formidable electoral challenge and the likelihood of another defeat in 1998. Now, with UCD leaders struggling to have their case heard outside of Cambodia, and Ranariddh still facing alleged criminal charges inside the country, the chances of an outright victory for Hun Sen and the CPP were greatly increased. With the support of international groupings known as the 'ASEAN Troika' and the 'Friends of Cambodia', Ranariddh, after being convicted in absentia in two sham trials in March 1998, followed by an almost immediate pardon by King Sihanouk, would eventually return to Cambodia just before the campaign period.[38] In the meantime, the various diplomatic and international groups directly engaged in the elections could continue with

---

37. Jason Barber and Huw Watkin, 'Hun Sen left seat-less at the UN', *Phnom Penh Post*, 10 October 1997.

38. The 'ASEAN Troika' was created by the foreign ministers of Indonesia, the Philippines and Thailand. The 'Friends of Cambodia' included: Australia, Canada, France, Germany, Japan, New Zealand, South Korea, United Kingdom, United States. Based upon a proposal put forward by Japanese representatives, what became known as the 'four pillars' plan, Ranariddh was able to return to Cambodia and participate in the elections. The Japanese plan involved four principles: a cease-fire and reintegration of FUNCINPEC forces into the RCAF, Ranariddh severing ties with the remaining Khmer Rouge leadership, a trial in absentia for the alleged crimes brought by Hun Sen and the CPP followed by a pardon from the king, and his guaranteed safe return to Cambodia. The plan was accepted by the ASEAN Troika and the Friends of Cambodia group on 15 February. After some initial resistance, Ranariddh accepted the plan's terms. Hun

preparations without the constant delays and frustrations caused by the infighting between the two prime ministers.

International Assistance for Elections Post-1997 Coup

Because of the crisis, the regular UNDP election coordination meetings had not taken place since 26 June. The German ambassador to Cambodia, however, convened two meetings of the 'high level' diplomatic contact group and international agencies to discuss 'their intentions to assist in the preparations in the light of the recent events'.[39] The details of the second meeting – attended by Co-Ministers of the Interior Sar Kheng (CPP) and You Hockry (F'pec) – demonstrated the donors' apparent eagerness to push ahead with the pre-July preparations. Although 'the recent events' were no doubt at the forefront of donors' minds, there was no specific mention of the plight of Ranariddh and other opposition leaders, and of the possible implications their continued absence had for the validity and credibility of the election preparations. Instead, discussions focused on donor expectations regarding the overall transparency of the electoral procedures. At the time, the various electoral laws expected to be enacted by September were under discussion at the 'Council of Ministers', chaired by Hun Sen.[40]

Given the dramatically changed political landscape, continued international engagement with the elections was in some ways more complex. To be sure, the deposing of Ranariddh and the flight of other opposition leaders had made their job somewhat easier insofar as the delays to the enactment of the legislative framework and other logistical issues could now proceed virtually unobstructed by political infighting. However, even if the return of Ranariddh and the UCD was not formally discussed, the coup and its bloody aftermath could not be ignored. In this sense, their job was made more difficult because continued support had to be based upon assurances and guarantees from the 'new government' that the elections would be 'free and fair'. The authorities in Phnom Penh interested in securing international endorsement were aware of the

---

Sen accepted it straight away. For more details see Sorpong Peou, http://www.c-r. org/accord-article/diplomatic-pragmatism-aseans-response-july-1997-coup.

39. UNDP. Note to the File on the Occasion of the adhoc Elections Coordination Meeting for Donors. 22 August 1997.

40. Ibid.

necessity to provide assurances to donors that the July fighting had not derailed the elections process. The Hun Sen–Ung Huot government was confident enough that international legitimacy could be conferred via elections that were conducted under minimal conditions, reflecting the nature of the political crisis before and after the coup.

Assurances guaranteeing minimal conditions were enough to keep international groups like the 'ASEAN Troika' and 'Friends of Cambodia' engaged. After several meetings between these groups a formal statement was sent by the Phnom Penh authorities to the UN Secretary General Kofi Annan, committing the government to 'maintaining and improving politico-socio-economic stability, and ensuring a peaceful environment conducive to free and fair elections in 1998'. The statement also committed the government to guaranteeing 'the physical security and safety of those members of the National Assembly and other political leaders who wished to return and resume their political activities'.[41] Some human rights monitors in Phnom Penh and elsewhere were not convinced by the assurances, arguing that the elections could not be 'free and fair' and would only serve to legitimize Hun Sen's 'de-facto' one-party rule. The systematic destruction of the NUF party's infrastructures and offices, the self-imposed exile of its leadership and the resulting 'pervasive climate of fear and intimidation' meant the elections would be anything but 'free and fair'. According to this understanding of the crisis, rather than focusing on support for elections, international governments and donors ought to have concentrated on bringing to justice those responsible for the March 30 grenade attack and the extra-judicial killings of F'pec personnel in the aftermath of the coup.[42]

The notion that political or other kinds of conditions, such as the withdrawal of financial and technical assistance for elections if minimal conditions were not guaranteed, was not something international donors were seriously prepared to consider. Anonymous foreign officials engaged in the elections process openly admitted in the English-

---

41. UN document S/1997/998. Annex I. Letter dated 22 October from His Excellency Mr. Ung Huot and His Excellency Samdech Hun Sen addressed to the UN Secretary-General. See http://www.geocities.com/khmerchronology/s.1997.998.htm.

42. Post Staff, 'Elections Debate: What's the alternative?' *Phnom Penh Post*, 12 September 1997.

language press that donors were primarily interested in political stability based on an assumption that Hun Sen was considered the only 'one who is going to run the country in the near future'. Presumably, the thinking was that conditions placed on electoral support would be destabilizing and thus diametrically opposed to donors' interests. According to this position, donors were not necessarily a 'bunch of knaves or fools'; legitimacy would not be conferred on Hun Sen by turning a 'blind eye to elections marred by violence and intimidation'. Rather, in the 'context of realpolitik', it was better to remain engaged rather than 'to lose influence' over the conduct of the elections process.[43]

Anonymous comments in newspaper articles did not necessarily amount to a clearly articulated donor policy of engagement in favour of conditions, but they did fairly accurately sum up the donors' approach to the crisis. Yet there were a number of problems with this position. First, it's difficult to imagine that powerful donor governments actually underestimated the amount of influence that could be brought to bear on Hun Sen with regard to the politically motivated killings before and after the July coup. Elections were a necessary component in Hun Sen's strategy to re-consolidate CPP power. Secondly, the idea that a Hun Sen led government would be legitimized by elections that were marred by violence and intimidation was difficult to sustain. This was highly problematic for various international agencies, including the UN, as levels of violence and intimidation increased as the elections preparations evolved. The question then became, what levels of violence and intimidation were acceptable or not to fulfil minimal conditions, and who among the international groups would make that judgment? Thirdly, this approach ignored or at best downplayed the significance of the emergence of non-state actors within Cambodian society who were genuinely interested in upholding human rights and democratic principles.

Donor Guidelines and Coordination

In an attempt to circumvent the thorny issue of possible conditions attached to electoral support, donors instead developed a set of principles or 'guidelines' intended to introduce government accountability and transparency into the process:

---

43. Ibid.

(a) An independent Election Commission (b) Creation of a political environment in which all parties have a free and fair chance to participate in the elections peacefully and the parties, candidates as well as voters enjoy the security of person and property (c) Parties to register themselves freely, choose their candidates freely (d) Every Candidate to respect the rights of others (e) Full respect for Human Rights by the State, the Parties, and the candidates (f) Free Campaign process, open equally to every party and candidate with due respect to their freedom of movement, assembly, association and expression and communication with the voters (g) Equal access by the parties and candidates to mass media (h) Effective, impartial and non-discriminatory registration of voters (i) Voting entirely by free choice and without intimidation or interference of any kind, and by secret ballot, without the presence of security forces in the immediate vicinity of the polling station (j) Cease-fire in areas where fighting may be continuing to allow citizens to vote freely and without fear (k) Total integrity of the ballot boxes and counting in the presence of representatives of the contesting parties as well as international observers (l) Acceptance of results by all parties (m) International observation to cover various stages of the election process (n) NGOs to be included in the election process as educators and as monitors (o) No use of State machinery to the particular advantage of any party or candidate.[44]

The 'guidelines' were significant for understanding the extent to which donors sought to influence the elections process beyond the provision of technical and logistical support. They were not considered to be strict conditions attached to financial support. Elections were expected to cost somewhere in the region of USD 23 million. It was emphasized at the time that they were in 'no way a list of demands or even the official position of any of the countries involved'. In a press interview, a member of the 'high level' diplomatic group was reported as saying that the guidelines 'had no official standing it is just a piece of paper that notes some of the issues of concern'.[45] Certainly donors and representatives of the foreign diplomatic community were careful to avoid the major political obstacles that had dogged the elections preparations for the previous two years. Those who had been involved from the

---

44. 'Diplomats Hand Over Election Guidelines', *The Cambodia Daily*, 27 November 1997.

45. Ibid.

beginning were fully aware of the political divisiveness and instability caused by the issues of concern. This explains to a large extent the less than sanguine pronouncements regarding the conduct of the process. While the elections were not expected to be 'free and fair', donors and diplomats were only prepared to offer a wish list of requirements, saying nothing about what specific actions would be taken if they were not met.

Aside from the guidelines and logistical and technical problems, UNDP election coordination meetings turned their attention to specific coordination issues including the important question of international observers and reporting. In December 1997, the UN Secretary General had agreed in principle to coordinate a joint international observer group alongside the UN's technical coordination efforts. Before the coup, representatives from the European Union had also been conducting assessments of the political situation with a view to developing a 'comprehensive project for the finance and support of election activities including responsibility for voter registration, training of election officials, legal assistance for journalists reporting electoral issues and the provision of long-term and short-term election observers'.[46] Along with Japan, the EU was one of the largest contributors to the elections process in 1998.

With so many different international entities, agencies and donors involved in the election preparations, the coordination of financial, logistical and technical support was complex. In an effort to simplify and streamline the process, the UNDP created a 'trust fund'; a mechanism through which each individual donor could contribute to whichever aspect of the elections process its government was interested in. More complex and troubling was the problem of collecting and controlling the analysis of information related to the political and human rights aspects of the electoral preparations. Collectively, as members of a so-called 'community' of disparate international actors, what was considered to be acceptable or not depended upon individual country interpretations and perceptions of the situation in the context of respective interests. In other words, international groups were bound together by a common goal to ensure the elections took place, but differed on exactly how this could and should happen.

---

46. Financing Agreement between The European Community and The Royal Government of Cambodia. Title: Support to the Democratic Electoral Process in Cambodia. Project Number: ALA 97/0513. October 1997.

This dual problem of technical coordination and politics was symptomatic of the UN's system-wide approach. As the first point of contact for technical assistance, the UNDP's role had up to this point been central to international support for the elections. However, under 'new policy arrangements' the RGC's 1996 request to the UNDP for the coordination of multilateral and bilateral assistance had to be cleared first by the UN Department of Political Affairs in New York (UNDPA).[47] Regardless of the deteriorating political situation, the UNDPA's needs assessment mission cleared the way for and formalized specialist coordination assistance in February 1997. The UNDP coordination meeting format satisfied 'the need for close coordination among the many interested partners: national authorities, bilateral and multi-lateral donors and national and international NGOs'. The meetings were intended to provide a forum for the receipt and exchange of information from interested partners and discuss concerns related to resource mobilization in the context of the political situation.[48]

The UNDP's role in coordinating the many partners' diverse interests was hampered by political obstacles upsetting the technical and logistical preparations prior to the July coup. The post-July political situation had the practical effect of galvanizing international efforts to push the process forward. Despite the apparent sense of urgency among the international groups, the political parties and electoral laws were subject to further delays, and only passed at the end of 1997. This included delays to the law on political parties concerning government control of the registration of political parties and the use of party names and logos. At the time, the KNP, led by Sam Rainsy, was 'officially' not considered a 'legal entity' by the government. Both the KNP and Son Sann's BLDP had been subjected to competing claims of ownership over the party name and logos as part of a broader CPP-inspired attempt to prevent them from running in the election. Further delays in the elections concerning the structure and powers of the National Election Committee (NEC) were ultimately resolved. The NEC's powers would be subjected to parliamentary approval, not that of the Council of Ministers, as was envisaged in previous drafts. Other issues related to the independence and recruitment of NEC

---

47. Report to donors on their contribution to the 1998 Cambodia Elections through the UNDP open trust fund, 28 December 1998, Phnom Penh.

48. Ibid.

members and the financing of the body would, however, continue to pose serious problems throughout the elections period and beyond.

UN coordination efforts after the July coup were extended further. First was the ASEAN Troika's request that the UN assist in and monitor the return of the UCD leaders and the 'unfettered' resumption of their political activities. The Safe Return Monitoring Operation was set up through the office of the Secretary General Special Representative to ensure the safety and security of UCD/NUF politicians when they eventually returned to Cambodia to rebuild party infrastructures in preparation for the elections.[49] The second and more controversial effort – in terms of political judgments about the freedom and fairness of the elections process – was the UN coordination of the Joint International Observer Group (JIOG) under the auspices of the Elections Assistance Secretariat (EAS). The JIOG was established in line with the UN's provision of electoral assistance for the 'coordination and support for international observers', which included a small secretariat to provide support to the JIOG. From the UN's perspective, this form of assistance had 'two major advantages'. It allowed the UN to 'retain a low political profile', and was the least politically intrusive 'while at the same time providing the benefits of an international observer presence'.[50]

With the addition of the JIOG and the EAS, international assistance for the 1998 elections after the July coup was extensive. The coup had simultaneously broken the deadlock that had previously frustrated international elections assistance efforts and had created new political dramas, the ramifications of which were uncertain. Hun Sen's triumph over his co-prime minister confirmed what most foreign diplomats in Phnom Penh had already concluded: that only he had the political and military wherewithal to run the country. Perceptions and interpretations of events related to the remnants of the Khmer Rouge provided Hun Sen a convenient recourse to realpolitik and the international communities' justification for its response. To be sure, the denial of a seat at

---

49. UN Office of the Secretary General's Personal Representative in Cambodia report: UN Assessment Meeting. 5 June 1998. UNOSGPRC 0750. CPY 222. NB: Benny Widyono was replaced as the UN Secretary General's Representative at the end of May 1997 by Lakhan Mehrotra with the title of UN Secretary General's Personal Representative in Cambodia, UNSGPRC.

50. UN General Assembly document A/50/332. III. Electoral Assistance, 7 August 1995, p. 23, paragraphs 67–72.

the UN, the postponement of Cambodia's entry into ASEAN and the UN-monitored return of the NUF politicians were temporary setbacks for Hun Sen. But in responding to the coup by insisting elections once again be used as a mechanism to resolve the latest phase of the conflict, international donors gave Hun Sen the room he needed to manoeuvre into a position where he could reach for the electoral victory he so desperately needed.

***

Continued international support for elections after the coup was on the surface at least intended to restore the democratization process begun in Paris in 1991. To endorse the political outcome of the coup would have been tantamount to writing off the UNTAC process as a complete failure. In a difficult and complex domestic political setting the interests of regional and international powers in political stability and security took precedence. This was based upon on the belief that by doing so further large-scale political violence and human rights abuses could be avoided. The question then became, to what extent was the resulting trade-off acceptable or not in the context of multi-party democratic elections? As laudable as the donor election guidelines were, the lack of specific conditions attached to electoral assistance was a tacit admission that the elections would be much less than free and fair.

CHAPTER 5

The 1998 Elections

Conflicts over the level of international involvement in and assistance for elections had divided the two co-prime ministers since the formal request for assistance was sent to the UN by the RGC in mid-1996. Ranariddh and F'pec's desire to have the UN observe and monitor the entire process was anathema to Hun Sen. In his dealings with UN officials throughout 1996–97, Hun Sen was only prepared to accept a minimal international observational role alongside UNDP technical and financial assistance. Ranariddh preferred a greater degree of international involvement to ensure what was hoped would be a genuine democratic contest. This type of assistance, known in UN parlance as 'verification' involves certifying the legitimacy of the various phases of the electoral process. International observers are deployed throughout the country for the election period producing reports on the conduct and integrity of the process. Based on these reports the UN makes a final judgment on the freedom and fairness of the process.[1] Although not as politically intrusive as other types of assistance such as the organization and conduct of the elections (UNTAC), or international supervisory roles, verification was apparently too politically divisive and destabilizing. With Ranariddh temporarily out of the picture and facing an uncertain future, the Hun Sen–Ung Huot 'coalition' was able to determine the modalities of engagement with the international observer coordination exercise without any real input or interference from the NUF/UCD leadership.

UN Coordination, JIOG and Political Violence

In October 1997, the government confirmed its readiness to cooperate with the UN in coordinating the observation of the electoral process.[2]

---

1. UN General Assembly document A/50/332. III. Electoral Assistance. 7 August 1995.

2. Copy of the text of a letter from UN Secretary General, Kofi Annan to Mr. Ung Huot. 2 April 1998.

Presumably, because of the controversy surrounding Ranariddh's predicament and the political and human rights situation more generally, the UN delayed its decision until December. It accepted the government's position and agreed in principle that the UN, 'acting in a strictly technical capacity, might coordinate an international observer force'.[3] The UN took a cautious approach before committing to the role of coordinator. Concerns about the implementation of the Japanese 'four pillars' plan and the investigations into human rights abuses and political killings since 1997 featured heavily in the deliberations. Under the terms of the plan, and after receiving a pardon from Sihanouk, Ranariddh finally returned to Cambodia at the end of March. An agreement between the UN and the RGC concerning the observer coordination was reached in early April.

Fears about the RGC's stated commitment to ensuring the freedom and fairness of the elections persisted. These fears surfaced during the visit of the UN High Commissioner for Human Rights, Mary Robinson, in January. The High Commissioner was there to discuss, among other things, the human rights situation and the future of the Cambodia UN Human Rights Office. Hun Sen's hostility towards the Center and its staff – who he considered to be politically motivated and biased against the CPP – was well known in Phnom Penh. In particular, the findings presented in an October 1997 report by the Special Representative for Human Rights, Thomas Hammarberg, implicating the military police and security forces in acts of political violence and killings, was severely criticized by the government for inaccuracies and lack of evidence. Although intimately familiar with the details of the report, the Special Representative was deliberately excluded from the meeting between the High Commissioner and Hun Sen. During the meeting, Hun Sen, in a blatant effort to discredit the Human Rights Office staff, produced four individuals who he claimed were reported as killed. Had he been present, the Special Representative would have been able to fully explain what turned out to be nothing more than administrative errors.[4] The continued presence of the UN Human Rights Office in Cambodia

---

3. UNDP. 9th Election Coordination Meeting. UNDP Service Center. 6 February 1998.

4. Elizabeth Moorthy. 'Robinson content with "full and frank discussion"', *Phnom Penh Post*, 30 January 1998.

presented a dilemma for the CPP. To seek its closure would be politically imprudent both nationally and internationally, especially as Hun Sen had invited the UN office to monitor, investigate and 'establish the facts' of all human rights abuses after the coup 'and report the findings to the government'.[5] At the same time, consistent links between human rights abuses and the military and security services, the police and local provincial and national authorities and the CPP reported by the office were politically damaging. Moreover, some international actors regarded the Human Rights Office as playing a vital role in the elections process. Many of the human rights abuses the office monitored, investigated and reported were of a political nature related to the elections process. Because of this, and Hun Sen's past experience with international agencies, the UN Human Rights Office was implicitly characterized as being part of the opposition against the CPP rather than an agency dedicated to supporting the government's efforts in combating the problem.

Although the government agreed to the continued operation of the office for a further two years, it sought to pressure the UN in circumscribing its role in the elections. This was evidenced in a letter of response to the UN Secretary General's formal acceptance of the invitation to co-ordinate international observers. Both Hun Sen and Ung Huot emphasized the government's continued efforts to investigate alleged human rights violations stipulated in the Special Representative's report, and stated that 'the perpetrators will be punished accordingly'.[6] As evidence of 'real progress' in the investigation, the letter cited the four individuals presented to the High Commissioner during her meeting with Hun Sen. Both the High Commissioner and the Special Representative had responded separately explaining the error.[7] Based on this supposed evidence, the government reiterated its 'legitimate request that UN officials be appointed as coordinators of observers and other officers, especially

---

5. Report of the Secretary-General of Human Rights in Cambodia. A/52/489. 17 October 1998. Para 42.

6. Copy of letter from Hun Sen and Ung Huot to United Nations Secretary General, Kofi Annan. Phnom Penh. 13 April. 1998.

7. Text of correspondence from UN Secretary General's Special Representative for Human Rights, Thomas Hammarberg to UN Secretary General's Special Personal Representative Lakhan Mehrotra. 'Comments on the Phnom Penh Response 13 April to SG's letter re UN co-ordination of observers'. 15 April 1998.

in the Center for Human Rights, which must maintain a cooperative and neutral attitude, and not at all pursue their own political agendas.[8] Just like other political forces perceived to be in opposition to the CPP, the UN Human Rights Office, if it could not be eliminated, had to be marginalized, neutralized or discredited. Attached to the UN Secretary General's acceptance of the RGC's invitation to coordinate the observers was a memorandum 'outlining the modalities and principles of the UN's role'. The memorandum covered the establishment of the Joint International Observer Group (JIOG) composed of observers 'sponsored by foreign governments and inter-governmental organizations to observe all phases of the election'. The Electoral Assistance Secretariat (EAS) was to serve as the 'focal point for harmonizing and supporting the JIOG, but it was understood that they play a purely administrative role and will not in any way participate as observers in the elections. In coordination with the National Election Committee, a small core group of international long-term observers would be deployed to monitor the pre-election period at the provincial level, including the political campaign, election polling day, the vote count, the convening of the new National Assembly and the establishment of a new government'. The memorandum further stated that the intention of the coordination exercise was to 'encourage a comprehensive and objective assessment of the electoral process by the international community'. However, it added that 'throughout the operation the UN maintains a clear public position of neutrality'. It made clear that it was the JIOG 'that normally issues a joint statement of their findings in the pre- and immediate post-election period'.[9]

While the memorandum was clear in proclaiming the UN's technical and administrative role and position of neutrality, the role of the JIOG as outlined in the document was more overtly political. It also stated that international observers under the auspices of the JIOG, would undertake private démarches with the National Election Committee and with the appropriate Government authorities. In addition to this, the JIOG could issue public statements on their findings to 'provide a col-

---

8. Ibid.

9. Copy of the text, 'Memorandum of Understanding between the United Nations and the Royal Government of Cambodia on the International Electoral Observers, 14 April 1998.

lective assessment' of the process. It was understood that the 'démarches and statements may include recommendations on how progress can be improved'.[10]

At the end of the memorandum the UN added that it 'reserves the right to withdraw or suspend' its observer activities 'if there is a fundamental deterioration in the political situation that would undermine the holding of credible and legitimate elections in accordance with internationally recognized criteria.' The UN accordingly said it would review its role under certain circumstances which included the following: restrictions of movements of observers, barriers placed in the way of the registration or participation of political parties or candidates, a general climate of intimidation, the absence of equitable access to the media by competing parties, and the 'inability of the constitutional council to exercise its authority as laid down in the constitution and in law'.[11]

The memorandum was sent to Hun Sen and Ung Huot after an upsurge in politically motivated killings of senior F'pec military officials. A spate of murders including F'pec General Kim Sang in March was characterized by human rights investigators as 'an orchestrated campaign to neutralize F'pec officials' in the run up to the elections.[12] Government officials including Ung Huot condemned the killings, but claimed they were likely non-political. Human rights workers however suggested they were part of a pattern of murders of F'pec officials that continued after the post-July murders, carried out by CPP security forces, 'possibly the government's anti-terrorist unit'.[13] In spite of government promises to do so, no serious investigations were conducted to establish what the motives or who the perpetrators were.[14] Kim Sang was killed two days before the 'ASEAN Troika' and 'Friends of Cambodia' (FOC) groups were due to meet in Manila in the Philippines to discuss the Cambodian situation. Both groups issued separate statements at the end

---

10. Ibid.

11. Ibid.

12. Khuy Sokheoun, Catherine Philp, Ham Samnag, Deutsche Presse-Agentur and Agence France-Presse, 'Murder Fuels Fears of Political Violence', *The Cambodia Daily*, 6 March 1998. See also Eric Pape, 'I believe we will be killed one by one', *Phnom Penh Post*, 27 March 1998.

13. Ibid.

14. Ibid.

of the meeting, welcoming the acceptance by all parties of the Japanese government's 'four pillars plan', which the 'ASEAN Troika' viewed as a favourable development 'in moving the process of creating conditions for the holding of free, fair, and credible elections forward'.[15] While it did not specifically refer to the upsurge in politically related violence, the FOC statement – as well as welcoming the four pillars initiative – made clear that urgent steps were required 'to ensure a climate free of human rights abuses and political intimidation'. In that regard, 'The "Friends" also expressed full support for the UN, including the UN Secretary General's Special Representative for Human Rights in Cambodia, Mr. Thomas Hammarberg.'[16]

The "Friends" group didn't specify what exactly the urgent steps were to be, but agreed to meet again with the 'ASEAN Troika' 'to look closely at the resolution of the issues and to draw appropriate conclusions'.[17] The stated support for the UN and its human rights representative Thomas Hammarberg in this regard was significant if a little vague. Clearly, the reports and findings provided by the Human Rights Center detailing abuses and political violence would be central in their deliberations. This was also true for the UN Secretary General's Personal Representative, Lakhan Mehrotra, regarding assessments and reports sent to his superiors in the UN Department of Political Affairs. Because of the nature of the Human Rights Center's monitoring and investigation work, it was very difficult for the UN to maintain a low political profile in the elections and its dealings with the Hun Sen–Ung Huot coalition.

This issue was illustrated by the government's response to the UN Secretary General's memorandum concerning the UN's role in coordinating the observers. The memorandum was returned with proposed amendments in the apparently erroneous understanding that it was a draft. Key paragraphs were proposed for deletion, including the section on JIOG démarches to the NEC and other relevant government authorities. In the paragraph dealing with the UN's right to withdraw or suspend its coordination activities key words and phrases such as 'credible and legitimate' and 'internationally recognized criteria' related

15. ASEAN Troika Statement. Manila, 6 March, 1998. Camnews.v001.n553.7

16. 'Friends of Cambodia' Meeting, Manila, 6 March 1998. Camnews.v001n553.8

17. Ibid.

to the elections were also proposed for deletion, and to be replaced with 'free and fair' and 'laws and regulations governing these elections'. In the list of five points or circumstances that may cause the UN to review its role, other phrases and words such as 'a general climate of intimidation' preventing the holding of free and fair elections were amended. The circumstance concerning the 'inability of the Constitutional Council to exercise its authority as laid down in the constitution and in law' was to be deleted.'[18]

The proposed amendments were an understandable cause for concern for the UN. Prior to receiving them, a meeting to discuss the UN's role in the elections was held in New York in early April. Following that meeting, in a communication to the UN Under Secretary General, Thomas Hammarberg pressed home the importance of having formal assessments of whether or not the criteria for free, fair and credible elections were met. Furthermore, he added that 'the possibility of suspension or withdrawal should be seen as real'. In this sense there would be 'an inevitable political dimension to the coordination role'.[19] The deletions by the RGC were indicative of the centrality of the political dimensions to international involvement. Commenting on the deletions, Hammarberg stressed that the document was not a proposal for negotiation and reiterated the significance of the possibility of withdrawal. The deletion of references to international standards and 'a general climate of intimidation' were viewed as unacceptable.[20] It was felt strongly that because the Hun Sen–Ung Huot coalition was actually a contender in the election, any negotiation with one of the contending parties could jeopardize and discredit what should be a strictly impartial role for the UN.[21]

In a carefully measured response to Hun Sen and Ung Huot, the UN Secretary General clarified that the memorandum was not intended as

---

18. Copy of text of proposed deletions to the 'Memorandum of Understanding between the United Nations and the Royal Government of Cambodia on the International Electoral Observers', attached to letter sent to UN Secretary General of the United Nations by Hun Sen and Ung Huot.

19. Copy of letter from The Special Representative of the United Nations Secretary General for Human Rights, Thomas Hammarberg, to the United Nations Department of Political Affairs Assistant Secretary General, Alvaro de Soto.

20. Copy of the text of 'Comments on the Phnom Penh Response 13 April to SG's letter re UN Co-ordination of Observers'. Thomas Hammarberg. 15 April 1998.

21. Ibid.

a draft. It was explained that it was 'merely to convey' the terms under which the UN would undertake the RGC's request for electoral coordination. He also pointed out that the previous guidelines provided to the government had never been formally endorsed by the UN General Assembly and are to be 'read and understood in the light of the circumstances prevailing in a particular country'. In assessing the political situation, he added that the UN 'can only abide by internationally recognized criteria'. Whilst the UN did not agree to the amendments, neither did it address what could be interpreted as a deliberate and conscious attempt to undermine the UN role. The UN's response suggested that any political judgments by the UN would be determined by events on the ground as they unfolded.

The NUF Boycotts

While the various international groups deliberated the role of the UN in coordinating international observers, NUF leaders were busy trying to re-build party infrastructures destroyed in the aftermath of the coup, and prepare to compete in the elections. For them, time was of the essence. Because of further delays in passing the election laws and the rules governing the creation and function of the NEC, the NUF sought to buy more time to wrest back some control over preparations from which they had been largely excluded. The actual election date had already been changed from the end of May to July 26 to allow more time for the logistical and technical challenges to be completed. The eleven-member NEC responsible for the elections was finally approved by the National Assembly at the end of January, leaving just under six months to administer the myriad of necessary tasks. To register their dissatisfaction and protest against the manner in which they felt the government was unfairly controlling the process NUF leaders began a boycott of the National Assembly at the end of April.

The boycott was intended to delay the National Assembly session to amend the election law. In effect this meant a delay in the voter registration process, giving more time for NUF grievances to be voiced. It was the first step in a broader effort to delay the date of the elections further. From their perspective, the elections could not be free and fair unless a whole series of problems and issues related to the legal framework, the independence and neutrality of the NEC and the Constitutional

Council (CC), fear and intimidation of opposition party members and voters, and equal access to the media were addressed. In essence, the NUF parties were struggling to reverse the reconsolidation of CPP control over the state and prevent a landslide victory for the CPP in the elections. Mobilization of CPP-dominated administrative and security structures in the rural areas to ensure such a victory was the NUF's biggest problem. It was precisely this conflict over control over rural administrative structures that precipitated the crisis between the two prime ministers in 1996, culminating in the July fighting.

For the most part, the NUF was unsuccessful in attempts to gain political support after rejecting the results resulting in a protracted post-election standoff, although some specific grievances related to the election law and the administration of vote counting were addressed. For instance, according to the election law, the votes were to be counted at the village level, leading to fears that the secrecy of the vote might be compromised. In an apparent compromise, Hun Sen and Ranariddh agreed to the counting of votes to be moved up to the commune level, alleviating fears to some extent.[22] The NUF thus ended the boycott of the National Assembly, allowing the registration process to begin in the middle of May.

Success in altering the ballot process was not matched in other areas of concern for the NUF. For example, there was no real discussion of issues related to the independence and neutrality of the NEC and the Constitutional Council, exacerbating a general feeling of distrust in the impartiality of both bodies. As a result, ten days after the National Assembly agreed on the membership of the CC, the NUF announced their intention to boycott the elections if no further progress could be made to assuage their fears. If the rationale for the boycott was to put pressure on international donors, it proved to be ineffective, even counter productive. After the political developments of the previous two years, there was no support among the donor community for the boycott.[23]

---

22. See for example Caroline Hughes, with Real Sopheap, 'Nature and Causes of Conflict Escalation in the 1998 Election', Cambodia Centre for Conflict Resolution under the auspices of the Cambodia Development Resource Institute, Phnom Penh, p. 19.

23. UN Secretary General's Personal Representative, Lakhan Mehrotra, 'Report: Friends of Cambodia – 20 June'. CPY 240, 22 June 1998, p. 2

The Constitutional Council

As the ultimate arbiter the Constitutional Council had a vital role to play in judging the freedom and fairness of the elections. In principle, as an independent body it would make the final decisions on the status of any electoral complaints the NEC was unable to deal with. Like the NEC, the legitimacy and authority of the Council was challenged from the very beginning by the NUF, who argued it was dominated by members closely associated with the CPP. In an effort to circumvent the problem, nine Council members would be appointed from three nominees submitted by King Sihanouk; one each from three parties represented in the National Assembly, and three from the Supreme Council of the Magistracy (SCM).

As the country's ultimate judicial body, the SCM was also considered to be overwhelmingly controlled by the CPP. For this reason, it was largely discredited as an independent and impartial institution both inside and outside of Cambodia.[24] Because of its proposed political composition, two of King Sihanouk's nominees, Son Sann and Chau Sen Cocsal, staged a boycott of their own, preventing the Council from convening its first meeting before the elections in May. Amidst allegations of political interference and intimidation from both Sihanouk and Hun Sen, the King's third nominee, Pung Peng Cheng, withdrew from the Council and left the country.[25]

The Council was not convened before the elections as international donors had hoped. For the most part, the donors' attitude towards the CC was ambiguous. While the integrity of the Council was considered paramount, it was recognized that it was 'loaded in CPP's favour but it was necessary to observe how it would actually perform once coming into being'.[26] It was felt by some in the donor community that 'the

---

24. At the time of the convening of the SCM in December 1997 a western observer was quoted as saying that: 'The concern is that, at this stage, (the SCM is) still 100 per-cent CPP members [sic].' Kimsan Chantara and Jeff Hodson, 'Supreme Council of Magistracy Convenes', *The Cambodia Daily*, Thursday, 4 December 1997.

25. Eric Pape, 'Hun Sen, King combine to convene council', *Phnom Penh Post*, 7/12, June 19–July 2, 1998. See also The Cambodia Daily and News Services, 'Hun Sen Holds Surprise Meeting With King', *The Cambodia Daily*, Tuesday, 9 June 1998.

26. UNOSGPRC 0701.Cryptofax. CPY212. From Lakhan Mehrotra UNSGPRC to Sir Kieran Prendergast USG/DPA New York. Subject: Meeting of the Informal

possibility of the CC performing impartially and independently should not be ruled out'.[27] This optimistic view was not shared by everyone. The UN's Special Representative of the Secretary General for Human Rights in Cambodia was said to be 'very pessimistic' 'about the prospect of having the Council's function be sufficiently respected in order to resolve outstanding conflict'.[28] Indeed, the Council's decision to reject the opposition's electoral complaints only served to reinforce the NUF's belief that the body was illegitimate, and unable to pronounce authoritatively on the integrity of the process.[29] The failure of the Council to adequately address this and related electoral problems precipitated the NUF's decision to reject the election results and take to the streets in protest after the polls.

The NEC

As the state agency responsible for organizing all aspects of the elections, the NEC and its provincial and commune counterparts, the PEC and CEC, were subjected to intense scrutiny and criticism by both opposition parties and civil society groups. As with other key state agencies in the post-July 1997 environment, the structure and performance of the NEC and its adjunct committees was highly politicized. The NEC itself was mired in controversy from the outset. For instance, senior CPP figures close to Hun Sen, such as Om Yentieng and Sok An, were reportedly involved in 'lobbying' the night before a vote to select the NGO sector's candidate for the NEC, leading to unsubstantiated accusations of bribery and vote-rigging. The winning candidate, Chea Chamroeun, Director of the Khmer Youth Development Organization and a well-known CPP supporter, defeated his main challenger Lao Mong Hay,

---

Group of Ambassadors on Cambodian Elections. 27 May 1998, p. 2. UNDP, Note to the file, 9th Elections Coordinating Meeting, UNDP Service Centre, 30 December 1997. During the meeting the UNDP resident representative Paul Mathews reportedly 'emphasized the importance of the Constitutional Council being in place, preferably at the start of the registration process'.

27. Ibid.

28. UNOSGPRC 0750.Cryptofax.CPY 222. From Lakhan Mehrotra UNOSGPRC to Kieran Prendergast USG/DPA New York. Subject: UN Assessment meeting. 5 June 1998.

29. See for example Caroline Hughes, with Real Sopheap, 'Nature and Causes of Conflict Escalation in the 1998 Election', pp. 49–51.

the then Director of the Khmer Institute for Democracy, the preferred candidate of the main Cambodian election monitoring organizations.[30] Although unsubstantiated, the involvement of such high ranking officials with the NGO candidate only served to perpetuate the already chronic lack of confidence in the capacity of the Committee to withstand any political pressure from the CPP.

Confidence in the Committee's independence and impartiality was eroded further in a bizarre episode in March. The NEC Chairman and former PRK Minister for Culture and Communications, turned artist, Chheng Phon, co-signed an agreement between the government and the Argentinian venture company Ciccone, which had links to an Israeli IT company worth approximately $26 million, to manage the elections. The agreement was described by Chheng Phon as 'a spare tyre' to provide a contingency if donor contributions did not cover the costs of electoral services and equipment.[31] At the time, the UNDP trust fund was open to receive donor contributions, and financing the elections was not a major concern for donors. What caused 'considerable concern' for them, however, was the fact that the negotiations with Ciccone had been carried out in secret and with an implicit suggestion that the failure to meet the 26 July election deadline might be attributable to the donor community. After the delays caused by the politicization of the election preparations, this was particularly vexing for donors, especially as the Australian government and the European Community had committed substantial funding to the voter registration system and related activities. In contrast, the RGC had yet to provide the NEC with the financial resources it had committed in its effort to be a viable counterpart in the elections alongside donors.[32] The episode was a clumsy attempt by elements within the government to put in place a contingency in the unlikely event that donor funding was withdrawn. For the most part, the NEC's overall performance highlighted technical and administrative achievements in the context of almost overwhelming technical and

---

30. Post Staff, 'Buying your way into democracy – NEC bribes alleged', *Phnom Penh Post*, 2 January 1998.

31. Marie-Christine Courtes, 'Between a hammer and an anvil', *Phnom Penh Post*, 27 March 1998.

32. UNDP. Note to the file. 12th Election Coordination Meeting. UNDP Service Center, 20 March 1998.

financial constraints and inexperience. At the same time however questions about the Committee's independence and neutrality persisted, perpetuating an ambiguous sense of developing technical competence but political partiality. This ambiguity was summed up by comments made at the May UNDP meeting which concluded that while the NEC 'was suspected of being pro-CPP', it had managed to 'generate a lot of confidence and trust among people'.[33] The basis upon which these comments were made was not clear. It seemed, however, that the reality was not simply a case of whether the NEC was pro-CPP or not, but rather whether there was the political will and courage to resist or counteract interference. In his post-election analysis of its performance, the NEC's Vice-Chairman, Kassie Neou, admitted that on a 'few important issues the CPP bore down' on the committee 'and had its way, 'compromising [its] neutrality and damaging the process as a whole'. He added that, although the spirit of the law called for a neutral election apparatus, the 'CPP managed to get partisans, including officials into the system's many levels'.[34]

NEC and Media Access Bias

Another of the principal justifications for the NUF boycott of the elections was unequal access to broadcast media outlets. After the July crisis, almost all of the country's private and state broadcast media, radio and TV, was owned by, controlled by or aligned with the CPP and its supporters. Summing up the media situation in his September report to the UN General Assembly, Thomas Hammarberg stated that 'Before and during the electoral period equal and equitable access to broadcast media did not exist in Cambodia.' To illustrate the extent of CPP control, he noted that not one TV or radio station covered the return of the ousted first Prime Minister Ranariddh when he arrived back in the country March 30.[35]

---

33. UNOSGPRC 0701.CPY 212. 'Meeting of the Informal Group of Ambassadors on Cambodian Elections'. 27 May 1998.

34. Kassie Neou, with Jeffrey C. Gallup, 'Conducting Cambodia's Elections', *Journal of Democracy*, Vol. 10, No 2, April 1999, pp. 153–64.

35. UN General A/53/400. Fifty-third Session. 'Situation of Human Rights in Cambodia. Report of the Secretary General'. 17 September 1998. Paras 42–67.

One of the major tasks of the NEC was to regulate media access for election purposes, including voter education. Under NEC regulations issued at the end of May, privately owned TV and radio stations were prohibited from broadcasting political party propaganda or any message that violated the electoral law. The NEC would therefore monitor broadcasts during the campaign period, scheduled to start on 25 June, to ensure they were free of propaganda that could incite violence, hatred and abuse, or promote fear or loss of confidence in the secrecy of the ballot. To deal with NUF and UN concerns, Thomas Hammarberg called for a new review of the media situation in June concerning the fairness of access. Each of the 39 registered parties would be allowed five-minute slots to broadcast their political platforms, and be able to join in roundtable discussions.[36]

The five-minute slots may have given the impression of 'equality' but they did not solve the broader problem of 'equity' in accessing broadcast media more generally. After the success of the UNTAC media and voter education campaigns in 1992–93, the CPP were acutely aware of the potency of broadcast media in getting a message across to a population with a high percentage of functional illiteracy. The popularity of the KNP – known after March 1998 as the Sam Rainsy Party (SRP) – among Cambodia's urban groups, such as teachers, students and garment workers, combined with F'pec's traditional royalist appeal in rural areas when channelled through radio and TV, posed an added significant threat to the CPP. The CPP was also very much aware of the popularity among Cambodian listeners of foreign radio broadcasts in Khmer such as the Voice of America (VOA) and Radio Free Asia (RFA), which were perceived to be sympathetic to the political line espoused by the SRP. It made sense therefore for the CPP to keep the NUF off the airwaves as much as possible.

Since 1996 the Ministry of Information had successfully blocked the former KNP's attempts to acquire a broadcast licence and open its own radio station, giving highly questionable technical and economic reasons for doing so. Both Son Sann's BLDP and F'pec were granted licences to re-open radio stations shut down in the aftermath of the July

---

36. UNOSGRC, 'The Special Representative of the United Nations Secretary-General for Human Rights in Cambodia appeals calls for a new review of the media situation.' 25 June 1998.

coup in May and June respectively, but were unable to have them up and running in time for the elections. After the July crisis and during the campaign, both state and private radio and TV news was dominated by the activities of Hun Sen and the CPP. The NUF parties were thus aggrieved at what they saw as their virtual exclusion from access to broadcast media in the months before the election, and the unfair CPP monopoly since July 1997. The gross imbalance in access between the parties was revealed in a detailed monitoring of radio and TV newscasts conducted by the UN Human Rights Office for June and the first two weeks in July.[37] This lack of media access was a clear disadvantage for the NUF, preventing them from fully participating in the elections and providing another reason to reject the results.

Fear, Intimidation and CPP Rural Control

The 1993 UNTAC elections experience demonstrated that CPP mass membership campaigns and related intimidation and violence were not enough to secure an outright electoral victory. Coming second to F'pec revealed that the party and its methods for delivering votes were not effective enough. Even without a large foreign presence, in 1998 a victory for the CPP was not guaranteed. Prior to the July crisis – and Ranariddh's bungled attempt to negotiate a deal with Khieu Samphan – the combined political forces of the NUF presented a formidable electoral challenge. In the absence of some form of direct intervention that challenge may have been insurmountable for the CPP. The July 1997 crisis was thus a catalysing event reducing the threat to more controllable proportions.

Psychologically, the impact of Hun Sen's military action on voters of all political stripes was profound. The dangers of challenging Hun Sen were firmly embedded in people's minds. Consequently, as in 1993, the 1998 elections functioned more as devices for ensuring stability and security, rather than instruments for delivering on substantive policy issues. Once again, fear of continued instability and war could be effectively exploited by the CPP. Successful manipulation of those fears in the face of countervailing forces of competition, opposition and international scrutiny nevertheless could still not guarantee the desired

37. Office of the High Commissioner for Human Rights, Cambodia, 'Media and the Elections: Updated Statistics', 23 July 1998.

outcome. Alongside official fear-control narratives, other bureaucratic and administrative means would need to be deployed for CPP control to be effective.

During UNTAC the mobilization of state employees in the service of the CPP's electoral strategy was effective up to a point. While UNTAC may have failed to create a neutral political environment, it was able to disrupt state–party structures enough to allow insurgent parties a competitive chance. The successful exclusion of F'pec from local level administrative positions by Hun Sen in 1996 was the first step in the CPP's reconsolidation of hierarchical control over rural networks. The destruction of NUF structures in the immediate aftermath of the July crisis followed by almost nine months of manufactured uncertainty and delays helped to keep them out of CPP rural strongholds long enough to prevent them from fully reorganizing.

The next step was to activate administrative mechanisms to systematically control and/or compromise voter autonomy to ensure enough votes for the party. To achieve this, the CPP developed a comprehensive nationwide strategy overseen by the senior CPP Standing Committee member Say Chhum. As in 1993, the strategy involved mass mobilization and recruitment campaigns to enlist potential voters into party ranks. By June, the CPP claimed it had recruited 3.1 out of a potential 5.5 million registered voters.[38] The strategy also included having party members on all provincial, commune and polling station committees. In doing so, according to Say the CPP hoped to win 73 seats out of the 124 available in the National Assembly.[39]

In and of itself, the strategy could have been viewed as fairly innocuous, but the methods and techniques used were viewed by local election observers and national and international human rights groups as compromising the integrity of the elections. NUF leaders complained that intimidation was widespread and systematic, but 'covert'.[40] In particular, as part of its mass mobilization efforts, the CPP's 'thumbprinting campaign' conducted in the months immediately before the elections was regarded not as legitimate canvassing for votes as claimed by the CPP,

---

38. Eric Pape, 'CPP master plan for poll victory', *Phnom Penh Post*, 5 June 1998.

39. Ibid.

40. Caroline Hughes, with Real Sopheap, 'Nature and Causes of Conflict Escalation in the 1998 Election', p. 56.

but rather a system that was used to coerce and intimidate potential voters. The UN Human Rights Representative described the campaign as 'an open invitation to coercion' and 'crossing the line between mobilization and harassment'.[41]

Many of the millions of individuals described by Say as having 'signed up' for the CPP were recruited through this system of thumbprinting which was reminiscent of a 'cell' system used by the PRK for social control in the 1980s. The system functioned by engaging local authorities and party members designated as leaders of small groups or 'cells' comprising approximately ten individuals. Cell leaders went door-to-door collecting the personal details of households including individuals' thumbprints which were recorded in specially provided booklets. It was expected that after having given a thumbprint, an individual would 'pledge' or promise his or her vote to the CPP. Once in the system, they were presented with a party membership card, had their voter registration temporarily confiscated and number recorded, and were eligible for CPP gifts, such as small amounts of money, *sarongs* and *kramas* (traditional skirts and scarves), and packets of monosodium glutamate (MSG) for cooking.[42]

The problem with the thumbprint campaign as described by the NUF, local human rights and elections monitoring groups, as well as the UN Human Rights Office, was the mobilization and exploitation of fear that underpinned it. Individuals who expressed neutrality or an unwillingness to be recruited into the system were subjected to threats and intimidation. The type and extent of threats varied. The UN Human Rights Office for example reported threats such as individuals being told that if they did not co-operate 'security could not be assured', that they might have problems registering to vote, or if they didn't support the CPP they would be accused of being a member of the outlawed Khmer Rouge. Other threats had a more pernicious ritualistic element involving a bullet being dropped into a glass of water; the potential voter was asked to pledge an oath to vote for the CPP before drinking the water, the inference being 'break the oath and the bullet ends up

---

41. Eric Pape, 'Will voters agree to bite the bullet'? *Phnom Penh Post*, 22 May 1998

42. For a detailed description of the thump print campaign, see Hughes, *The Political Economy of Cambodia's Transition*, pp. 67–76.

in your body'.[43] In other instances, whole villages were threatened with withdrawal of development and humanitarian aid after the election if the village did not deliver a sufficient number of votes for the CPP.[44]

The issues of thumbprinting and intimidation and coercion were raised by Thomas Hammarberg at a meeting with Hun Sen in early May. According to Hammarberg, although Hun Sen gave the 'impression he was not in favour' of the procedure, it was not clear what action if any he would take to deal with the problem. In subsequent speeches, Hun Sen reportedly said that the thumbprints were a way of checking the numbers of party members, complaining that the CPP was being 'unfairly singled out by the human rights workers for wrongdoing'.[45] Subsequent comments on the matter by a government adviser repeated Hun Sen's explanation, adding that in 1993 the CPP had recruited 3 million members and yet only received 1.5 million votes. They therefore wanted to check the numbers 'to avoid another embarrassing defeat'. The comments reinforced the belief expressed by the CPP's electoral strategist Say Chhum that the party was usurped from power in 1993 by an 'international conspiracy'.[46]

It was evident from the results in 1993 that the CPP mobilization and recruitment campaign had largely failed to produce the expected outcome. Assuming the stated numbers of CPP members was accurate, this suggests that in the absence of widespread fraud and irregularities – but in an environment of intimidation and violence – UNTAC's efforts to educate and persuade voters of the secrecy of the vote had been fairly successful. Again as in 1993, the secrecy of the vote was uppermost in the minds of local and national human rights and observer groups. However, the heightened sense of insecurity and violence in the wake of F'pec's military defeat, the routing of the NUF leadership and Ranariddh's public humiliation and pardon served to limit the perceived options and choices available to many voters. During their mobilization and recruitment campaign, the CPP were able to press home the idea

---

43. Eric Pape, 'Will voters agree to bite the bullet?' *Phnom Penh Post*, 22 May 1998.

44. Examples of threats from UN report cited in Hughes, *The Political Economy of Cambodia's Transition*, p. 68.

45. Marc Levy, 'Poll Authority Eyes CPP Thumbprint Campaign Program', *The Cambodia Daily*, 18 May 1998.

46. Eric Pape, CPP master plan for poll victory', *Phnom Penh Post*, 5 June 1998.

that they alone could guarantee security and provide the necessary resources for development. The message was clear; by not voting for the CPP you risked exclusion from the political and socio-economic protection being offered, the consequences of which could be dire for you and your family.

Voters, NGO Election Observer Coalitions and Education

With technical and financial support through the UNDP trust fund – mainly from the EU and Australia – the NEC managed to register over 5 million voters representing about 93 per cent of the electorate. Most observers reported that the process was generally free from violence but plagued by intimidation and procedural problems. The work of the NEC and its provisional and commune committees were scrutinized by NGOs grouped under two main election observer coalitions, COMFREL and COFFEL, and a third smaller organization, NICFEC. From the earliest beginnings of the preparations in 1995, these coalitions were expected to play an important role in the conduct of the elections. Because the elections infrastructure was once again being built virtually from scratch in a hostile and dangerous political milieu, the work of the observer groups required more than just the observation of distinct phases of the process. Out of necessity, they saw themselves as educators and advocators as well as impartial and neutral monitors and observers.[47]

As regular participants at the UNDP coordination meetings, various NGOs grouped under the election coalitions were viewed by international donors as an integral part of the elections preparations. As such they could attempt to exert some, influence over the integrity, freedom and fairness of the process. With international backing and support, they set out to do this in a variety of ways, implementing strategies and programmes designed to engage state authorities on issues as they arose, and mobilizing networks of rural activists and volunteers for civic voter education initiatives. Strategies included the issuance of joint press statements and briefings in Phnom Penh expressing concerns about the process. COMFREL in particular, between November 1997 and September 1998, issued 21 separate statements criticizing, protesting,

47. See for example Caroline Hughes, 'Strategies and Impact of Election Observer Coalitions in Cambodia'. Phnom Penh: Experts for Community Research (ECR), Report No. 38, 2000. With assistance from Chhor Bonnaroath.

condemning and reporting on the progress of the elections at every stage, including the drafting of the elections laws, the composition and impartiality of the NEC and CEC, unequal media access, and politically related violence and intimidation in the pre-election period, registration process, campaign, polling, counting and post-election period.

In terms of programming, attention was focused on public participation through training, education and monitoring of the general situation. Building upon experience garnered during UNTAC, the leaders of the main human rights and democracy NGOs knew full well the importance of their role as mediators and educators. Post-July 1997, the dissemination of good quality information related to the elections and the rights and responsibilities of voters, supplied directly to the electorate, especially in rural areas, was perhaps more important than ever. Much like the NEC itself, these coalitions were poorly resourced in terms of time, skills and funding, and relied heavily on foreign donor support for their activities. A host of international organizations and agencies like The Asia Foundation, USAID, the NDI, the EU, the Dutch and Swedish development agencies NOVIB and Forum Syd, the Canada Fund, the Embassy of New Zealand, Oxfam America, and the UN Human Rights Office were actively involved in coordinating and supporting the voter education efforts of the observer coalitions.[48]

In spite of constraints, over a six month period between January and June 1998, election observer coalitions were able to recruit and train thousands of provincial and commune volunteer-educators and village level observers. According to COMFREL's figures, between May and July volunteers and village observers held 'a total of 12,434 village level workshops to explain the electoral process and inform voters of their rights'. 'These workshops were attended by approximately 870,000 individuals.'[49] COFFEL also trained people to become election observers and conduct voter education sessions, reaching out to 315, 806 people in 11 provinces.[50] Workshops covered all aspects of elections including intimidation, vote buying, thumbprinting, voter rights, secrecy of

---

48. COMFREL. Final Report, the 1998 National Assembly Elections in Cambodia. Phnom Penh. February, 1998, pp. 4–5.

49. Ibid., p.14.

50. Hughes, 'Strategies and Impact of Election Observer Coalitions in Cambodia', p. 22.

the ballot, election laws, voter registration, the campaign, polling and counting. Informational and other educational materials such as leaflets, posters, booklets on election fraud, voter guides, comic and picture books, video and audio tapes were produced by COMFREL and other national NGOs and international organizations like the Center for Social Development (CSD), the Cambodian Institute for Human Rights (CIHR), the Khmer Women's Voice Center (KWVC) and the EU. Tens of thousands of these materials were disseminated across the country. Throughout May and June voter education topics and issues were broadcast on national radio and state television broadcast programmes. COMFREL also used newspaper articles to get the information across to the electorate.[51]

Given the dangerous political conditions, the work of the election observer coalitions was impressive. Their close working relationship with international donors and participation in the preparations from the outset were a key factor in ensuring enough political space within which they could operate. Public statements and reports criticizing the formation and operation of the electoral bodies and the CC demonstrated their potential as a countervailing force in the political landscape. Countrywide networks of activists and volunteers were able to provide credible reports of election-related violence, intimidation and partiality of local authorities such as village and commune chiefs. In the absence of systematic studies, it is difficult to assess the overall impact the coalitions' voter education programmes had on the behaviour of the electorate.[52] That said, the high rates of voter registration and turnout at the polls, combined with the weakness of the NUF parties and the dominance of the CPP in the rural areas suggest that they were effective. Furthermore, in spite of the difficulties faced by F'pec and SRP in organizing their campaign in the months leading up to the actual polls, together they received almost one quarter of a million more votes than the CPP. In total, 60 per cent of the electorate voted for a party other than the CPP, reinforcing anecdotal evidence that suggests that the work of election observer coalitions must have had significant impact on the outcome.

---

51. COMFREL, Final Report, pp. 14–15.

52. For a detailed discussion of the impact of the election observer coalitions see Hughes, 'Strategies and Impact of Election Observer Coalitions in Cambodia', pp. 27–30.

Political Parties, Violence and Intimidation

Of the 44 political parties that registered with the Ministry of Interior before the official 26 March deadline, 39 competed in the elections; 19 more than in 1993. Factional infighting and engineered splits before the elections produced a number of new parties led by personalities who had previously held senior positions in the three main NUF groups. Senior former F'pec dissidents Ung Huot, Toan Chhay and Loy Sim Chheang formed their own parties. To protect themselves from any possible future legal disputes over ownership of party names and logos, the Son Sann faction of the BLDP and Sam Rainsy's KNP competed under the eponymous Son Sann Party and Sam Rainsy Party. Many of the smaller parties were politically inactive or had limited budgets. Only the main three parties, CPP, F'pec and SRP won any seats.

The 1996 struggle over power-sharing at the district level had prevented F'pec and other opposition parties like the SRP from strengthening rural networks of party activists and supporters. The destruction of NUF party structures after the coup left them vulnerable in areas controlled by local authorities and police and security forces loyal to the CPP. While most NUF leaders remained in exile in the months following the coup, local party members lived in fear for their lives and livelihoods. When they did eventually return to pick up the pieces and try to reorganize, they were offered a modicum of safety under the terms of the UN safe return monitoring plan. However, party members and workers were still subjected to political violence and intimidation. The UN Center for Human Rights working in collaboration with local human rights organizations and election observer groups like LICADHO, ADHOC and COMFREL received, investigated and reported numerous credible cases of election-related violence and/or intimidation against opposition party candidates, activists and supporters.[53]

In a final assessment of the elections, COMFREL reported that despite messages broadcast on TV by the CPP leadership calling for its

---

53. See for example 'The Human Rights situation in Cambodia': Note on apparent instances of politically motivated violence and intimidation, prepared by the Cambodian Office of the High Commissioner for Human Rights. May 20-June 15, 1998; Cambodia Office of the High Commissioner for Human Rights Fortnightly report, June 1-June 18, 1998. Also, 'Monitoring of Intimidation and Violence', Report 10–17 July 1998.

cessation, politically related violence claimed 40 lives from the beginning of 1998 up to polling day.[54] Incidents of election-related violence and intimidation of opposition party members and workers were widespread, with cases reported by human rights groups and other monitors and observers in every province. In addition to its six provincial offices, the UN Human Rights Office deployed six mobile monitoring teams during the election period covering all provinces except the remote north-eastern province of Ratanakiri. The UN Office defined different types of political violence and intimidation it encountered during its monitoring work, including: harassment; direct threats verbal or accompanied by the use of weapons related to loss of land, employment or status; discrimination of individuals based on their political affiliation; destruction or damage to homes or property; torture or physical abuse; killings and attempted killing; missing persons; disappearances of individuals; illegal arrest and detention.[55]

In most reported incidents, local authorities including village and commune chiefs, local militias, police and security forces were either directly involved or complicit in the political violence and intimidation. Involvement of local officials and authorities in election-related crimes further entrenched a climate of fear and impunity. For example, in Tbong Khmum district in Kompung Cham province, witnesses reported the arrest of a SRP member by six men including the village chief and the commune police and militia chiefs. Witnesses saw him handcuffed, blindfolded and led to nearby rubber plantations where he was later found dead in a shallow grave. The night before the murder the village chief invited people to his home where he declared that anyone joining a party other than the CPP would be killed. According to witnesses, 'the threat was repeated after the murder at a gift-giving ceremony when the chief reportedly warned that Sam Rainsy supporters would be killed one by one'. As COMFREL noted, in spite of the government and the CPP's reassurances and obligations to provide a safe and secure environment for the elections, they failed to undertake serious investigations of these killings.[56]

---

54. COMFREL, Final Report: 1998 Election in Cambodia, p. 16.

55. 'Monitoring of Intimidation and Violence', p. 6.

56. COMFREL, Final Report: 1998 Election in Cambodia, p. 15.

Another form of intimidation directed at political parties was attacks on party offices and the destruction of party signposts. Prior to registration at the end of March, political parties were denied the right to open offices and start political activities in preparation for the election campaign. After registration, parties could open party offices and commence work. Although the main NUF parties were able to open provincial offices in most areas, party workers attempting to do this at the district and commune levels faced considerable resistance from local authorities. The UN mobile monitoring teams reported numerous incidents of attacks on party offices and the destruction or removal of party sign boards by local authorities. Sign boards were either shot at or physically uprooted and removed. In other cases, party workers were intimidated by local authorities and security forces removed the boards.[57]

Political violence and intimidation continued throughout the campaign period, although not at the same level as before.[58] COMFREL cooperated with provincial and some commune election committees to bring together political party candidates, party agents and local authorities for roundtable discussions focused on reducing electoral violence and intimidation in 16 provinces. Despite these initiatives, COMFREL monitors continued to report violations of the campaign regulations, including: incidents of vote buying, obstruction of opposition parties' campaign activities, use of state resources by the CPP, and a general 'lack of neutrality among local authorities, police and military'.[59]

The Campaign

The campaign got underway on 25 June. Thousands of supporters from the main parties took to the streets of Phnom Penh with great exuberance and fanfare. For the most part, campaign activities such as party rallies, gatherings and meetings took place in a relatively peaceful atmosphere. In terms of what the political parties had to offer, voter choice and preferences were heavily influenced by the events of the preceding

---

57. Situation of human rights in Cambodia. Report of the Secretary-General. A/53/400. 17 September 1998, pp. 42–67.

58. Special Representative of the United Nations Secretary-General for Human Rights in Cambodia Monitoring of Intimidation and Violence. Report (10–17 July 1998).

59. COMFREL, Final Report: 1998 Election in Cambodia, p. 18.

twelve months. Since the breakdown of relations between the two prime ministers in March 1996, national politics and government functions had been hamstrung by instability and uncertainty. To be sure, between 1991 and 1995 Cambodia's macro-economic situation had stabilized, but this was mainly due to foreign intervention and aid. From a limited base – mainly garments and the service industry – the economy had grown on average 6.6 per cent in that period.[60] Bland statistics, however, could not disguise the formidable socio-economic challenges that the country continued to face in all sectors. Public finances were in disarray, exacerbated by deepening corruption and dependent on foreign support. Average per capita income was among the lowest in the region at $270. In 1996, public spending on health and education was 1 and 0.7 per cent respectively, compared to a staggering 50 per cent on defence. Mortality and illiteracy rates were among the highest in the region. Huge investments were needed in agriculture, rural development, transport and infrastructure. Illegal logging and exploitation of freshwater and land resources were becoming a serious problem, compromising the country's comparative advantages in natural resources.[61]

Political leaders of all stripes were under no illusions about the extent of the problems the country faced. Gaining support at the ballot box, however, depended upon voters' perceptions of and responses to the political and socio-economic realities within which they lived. The July 1997 military action coupled with Ranariddh's criminal conviction, followed by a repressive and intimidating recruitment campaign and continued violence directed at CPP opposition, left the majority of Cambodian voters in no doubt about Hun Sen's dominant political position and military power, not to mention CPP control over the attendant economic benefits in the context of international aid for reconstruction and development. As in 1993, fear of continued political instability and economic insecurity were uppermost in many voters' minds.

Voters were fearful of a repeat of the 1993 experience when the CPP refused to accept the results and threatened a return to armed conflict. Since then, Hun Sen and the CPP had worked hard to reconsolidate

---

60. Chan Sophal et al., 'Cambodia: Challenges and Options of Regional Economic Integration'. Conference Papers. Cambodia Development Resource Institute (CDRI), pp. 10–21. Phnom Penh. October 1998.

61. Ibid.

authoritarian control over state structures, especially in the districts, communes and villages by keeping the opposition weak and excluded. Voters were therefore largely sceptical that win or lose the CPP would relinquish or share power in a meaningful way with the opposition. And yet discontent with the prevailing political-economic system among rural and urban voters was growing. This was manifested in protests and strikes by garment factory workers in Phnom Penh in May and a SRP demonstration in June, as well as in commonplace complaints by voters over the misappropriation of natural resources by the military, which threatened livelihoods. [62]

Notions of political choice and representation of voter interests in the campaign rhetoric of the three main parties differed very little from each other. In terms of specific issues and policies, all three put forward particular visions for tackling socio-economic problems such as corruption and poverty, and promised to promote democracy and human rights and attract foreign investment. All professed commitment to institutional reform, especially in the armed forces, and raising civil servant salaries. Other issues such as national reconciliation, protecting territorial integrity, and tackling illegal immigration also featured in campaign platforms.[63]

From weakened positions, both F'pec and the SRP resorted to populist themes and issues related to anti-Vietnamese sentiment and focused on the events of July 1997 and the earlier March grenade attack on the SRP demonstration. As in the 1993 campaign, F'pec relied heavily on its royalist credentials while at the same time exploiting grievances concerning land issues and border disputes between Cambodia and Vietnam.[64] Sam Rainsy staged a particularly aggressive anti-Vietnamese campaign, claiming that thousands of illegal Vietnamese immigrants had been allowed to register to vote, but without providing much evidence.

---

62. See for examples: Saing Soenthrith, '200 Garment Workers Protest Low Wages Forced Overtime', *The Cambodia Daily*, 13 May 1998; Caroline Hughes, 'Political Parties in the Campaign', in John L. Vijghen (ed.) *People and the 1998 Elections in Cambodia: Their Voices, Roles and Impact on Democracy*. Experts for Community Research (ECR). Phnom Penh, January 2002, p. 19.

63. See Sorpong Peou, *Intervention and Change in Cambodia?*, pp. 316–17.

64. See for example Samreth Sopha and Elizabeth Moorthy, 'Funcinpec relies on royalty, anti-VN rhetoric', *Phnom Penh Post*, 17 July 1998.

The CPP were again portrayed by Ranariddh and Rainsy as 'communists and puppets of the *youn*'. Rainsy linked the problem of corruption in the trade of the country's natural resources to the CPP and Vietnam. Both leaders drew criticism from human rights groups and international organizations like the UN for the inflammatory nature and racist overtones of their anti-Vietnamese propaganda.[65]

The CPP by contrast deliberately avoided any confrontation over the issue. Party activists and candidates were confident that mass mobilization and education campaigns would be enough to secure a win for the CPP. Party campaign rhetoric recycled familiar themes of national liberation from the Khmer Rouge. Candidates emphasized the party's role in national reconciliation, reconstruction and development and as the provider of public works, health centres and schools. Hun Sen, as in 1993, did not formally campaign, explaining to reporters that his self-appointed role as guarantor of 'free and fair' elections meant he did not want to be both 'referee and player'.[66] His apparent reluctance to campaign could be explained by informal surveys conducted by the CPP in 1993 and 1998, revealing the party's apparent unpopularity in areas considered to be pro-CPP.[67] It was also the case that the CPP felt confident enough to expect, if not a two thirds majority, then a dominant position in what seemed to be the inevitable formation of another coalition government.

Polling, Counting, Results

The month long campaign ended in Phnom Penh as noisily and colourfully as it began. Polling and counting of votes took place on 26–27 July. Voter turnout was spectacularly high with over 5 million votes cast, representing 93.7 per cent of all registered voters. Almost all national and international observer groups concurred that the polling and counting processes took place without any serious widespread problems. COMFREL provided the largest coverage, having trained observers at 10,265 polling stations or 93.1 per cent of the total number. Based on

---

65. Post Staff. 'UN rights envoy appeals for end to VN bashing', *Phnom Penh Post*, 17 July 1998.

66. Mathew Grainger, 'UN blasts CPP's domination of state-run media', *Phnom Penh Post*, 3 July 1998.

67. Kate Frieson, 'The Politics of Getting out the Vote', p. 188.

observer reports, they concluded that the process was generally free from serious irregularities. Those that did occur were considered to be isolated, and would not have affected the overall outcome. Likewise, the counting of votes also took place without incident and in a reasonably acceptable manner. The biggest problem COMFREL reported was the early morning crowds of anxious and enthusiastic voters waiting outside the polling stations.

As relatively trouble free as the administration of polling and counting appeared to be, it belied the serious problems underlying the conduct of the process as a whole. Because of the manner in which the elections had been organized, it was expected that NUF parties would reject the elections results in the event of a CPP win. Indeed, no party won a two thirds majority to form a government alone, but the distribution of seats gave the CPP an absolute majority in the National Assembly. Under the proportional representation system used by the NEC to allocate the 122 seats in the National Assembly, the CPP won 64, F'pec 43, and the SRP 15. The CPP secured more votes than its two main rivals in all provinces except Kandal, Kampong Cham, and Kratie, where F'pec won the most. F'pec also won in Phnom Penh with 33.5 per cent, and SRP won in the municipality of Pailin with 48.8 per cent. Events in the post-election period beginning with national and international assessments of the polling and counting were, however, far from straightforward.

International Assessments and Electoral Authoritarianism

In 2002, the former 'EU Special Representative for the 1998 Elections in Cambodia' and UK Member for the European Parliament, Glenys Kinnock, in a previously unpublished report issued a damning indictment of the JIOG's role in assessing the elections process. The report called into question the 'efficacy and integrity' of the group and singled out foreign diplomats and politicians who in her view had a clear political agenda of their own, issuing statements that were clearly being used as a political tool'. According to the report, this agenda was driven by 'outside pressure' to allow Cambodia 'to join ASEAN, gain a UN seat and join in a partnership with the EU' at the expense of a credible elections process.[68]

---

68. European Union Special Representative's report on Elections in Cambodia, 26 July 1998. See also Mathew Grainger, 'Lessons from the 1998 national election', *Phnom Penh Post*, 1 February 2002.

Mrs Kinnock added that the position of the EU chief long-term observer and chair of the JIOG, Sven Linder, was undermined and became politicized when his role should have been purely a technical one.[69]

Harsh criticisms of the EU's role in the elections noted in the unpublished report contrasted sharply with Kinnock's more sanguine statement given at a press conference in Phnom Penh on 29 July 1998. At the conference, she described the elections as 'unprecedented in Cambodia's history' and the responses of the electors as 'vindicating the EU's difficult decision to opt into the elections process in the first place'.[70] The statement came two days after Linder issued a highly controversial press release immediately after the official polling and counting period had come to an end but before a fully informed and complete assessment could be made. Carefully worded, the statement concluded that 'what could' be observed by JIOG observers on the polling and counting days 'was a process which was free and fair to an extent that enables it to reflect in a credible way the will of the Cambodian people'. It added that in the end, 'efforts to intimidate sections of the Cambodian population appear not to have significantly influenced the conduct or climate of polling day itself'. Linder explained that the statement was based upon reports of the almost 500 international observers. He also added that he and the JIOG 'believed that all parties should accept and honor the results of the election without any attempt to undermine the original outcome.'[71]

The timing and content of the press release astonished both national and international observers, including some members of the JIOG not involved in the drafting process. JIOG had previously agreed to form a 'Reference Group' of six members from ASEAN, Australia, Canada and the EU, including member countries Japan and the US, to act as a committee for drafting statements.[72] In spite of reservations related to

69. Ibid.

70. Statement by European Union Special Representative, Glenys Kinnock MEP. 29 July 1998. Phnom Penh. See also Jeff Smith, 'EU Say Wait on Final Verdict for Credible Poll', *The Cambodia Daily*, 30 July 1998.

71. United Nations Electoral Assistance Secretariat (UNEAS). Joint International Observer Group (JIOG) Press Release. Phnom Penh. 27 July 1998.

72. United Nations Electoral Assistance Secretariat (UNEAS).'First meeting of the Join International Observer Group (JIOG). 1 June, 1998. Phnom Penh.

'logistics' expressed by Linder, it was decided in June after the 'Friends of Cambodia' meeting that a statement should be released as early as twenty-four hours after the end of the counting day. There was concern that a JIOG statement might be 'drowned out' by earlier statements from independent observer groups such as the US-based NDI and the International Republican Institute (IRI), who had publicly expressed the view that the elections were 'fundamentally flawed'.[73] The JIOG release did include the caveat that its final conclusions 'were subject to the 'appropriate conduct in the post-election period', vote tabulation and the complaints and appeals process.[74] Critics argued that statements made before the actual counting process was completed, and before JIOG observers had been debriefed, were premature and 'illogical'.[75] Matters were made worse for the JIOG when it became apparent that the NEC itself had on the same day announced that it intended to delay the preliminary results. In spite of growing criticism, the JIOG released a further statement two days later saying that it stood by its previous findings.

JIOG, Politics and Human Rights

As the official voice of the international community involved in the elections on the ground in Cambodia, the JIOG's judgment carried a great deal of political weight. For this reason, its role from the beginning was a source of tension between the RGC and the UN agencies. Hun Sen and Ung Huot's failed attempt to negotiate deletions of key paragraphs and lines in the April memorandum of understanding between the UN and the RGC regarding the UN's role in coordinating international electoral observers set the tone for subsequent assessments and public statements. UN coordination of the JIOG was intended to 'encourage a comprehensive, objective assessment of the electoral process by the international community from the pre-election period' to the confirmation of the official results and their acceptance by all participating political parties. The JIOG was 'normally' expected to issue statements and

---

73. UNOSGPRC report 0823: 'Friends of Cambodia – June 20'. CPY 240. 22 June 1998.

74. JIOG Press Release, 27 July 1998.

75. Mathew Grainger, 'Critics say JIOG statement jumps the gun', *Phnom Penh Post*, 31 July 1998.

reports of their findings in the pre- and immediate post-election period. There was an expectation that it would undertake private démarches to the NEC and the government to address concerns related to the terms and conditions laid out in the memorandum.[76]

The JIOG's relationship with UN agencies and the interpretation of its political role in the context of the memorandum proved to be problematic. Such problems were illustrated by the reaction to a UN EAS situation report presented at a JIOG meeting at the end of June. As part of its terms of reference the EAS was responsible for compiling and analysing JIOG information collected by the foreign Long Term Observers (LTO) and UN agencies including the UN Center for Human Rights.[77] The content of the report was severely criticized by some indignant foreign ambassadors at the meeting for being 'too political and based too much on human rights'.[78] They incorrectly felt it was not in the EAS mandate to provide political analysis nor to make démarches to the NEC or other relevant government authorities. The report was suppressed and the meeting agreed that the content of future reports be technical in nature only.

The episode exposed the politicization of the JIOG and the agendas of some of its diplomatic members referred to in the later damning Kinnock report. The original UN Secretary General's April memorandum was clear enough. The JIOG 'will undertake private démarches' with the NEC and the government with the findings of its reports. It was also clear in stating that the UN 'reserved the right to withdraw or suspend its activities if there was a fundamental deterioration in the political situation that would undermine the holding of credible and legitimate elections'. Misunderstandings or wilful ignorance of mandates created serious political divisions and discontent within the international groups involved. Staff at the UN Center for Human Rights for example were angry and frustrated that the contents of their reports

---

76. 'Memorandum of Understanding between the United Nations and the Royal Government of Cambodia on the International Observers'. Copy in author's possession.

77. Issuance of a Directive regarding the UN role in coordinating International Observation of the Elections in Cambodia.

78. UNEAS. Weekly Report 23–29 June. 30 June 1998. Phnom Penh. See also Mathew Grainger, 'International observers' report 'too political', *Phnom Penh Post*, 17 July 1998.

were sidelined in favour of bland press statements that acknowledged ongoing concerns but offered little in terms of concrete steps to bring the RGC to account.[79]

By mid-July it was clear that diplomatic efforts through the FOC and the Troika, and the various UN Envoys and ambassadorial groups on the ground in Cambodia, had largely failed to push the RGC to create a climate conducive to holding free, fair and credible elections. In his briefing to the UN Security Council two weeks before polling, the Asia Pacific Director of the UNDPA acknowledged both the Secretary General's and the FOC's concerns, including the CPP monopoly of the media before the campaign, lack of coverage of opposition activities, widespread voter intimidation during the registration period, political imbalances in the Constitutional Council, the 'overwhelming presence of CPP officials in the election authorities', and the 'continuing climate of impunity derived from the lack of serious investigation into apparently politically motivated killings and disappearances'.[80]

At the same time, he expressed the view held by other diplomatic groupings that positive developments including the technically successful voter registration process, the willingness of all parties to participate in the elections and a comparatively peaceful campaign 'gives grounds to hope' that the elections can provide 'a free expression of the will of the Cambodian people'.[81] Ten days after the Security Council briefing and two days before the polling, the JIOG issued a similar public statement denouncing the negative political climate in which the elections were going to be held, but felt justified in anticipating 'that reasonable conditions exist for the elections that can be broadly representative of

---

79. Personal communications between UN Center for Human Rights and the UN Special Representative for Human Rights in Cambodia. July 1998.

80. UN outgoing cable to Mehrotra, SGPRC, Phnom Penh from Prendergast, United Nations New York. 'Briefing to the Security Council'. 1447. CYP 102. 14 July 1998.

81. Ibid. Politically motivated killings continued to be investigated by the UN Center for Human Rights during the campaign period. On July 17 several electoral workers were injured and two government soldiers killed in Anlong Veng in what was believed to have been an attack by Khmer Rouge guerrillas linked to Ta Mok. On July 27 the Khmer Rouge staged an assault on a RCAF outpost in Anlong Veng, killing two soldiers and eight villagers. Both incidents were considered isolated and did not unduly affect the elections process.

the will of the Cambodian people'.[82] In sum, irrespective of a political climate underpinned by fear and election-related human rights abuses, if the polling and counting days were free from violence, intimidation and obvious fraud, international diplomats and then donors were happy to stamp their approval on the process.

Other assessments from independent international and national observer groups were mixed. As well as the JIOG and the EU observer unit, the Volunteers of the Cambodian Elections (VOCE) led by the controversial former Australian Ambassador to Cambodia Tony Kevin, the NDI, the IRI, and a regional group, the Asian Network for Free Elections (ANFREL) deployed small groups of observers. With the exceptions of the JIOG and VOCE – both of whom hyperbolically described the elections without the necessary detailed clarification as 'free and fair' – all other groups expressed varying degrees of caution, preferring to wait until after the complaints and grievances process had been carried out to everyone's satisfaction before making definitive judgments. The three main national observer groups, COMFREL, COFFEL and NICFEC, who did the bulk of the observing country-wide, also refrained from making any sweeping statements until the post-election process was complete.[83]

Positive assessments of polling and counting days were tempered by pre-election problems and the uncertainty of the final outcome. Unfortunately for the NDI and IRI, who had been highly critical of the pre-polling phases, the co-leader of its observer group, former US congressman Stephen Solarz, speculated that if the complaints procedure and the formation of a new government proceeded smoothly, the elections could be considered a 'miracle on the Mekong'. His off-the-cuff remark was seized upon by the CPP and the international press as being a resounding endorsement of the elections as a whole.[84]

Post-Election Turmoil

Opposition parties immediately rejected the outcome. Ranariddh and Sam Rainsy held a press conference where they refused to accept the

---

82. Ibid.

83. For copies of all observer group press statements see National Democratic Institute for International Affairs (NDI). 'The July 26, 1998 Cambodian National Assembly Elections'. Appendices.

84. Ibid., p. 40.

results until recounts and re-polling had taken place in areas where they claimed serious irregularities had taken place. They threatened to boycott the National Assembly to prevent the formation of a new government if the irregularities were not thoroughly investigated. Complaints about irregularities included: a lack of access by party agents to the commune level counts, suggesting numbers had been changed or incorrectly recorded, ballots unfairly declared as spoiled, covering up of missing ballots, improperly sealed ballot bags, and intimidation of voters and instances of passing pre-marked ballots, known as 'telegraphing'.[85] As far as the international community assessments were concerned, on August 4 Sam Rainsy issued a press statement criticizing the JIOG assessment, calculating that its observers covered 'barely one per cent of the polling, which hardly qualified 'the JIOG or its chair to make sweeping statements about the fairness of the polls let alone to say that the outcome of the elections reflects in a credible way the will of the Cambodian people'.[86]

NEC and CC mishandling of the complaints procedure led to a lengthy political impasse involving demonstrations and violence before a new coalition government was finally formed at the end of November. Most observer groups concurred that although there were many irregularities, they were not numerous enough to significantly alter the overall results. Nevertheless, under pressure from the CPP to conclude the process as quickly as possible, the NEC's behaviour only served to reinforce accusations of political bias and fraud. In frustration over administrative and management difficulties the vice-chairman of the NEC resigned as chair of the sub-committee set up to handle complaints and recounts.[87] Recounts were conducted in a handful of communes in four provinces with no major discrepancies found. After only a week since the formation of the sub-committee on August 11, the NEC formally rejected all of the 800 and more complaints submitted by F'pec and the SRP without an explanation.

---

85. Ibid.

86. Sam Rainsy Party Statement. 'Linders one Percent Solution'. 4 August 1998.

87. Cited in NDI, 'The July 26, 1998 Cambodian National Assembly Elections', p. 43. See also Kassie Neou with Jeffrey C. Gallup, 'Conducting Cambodia's Elections', *Journal of Democracy*, Vol. 10, No 2, April 1999. p. 161.

Mistrust and lack of belief in the NEC's capacity to act impartially was entrenched further when it became apparent that the formula chosen for allocation of parliamentary seats by the NEC was not the same as the one used by observers and the political parties. Observer groups and NUF leaders, among others, were astonished when it was announced that the formula indicated in the NEC regulations distributed to political parties and NGOs on May 6 and again on May 25 had changed. Using another formula meant the CPP received 64 seats instead of the 59 it would have won using the original calculations, giving it a majority in the legislature. The NEC later claimed a version of the regulations dated May 29 distributed to party agents at the beginning of June contained the different formula, and blamed them and the observers for not noticing the change. NEC claims that a decision had been made at a meeting on May 29 were rejected by national observers and the political parties. The controversy escalated when a Canadian government-funded NEC adviser admitted at a press conference on August 8 that he had made errors in omitting certain steps in the calculation process that he later introduced in the formula used by the NEC. Matters were made worse when it was later revealed that the adviser, in a letter to the Canadian government explaining his position, had stated that the NUF parties 'should now accept the results of the election gracefully and should stop identifying scapegoats to cover up their division and weaknesses'.[88]

The NEC's response to the formula controversy followed by the Constitutional Council's decision on August 14 to refuse all but 16 complaints submitted to it by F'pec and the SRP exacerbated a looming crisis. On August 20, at a vigil staged by the SRP to protect ballot bags, a Kyodo news agency driver was killed when bullets were fired and a hand grenade thrown outside the entrance to the Ministry of Interior in what was believed to be an attempt to assassinate Sam Rainsy.[89] The attack came two days before a planned protest march calling for an investigation into the election complaints. In spite of efforts by the Phnom Penh authorities to prevent the march, rallies continued and quickly transformed into a full time 'sit-in' on a site opposite the National Assembly

---

88. NDI, 'The July 26, 1998 Cambodian National Assembly Elections', p. 46.

89. Stew Magnuson and Pin Sisavann, 'Rainsy, Interior Trade Accusations', *The Cambodia Daily*, 22 August 1998.

building symbolically dubbed "Democracy Square".[90] Thousands of protesters gathered at the site to hear speeches by Ranariddh and Sam Rainsy, calling for a proper investigation into the complaints and denouncing Hun Sen as a puppet or lackey of the Vietnamese. More or less at the same time, the Constitutional Council announced there were no 'reasonable grounds' for further investigations into the complaints, summarily dismissing them all.[91] The terse dismissal of the grievances without due process by NEC and CC fuelled further protests.

Vitriolic and racist overtones of speeches given at Democracy Square did little to help Ranariddh and Sam Rainsy's plight. Strong anti-Vietnamese and anti-Hun Sen feelings were expressed at the end of a march in August attended by an estimated 15,000 protesters. A small group of protesters chanting anti-Vietnamese slogans damaged and attempted to set fire to the Cambodian–Vietnamese friendship monument erected to memorialize the CPP leadership's role in the overthrow of the Khmer Rouge by the Vietnamese in 1979. In the tense atmosphere of anti-Vietnamese sentiment, rumours circulated that people had died drinking wine poisoned by Vietnamese food sellers. In retaliation several ethnic Vietnamese were killed and others seriously injured.

As tensions grew, the prospect of further unrest turning violent intensified the need for a negotiated solution to the impasse. As analysts and commentators expected, everyone looked to King Sihanouk for a solution. A series of negotiations mediated by Sihanouk and representatives from the main political parties including the electoral authorities began on September 5 in an effort to meet the deadline for the swearing in of the new National Assembly on the 24th. The talks started after the NEC declared the results of the elections official on 1 September. Just before negotiations began, Hun Sen and the CPP leadership visited the King – who was experiencing health problems – in Siem Reap to discuss a swift resolution to the impending impasse in the form of a three-way coalition government. When it became clear that Ranariddh and Rainsy were united in rejecting this idea, Hun Sen instead sought a constitutional amendment to allow a government to be formed with a simple rather than a two thirds majority. As well as demanding a full and

90. Lor Chandara and Stew Magnuson, 'Protesters Dig In at "Democracy Square"', *The Cambodia Daily*, 27 August 1998.

91. See NDI, 'The July 26, 1998 Cambodian National Assembly Elections', p. 46.

impartial investigation of election irregularities and a resolution of the seat allocation issue, Ranariddh and Rainsy in turn sought to exclude Hun Sen from any coalition deal.

By September 7 negotiations were no closer to ending the impasse than when they had started. Meanwhile at mid-morning that day, three hand grenades were thrown into the courtyard of Hun Sen's residence in Phnom Penh. No one was injured. However, eye witnesses reported that the perpetrators, in trying to make good their escape, had crashed the motorcycle they used in the attack. In attempting to continue their escape on foot, the alleged grenade thrower was seized by unidentified individuals and beaten to death. It was later reported he had documents in his possession showing he was a police intelligence agent. According to a UN Secretary General report, the results of any investigation were not known and the killers of the alleged grenade thrower were not charged.[92]

Hun Sen and his close ally, Director General of National Police Hok Lundy, accused Rainsy of inciting the perpetrators in what was seen by them as an attempt on his life. Fearing arrest, Rainsy sought refuge at the UN Secretary General's Special Representative Lakhan Mehrotra's office, situated in the Cambodiana Hotel. A man was killed and several others injured when police fired shots into the air and at the feet of a group of about 1,000 protesters who had gathered outside the hotel to support Rainsy. In the early hours of September 8, riot police moved into Democracy Square and forcibly broke up the protesters' encampment. Later that day, the government imposed a travel ban prohibiting all outgoing and incoming non-CPP members of the National Assembly from leaving the country on the pretext the perpetrators of the grenade attack might slip through the net.

The crackdown did not deter protests. In the following days, marches continued, and groups of protesters including monks and students gathered outside the US Embassy, where they were met with more heavy handed police and security service tactics and gunfire. Violence escalated when truckloads of CPP supporters arrived from outside the city to stage counter-demonstrations. Running street battles were

---

92. Situation of Human Rights in Cambodia. 'Report of the Special Representative of the Secretary-General for Human Rights in Cambodia, Mr Thomas Hammarberg'. E/CN.4/1999/101. 26 February 1999. Para 24.

fought in some parts of the city between rival gangs of protesters and CPP supporters. Violence, according to the UN Human Rights Office, was instigated by members of the security services acting as *agents provocateurs* dressed in civilian clothes and brandishing handguns. As the violent atmosphere intensified, human rights organizations received numerous reports of intimidation and beatings by armed police and soldiers using batons and cattle prods; reports came especially from monks, who it seemed were singled out by the authorities. Many protestors were arrested and detained by gendarmes and 'flying tiger' police units. After a week of unrest and detentions, dead bodies, including those of monks, were found floating in rivers and in shallow graves around the city. The UN Human Rights Office confirmed the violent deaths of twenty-four individuals, including women and monks, but was unable to establish any links between the deaths and the protests.[93]

End Game: the Formation of a New Government

By the middle of September, as the numbers of dead bodies increased, there were signs that the political parties were ready to attempt further negotiations to break the deadlock. It would, however, be almost another three months before a final agreement on a new coalition government was reached. In the meantime, the political theatre continued. In return for a partial lifting of the travel ban, street protests stopped. Ranariddh and other NUF leaders agreed to attend the swearing-in ceremony for the newly elected members of the National Assembly in Siem Reap as scheduled on 24 September, thereby protecting parliamentary immunity and the threat of possible arrests made by Hun Sen. Nonetheless, they publicly remained committed to demands for impartial investigations into electoral problems and the removal of Hun Sen as the CPP's prime ministerial candidate. Hun Sen responded by reiterating the threat of military action if any moves were made to prevent him from becoming sole prime minister. Any further signs that a compromise could be reached were dashed when an improvised explosive comprised of B40 rockets was detonated as politicians made their way to the swearing-in ceremony. According to sources at the time, one rocket narrowly missed Hun Sen's motorcade,

---

93. Ibid.

instead hitting a house and killing one of its occupants.[94] The identities of the perpetrators have never been established, but Hun Sen nevertheless concluded the incident was another attempt on his life. Immediately after the swearing-in ceremony, both Ranariddh and Sam Rainsy, fearing for their safety, left Siem Reap for the Thai capital Bangkok.

While overseas, the NUF leaders attempted to internationalize their cause further. Draft non-binding resolutions passed in the US House of Representatives calling for Hun Sen to personally account for alleged humanitarian crimes and human rights abuses did little to divert the attention of Cambodia's donors, including the US administration, away from a speedy resolution. Cambodia's seat at the UN, their long awaited entry into ASEAN and the resumption of international aid and investment were all contingent upon ending the deadlock and forming a new coalition government as soon as possible. By mid-October it seemed clear that the NUF leaders could bring no international pressure to bear in support of their earlier demands for an independent investigation of election irregularities, including the seat formula and the removal of Hun Sen. Instead, as concerns about the worsening socio-economic conditions mounted, they found themselves under increasing international and national pressure to join a coalition with Hun Sen as the sole prime minister.

In what was reported at the time as a surprise move, Ranariddh returned to Cambodia without Sam Rainsy two days before Sihanouk was due to leave for medical treatment in China on November 14. This apparently allayed earlier fears that Sihanouk's departure before the deadlock could be broken would leave Cambodia without a head of state. Thus, after months of delays and faltering attempts, a compromise between F'pec and the CPP, without any real input from the SRP, was finally reached, and Sihanouk departed for Beijing as scheduled. For F'pec and Ranariddh, on the surface at least, the final terms and conditions of the compromise were the best deal they could have hoped for. As for the SRP, they were resigned to playing the role of the only opposition in a CPP-dominated government strengthened by its successful marginalization of the NUF before, during and after the elections.

Ranariddh succeeded in getting the position he wanted as president of the National Assembly but only by agreeing to the formation of a

---

94. Kimsan Chantara and Jeff Smith, 'B-40 Rocks Siem Reap Motorcade', *The Cambodia Daily*, 25 September 1998.

controversial new upper house or Senate. In doing so, he forfeited the right to act in that position as head of state in the King's absence, which was passed to the new chairman of the yet to be created Senate, the former assembly president Chea Sim. The powerful ministries of Interior and Defence were still shared by the two parties while other ministerial portfolios were headed by individual party members. Other significant ministries for F'pec included the ministries of Justice and Information. Out of the nine parliamentary committees responsible for various areas of legislation, eight were divided between the two parties and one, the Committee of Public Works and Transport was allocated to the SRP. The deal also included amnesties for F'pec generals Nhek Bun Chhay and Serey Kosal, who had continued military operations on the Thai–Cambodia border after escaping from Phnom Penh in the aftermath of the 1997 coup. Prince Sirivudh, accused of plotting to kill Hun Sen in 1995, was also given an amnesty.

***

With significant international, financial and technical assistance, the 1998 elections delivered for Hun Sen and Cambodia's principle donors what they wanted: a relatively stable coalition government presided over by a single prime minister. Procedurally the elections ultimately served their purpose in producing a new government. In terms of control they functioned as instruments for the reconsolidation of Hun Sen and the CPP's authoritarian control. In the twelve-month period between the coup in July 1997 and the actual polls, Hun Sen had been able to manipulate international and domestic politics and avert what was likely another electoral defeat.

Hun Sen's animosity towards the UN Center for Human Rights was instrumental in setting the tone for international donor engagement with the RGC and the elections. The work conducted by the Center exposed the CPP top leadership's total disregard for publicly stated commitments to serious investigations into human rights abuses and murders in the months after the July fighting leading up to the elections. The Center was thus perceived as part of the opposition to Hun Sen's plans to reconsolidate power through the elections process. Because of past experiences in Cambodia, there was no political will at UN HQ in New York or among the high-level diplomatic group in Phnom Penh to push Hun Sen too far. To do so would destabilize the situation further and threaten the election preparations.

This had three practical effects. First, it sent a clear message to the government that a lack of action on the investigations would be tolerated by the 'Troika' and 'Friends of Cambodia' groups provided democratic procedures for the elections were put in place, even if in practice they were not adhered to. Second, it circumscribed the work of the UN Human Rights Office, placing it at odds with other UN agencies and the JIOG coordinated by the UN. Third, it circumscribed the work of the JIOG and its pre- and post-election assessments that carefully downplayed human rights abuses and the undemocratic manner in which democratic procedures were enacted. The reluctance of UN and foreign diplomats to follow through on the five conditions laid out in the memorandum of understanding and principles for international involvement in the elections demonstrates the point concretely.

Under these conditions, Hun Sen and the CPP could maximize the renewed advantages of incumbency after the coup and manipulate further the domestic political situation and the elections process. Realistically, all sides were fully aware that credible elections could not take place without the NUF leaders. The NUF leadership would eventually return to compete only weeks before the polls and after having been subjected to pseudo-legal manoeuvres and veiled threats to their safety, preventing them from re-building party structures and competing on a level playing field. Key electoral legislation was passed in their absence. The newly created election administrative and bureaucratic structures, the NEC and its provincial and commune counterparts, were ultimately in thrall to the CPP as was the Constitutional Council. Access to broadcast media throughout the elections process was tightly controlled and dominated by the CPP.

Leaving nothing to chance, the CPP membership drive and thumbprint campaign along with the collection of voter registration cards intensified the atmosphere of fear and insecurity already present after the ruthless display of Hun Sen's intent to destroy any opposition after the 1997 coup among large numbers of the electorate. Intimidation and violence directed mainly at NUF party activists, but also at individual voters who disavowed CPP entreaties, was carried out by officials and security personnel connected to local CPP networks. NUF attempts to influence international responses to these problems through boycotts did little to help their cause among donors eager to see a new, stable government formed as quickly as possible. Likewise, the stoking of ethnic tensions through anti-Vietnamese rhetoric only served to damage the NUF's reputation and alienate others in the international community who may have had some sympathy for their plight. All of these issues no doubt helped shape the early controversial JIOG assessments which largely ignored the problems and focused instead on a comparatively trouble free polling and counting phase.

Given the relatively huge amount of time, energy and resources invested by international donors to push the elections forward since 1996, it was unlikely that they would support the NUF demands in the post-election period. Provided the situation remained politically stable enough, the pressure would always be on the NUF to accept the results and join the CPP in a coalition government, allowing aid and investment to flow back into the country. In the end, international donor support for the 1998 election enabled authoritarian elements to prevail, thus undermining in practice the democratic principles embodied in multi-party competitive elections; a situation that some scholars describe as electoral authoritarianism. Indeed, Hun Sen and the CPP were able to apply authoritarian controls to avert an all-out defeat and reduce uncertainty.

The actual polling results however clearly demonstrate that despite the authoritarian constraints, the elections were not meaningless. Voting patterns and the role played by election monitoring organizations suggest that under certain conditions authoritarian elements can be challenged through electoral politics. Authoritarians within the state accept the necessity of holding multi-party elections for both domestic and international purposes. But there are limits to how far they can go in manipulating the outcomes. Opportunities therefore exist for opposing political and civil society forces to exploit those limitations even if the competition is rigged against them. Almost immediately after the formation of the new coalition government the CPP began preparations for the postponed commune elections. The new government would look to the international community for technical and financial support, and elections would once again become a key site of contestation as civil society groups and political opposition continued the struggle to reform the electoral system.

CHAPTER 6

Commune Elections Revisited

onditions for the preparation of the postponed commune elections were fundamentally different from previous elections planning. The destabilizing effects of the 1998 elections process from late 1995 onwards had, despite the problems, ushered in a period of relative political stability. The new government with a single prime minister could now fully engage with international partners in tackling Cambodia's dire socio-economic problems. Central to that partnership was a number of long-standing reform initiatives in the areas of public administration and finance, demobilization of the armed forces, and forestry and environmental reforms, among others. Whether or not the necessary reforms that were needed to address the economic problems would be enacted and implemented remained to be seen.

A key element of public administration reform was the decentralization and deconcentration of political and financial powers to commune authorities via elections. The goal was to hold commune elections to create councils responsible for the institutionalization of local, autonomous political and financial structures. Elections were thus regarded by technical experts as a crucial step in the expansion of existing multi-donor-funded rural development programmes. Decentralization and deconcentration via elections were part of popular ideas at the time that attempted to theoretically link local processes of democratization and poverty alleviation. For these ideas to be meaningful in practice, much would depend upon the performance of the prevailing institutional arrangements at the centre in Phnom Penh. Politically, this presented serious challenges and potential problems for the CPP.

Inflows of economic resources were accompanied by political ideas associated with multi-party democratic elections, adding an important political dimension to transformed patron–client relationships in rural areas. In this context, the relationship was inverted as the patron became dependent on the client for political loyalty on polling day. Because of

163

transformed economic relationships and the offer of political choice through elections, political loyalty was not automatically guaranteed. To reduce uncertainty and ensure loyalty the CPP resorted to the kinds of overt and covert strategies of fear, intimidation and violence used during the 1993 and 1998 elections. At the same time, CPP networks were dependent to various degrees on donor aid flows and development assistance linked to decentralization reforms. Thus, widespread abuses of power, and political violence and intimidation, took place in the presence and under the scrutiny of international observers and commentators. This had the practical effect of curbing the extent of the abuses and helped to create enough space for political participation and activism to take place, but only to the point where it did not threaten to destabilize the dominant networks of power, aid delivery and development.

The introduction of the decentralization concept via commune elections brought to the surface many of the issues that the architects of the 1998 elections had attempted to suppress. Official government rhetoric concerning greater participation in decision making processes and the improved performance of national institutions were to be tested during the course of the preparations for the commune elections. Theorists and practitioners alike recognized the importance of clearly defined, transparent and accountable legislative and political frameworks necessary for effective commune reform. They were also acutely aware of the important roles NGOs and other civil groups would play if the reforms were to be successful. Once again, the legislative and political infrastructures for the elections had to be built from scratch, with significant international technical and financial support. This provided fresh opportunities for civil groups, in particular the election monitoring organizations, to engage the state in a debate over the content of the new legislation and to push their own advocacy and reform agendas related to voter education and the existing electoral bodies created for the 1998 elections.

The elections would replace CPP-appointed commune chiefs with elected councillors in all of Cambodia's 1,621 communes. A re-structuring of rural power structures had profound implications for future national elections, given the importance of the rural vote. At the same time, commune elections provided an opportunity for the new RGC and international multi-lateral agencies like the UNDP to fulfil commitments made in 1996 to hold elections as part of the next phase in Cambodia's development. From the perspective of political development outside of state structures, the elections also provided opportunities for NGOs, in particular the election monitoring organizations, to build upon experiences from previous elections in acting as independent intermediaries between political parties, the state and wider society.

For the main political parties, especially the SRP, commune elections presented new opportunities to penetrate further into rural areas after their electoral successes in 1998. However, because of the inherent threats and opportunities, legislative, institutional and political problems persisted. Although the new events of 1997 and 1998 had reduced the possibility for further widespread instability and unrest, the elections were still a potential source of conflict. Persistent problems resulted in yet another protracted struggle between the new government, political parties and NGOs mediated by international donors over the form and conduct of the elections process.

Decentralization and Elections

Since 1998 the international community, including the EU and the UN, had encouraged the new government 'to pursue a policy of decentralization and deconcentration as the most effective means to extend democracy and improve delivery of services and infrastructure in Cambodia'.[1] Commune elections were central to this process. Pinning down exactly what was meant by these terms and how they could be applied to the Cambodian context was, as development practitioners pointed out at the time, 'a task fraught with conceptual and practical difficulties'.[2] In simple terms, decentralization is used to refer to a programme of 'political decentralization where additional levels of democratically elected 'government' are formed; whereas deconcentration refers to a process of delegating responsibilities to new levels of local government.[3] In practical terms, both elements of reform are concerned with accountability and the empowerment of citizens to participate in local decision making

1. United Nations Development Programme (UNDP), 'Report on the Elections of the Commune Councils'. Phnom Penh, March 2002, p. 10.
2. D. Ayres, 'Decentralisation: A Review of Literature'. Phnom Penh, August 2001, p. v.
3. Ibid.

processes and the setting of local agendas. Government officials like the Secretary of State for the Ministry of Interior, Prum Sokha, stated that people 'must take a greater part in decision[s] affecting their lives', and that government itself 'must be more responsive to its citizens'.[4]

Government rhetoric concerning citizen participation in decision making and government responsiveness masked realities on the ground in rural Cambodia. The concept of decentralization was not necessarily new. In 1996 the multi-donor funded Seila (foundation stone) project was established by the RGC policy experiment in poverty alleviation linked to decentralized governance. Focused on Commune Development Committees (CDC), the project was intended to provide citizens with opportunities for local input into plans for the investment of annual development funds to address the needs of the commune. Independent evaluations of the project suggested that assumptions about decentralization, bringing government closer to the people and allowing for greater participation, do not always hold true. In many cases villagers did not know that the CDC or development funds existed.[5] Further, studies by development practitioners suggested that it cannot be assumed that the closer the government is to the people the more they are able to participate in decision making processes or the more likely it is that they will see an improvement in their livelihoods. In addition, in situations where governments are committed to decentralization 'there is no evidence to show that [it] automatically results in increased democratisation or reduced poverty'. Indeed, governments may want

---

4. Sokha, P. (2000) cited in Ayres, D. (2001), p. 2.

5. R. Biddulph, *Decentralisation and Commune Council Reforms: Immediate Opportunities for Cambodian NGOs*. Phnom Penh: Oxfam GB in Cambodia. December 2000, p. 11. With the influx of development aid during the UNTAC period and small international NGOs, the concept and practice of Village Development Committees (VDCs) was introduced to organize aid activities. The idea was taken up by the UN's CARERE Resettlement and Regeneration project for infrastructural development projects. This was followed by the Seila project that seeks to build the capacity of provincial, district and commune authorities for local governance and development. See J. Ledgerwood and J. L. Vijghen, 'Decision-Making in Rural Khmer Villages', in J. Ledgerwood (ed.) (2002) *Cambodia Emerges from the Past: Eight Essays*. Southeast Asian Publications, Center for Southeast Asian Studies, Northern Illinois University.

to decentralize for other 'unstated reasons' than democratization or poverty reduction.[6]

In October 1998, the MoI approached the UNDP for specialist assistance in drafting the necessary basic legislation for the reforms. International consultants working as part of a drafting commission to govern the new commune authorities did not receive a 'fully authoritative statement of policy' explaining the government's thinking concerning decentralization.[7] It was difficult therefore to discern exactly where the motivation for the government's broader decentralization policy came from, casting some doubts about the government's overall commitment to the process.[8] By contrast, the MoI position on elections for the communes was more definitive and clear. Ideas for commune elections at the MoI dated back to late 1995, when co-Minister of Interior Sar Kheng took the initiative with the support of the German Konrad Adenauer Foundation.

Because of the scale and complexity of the elections, the RGC again turned to the international community and donors for technical and financial support. At the end of 1998, with the support of the UN system, the government began formulating the basic legislation and political framework that would underpin the decentralization process and determine how much it would cost. It was initially expected that elections would be held at the end of 1999. Due to a lengthy delay in the drafting process, the two basic laws, the Commune Election Law and the Law on the Administration of the Communes, were not passed by the National Assembly until January 2001.[9] Under the implementing regulations of the election law, the elections would replace existing commune chiefs with councils made up of between 5–11 representatives, depending on demographic and geographic circumstances. Councillors were to be elected using a proportional system, and would be drawn from political party candidate lists. The first choice candidate from the

---

6. Biddulph, *Decentralisation and Commune Council Reforms: Immediate Opportunities for Cambodian NGOs*, p. 4.

7. See, for example, P. Roome, Project CMB/97/C01: Assistance to the Ministry of Interior on Basic Legislation for Decentralised Commune Councils with the support of United Nations Capital Development Fund. December 1998.

8. Ayres, *Decentralisation*, p. 51.

9. Mhari Saito, 'Commune Election Law Sent Back for Changes, *The Cambodia Daily*, 24 November 1998.

list that received the most votes would be appointed head of the council. Two deputies, coming second and third on the list respectively, would also be appointed.

As envisaged in the legislation, the roles and objectives of the councils were to be extensive. According to the commune administration law, the councils would serve a five-year mandate 'to serve the overall interests of the commune'.[10] These interests would range from the maintenance of local security and public order to the management of public services and socio-economic development. In the initial stage of the process, these activities would be funded by the Ministry of Economy and Finance with support from the MoI through a commune revenue fund. In the longer term, the councils would be expected to raise their revenues through taxation. In addition to these activities, the councils would also act as agents of central government, having both legislative and executive powers.

Political Implications

Reflecting upon their performance in difficult and dangerous circumstances, both F'pec and the SRP would have been encouraged by the numbers of votes received in 1998. CPP control over internationally supported and scrutinized elections would never be absolute. Elections had to be competitive enough to be seen as credible in the emergent post-1998 political system. Political opportunities for change through elections thus continued to exist, provided opposition parties were prepared and able to take full advantage of them. The existence of those opportunities and the potential threats they posed to CPP control meant electoral conflicts were inevitable, especially at the local level.

While it may have been difficult for some analysts to determine the RGC's motivation for its decentralization programme, the political implications of its implementation for local power structures were readily identified. One of the main reasons for the postponement of the local elections in December 1997 was because disruption to the existing power structures at the time had great potential for violence and instability. At the same time, commune elections and the accompanying decentralization reforms allowed opportunities for broader political

---

10. Law on Administration of Communes (English). NS/RKM/030/05. Chapter two. Article 9.

participation and debate in circumstances where, without them, they would probably not exist. However, the threat that this posed for local authorities and elites bound up with CPP networks restricted the extent to which those outside of the networks could capitalize on and widen the space for political activity.

Inflows of foreign development aid and assistance since 1993 were beginning to have a noticeable impact in rural areas. Interactions between outsiders, local authorities and economic elites introduced new social dynamics, disrupting and transforming pre-existing patron–client relations. Under these new patron–client relations, social science researchers found that powerful and wealthy patrons are less likely to turn resources back to local networks of clients.[11] In many cases it was noted that wealth was being moved out of the community and re-invested in nearby market towns of the capital. As a consequence, patrons seemed to be less dependent upon clients, but the clients remained dependent upon their patrons.[12]

NGOs and Commune Reforms

Following the government's lead, civil society groups who had demonstrated their worth before, during and after the 1998 elections were preparing to take the opportunities presented by the commune reforms to further their own interests in acting as intermediaries between the state, political parties and the electorate. As the elections 1993 and 1998 had shown this was far from straightforward. Given the manner in which Hun Sen had come to control the political landscape in the 1996–98 period space for direct political action outside of the state was becoming increasingly narrow and more dangerous. NGOs working in the fields of human rights, elections and democracy promotion had to work hard to maintain independence and avoid being perceived as direct opponents of the CPP.

One way of protecting themselves was to rely on international support and oversight from donors in promoting NGO engagement with government.[13] While it was the case that a large international donor

---

11. J. Ledgerwood and J. L. Vijghen, 'Decision-Making in Rural Khmer Villages'.

12. Ibid., pp. 144–45.

13. Personal interviews with Koul Panha, Director of COMFREL, and Hang Puthea, director of NICFEC, Phnom Penh, February 2002.

presence in Cambodia to some extent protected the space in which local NGO and civil organizations could operate, there was frustration among some organization heads that insufficient pressure was being applied on the government to address electoral reform. One well known Cambodian commentator and activist felt that after a period of relative stability following the 1998 elections, foreign donors were 'losing interest' in Cambodian politics.[14] After the international endorsement of the flawed 1998 elections, there was a growing sense that future elections were in danger of becoming meaningless in the face of CPP dominance and donor apathy. It was generally felt among many within the NGO sector that their organizations had a crucial role to play in actively promoting advocacy and capacity building at the grassroots level in rural areas if future electoral contests were to have any substance.[15] The commune reforms and elections were therefore seen as fertile ground for the active promotion of these goals through advocacy campaigns in rural areas and lobbying of the government at the centre.

Advocacy and Lobbying

Electoral monitoring organizations (EMOs) were at the forefront of these efforts. The advocacy and lobbying campaign they conducted was seen as a natural outgrowth of the experience gained since 1993. In that time, they had established themselves both internationally and nationally as credible independent observers. They had also demonstrated a willingness to challenge government policy concerning the institutionalization of electoral practices. In early 1999, they issued a number of recommendations that formed the core of their activities during preparations for the commune elections. Central to the recommendations was the restructuring of the NEC, reducing the number of members from eleven to five with a 'credible neutral political standing'. They also called for a review of the composition of the PECs and CECs and recommended that voter education be carried out on an ongoing basis. They argued that voter education should not only inform the

---

14. Personal interview with Dr Lao Mong Hay, former Director of the Khmer Institute of Democracy (KID).

15. Ibid.

public about correct voting procedures and rights on polling day, but also on the wider subject of the democratic process as a whole.[16]

These recommendations clearly demonstrated the EMOs' readiness to follow up on their previous successes and play an important democratizing role as a non-partisan link between elections and wider society. To achieve this, they developed a number of strategies and approaches intended to galvanize the democracy-promotion NGO sector and its international sponsors, and engage the public in challenging key aspects of the government's plans for decentralization. Between May and December 1999, the three main EMO networks, COMFREL, NICFEC and COFFEL, organized a series of seminars and workshops to discuss with other local organizations, government officials and international agencies the potential problems and conflicts associated with the elections and decentralization.[17]

The prospect of political party violence and an insecure environment was uppermost in the minds of the attendees. In an effort to mitigate these threats to the integrity of the elections, EMOs put forward a number of proposals for inclusion in the draft legislation. As well as lobbying for the restructuring of the NEC, they pushed the idea of expanding the powers of EMOs to play a greater role in the complaints-resolution process, which was a major source of conflict between the political parties and the NEC. To minimize the prospect of violence, they advocated the inclusion of individual candidates able to stand for a council seat. It was felt that measures like these would lessen conflicts between political parties, and introduce an element of accountability between people and council members, rather than promote allegiance to party hierarchies. For similar reasons, they also placed great emphasis on the inclusion of female candidates who they felt were less likely to resort to violence to solve political problems.[18] These initial attempts had little impact. Delays in the drafting of the laws meant they were unable to obtain 'working

---

16. Cited in Hughes, 'Strategies and Impact of Election Observer Coalitions in Cambodia'.

17. Phelim Kyne, 'Commune elections back to the future', *Phnom Penh Post*, Issue 8/16, 6–19 August 1999.

18. Committee for Free and Fair Elections in Cambodia, COMFREL, 'Annual Narrative Report for the year 2000: Activities, Achievement and Impact', p. 11.

copies' of the drafts, having to rely instead on piecemeal information from the MoI.[19]

By the end of 1999, neither of the two commune council election laws had gone before the Council of Ministers or the National Assembly. In the meantime, as part of their strategy to supplement advocacy in Phnom Penh, EMOs in conjunction with KID organized public forums in 13 provinces. The forums had two simple goals. First, they aimed to introduce and explain to voters in rural areas the idea of the commune councils and how they would be structured. In particular, they emphasized the differences between the government's proposed electoral system of proportional representation with closed party lists, and voting for individual candidates. Second, at the end of the forums, participants were encouraged to fill out questionnaires designed to gauge their attitudes and opinions about the election laws and decentralization more generally.

The outcome of the forums encouraged the networks to lobby hard for changes to the draft law as they headed into a new year. Results from the questionnaires found that sixty-eight per cent of participants preferred that the deputy commune chiefs be nominated from outside the council. This sent a clear message that many people were concerned that councils would become tools of existing local authorities, especially if the extant CPP-appointed chiefs were to retain their positions as heads of the new councils. This analysis appeared to be confirmed by the 'overwhelming' support for the election of individual candidates; according to COMFREL, eighty-eight per cent of participants opposed proportional representation. Based on the data generated by the forums in 13 provinces, it was clear that a representative majority of people were in favour of the new councils, and wanted to see a replacement, or at the very least a restructuring, of local authority structures.[20]

Emboldened by the results of their early activities in 1999, the EMO and NGO networks turned their attention to lobbying the leaders of the three main political parties. From March to May 2000, delegations from the EMOs met with Hun Sen, Ranariddh and Sam Rainsy as well as co-Ministers of the Interior to present their ideas concerning the commune reforms. The broad aim was to intensify dialogue with key of-

---

19. Ibid., p. 8.
20. Ibid., p. 11.

ficials over the changes they were proposing. Specifically, they wanted to ensure that 'civil society' input into the legislative process was included before the commune laws went before the National Assembly.[21] Perhaps unsurprisingly, given the public nature of the dialogue, all party leaders were, in principle, in agreement with the proposals and recommendations put forward.

Hun Sen, however, was clear that reform of the NEC, if it had to happen, would not take place before the end of its existing mandate, which would be just before the 2003 parliamentary elections. His attitude, although unsurprising, highlighted the relatively weak position the EMOs realistically had vis-à-vis the government. Undeterred, EMO networks continued to push their demands for change, holding more public meetings and provincial forums. Regardless of the short shrift from the government, they were convinced that the meetings and forums were viable 'means to get grassroots people's voices heard through democratic participation'.[22] Without doubt, activities like public meetings and forums provided opportunities for many people to express political views, but by the end of 2000 COMFREL had concluded that 'the results of the advocacy and lobbying activities had fallen well short of expectations'.[23] After almost two years of attempting to bring pressure to bear, the National Assembly finally passed the election laws in January 2001 without any of the changes put forward by the EMO networks.

Lack of success in directly influencing the outcome of the legislative process, however, did not necessarily mean the NGO networks had no effect. Although the impact was difficult to measure at the time, the advocacy activities in particular were new and potentially empowering avenues for independent participation outside of political party structures. Certainly from an educational perspective, by providing information and raising awareness of the issues surrounding commune councils the provincial forums and public meetings were a positive step. In providing alternative sources of information and education, they were

---

21. Ibid., p. 13.
22. Ibid.
23. Ibid., p. 21.

consciously making a positive contribution, strengthening alternative forms of representation within Cambodia's nascent civil society.[24]

EMO activism and advocacy was fraught with difficulties and danger. It was no coincidence that the reforms and proposals put forward were fully endorsed and supported by opposition political parties. As such, there was a real danger that in vigorously pursuing specific reforms, they would be perceived by elements within the government as part of the opposition. They had to tread very carefully in their efforts to give a democratizing voice to avoid creating the very same conflicts they were attempting to prevent. These organizations were very much aware of both the opportunities and constraints that the new post-1998 election political arrangements had to offer. Now more than ever since 1993, the commune election process offered significant opportunities to free up crucial political space in the countryside. However, the threat that this and the electoral reforms posed to CPP power at the local level placed considerable obstacles in the way of the democratizing activities of NGO networks.

International Re-engagement and National Politics Post-1998

NGO dialogue with the new government at this time was part of a broader engagement with all stakeholders including international donors. Under the new coalition arrangements, the CPP now had to manage and control renewed demands and expectations of donors, coalition partners, the SRP and an internationally supported and emboldened NGO sector. At his inaugural speech in the National Assembly in November 1998, Hun Sen outlined the government's commitment to human rights, freedom of the press, the rights of opposition parties, reform and economic development and the fight against corruption.[25] Not long after, in December, Cambodia reclaimed its seat at the UN. In February 1999, donors pledged to disburse $470 million contingent upon the government reviewing its reform efforts on a quarterly basis.[26]

---

24. Hughes, 'Strategies and Impact of Election Observer Coalitions in Cambodia', p. 34.

25. Post Staff, 'Hun Sen gives new cabinet its tasks', *Phnom Penh Post*, Issue 7/27, 11–24 December 1998.

26. Sarah Stephens, 'Government agrees to quarterly aid review meetings', *Phnom Penh Post*, Issue 8/5, 5–18 March 1999.

Shortly after that, Cambodia was finally accepted as the tenth member of ASEAN. Such was the optimism that Cambodia was now on the path to democracy and development, that the UN's Special Representative in Cambodia, Lakhan Mehrotra, stunned some observers of the Consultative Group meeting in June 1999 when he described Hun Sen as 'a champion of democracy'.[27]

Just how representative the views of Mehrotra were was not clear, but such an astonishing characterization highlighted the enthusiasm among some donors that the international endorsement and legitimization of Hun Sen could be turned into sustained, concrete action. Many political challenges in the areas of human rights, judicial reform, democratization of state institutions and tackling corruption remained, however. Not least of these was the question of international involvement in tribunals to bring surviving leaders of the former Khmer Rouge to account for genocide and crimes against humanity.

Following up on the 1997 request by Hun Sen and Ranariddh for assistance with possible trials for individual Khmer Rouge leaders, the UN in November 1998 sent a team of three independent legal experts to Cambodia to assess the situation. Their report, presented to the government in February 1999, concluded that the existing judicial and court systems lacked the necessary political independence to deal with crimes committed during DK rule. It thus proposed that the UN 'should "establish an ad hoc international tribunal" similar to the ICTY/ICTR, to deal with crimes against humanity and – if it could be proven through further investigation – international genocide'.[28] Hun Sen rejected this and other later proposals for a 'mixed tribunal' under international control on the basis that the political and military situation had changed since 1997. Instead, Hun Sen proposed a domestic court under his control but with some of the international elements put forward by the UN.[29]

Retaining tight control over the judiciary and courts was essential for helping protect the CPP as it reconsolidated power after the 1998

---

27. Sarah Stephens, 'UN rep causes upset at CG meet', *Phnom Penh Post*, Issue 8/13, June 25–July 8, 1999.

28. Cited in S. Heder, 'Hun Sen and Genocide Trials in Cambodia', p. 204. ICTY/ICTR are acronyms for International Criminal Tribunal former Yugoslavia and Rwanda.

29. Ibid., p. 178.

elections. With the surrender of Khieu Samphan and Nuon Chea in December, followed not long after by the arrest of Ta Mok in March 1999, any real or concocted military threat to a Hun Sen government from the Khmer Rouge was effectively over, although potential political manoeuvring was possible. So too was any threat from F'pec resistance forces after amnesties for senior commanders like Nhek Bun Chhay were agreed upon as part of the post-election deal between Ranariddh and Hun Sen, allowing the re-integration of F'pec loyalist forces back into the RCAF. For all intents and purposes, Cambodia was considered to be at peace. After Hun Sen's display of military power in July 1997, any challenges to the Hun Sen government therefore would likely be political in nature. The electoral threat after the events of July 1997 had been effectively managed and contained, but, because of international relations, could not be eliminated altogether. Control of political processes and events through the judiciary and the electoral authorities were thus of the utmost importance to the consolidation of Hun Sen's power.

National Politics and Discontent

Reflecting upon their performance in difficult and dangerous circumstances, both F'pec and the SRP would have been encouraged by the numbers of votes received in 1998. CPP control over internationally supported and scrutinized elections would never be absolute. Elections had to be competitive enough to be seen as credible in the emergent post-1998 political system. Political opportunities for change through elections thus continued to exist, provided opposition parties were prepared and able to take full advantage of them. The existence of those opportunities and the potential threats they posed to CPP control meant electoral conflicts were inevitable, especially at the local level.

At the national level throughout 1999, as well as with commune elections the new coalition government was pre-occupied with a number of other pressing political issues, including the formation of the new senate, the Khmer Rouge tribunals and donor reform agendas. Technical and administrative delays to the commune election legislation therefore probably suited all parties. F'pec and the Sam Rainsy Party in particular would welcome more time to re-organize themselves in preparation for the local polls. For F'pec, this was easier said than done.

By mid-1999, rumours began to circulate among F'pec party members of continued dissatisfaction with Ranariddh's leadership. Insiders reported Ranariddh's apparent acceptance of Hun Sen as sole prime minister, resulting in what they described as self-interested 'cronyism and corruption' within the Prince's inner circle.[30] In an echo of party member complaints before the March 1996 party congress, Ranariddh was again accused of being indifferent to the party's interests and those of grassroots supporters.[31] Weaknesses and dissent within the party worsened after Ranariddh supported the idea of 'reintegrating' former F'pec officials who had remained behind after the 1997 fighting, and had formed separate political parties to compete in the 1998 elections. These included Ung Huot, the leader of the Reastr Niyum party and former co-Prime Minister, installed by Hun Sen after July 1997.[32]

Ranariddh and senior F'pec members felt that the reintegration of the renegades could actually strengthen the party ahead of the commune elections. This stemmed from a belief that they stood a good chance of taking political ground from the CPP.[33] The allocation of district chief positions to F'pec as part of the post-1998 election negotiations reinforced this belief. The creation of mixed CPP-F'pec working committees, intended to help prevent electoral violence and intimidation, also contributed to a general sense that political relations between the two coalition partners were stable. Sceptics, however, were not convinced by the positive spin Ranariddh and others were putting on the idea of bringing what many F'pec members saw as 'traitors' back into the fold. Criticism about Ranariddh's leadership and a lack of purpose and direction for the party was hard to shake off.

Moreover, with elections initially expected to be held sometime in 2001, there was a marked increase in unrest and violence throughout 2000. While relations between the coalition partners may have been cordial on the surface, the government was faced with continued rural and urban discontent. This was fertile ground for the SRP to make political

30. Post Staff, 'Inside Funcinpec: Cracks Apparent', *Phnom Penh Post*, 30 April 1999.

31. Ibid.

32. Thet Sambath, 'Funcinpec Divided over Possible Return of '97 Renegades', *The Cambodia Daily*, 8 March 2000.

33. Kevin Doyle and Thet Sambath, 'Funcinpec Predicts Commune Election Win', *The Cambodia Daily*, 21 March 2000.

headway, championing the plight of the rural dispossessed and urban garment workers, but it also ran the risk of a backlash from the CPP and government supporters. In early 2000, farmers protesting against illegal land grabs joined the SRP in calling for donors, in particular the EU, to exert influence and push the government to land reform.[34] Over the summer, two people were injured when security guards fired shots over the heads of striking garment workers demanding better pay and conditions in Phnom Penh. The strike followed a number of garment worker protests in May involving 29 of Cambodia's 178 garment factories that existed at the time.[35]

Protests and demonstrations by garment workers in Phnom Penh were perceived as being part of anti-government activities of the SRP. In two separate incidents in May, a mob attacked the SRP headquarters and destroyed a memorial erected outside the National Assembly to commemorate those killed in the 1997 grenade attack on a SRP demonstration. In June, a newly appointed F'pec commune councillor candidate and his wife were shot dead in what was believed to be a politically motivated killing. National and international human rights groups reported cases of extra-judicial killings carried out by the military on individuals suspected of being members of anti-government movements, and numerous instances of violence throughout 2000 against local commune leaders, mostly directed at members of the SRP.[36]

Violence in Phnom Penh reached a peak in November when an anti-government group calling itself the Cambodian Freedom Fighters (CFF) launched botched attacks on government buildings, a TV station and an army base. The attacks were ill-conceived and poorly executed; eight people were killed and over a dozen injured. Little was known about the group outside of Cambodia at the time other than that they claimed to be an anti-communist organization funded through Cambodian-American sources intent on overthrowing the government, which they characterized as communist and a Vietnamese puppet regime. The apparent mastermind behind the CFF, which was officially

---

34. Bou Saroeun, 'Calls for Land Reform', *Phnom Penh Post*, 4–17 February 2000.

35. Post Staff, 'Striking workers shot', *Phnom Penh Post*, June 23-July 6, 2000.

36. See for example Anette Marcher, 'Rights groups face prosecution'. 1 September 2000, Human Rights Watch 2000, Cambodia Report, http://www.hrw.org/wr2k1/asia/cambodia.html.

formed in October 1998, was a Cambodian-American citizen, Chhun Yasith, an accountant based in Long Beach, California. Yasith was a former member of the SRP who had been expelled from the party in 1998.

The CFF episode contributed to a growing atmosphere of fear and insecurity in Phnom Penh and in the countryside as 2000 drew to a close. In the weeks after the attacks, over 200 individuals suspected of being involved with the CFF were arrested or detained, and another fifty were arrested a year later. Many of those arrested or detained were members of the SRP or F'pec, suggesting to human rights and civil groups that the CFF incidents were being used a pretext to target and intimidate non-violent government opponents.[37] As amateurish and bungled as the attacks were, they nonetheless highlighted the lengths some groups were prepared to go to register their discontent with the new coalition government. This, combined with rural protests against a steady increase in land grabs and continued industrial unrest in the garment factories, would require a determined response from those within the CPP and the government whose interests were once again threatened by elections.

International Electoral Support

Amidst growing concerns about electoral violence and continued CPP control of the election administration, the two elections laws, after considerable delays, were adopted by the National Assembly and the new Senate in March 2001, and the date of 3 February 2002 was set for the elections. With electoral legislation in place, the UNDP and the government were ready to invite the UN Electoral Assistance Division (EAD) to conduct a needs assessment mission. The mission took place from the end of May to the middle of June 2001, and concluded after taking into consideration the findings of the UNDP consultants 'that conditions in Cambodia were right for holding successful elections'. The EAD optimistically added that 'with the appropriate and relevant advice the NEC had the capacity and planning in place to undertake the challenging process.'[38]

---

37. See for example 'Cambodia: Information on Cambodian Freedom Fighters (CFF)' and Michael Hayes, 'The CFF attack: schools of thought', *Phnom Penh Post*, 8–21 December 2000.

38. UNDP, 'Report on the Elections of the Commune Councils', p. 10.

An agreement between the UNDP and the NEC was signed shortly afterwards. The UNDP then established an Electoral Support Unit (ESU), 'to work closely with the NEC and election related organizations to further strengthen capacity and skills aimed at achieving a free, fair and transparent election process'.[39] The ESU comprised legal, education, training, media, information and financial advisers. In addition, the EU also provided advisory support to the NEC in the areas of logistics and election administration including complaints and appeals procedures. As in the 1996–98 process, the UNDP resident representative continued regular coordination meetings with donors, the NEC and civil and other groups involved in the process to monitor the mobilization of donor funds and other technical activities. The UNDP reported that twelve donors contributed a little over $10 million to the elections through a cost sharing agreement, the largest being Japan and the EU. Significant contributions were made by Australia, Belgium, Denmark, France, the Netherlands, New Zealand, Sweden and Switzerland. Germany and Japan contributed $3.2 million directly to the NEC. The government was expected to contribute $6.9 million to cover the overall expected cost of $17 million. However according to the head of the ESU the actual figure may have been closer to $15 million.[40]

The UNDP/EAD's positive portrayal of the NEC's capabilities, albeit with caveats attached, was in stark contrast to that of a majority of concerned civil and international organizations. For these groups, nothing had changed since the controversies surrounding the formation and performance of the NEC in 1998. The NEC and its provincial and commune counterparts remained as politically divisive, partial and lacking in credibility as they were then. In an attempt to appease donors' apparent dissatisfaction with the government's lack of progress, at a donor meeting in January 2001, Hun Sen implicitly acknowledged the problems with the NEC but stood by his earlier position not to agree to its reform until its current mandate had expired before the 2003 parliamentary elections.[41]

---

39. Ibid.

40. Ibid. The figure of $15 million was given during author's personal interview with the head of the ESU, Phnom Penh, 15 July 2002.

41. See for example National Democratic Institute for International Affairs (NDI), 'The 2002 Cambodian Commune Council Elections', Phnom Penh, 20 March

Technically and logistically, provided both donor and government funds were disbursed in a timely fashion, with the support of the UNDP/EAD experts and consultants, the NEC, as the Vice-Chairman stated, was ready to organize the elections.[42] Technical and financial assistance from donors was contingent upon the preparation of plans and budgets by the government. By April, the NEC had produced a 'Master Plan' including a detailed timeframe and costings. Budgets were broken down into four 'general activity' sectors: voter registration, polling, voter education and computer systems. The NEC also nominated staff for provisional and commune elections committees. The commune committees were responsible for registering voters, actual voting and counting and the recruitment of staff.

NEC Practice and Performance

Minor changes were made to the 11-member committees, but these did nothing to affect the overall influence and control that could be exerted by the CPP. Civil groups and NGOs who had lobbied hard for the reduction in the number of members from 11 to 5 in an effort to de-politicize and professionalize the committee had a total lack of confidence in its capacity to oversee a fair and impartial process. They were concerned that the MoI was controlling the list of nominees and that most of them had a clear affiliation with the CPP. They argued that this political imbalance was also reflected at the provincial and commune levels. In an effort to appease detractors, the commune election law was amended in January 2001 to allow SRP representation on the committee and the replacement of some members who were no longer represented in the National Assembly.[43] After some lengthy political theatre, including an initial rejection by a National Assembly vote and an endorsement from Hun Sen, the SRP candidate finally took his seat on the committee in

2002; Michelle Vachon, 'Donor Meeting Looks at Wide Range of Reforms', *The Cambodia Daily*, 16 January 2002.

42. Samnang Ham, 'Date of Commune Elections Moved to Feb 3', *The Cambodia Daily*, 23 March 2001.

43. Committee for Free and Fair Elections (COMFREL), 'Report of the Commune Council Elections (February 03, 2002)', March 2002, Phnom Penh, p. 8.

August, months after the preparations for the elections had officially begun.[44]

As the case of the SRP NEC candidate illustrated, after the promulgation of electoral legislation, the opposition and civil society groups were engaged in a constant struggle to remove bureaucratic, administrative and legal obstacles laid down by the electoral authorities. In all areas of the electoral process, from voter and candidate registration, media access and voter education, to the accreditation of observers, resolution of electoral conflicts and law enforcement, barriers and problems were encountered. Most issues stemmed from the electoral legislation itself, which despite the lengthy drafting process, was approved with what UN officials described as 'obscure requirements' in areas of the law that had not been fully developed, requiring further interpretation and clarification. Working with the UN, the ESU and UNDP legal advisers, the NEC was compelled to issue separate directives and regulatory clarifications as issues arose.[45]

One of the major criticisms of the NEC's performance was its handling of the voter registration process, conducted between 21 July and 16 August. The NEC budget of approximately $3 million included donor technical support and a new networked computer system for the National Election Computer System (NECC). At the end of the process, EMOs complained that significant and surprising numbers of eligible voters had not registered. Based upon reports gathered from their networks, they felt many people were prevented from registering, prompting them to lobby the NEC to extend the registration period in some parts of the country. The NEC complied, extending it for a further three days. However, the NEC's final figures showed that out of 6.2 million eligible voters, only 83 per cent actually registered, leaving approximately one million people unrecorded. Reasons given by the NEC and the UN for the low turnout during registration when compared to the 98 per cent in 1998 were various, including the impact of seasonal flooding, poor cash flows and last minute procurements of materials. Observers from

---

44. Pin Sisovann and Matt Reed. 'Assembly Allows Opposition to Join NEC', *The Cambodia Daily*, 28 July 2001.

45. UNDP, 'Report on the Elections of the Commune Councils', pp. 26–27.

the EU mission concluded that they were unable to 'identify significant numbers of eligible voters excluded from the process'.[46]

By contrast, EMOs and other civil groups who had a far superior knowledge and understanding of the situation on the ground to EU observers attributed the problem to other politically related factors. COMFREL for example cited a general lack of political commitment on behalf of the NEC, a lack of resources, poor training of election officials and failure to finalize regulations in a timely fashion, which contributed to preventing many people from registering. They added that, for politically motivated reasons, many voters were unable to register on scheduled days or at their designated registration stations because of confusion over personal requirements. In some instances, the PECs, CECs and Registration Officers disseminated information inequitably, whereas local authorities were well informed and well placed to ensure that groups of CPP supporters were able to register in large numbers early. Furthermore, at the outset of the process, the NEC required voters to register in their home communes, although after complaints the NEC reversed this decision half way through. Many students and migrant garment workers residing outside of their homes in the provinces, who were likely to vote for opposition parties, were thus prevented from registering in time.[47]

Similar issues were raised and problems encountered with the registration of candidates, held from 14 to 16 October. The NEC officially accepted 75,287 candidates for 8 political parties in all of the 1,621 commune councils to be contested. As well as the main three parties, there were also candidates from the Khmer Angkor Party, Vongkot Khmer Party, Khmer Progress Party, Khmer Democratic Party, and the Cambodian Women's Party. Prior to the registration of candidates, EMOs registered their concerns about the CPP's use of surveys to assess the political opposition faced by their candidates. While the election law has nothing to say about these activities, civil groups suspected that state officials and resources were being used to conduct the surveys, and the nature of the questions asked contributed to an atmosphere of fear

---

46. Ibid., p. 12.
47. COMFREL, 'Report of the Commune Council Elections', p. 13. See also NDI, 'The 2002 Cambodian Commune Council Elections', pp. 14–15.

concerning the secrecy of the vote.[48] Other legal matters concerning the power of the CECs to reject whole lists of party candidates and the interpretation of election laws regarding the nationality and literacy of candidates were brought to the attention of the NEC. On receiving these concerns the NEC issued directives and clarifications, thereby forestalling any serious disputes.[49]

NEC Voter Education and Media Access

While some groups downplayed political factors in favour of technical problems and a lack of human and other resources to account for the NEC's shortcomings, when problems in other areas were also taken into account, patterns of control could be discerned. As in previous elections, control of information and media access were two areas in which these patterns were readily identifiable. From early on in the process, the NEC regulations relating to the control of voter education materials were criticized as being unconstitutional, amounting to the curtailing of freedoms of speech and expression. Under the regulations, all local and international NGOs or groups engaged in election education had to have materials including documents, video tapes, leaflets, books, images appearing in newspapers and slogans appearing on hats and T shirts approved by the NEC in advance. After considerable pressure was brought to bear by local and international NGOs, the NEC agreed to amend the regulations and 'establish a process of voluntary approval from the NEC'. In the days before the election, however, the NEC appeared to reverse its decision, instructing PECs and CECs to approve materials, thus causing further delays and additional costs to the organizations involved.[50]

After the 1998 elections experience the NEC gave explicit assurances that all political parties were to have equal access to state-owned TV and radio during the 15-day campaign period. The UN Secretary General's Special Representative for Human Rights in his final assessment of the

---

48. Ibid., p. 15.

49. See for example UNDP, 'Report on the Elections of the Commune Councils', pp. 13–14.

50. NDI, 'The 2002 Cambodian Commune Council Elections', p 11; see also COMFREL, 'Report of the Commune Council Elections', p. 11.

commune elections, stated that this 'did not happen'.[51] Indeed, almost all observer groups, domestic and international, who made statements about media access, including the European Union Election Observer Mission (EUEOM) found that state media coverage was overwhelmingly given to the government.[52] The UN Human Rights Office concluded in its final report that media access was actually 'less fair than in 1998'.[53] COMFREL concluded that 'the media has never provided equal access to political parties' and the NEC did not make a proper effort to 'inform the voters'.[54]

Lack of equal access to state media was compounded by the NEC's reversal of its decision to broadcast 15 voter education programs involving political party roundtable question and answer sessions. The programs were cancelled after the NEC charged F'pec Minister for Women's Affairs, Mu Suchua, with taking personal credit for a successful initiative led by her ministry, during the recording of one of the programs. The NEC's media representative, Prum Nhean Vichet, argued that the minister's behavior was improper and that the initiative was led by the government. The minister was forced to write an apology to the Prime Minister which was widely broadcast on state TV To reinforce its position, the government dropped from an aircraft thousands of copies of a press release criticizing the minister.[55]

The situation deteriorated when the NEC blocked both state and private TV from airing taped commune candidate debates organized and paid for by NDI and KID. The debates provided an unprecedented opportunity for candidates to publicly and directly engage each other and local audiences with questions concerning local issues. The reasons for the ban were not clear. NEC members and Deputy Prime Minister

---

51. Special Representative of the Secretary General for Human Rights in Cambodia, 'Commune Councils Elections 2002. Media and Freedom of Expression', p. 10.

52. EU Election Observer Mission (EUEOM Cambodia), 'Final Report on the Commune Elections', 2002, pp. 15–23.

53. UN Office for Human Rights in Cambodia, 'Commune Councils Elections 2002', p. 11.

54. COMFREL, 'Report of the Commune Council Elections', p. 9.

55. See for example NDI, 'The 2002 Cambodian Commune Council Elections', p. 13.

Sar Kheng promoted the idea that the election law did not require the NEC to take responsibility for broadcasting such programs.[56]

The NEC's decision to ban the broadcasts caused an uproar among the opposition parties, EMOs, international agencies and members of the diplomatic community. In an apparent attempt to defend and 'clarify' its role in assisting and advising the NEC, the UNDP after the elections sent a memorandum to diplomatic missions expressing its view that the 'NEC is not, and should not be, the vehicle or the electoral platform of political parties'. The UNDP's legal adviser argued that there was no 'legal basis for the NEC to get involved in the preparation or broadcasting of a debate between political parties aimed at informing the voters about substantive programs of each party'.[57] Critics argued that the UNDP had overstepped its mandate by trying to protect the NEC from criticism over a serious electoral issue.[58]

The UNDP offered an extremely narrow and rigid legal interpretation to justify its position and its attempt in portraying the NEC as a neutral body. According to its final report, the problem lay with the NEC's Public Information Bureau (PIB), which it was claimed worked in isolation and without consultation with the ESU. The ESU, it added, deplored the bureau's decision to take on a legally authorized role in controlling media for the elections. As the ESU saw it, problems could have been resolved with a timely appeal to the Minister of Information, who could have reversed the decision and allowed the programs to be broadcast. In its efforts to portray the NEC as a neutral state institution, the UNDP's criticism of sub-committees within the NEC only served to underscore the partial nature of the institution as a whole. As a consequence, almost all domestic and international assessments concurred that the NEC's handling of media issues worked to the advantage of the CPP and likely restricted the chances of voters from making educated and informed choices on polling day.[59]

---

56. Cited in NDI, 'The 2002 Cambodian Commune Council Elections', p. 14.

57. Cited in Rajesh Kumar, 'UN agency condemned for lobbying tactics', *Phnom Penh Post*, Issue 11/4. 15–28 February 2002.

58. Ibid.

59. EUEOM, 'Final Report on the Commune Elections', p. 22.

De-politicizing Electoral Violence and Intimidation

After two elections marred by violence and intimidation of voters and members of political parties involving local authorities, the police and the military, the new coalition government was aware of the need to demonstrate to donors a commitment to prevent a re-occurrence of problems during the commune elections. There was also a desire to de-politicize the violence and intimidation related to the elections in an effort to divert attention away from political causes and effects. This was illustrated during the first visit of the UN Secretary General's Special Representative for Human Rights, Peter Leuprecht, to Cambodia at the end of 2000. In a January 2001 report, he stated that political violence and intimidation presented 'a serious danger' as the commune elections approached and thus requested that the Prime Minister issue 'a clear and firm message condemning all acts of political violence and intimidation'. Hun Sen, known for his animosity towards the Human Rights Office in Cambodia, responded to the request by expressing the view that political violence did not occur in Cambodia.[60]

Hun Sen's stance was a reminder of the importance he attached to the international legitimacy of the new coalition government under his control. Central to this was the manner in which he and his coalition partners were perceived to be conducting the elections. In May, a month before a donors meeting with the government to discuss progress on reforms and aid disbursements, the CPP and F'pec signed an accord which Hun Sen claimed would ensure the elections would be held 'peacefully, transparently and without violence, sending a clear message to voters and the international community'.[61] Ranariddh expressed his view that the agreement would have a positive effect on the June donor meeting by showing the extent to which both parties were committed to ensuring stability.[62]

By presenting a united front on the issue of violence and intimidation, the government sought to manage international perceptions and take the politics out of electoral conflicts. The political realities on the ground however made this an impossible task. Local and international

---

60. Report of the Special Representative of the Secretary General for Human Rights in Cambodia, Mr. Peter Leuprecht. E/CN.4/2001/103, 24 January 2001, paras 23–24.

61. Lor Chandara. 'CPP, Funcinpec Ink Accord', *The Cambodia Daily*, 25 May, 2001.

62. Ibid.

human rights groups had reported an increase in politically-related violence since 2000, reaching a peak with the CFF attacks in November. The international organization Human Rights Watch (HRW), for example, stated that 'between February 10 2001 and January 5 2002 nineteen F'pec and SRP party members, the majority of whom were either prospective or confirmed commune council candidates were killed'.

In addition, HRW also reported that human rights organizations working in Cambodia had documented more than 267 cases of alleged violence and intimidation from 1 January 2001 to 5 January 2002. These included familiar types of offences and violations recorded in previous elections such as harassment, arbitrary arrest and detention, restriction of assembly, property violations, destruction of party signboards, physical assaults and other violent acts.[63] COMFREL and other monitoring groups recorded numerous incidents of government and party officials confiscating voter registration cards, creating the impression among voters that their votes would be recorded. There were also widespread cases of commune and village chiefs collecting thumbprints and coercing voters into supporting the CPP using allegiance-swearing ceremonies similar to those used during the 1998 elections process. Vote-buying using gifts and small amounts of cash and other incentives was also prevalent. EMOs reported that all parties engaged in these activities, but that the majority of violations were committed by CPP officials who had considerably more resources at its disposal.[64]

Hun Sen made numerous statements throughout the various stages of the process, denouncing political violence and ordering authorities to arrest perpetrators regardless of their political affiliation. Prime Ministerial pronouncements, however, did little to stop the violence and intimidation. Some investigations and arrests were conducted for some of the more serious cases of murder, but according to the UN human rights representative, as of May 2001 he was only aware of six convictions out of a total of nineteen election-related deaths. In addition, many of the investigations were seriously flawed by claims that authorities used beatings to obtain confessions.[65]

---

63. Human Rights Watch, 'Cambodia's Commune Council Elections: A Human Rights Watch Backgrounder', January 2002, pp. 3–4.

64. COMFREL, 'Report of the Commune Council Elections', p. 24.

65. Report of UN Secretary General's Special Representative for Human Rights in Cambodia. A/57/230. 27 September 2002, paras 46–47.

In similar ways, the NEC failed in its duty to enforce directives giving it and its PECs and CECs powers to hold hearings and enforce sanctions in cases of complaints and contraventions of the commune election law. Chapter 16 of the Commune Election Law provided clear and comprehensive sanctions and penalties for anyone involved in the kinds of illegal electoral practices utilized in previous elections, for example the collection of voter registration cards, vote buying, the removal or destruction of party signs and property, threats including death, physical harm or denial of economic resources and aid, loss of land, the swearing of oaths of allegiance to the CPP and thumbprinting, among others. The law failed to specify which authority was responsible for offences of this nature and how they were to be dealt with. To circumvent this problem, the legal department of the NEC, with legal advice from the UNDP, issued a series of directives to fill yet another 'legal vacuum'.[66]

Directives equipped the NEC, PECs and CECs with 'quasi-judicial' powers and procedures for addressing complaints and resolving electoral conflicts as they arose. Failure of local electoral authorities to use these powers was chiefly attributed to a lack of official complaints due to fear of confronting the powerful local authorities that either perpetrated or were complicit in most of the violations.[67] The majority of reported cases of voters being intimidated and harassed to vote for the CPP involved village and commune chiefs. In an effort to deal with the problem, the MoI drafted a code of conduct for 'chiefs of village, chiefs of commune', outlining their role in ensuring a neutral and secure political environment for the elections. Even though the instruction was approved by the MoI in a timely fashion, as the UNDP pointed out, Hun Sen failed to approve it in time for the elections.[68] In the end, complaints and conflicts were subject to a highly unsatisfactory system of extra-judicial conciliation meetings. These involved the complainant meeting with the alleged perpetrator and the electoral authorities to arrive at a compromise, often resulting in nothing more than an apology.[69]

---

66. UNDP, 'Report on the Elections of the Commune Councils', Annex 6, p. 53.

67. Ibid., pp. 53–55. See also UNSRSGHRC 2002, pp. 4–10.

68. UNDP, 'Report on the Elections of the Commune Councils', p. 44.

69. NDI, 'The 2002 Cambodian Commune Council Elections', p. 10.

The Campaign

The 15-day campaign period from 18 to 31 January was overshadowed by more reports of violence, intimidation and last-minute vote buying. During the usual noisy street parades and party rallies, the mutilated body of an election observer from the monitoring organization NICFEC was found in Svay Rieng province two days before polling day. EMOs also recorded more instances of widespread and systematic coercion and buying of votes by CPP officials and activists on the eve of the elections, and in some cases actually on polling day. COMFREL concluded that these 'tactics were undoubtedly more prevalent' than in the 1998 election campaign.[70] Other problems included the confiscation of SRP campaign materials. These consisted of audio extracts of Sam Rainsy speeches and printed material of audiences with the King. Local election authorities deemed the materials illegal for contravening the election law, and an NEC directive to reinforce articles within the law concerning the campaign was issued in late January. NEC authorities justified the decision arguing that the tapes used illegal images of the King for political purposes and criticized the 'two parties forming the government', claiming they were in direct contravention of the law.[71]

Although this like other NEC decisions was reversed and the materials returned, the episode highlighted the general lack of engagement by all political parties in specific local issues and ways to address them during the campaign. Confiscated SRP speeches, for example, were copies of earlier recorded speeches, some of which had previously been aired on television as part of state TV's coverage of proceedings in the National Assembly.[72] Party political rhetoric tended to focus on issues drawn from their national political platforms.[73] Moreover, EMOs complained that the parties failed to generate sufficient interest among the electorate, and that information about policies and manifestos was thin and delivered in 'sound bites' rather than in a substantive and coherent way.[74] Part of the problem could be attributed to the fact that at the time

70. COMFREL, 'Report of the Commune Council Elections', p. 20.

71. For a full explanation of the NEC's position, see UNDP, 'Report on the Elections of the Commune Councils', pp. 64–65.

72. Ibid.

73. NDI, 'The 2002 Cambodian Commune Council Elections', p. 16.

74. COMFREL, 'Report of the Commune Council Elections', p. 19.

of the elections, the government had not finalized details about how the councils were to be run and what specific powers they would have. Unequal media access and the NEC's failure to support voter education initiatives was another contributing factor that served to undermine the campaign.

Polling and Results

After a two day cooling off period at the end of the campaign, voters went to the polls on February 3 as enthusiastically as they had in previous elections. At 86 per cent the turnout of registered voters was notably less than in the 1998 national elections. Voter registration problems that may have contributed to as many as one million eligible voters not registering certainly had an impact on the numbers of actual voters. Poor dissemination of information and education related to the concept of local governance and the structure and function of the councils could have also been a factor. Undoubtedly, fear, caused by widespread intimidation, coercion and violence, played a major role. When viewed as a whole, these factors may have resulted in the onset of a general feeling of apathy among large sections of the electorate.

Procedurally, polling and counting phases were conducted satisfactorily, with minor irregularities and problems recorded. Out of a total of 1,621 commune council chief positions available, the CPP secured an overwhelming 1,598, followed by the SRP with 13 and only 10 for F'pec. The CPP also won the majority of first and second deputy chief positions, taking 789 and 154 respectively. F'pec won 457 deputy and 154 second deputy positions, and the SRP 285 and 615. Overall, these represented sixty per cent of the vote for the CPP, twenty per cent for F'pec and sixteen per cent for the SRP. Out of the other five political parties, only one other, the Khmer Democratic Party, won a seat on a council.

Domestic and International Observation and Assessments

Domestic observation of the elections was another contentious issue. The creation of the NGO Coordinating Committee (NGOCC) to accredit local and international observers was viewed as yet another attempt to control and obstruct the work of the established EMO networks. Initially afraid that their independence as monitors would be compromised, they threatened to boycott the committee. They also ran the risk of being excluded from the elections altogether. Nonetheless, after lobbying the NEC and the government, they received assurances that their independence would be preserved. These pledges, however, did not stop the new, inexperienced committee from placing bureau-cratic and administrative obstacles in the way of the EMOs, creating unnec-essary repetition of 'pedantic' procedures and causing delays and anxieties.[75] Many international observers including the EU felt the NGOCC was an unnecessary additional layer of bureaucracy that hindered rather than facilitated domestic election observation.[76] At the end of a fraught process, the NEC through the NGOCC managed to accredit almost 40,000 local observers and 624 international observers from the European Union, NGOs and UN agencies.

Post-Election Events, Complaints and Resolution

Two days after the elections, Sam Rainsy indicated that his party would accept the results and not stage any protests if international observers did not report 'a very black picture'.[77] However, both the SRP and F'pec, as well as the EMOs, did submit a large number of complaints to the NEC, but these were considerably less than in 1998.[78] The majority of complaints focused on communes where the margin of difference between the winning and losing parties had suspiciously high numbers of invalid ballots.[79] The NEC agreed to hold recounts in three such communes, resulting in a reversal of the outcome and the awarding of the commune chief position to the SRP. Encouraged by this outcome, the SRP pushed the NEC for more recounts. After a vote of its members,

---

75. COMFREL, 'Report of the Commune Council Elections', p. 12.

76. European Union Election Observation Mission Cambodia. 'Cambodia Commune Council Election 3 February 2002', p. 36, http://www.ecoi.net/file_upload/625_tmpphpwkuMbS.pdf.

77. Jody McPhillips. 'Sam Rainsy Says He Will Accept Results if Observers Do', *The Cambodia Daily*, 5 Feb 2002.

78. According to the NDI's final election report, the SRP submitted 91 complaints, F'pec 57 and the CPP 1. NDI, 'The 2002 Cambodian Commune Council Elections', p. 21.

79. Ibid., p. 21.

the NEC refused to conduct any more recounts, arguing that specific complaints had not been administered correctly and were submitted after the official deadline. Sam Rainsy contested the decision and organized the only demonstration of the post-election period to contest the results.[80]

Recounts and the award of an additional SRP commune chief position represented a small technical victory for the opposition, but this was overshadowed by the NEC's inability and unwillingness to address the more serious complaints of a political nature related to coercion, intimidation and vote buying. Many of these complaints were not formally reported, and most of those that were never went further than a conciliation meeting conducted by the CECs and PECs. For the most part, this was due to a lack of evidence as victims were reluctant to lodge complaints, fearful of reprisals from perpetrators who were often local officials affiliated with the CPP. Instances of reprisals against villagers who had voted for opposition parties were reported by the UN Human Rights Office monitoring teams and the EMOs.[81] When concrete evidence was presented in the more serious cases, there was legal confusion over which authority was responsible for hearing the cases. In many instances, CECs and PECs refused to handle the complaints, referring them instead to the NEC, who duly sent them back. Many serious cases were thus left unresolved.

Final Assessments

Election observer groups were faced with a dilemma. How to assess and judge a process financed and supported by international donors that was clearly manipulated by authoritarian elements within the state, and yet had the potential for political and social change? Striking a balanced view between authoritarian control and democratic possibilities was no easy task. After the debacle surrounding the JIOG assessments in 1998, most international observer groups, especially the EU, were cautious and guarded in their final assessments, avoiding the use of the term

---

80. Kay Kimsong, 'Opposition Demonstrators: NEC Controlled by the CPP', *The Cambodia Daily*, 25 February 2002.

81. Special Representative of the Secretary General of the United Nations, 'Commune Council Elections 2002', p. 6; COMFREL, 'Report of the Commune Council Elections', p. 23.

'free and fair'. They nonetheless drew attention to the stark and inherent contradictions and inconsistencies of Cambodia's internationally supported authoritarian elections. Simultaneously, elections brought to the surface the differences in approach, perception and understanding of Cambodian political realities within and between the international community, domestic groups and political parties engaged in the process.

The European Union fielded the largest international observer mission from late December 2001 until the end of February 2002, deploying 30 long-term observers in 15 teams of two people in 15 provinces. A further 60 short-term observers made up of individuals from all European states were deployed for the actual election days.[82] In a comprehensive final report, the EU mission reiterated its conclusion in a preliminary statement issued on election day that the 2002 commune elections 'marked progress in the consolidation of democracy in Cambodia'. It added the caveat that further 'democratic possibilities' might be limited if the irregularities and malpractices that 'blighted' the elections were not dealt with.[83]

In an attempt to provide a balanced assessment, it was not immediately clear from the EU report – beyond the fact that the government had agreed to hold local elections in the first place – exactly which aspects of democracy had been consolidated. The list of recommendations provided in the report illustrates the point. Firstly, it recommended that 'all parties and stakeholders' demonstrate the necessary 'political will' to honour the letter and spirit of the law if elections were to meet international standards. In addition, it recommended that guidelines be established and adhered to, to check the behaviour of government at national and local levels during an election period, 'ensuring an end to the misuse of state resources or abuse of State authority'.[84] Quite apart from the fact that no connection was made between the abuse of state power outside of an election period and elections, the reality on the ground suggested it was authoritarian control of elections that had been consolidated and democratic possibilities repressed.

---

82. European Union Election Observation Mission, 'Cambodia Commune Council Election', p. 3 http://www.ecoi.net/file_upload/625_tmpphpwkuMbS.pdf.

83. Ibid.

84. Ibid., p. 35.

Like the EU, all other principal international and national organizations and observer groups directly involved in the elections who produced public statements, such as UNDP, UN Special Representative of the Secretary General for Human Rights in Cambodia, NDI, IRI, the Asian Network for Free Elections (ANFREL) and Cambodian EMOs, more or less agreed that despite serious problems in virtually all areas of the elections, they nonetheless held out hope for future democratic development. Only the IRI, based on its preliminary assessment of the pre- and post-election periods, described the elections as not being 'free and fair', failing to meet international standards.[85] By contrast, the Japanese embassy observer mission, based on its assessment of polling and counting, considered the elections to have been 'held in a free and fair manner'.[86]

Having partnered with the NEC and coordinated technical and financial donor resources for the elections, the UNDP carefully avoided explicit political statements in its final reporting. Instead, it presented a politically sanitized description of each aspect of the elections process, concluding that the NEC's 'technical performance was strong'.[87] Problems were acknowledged, but in such a way as to suggest that with more technical tweaking they could be resolved. In stark contrast, the UN human rights special representative concluded that the elections 'exposed continued serious underlying problems that more than ever need to be addressed with determination and urgency'.[88] It added that the 'institutions responsible for ensuring the neutrality of the election environment and for ensuring justice is upheld failed to do so'.[89] The differences in interpretation and approach could not have been more clear.

After the failure of the lobbying and advocacy campaigns in 1999 and 2000, Cambodia's EMOs were under no illusions about the seriousness

---

85. International Republican Institute (IRI), 'Preliminary Statement on Cambodia's February 3, 2002 Commune Council Elections', 4 February 2002.

86. Embassy of Japan. 'Statement of the Japanese Election Observation Mission on Commune Council Elections in the Kingdom of Cambodia February 3rd, 2002', Phnom Penh, 5 February 2002.

87. UNDP, 'Report on the Elections of the Commune Councils'.

88. UNSRSGHRC, 2002, p. 15.

89. Ibid.

and extent of problems affecting electoral politics. Looking ahead to the 2003 elections, they therefore emphasized some of the more positive aspects of the first commune elections, such as the greater participation of women candidates, fewer technical irregularities and the reduction in numbers of election-related killings compared to previous polls.[90] Like many of the intentional observer groups, despite the CPP's clear reassertion of control of the communes, EMOs felt the presence of SRP and F'pec members on the councils was nonetheless a small but important step in the right direction.

As far as the main political parties were concerned, the outcome for them was mixed. The CPP had achieved the objective of satisfying donors' expectations by staging the elections and holding on to virtually all commune chief positions. In response to statements that the elections were not free and fair and did not meet international standards, Hun Sen publicly mocked international observers, stating that the elections were 'free and fair' enough and that 'international standards only exist in sports'.[91] Such comments underlined the glaring inconsistencies and contradictions in the international donors' approach to Cambodian elections. F'pec's performance was nothing short of disastrous, confirming the discontent felt among grassroots supporters with the party's leadership. The SRP did not take as many votes away from F'pec as they had hoped, but were nonetheless satisfied that the overall increase in votes was a positive sign for the future. With the 2003 parliamentary elections just over a year away, it remained to be seen whether or not the government would make good on its promises to address electoral problems and issues. If the 2002 experience was anything to go by, the likelihood was that elections would remain a key site of struggle between authoritarian forces and those hoping to make the democratic possibilities talked about by international observers a reality.

---

90. COMFREL, 'Report of the Commune Council Elections', p. 1.

91. Rajesh Kumar, 'Election winner: "the grassroots"', *Phnom Penh Post*, 15 February 2002.

CHAPTER 7

The 2003 Elections

*T*he startling recommendation by the 2002 EU observer mission that government behaviour be checked to ensure an end to the use of state resources and abuse of authority at election time revealed how much international authorities like the EU understood about Cambodian electoral politics. In recommending the establishment of guidelines to help prevent these abuses the EU simultaneously acknowledged that government was both part of the problem and the solution. Furthermore, it explicitly acknowledged that there was a 'gap between the willingness to put such guidelines on paper and the willingness to ensure their implementation and adherence on the ground'.[1] Although it was not expressed overtly in the report, the mission clearly understood how state resources and authorities were used illegally to help secure electoral victories for the CPP. The real problem for the EU and other international agencies directly involved in supporting Cambodian elections was how to manage the problem.

This was nothing new. Attempts by international agencies to separate the CPP from state institutions, beginning with UNTAC in 1993, proved to be an almost impossible task. In 1997, when it was evident that the government would not adhere to conditions set out in the UN memorandum of understanding, such as the threat of withdrawal of electoral support, diplomats in Phnom Penh instead introduced guidelines as a way of addressing ongoing electoral abuses involving the use of state resources and officials.[2] In both instances abuses continued. The 2002 elections were plagued by the same kinds of problems encountered in 1993 and 1998, clearly demonstrating the emergence of disturbing patterns of government behaviour. Because of past experiences, there were plenty of reasons to suspect that the same patterns would emerge during the 2003 parliamentary elections. However, the political and

---

1. EUEOM, 'Final Report on the Commune Elections', p. 35.

2. See chapter 4, p. 117.

economic implications of tackling these problems with the government head on was not something the UN or the EU were realistically prepared to countenance. Seemingly intractable political problems posed themselves, to be circumvented through the technical management of internationally proposed and supported governance reforms, including elections.

Elections and Governance

In early 2003, 'a team of experts from the UNDP Bureau for Development Policy' conducted 'a critical analysis and review of governance issues and challenges' facing Cambodia. They concluded that governance, more than any other area of development, 'requires societal transformation, which is not achievable without strong and visionary leadership and civic engagement'. This was linked to broader notions espoused by the chief UNDP administrator that the consolidation of democracy in places like Cambodia was 'not just about an election, but a long term process'.[3] In this way, elections were viewed as important events, but only in a longer term effort to promote reform through good and democratic governance. 'Electoral systems and processes' became one component in the UNDP's efforts to strengthen governance institutions in other areas such as 'parliamentary development, justice and human rights, decentralization and local governance as well as public administration reform'.[4] Elections in Cambodia were thus bundled up with wider UNDP and government initiatives and programmes aimed at poverty reduction, Millennium Development Goals (MDG) and Governance Action Plans.

Attempts to reduce the elections process to a donor reform objective in part stemmed from western liberal concerns over 'illiberal' or non-democratic outcomes of internationally supported elections held in authoritarian regimes undergoing political transition in the early 1990s. It was argued that elections could wait until other aspects of liberal democratic society had been consolidated, like the rule of law, accountable and transparent parliaments and vibrant civil societies, with the help and

3.   United Nations Development Programme, 'Cambodia Annual Report 2003', Phnom Penh, p. 8.

4.   Ibid.

support of foreign development experts and consultants. This position was countered by the argument that early elections, for good or bad, were in actual fact an important part of the long-term democratization process.[5] By the beginning of the 2000s it appeared that, by including electoral systems and processes in a donor-backed liberal governance reform agenda, a compromise between the two positions had been struck.

This was nonetheless problematic for donors. Another consultant report in 2003 analysing the RGC's policy process concluded that donor-led reforms begun in the 1990s were 'by and large unsuccessful'. This was because donors were attempting to rationalize and legalize, along liberal democratic free market lines, an existing exploitative and extractive state system that primarily served the dominant interests of the CPP.[6] According to this view, donors presumed that state resources extracted from rent-seeking and international aid could, by improving and rationalizing policy formulation and reform implementation processes, generate enough revenues and profits from extractive industries and business activities that would eventually trickle down to the poor. The presumption however that the state could somehow be disciplined in this way was wrong, and failed to account for political realities. In reality, it was argued that the main priority of 'Cambodian leaders' was to stabilize the situation by consolidating networks of loyalty underpinning the state, rather than to implement a western liberal democratic-style bureaucracy. This implied that existing networks loyal to the CPP within the state system were actually being strengthened, thereby creating more opportunities for exploitative, illegal and coercive entrepreneurial activities.[7]

This situation by no means implies that all donors are naïve or ignorant of the context within which they operate, although this may be the case in some instances. Neither does it imply that all Cambodian leaders and state power holders are necessarily predatory and self-interested in nature, although these do exist in great numbers. It is rather a situation of 'engaged detachment', whereby outside ideas about how to organize and run a modern, rational, state system are accommodated but manipulated for the purposes of international aid and legitimacy; and as a means to

---

5. See Introduction, p. 3.

6. C. Hughes and T. Conway, 'Understanding pro-poor political change: the policy process'. London: Overseas Development Institute (ODI), 2003, pp. 26–27

7. Ibid., p. 27

divert attention away from the exploitative and criminal activities of a small, predatory elite operating within formal state institutions. Donors and government officials thus engage often in good faith, but do so within a system that, despite its outward appearance of rationality and formality, functions in quite a different way.

Some scholars and analysts of Cambodian politics refer to this situation in terms of a modern 'theatre' state where there are 'patterns of discrepancies between appearances and reality'. In this characterization, what appears to be genuine donor–government engagement and accommodation is in fact an elaborate and deceptive but abstruse 'façade'.[8] Evolving from PRK interactions and accommodation with Vietnamese patrons in the 1980s, the façade was created and developed as a way of protecting CPP interests and counteracting UNTAC's control mandate. By adopting a policy of 'false' or 'superficial' cooperation with UNTAC, especially on security issues after the Khmer Rouge withdrew, the CPP systematically subverted the election process through violence and intimidation, and financed it through the sale of public assets.[9] In early 1993 UNTAC authorities had come to realise that they had been duped, concluding that the ministries and officials with whom they had been dealing in Phnom Penh functioned as 'shells and screens'.[10]

From this perspective, real political power and decision making lies behind, above and below this façade orchestrated and controlled by 'shadow networks' of allegiance to Hun Sen, 'his cronies and henchmen'.[11] Between the end of 1993 and 2003 these shadow networks working behind the façade had successfully marginalized or destroyed any opposition and accommodated donor demands, but stopped short of any meaningful reform that threatened the dominance of the networks. During that time, international donors continued to support the system with aid and assistance, despite the growing amount of evidence from

8. Steve Heder, 'Political Theatre in the 2003 Cambodian Elections: State Democracy and Conciliation in Historical Perspective', in Julia C. Strauss and Donal Cruise O'Brien (eds), *Staging Politics: Power and Performance in Asia and Africa*, 2007.

9. Ibid., p. 24

10. Ibid.

11. Ibid., p. 29

scholarly work and consultant reports about how it actually functioned to the detriment of reform agendas.

Arguments and reasons why donors were reluctant to challenge this system head on typically revolve around interpretations of recent Cambodian history, which help to inform and shape the ideological underpinnings of international liberal democratic and 'good governance' agendas. Hun Sen's ascension to the position of Cambodia's 'strongman' dovetails to some extent with the UNDP administrator's view that societal transformation cannot happen without strong leadership. Portrayed by former ambassadors and senior UN officials as democratic, Hun Sen is seen by some in the international donor community as having the necessary 'vision' and personal qualities needed to lead Cambodia out of its deeply troubled past to a more peaceful and prosperous future.[12] At the very least in the short term, from a good governance viewpoint, political stability and security is an obvious and essential prerequisite for the following phases in the construction of strong, viable democratic states. This suggests that the longer-term enterprise in places like Cambodia is bound to be, because of its violent past, problematic in the short term, but with the right kind of technical interventions in areas like electoral systems and processes, a democratic culture can evolve. The evident failure by donors to push the government along the path of reform from late 1998 onwards, and the persistence of the same kinds of electoral problems during the 2002 commune elections, suggested that technical interventions alone would not move Cambodia in a democratic direction.

UNDP 'Improving' Elections: the NEC

In light of criticisms and recommendations made by both international and national observer groups, the stated 'primary objective of UNDP support was to assist the different departments of the NEC to assume ownership, leadership and accountability with regard to various aspects of the electoral process.'[13] Technical assistance took the form of an eleven-member team that worked with the NEC over a period of 18 months

---

12. See Chapter 5.
13. UNDP, 'Cambodia Annual Report 2003', p. 9.

in the run up to the elections on areas related to legal aspects, media training, voter registration, civic education and complaints.[14]

Five months after the commune elections the Ministry of Interior in consultation with the UNDP proposed an amendment to the 1997 Law on the Election of Members of the National Assembly (LEMNA). The amendment included a reduction in the number of NEC members from 11 to 5, and a new regulatory framework to ostensibly address the problems encountered in previous polls. Included in the framework was the incorporation into the body of the law the seat allocation formula that had caused bitter controversy during the 1998 elections. The voter registration system was improved to provide clearer guidelines on requirements related to identity, residence, age and citizenship. A bylaw and code of conduct to govern the structures, roles, responsibilities and duties of NEC and other officials, including rules to strengthen the sanctions, complaints and appeals procedures was introduced. According to the UNDP, the consultative process was open and transparent, involving regular consultation with all 'stakeholders' at every stage, representing what was viewed as a significant improvement in NEC public relations.[15] The amended law was adopted and promulgated by the National Assembly on September 17, in time to begin the first stage of preparations for the elections when the new members of the NEC took office in November.

The UNDP's positive assessment of the consultative process, when compared to previous legislative exercises involving elections, couldn't mask the continued frustration and discontent felt by some with the final outcome. In the same month that the MoI released the proposed amendment, EMO networks reissued statements calling for the kinds of electoral reforms they had lobbied hard for in 1999–2000, perhaps now sensing that their concerns and recommendations might be fully addressed.[16] While they acknowledged the international contribution made by the UNDP in framing the amendments and the NEC's invitation to civil groups to participate in the consultative process, they

---

14. Ibid.

15. UNDP, 'Cambodia Annual Report 2003', pp. 5–6.

16. COMFREL, 'Statement on Election Reforms in Cambodia', 8 July 2002.

argued that important recommendations and suggestions had either been ignored or were not incorporated into the final framework.[17]

Once again, the central concern was the form, function and independence of the electoral authorities. The reduced membership of the NEC itself was welcomed, but the manner in which members were to be selected did little to boost confidence in its neutrality and independence among most civil society groups. According to Article 13 of the amended election law the MoI remained in control of the selection procedure, which, unlike in previous years, involved non-political party candidates. Instead, the new five member committee was to be made up of suitably qualified 'dignitaries', an idea that was rumoured to have been put forward by Hun Sen and passed on to the two co-Ministers of the Interior, Sar Kheng and You Hockry of F'pec. Both F'pec and the SRP along with civil society groups were for the most part supportive of the new arrangements, provided the dignitaries were selected under certain conditions and in open consultation via a specially formed selection committee.[18]

The government's decision to select members in accordance with Article 13 of the amended law and not by an all-inclusive selection committee unsurprisingly met with considerable resistance. Despite attempts by opposition parties, including some F'pec parliamentarians, to boycott the required vote in the National Assembly, the CPP secured enough support to ensure the new members were approved. The announcement of the names of the new committee members in September seemed to confirm earlier speculation that the five 'dignitaries' suggested by Hun Sen would be three CPP-affiliated individuals, including the then Secretary General of the NEC Im Sousedy, and two aligned with F'pec. The selection of the NEC members in this way was

---

17. COMFREL, 'Assessment Report on the Cambodian National Assembly Elections 2003', p. 12. Available at http://www.comfrel.org/eng/components/ com_mypublications/files/79153401_Result_Report_2003_NA_Election_ Report_COMFREL_2003_En_Fina.pdf.

18. See for example Yun Samean, 'Comfrel Unveils Plan for Reforming NEC, *The Cambodia Daily*, 14 August 2002. Also, 'Joint Statement of Concerns over the Selecting Procedures of the National Election Committee Members for the 2003 National Assembly Elections' by COMFREL, NICFEC, Cambodian Human Rights Action Committee (CHRAC), and Star Kampuchea, Phnom Penh, 10 October 2002.

a blatant attempt to fudge the long standing and highly divisive issue of neutrality and transparency, and to legitimize it within the framework of the amendment to the law.

Rather than placating critics, the restructuring of the NEC along these lines generated further controversy before the preparations for the 2003 polls had officially begun. Because of the extent of international involvement in the elections process, the role of the international agencies came under the spotlight. Sam Rainsy, by then well known for his vocal and active efforts to solicit international support, had unsuccessfully sought clarification from EU and UN officials regarding their position on NEC reform. Representatives from the EU commission in Phnom Penh refused to be drawn into the controversy, telling reporters instead that the EU's role was solely technical and the NEC reform was an internal matter that shouldn't be influenced by outsiders and should be left to Cambodian politics and civil society.[19] Clearly irritated by the EU response, COMFREL's director was reported as saying that he felt donor support was often manipulative and presented a false front of free and fair elections. At the time, the UNDP spokesperson did not comment.[20] It was clear from comments like these that civil society groups felt that they and their concerns were being ignored by both Government and its international supporters like the EU, who frequently paid lip service to notions of democratic possibilities but in reality helped to contribute to their suppression. Put another way, as one senior western institutional capacity adviser working for a government ministry did, donor involvement in Cambodia had less to do with democracy via elections and more to do with 'governance via international expertise'.[21]

Elections Preparations, Progress and Achievements?

In the eyes of opposition parties and civil groups who had actively campaigned for electoral reform since 1998, a renewed lack of confidence in and mistrust of the newly restructured NEC did not bode well for the elections preparations. By contrast, the UNDP and EU were satisfied

---

19. Bill Myers, 'Two Large Election Donors Stay Out Of Debate', *The Cambodia Daily*, 16 August 2002.

20. Ibid.

21. Author anonymous interview, 3 March 2002, Phnom Penh.

that, through the consultative process, progress had been made, and that the NEC had demonstrated 'genuine commitment in clarifying and strengthening the legal framework'. Progress was thus measured by positive changes to the legal framework and by what the UNDP saw as the overall improvement in election administration. Included in a list of achievements was the reduction in the cost of administration, measured by each registered voter, from $4.82 in 1998 to $1.98. Others included: the permanent voter registry administered by the commune councils allowing for the registration of 93 per cent of eligible voters, better implementation of codes of conduct and education programmes covering technical voting issues, and the introduction of an equity news campaign.[22]

Technical and administrative plaudits showered on the NEC by the UNDP and EU were however at variance with the overall assessments of opposition political parties, EMOs and other international observer groups. To be sure, almost without exception, all of the principal observer missions concurred that legislative and administrative improvements were positive signs, but these did not prevent the same kinds of problems experienced in previous elections from reoccurring. At the same time, both the EU and UNDP acknowledged that problems existed, but the EUEOM observers in particular denied accusations by the opposition and some civil groups that the NEC lacked independence and were biased in favour of the CPP.[23] The EUEOM maintained that the NEC had worked in a transparent fashion, and had sought 'contact with political parties and civil society'.[24] By portraying the NEC as accountable and transparent while also accepting that problems persisted, the EUEOM failed to adequately address the issue of separating the CPP from the state, something they had alluded to in the previous 2002 election report.

This incongruous mix of technical improvement and the persistence of familiar problems was encountered from the outset of the formal process beginning with voter registration. On the positive side, allowing for demographic changes since 1998, improved procedures enabled more voters to register than previous elections. With the introduction of a permanent register, the numbers from 2002 were used to register

22. UNDP, 'Cambodia Annual Report 2003', p. 9.

23. EUEOM, 'Final Report on the Elections of the Members of the National Assembly, 27 July 2003', 2003, p. 10.

24. Ibid.

approximately 6.3 million voters, almost 1.2 million more than in the commune elections. Observer groups also welcomed the relaxation of provisions that previously restricted workers and military personnel from registering at their place of work and allowing others to take time off if they had to register elsewhere. The NEC, again urged by observers groups, extended the registration period to allow for the registration of newly eligible voters, estimated to have risen to one million since 1998.

As welcome as these improvements were, civil groups and their international supporters were concerned that impressive voter registration figures did not tell the whole story. Based on its findings, COMFREL suggested that perhaps as many as 400,000 new voters had not or were unable to register to vote. While they didn't rule out voter apathy and other more prosaic explanations, they believed that, on the basis of demographic data, these voters may have been deprived of the right to vote. It was argued that the data suggested that many were from disadvantaged groups, including the poor, students, youths and monks; groups often drawn to opposition parties like the SRP. Due to procedural barriers, issues related to access, timing, confirmation of identity, inadequate training and poor selection of registration staff, many individuals from these groups were prevented from registering. Monks from one of Cambodia's two Buddhist sects were particularly affected after spiritual leaders issued instructions for them not to vote in elections.

Another major concern was the integrity and accuracy of the Official Voter Lists (OVL). SRP parliamentarians in April had called for an independent audit of the lists. The NEC, legally obliged to respond, initially refused to provide the SRP and COMFREL with copies, eventually releasing them in June. With very little time before the actual polls, COMFREL with the support of the The Asia Foundation and NDI conducted a sample 'people to list survey' of voter names, which revealed serious discrepancies and inconsistencies.[25] It was possible, according to the findings, that the NEC's official registration figures could differ from the actual lists by as much as 4 per cent, meaning that there could be as many as 253, 673 'ghost voters' or names that didn't appear on the lists. If the samples were representative and extrapolated across the country, the discrepancies could have had a major impact on the outcome of the

---

25. COMFREL, 'Assessment Report on the Cambodian National Assembly Elections 2003', pp. 21–22

elections, especially in marginal areas, casting overall doubts on whether or not they genuinely represented the people's choice.[26]

Voter Education and Media Access

Conflicts between civil groups, political parties and the authorities over voter education and media access continued despite changes to NEC regulations and guidelines. The NEC ran a voter education programme during the voter registration phase, producing public announcements, audio and video spots, leaflets and posters. These included information on the secrecy of the vote, prevention of violence and intimidation and the complaints process. EMOs for the most part felt that these efforts were inadequate and of poor quality.[27] There were complaints that in some remote areas no voter information was provided. On the positive side, most assessments concurred that there was an overall improvement in access to information, albeit limited, partially due to a Ministry of Interior directive sent to local authorities in February instructing them to facilitate NGO voter education efforts. NGO and EMO voter education activities included radio and TV spots and drama performances 'in almost all districts and communes', and information guides about political party platforms. NDI provided 'special programs' broadcasting political party debates. Overall, it was generally felt that voters were reasonably well informed, but this was largely due to the activities of NGO and EMOs who relied heavily on international funding. With international funding for NGO activities likely to be drastically reduced in future elections, concerns arose among civil groups that inadequate state provision would mean that voter education would suffer.[28]

Despite improvements, access to broadcast media continued to be controlled by the CPP. In an effort to avoid a repeat of previous controversies surrounding these issues at election time, NEC regulations clearly stated that both state and private media were obliged to ensure the right of voters to make an informed choice by abiding by the NEC

---

26. Ibid., p. 23

27. EUEOM, 'Final Report on the [2003] Elections', p. 11.

28. COMFREL, 'Assessment Report on the Cambodian National Assembly Elections 2003', p. 19.

media guidelines.[29] They also made it clear that it was the responsibility of state media to ensure the 'principles of equity and distinguish between government and party activity' in its coverage of news.[30] However, it was still not clear how the guidelines regulating private media would be enforced.

Article 75 of the amended election law nonetheless empowered the NEC to take necessary measures to publicize the platforms of the political parties through equal and orderly access to the media. On this basis, a UNDP initiative facilitated the introduction by the NEC of 'Equal Access Programming' and 'Special Elections News Bulletins', which were incorporated into state news broadcasts. Political parties were allocated free time in the bulletin using an 'equity' formula based upon the percentage of valid votes and number of National Assembly seats won in previous elections. A similar formula was to be used for private media outlets. However, none of the six private TV stations responded to the initiative, and they continued to devote almost all political coverage to the activities of the Prime Minister and CPP members of the government.[31]

The equity news concept, while welcomed by opposition parties and civil groups, was not necessarily what the UNDP described as a 'revolution in state media'. Media monitoring exercises carried out by COMFREL and the EUEOM did note an improvement in the availability of election-related information on state TV during the campaign period, but even then, they recorded imbalances with coverage almost exclusively in favour of Hun Sen and CPP officials. Lengthy Hun Sen speeches and images of gift-giving ceremonies and the inauguration of new development projects and public facilities like new school openings featuring the prime minister and senior CPP officials received a disproportionate amount of air time, and had a powerful impact on the shaping of public perception and opinion.

It was a similar with radio broadcasts. National Radio of Cambodia (FM 96) provided coverage using the 'equitable' formula during the campaign but reverted back to exclusive coverage of Hun Sen and CPP once it was over. Unlike private TV stations, some private radio stations

---

29. Ibid., p. 42.

30. Ibid.

31. EUEOM, 'Final Report on the [2003] Elections', pp. 43–45.

were more accessible and did provide broader coverage of all political party platforms and political debate. F'pec for example had finally been granted a licence for its own station. Beehive Radio, owned by the anti-government activist Mam Sonando, on FM 105, considered the only really independent outlet in Cambodia, was the only station to provide fairly balanced coverage of all parties engaged in the elections. Problems remained however. Beehive Radio was targeted by elements within the government for being part of the CPP opposition because of the station's re-broadcasting of Voice of America (VOA) and Radio Free Asia (RFA) programming in Khmer. Considered to be anti-Hun Sen and CPP, these stations drew large audiences but were not permitted to operate inside Cambodia, broadcasting instead from neighbouring countries. Mam Sonando had been ordered by the government in November 2002 to stop the re-broadcasting of VOA and RFA programs.[32] Meanwhile, the SRP was still unable to obtain a licence for its own radio station.

Security and the Anti-Thai Riots

As important as voter education and media access were, the security environment had a profound impact on Cambodian voters' perceptions and arguably choices made at the ballot box. Since 1993, the security situation had been a central concern, having a demonstrable negative effect on preparations for elections. Whether it was the threat posed by the Khmer Rouge before elections in 1993 and 1998, or armed dissident groups like the CFF seeking to overthrow the state before local elections in 2002, voters had had to contend with a heightened sense of fear and insecurity before, during and after elections.

After the 9/11 terrorist attacks in New York in 2001, followed by the Bali bombings in Indonesia in 2002, security inside Cambodia took on international and regional significance. The presence in Cambodia of the suspected Bali bomber Hambali Abdullah between 2002 and early 2003, before his arrest in Thailand, focused international and especially US attention on the security of Cambodia's porous borders and its place in the so-called 'war on terror' in Southeast Asia.[33] Before the bombing

32. Yun Samean, 'Beehive Radio Founder Mulls Reviving His Dormant Party', *The Cambodia Daily*, 26 November 2002.

33. Post Staff, 'Hambali was here', *Phnom Penh Post*, 29 August 2003. Also, 'Terrorism in Southeast Asia' Congressional Research Service Report for Congress. The

in Bali, at an ASEAN Police-Chief conference held in Phnom Penh in May 2002, co-Minister of the Interior Sar Kheng was reported as telling delegates that member states should 'think globally as they act locally' in the fight against terrorism in the region.[34] Later that year in November, weeks after the attack in Bali, Cambodia hosted the eighth ASEAN Summit where commitments and pacts were made between member states to combat regional terrorist threats and crime.[35]

Despite events in Bali, ASEAN leaders at the summit were critical of what was perceived as western 'fear mongering' about the threat of terrorism in Southeast Asia; which at the time seemed to them to be more 'phantom than real'.[36] They nonetheless issued formal statements agreeing to step up efforts to counter terrorist threats, and agreed to share information about suspected terrorists. Such statements issued by ASEAN leaders were a serious concern for both regional and Cambodian human rights groups, who feared that anti-terror measures could be used to silence government critics, stifle dissent and place limits on personal freedoms. The Director of the Center for Social Development in Phnom Penh for example recalled that one week after the September 11 terror attacks in the US, Hun Sen announced a 'crackdown' on those the government suspected of being connected to the CFF. Subsequent arrests of suspects included members of F'pec and the SRP, who had no links with the CFF.[37]

Not long after the ASEAN summit, in December the government announced a joint police and military strategy to boost security during the voter registration period, scheduled to begin on January 17. The strategy involved deploying more police from national headquarters into Phnom Penh and surrounding areas and villages to provide security for voters to reduce everyday crime. Government officials were concerned

---

Navy Department Library. Updated 18 November 2003. http://www.history.navy.mil/library/online/terrorism%20in%20southeast%20asia.htm.

34. Saing Soenthrith, Kay Kimsong, 'Region Needs To Fight Terrorism, Sar Kheng Says', *The Cambodia Daily*, 29 May 2002.

35. Kevin Doyle, 'Stalking Terrorism Will Test Inter-Asean Trust', *The Cambodia Daily*, 12 November 2002.

36. Ibid.

37. David Kihara, 'Rights Officials See Flaws in Terror Pledge', *The Cambodia Daily*, 13 November 2002.

that criminal acts like robbery would be politicized and linked to the elections process by political parties like the SRP. This was a familiar tactic employed by the CPP to manipulate the security situation to divert attention away from military, police and local authority involvement in election-related crimes. In the absence of a Khmer Rouge or CFF threat, it would be difficult to connect election violence and intimidation to the actions of insurgents and so-called subversives. Therefore, according to the 'security strategy', ordinary everyday crime was to be expected, but could be stopped or deterred by the presence of increased numbers of police and military, thereby reducing the possibility of politicization by opposition forces. Comments reported in the English language press at the time appeared to sum up the government's position when the Director of National Police, Hok Lundy, asserted that it was 'impossible to guarantee an incident-free registration period because some political parties turn robbery cases into political killing and intimidation'.[38]

This strategy failed spectacularly two weeks before the end of the voter registration period when police stood by as an angry mob of about 100 'students' smashed their way into the Thai Embassy in Phnom Penh, forcing the ambassador to flee over a back fence shortly before the building was ransacked and set on fire.[39] After some considerable time had passed, riot police eventually intervened, but were unable to prevent the mob of rioters, having dispersed from the embassy, from causing the further systematic destruction of several Thai businesses and commercial interests in the city. Costs of damages to Thai-owned business interests were estimated to be somewhere in the region of USD50 million.

The origins of the riots were never clearly established, but were attributed to reactions to long-standing, unsubstantiated rumours reported in a pro-government newspaper, *Reaksmei Angkor*, on January 18 that a Thai actress had remarked that she 'would perform in Cambodia only after Cambodia returned the Angkor Wat temples to Thailand'. Two days before the riots, Hun Sen, during a widely televised public ceremony, referred to the actress's comments, remarking that she was

---

38. Thet Sambath, 'Security Stepped Up Ahead of Voter Registration Period', *The Cambodia Daily*, 10 December 2002.

39. Post Staff, 'Mobs go berserk in anti-Thai frenzy Thai embassy torched; businesses gutted', *Phnom Penh Post*, 31 January 2003.

not 'even worth the blades of grass at Angkor Wat'.[40] Later claiming that the PM's comments had spurred them on, students staged what was initially a peaceful protest outside the Thai embassy on the morning of January 29. Eyewitnesses reported that later in the day, the protests were taken over by members of a pro-CPP quasi-youth association called the 'Pagoda Boys', known to take part in anti-opposition counter-demonstrations. Protesters stormed the embassy after false rumours circulated among the crowd that the Cambodian embassy in Bangkok had been attacked and Cambodian diplomats killed.[41]

Although the attacks on Thai interests constituted a major international incident, the damage done to bi-lateral relations between the two countries was short-lived. The RGC accepted conditions set by the Thai government for the normalization of relations, admitting it had misjudged the situation and had failed to provide adequate security. Full diplomatic relations were resumed in April.[42] In light of the previously announced security strategy in December and the subsequent failure of police and military to intervene and prevent the attack on the embassy and Thai business interests, questions were raised about whether government officials were deliberately slow to react or even manipulating and controlling events on the ground.[43] Based on the available evidence, the US Department of State report to Congress could only conclude that 'the Cambodian government authorities were irresponsible with nationalist rhetoric and incompetent in handling the unfolding crisis'.[44] Charges of incompetence are difficult to sustain. Recent history has shown that government security forces and the police have been highly capable and diligent when required. Ironically, the Thai embassy is situated directly opposite the CPP headquarters and metres away from the Ministry of Interior responsible for national security. Whether incompetence or manipulation, or a combination of both, the episode heightened a general sense of fear and insecurity in the months preceding the elections.

---

40. US Department of State. 'Report to the Congress on the Anti-Thai Riots in Cambodia on January 29, 2003.' 14 May 2003. http://2001-2009.state.gov/p/eap/rls/rpt/20565.htm
41. Ibid.
42. Ibid.
43. Ibid.
44. Ibid.

Security, Violence, Intimidation and Elections

Less than a month after the riots, Lundy announced further security measures to deal with protests and demonstrations before and after the elections. These included the creation by the MoI of a Central Security Bureau for the Defence of Elections that would train national and military police in crowd control and demonstrations. At a meeting at the end of February Lundy told a large gathering of national and military police officers that the 'masterminds of the [riots] will be shown the strength of the police force', and after the elections 'if any political party refuses to accept the results of the election and affects national security...we will take down the demonstrators'.[45] Given the speculation surrounding official complicity in the orchestration of the riots, Lundy's comments had a deeply disturbing effect among human rights and opposition political party activists.[46] It was evident that the anti-Thai riots would be used as justification for the suppression of any dissent, organized or otherwise, concerning the elections. The fact that state officials, including the police and military, had a history of involvement in election-related violence and intimidation only served to heighten fears of further repression and possible political violence in the build-up to the elections.

Indeed, previous patterns of politically linked violence and intimidation continued throughout the election period. Although much was made of a reduction in the number of serious incidents when compared to past elections, including killings, the overall atmosphere of fear and intimidation among the electorate remained intense. The high-profile assassination outside a Phnom Penh restaurant of senior F'pec official and advisor to Ranariddh, Om Radsady, in early February had a particularly deleterious effect on the political climate.[47] Known for his unimpeachable character and uncomplicated lifestyle, his murder immediately raised suspicions that the motives were political and not a simple robbery of his mobile phone, as officials from the MoI had initially

---

45. Michael Coren, 'Elections Hok Lundy reads the riot act', *Phnom Penh Post*, 28 February 2003.

46. Ibid.

47. Saing Soenthrith and Teth Sambath, 'Senior Advisor to Ranariddh Shot, Killed', *The Cambodia Daily*, 19 February 2003.

claimed.[48] At the time, he was linked to a dispute between Hun Sen and F'pec parliamentarian Princess Veachera, King Sihanouk's half-sister. The Princess had challenged Hun Sen to account for the government's handling of the anti-Thai riots before the National Assembly.[49] After the riots, Hun Sen had come under pressure from civil society groups that had planned but subsequently cancelled protests calling for his resignation.[50] Demands by F'pec that Hun Sen address the National Assembly over the issue were also later dropped.[51] Two individuals were arrested and sentenced for the killing of Radsady, and the MoI later admitted that the killing was more than just a robbery, but no further action has been taken since.[52]

High profile killings in Phnom Penh were followed by familiar and anticipated incidents of violence and intimidation directed at voters and political party activists elsewhere in the country. The UN Human Rights Office reported 13 additional suspected political killings of known activists and members of the three main political parties between the February 2002 commune elections and the end of the 2003 election campaign period on July 25. COMFREL recorded a total of 31 suspected political killings between January and the end of July in 16 out of Cambodia's 24 provinces and municipalities, including 11 individuals connected with the CPP, 12 with the SRP and 8 with F'pec.[53] The difference in figures can be attributed to whether or not it could be established that the motivations were political or due to some other

---

48. Ira Dassa, Keith Schultz, Evan Gottesman and Brad Adams, 'Murder of a man with no enemies', *Phnom Penh Post*, 28 February 2003.

49. Lor Chandara and Kevin Doyle, 'Ranariddh Drops Demand on Riot Explanation', *The Cambodia Daily*, 14 February 2003.

50. Kate Woodsome, 'Coalition of Unions Cancels Planned Strike', *The Cambodia Daily*, 12 February 2003.

51. Chandara and Doyle, 'Ranariddh Drops Demand on Riot Explanation'.

52. A briefing Paper by Human Rights Watch June 2003. 'The Run-Up to Cambodia's 2003 National Assembly Election: Political Expression and Freedom of Assembly Under Assault'. See also, Human Rights Watch, '"Tell Them I Want to Kill Them": Two Decades of Impunity in Hun Sen's Cambodia', 2012, p. 50. Available at http://www.hrw.org/sites/default/files/reports/cambodia1112webwcover_1.pdf.

53. COMFREL, 'Assessment Report on the Cambodian National Assembly Elections 2003', p. 50.

reason unrelated to the elections. In keeping with what appeared to be a deliberate attempt to de-politicize serious crimes committed during the various election stages, government officials were reluctant to attribute political causes to many of the killings.[54]

Alongside the killings, voters, party activists and supporters were again subjected to a variety of forms of intimidation and coercion. Human rights groups and EMOs reported numerous and widespread cases of death threats and threats of physical violence, use of firearms, illegal arrests and detention, confiscation of voter registration cards, removal or damage to party signboards and property, and threats of economic sanctions and social exclusion.[55] Buddhist oath-swearing ceremonies resembling those used in previous elections, and vote buying through gift-giving including money, seriously compromised the integrity of the process and created a climate of fear, coercion and insecurity. Local authorities aligned with the CPP were either directly or indirectly involved in the vast majority of incidents of intimidation and coercion. Civil groups and the UN did acknowledge that, following government directives instructing security forces and authorities to remain neutral, there was a reduction in the involvement of the military in these activities. However, government directives did little or nothing to prevent village chiefs from engaging in most of the reported cases of intimidation and coercion.

Accountability, Complaints and Reconciliation

Intimidation and coercion of voters by village chiefs underscored ongoing problems with a lack of accountability and impunity for local authorities who violated elections laws or engaged in election-related criminal acts. MoI rules and regulations, intended to facilitate the selection of village chiefs by commune councils that could potentially introduce an element of accountability, were not enacted before the elections. Many election-related complaints and reported violations of

---

54. Ibid., p. 8.

55. United Nations Cambodia Office of the High Commissioner for Human Rights (,), Special Representative of the Secretary for Human Rights in Cambodia, 'The 2003 National Assembly Elections', December 2003, p. 5. See also COMFREL, 'Assessment Report on the Cambodian National Assembly Elections 2003', pp. 7–10.

the election law thus involved village chiefs and commune authorities. According to the UN Human Rights Office, commune police were either complicit or refused to investigate complaints, allowing village and commune authorities to get away with violations with impunity.[56] In the more serious cases of politically motivated murder, the UN reported only four convictions in the 13 cases recorded from the commune elections to the end of the campaign period in July 2003. In these and other earlier cases related to the commune elections, investigations and court proceedings were, according to the UN, flawed, raising serious doubts about the veracity and 'reliability of some of the convictions'.[57]

Continued problems with police investigations into politically motivated murders and election-related crimes, combined with weak judicial and courts systems, perpetuated a climate of impunity. Because these problems had been persistent features of elections since 1993, a great deal of attention was focused on the capacity of the electoral authorities to manage and resolve conflicts and punish violations of the electoral law in 2003. In an effort to minimize some of the past criticisms and reduce its direct administrative burden, the NEC with UNDP and EU technical support introduced 'conciliation' into the existing electoral complaints and appeals procedures. Commune Election Committees were authorized to investigate and seek the resolution of minor violations of the electoral laws through 'conciliation meetings' between plaintiffs and the accused. They were not authorized to hold 'hearings', but rather to facilitate a mutually acceptable settlement of a dispute through 'conciliation'.[58] If conciliation failed at the CEC level, the case was passed onto the PEC who had 'jurisdiction to resolve all complaints related to offences' covered in Chapter 11 of the amended electoral law. Flagrant cases of electoral law violations were to be sent by the CECs directly to the PEC, and outright criminal acts to the local authorities and courts.

Complaints and appeals procedures and conciliation processes were highly problematic. First of all, there was confusion over which authority was responsible for what in prosecuting violations of the electoral law and imposing sanctions on offenders. Both the NEC, the police and the

56. UNCOHCHR, 'The 2003 National Assembly Elections', p. 7.

57. Ibid.

58. EUEOM, 'Final Report on the [2003] Elections', p. 20.

courts had parallel powers to do so in election-related cases, as stated in Chapter 11 of the electoral law, resulting in what the UN Human Rights Office described as 'buck passing'.[59] With the exception of sanctions imposed upon three village chiefs two days before polling day, the NEC failed to take measures against offenders in numerous cases of intimidation, reverting instead to issuing directives.[60] This did little to build confidence and trust among opposition parties, civil groups and voters. The EMOs for example recorded far more incidents of threats, intimidation and partiality among electoral authorities than officially recorded by the NEC.[61]

The EU in its final report acknowledged that the complaints and appeals procedures did not function as expected, with 'reconciliation rather than law enforcement' determining outcomes. Stated reasons for this included reluctance on behalf of victims to lodge complaints, 'difficulties in substantiating cases' and a 'reluctance of officials to take action'. Irrespective of these problems, it concluded that the 'conciliation' processes at the level of the CEC seemed to have 'efficiently acted as expected', operating as filters to prevent too many cases from reaching the hearing stage.[62] By contrast, EMOs found that the majority of the complaints they recorded were not of a minor nature and should not have been handled by conciliation at a CEC. Moreover, when hearings at the PEC were held, 'they did not conform to the expected standards for such proceedings'.[63]

EU and UNDP praise for the conciliation process in the context of other identified problems, such as the lack of law enforcement and involvement of local officials and civil servants in transgressions, suggested a misreading and misunderstanding of the traditional practice of conciliation, or *sâmroh-sâmruol* in Cambodia. Scholarly research in

59. UNCOHCHR, 'The 2003 National Assembly Elections', p. 7.

60. The MoI issued a directive five days before polling day prohibiting village chiefs from acting as party agents. See UNCOHCHR, 'The 2003 National Assembly Elections', p. 7.

61. COMFREL and NICFEC, 'Pre Election Assessment Joint Statement', 25 July 2003.

62. EUEOM, 'Final Report on the [2003] Elections', p. 20.

63. COMFREL, 'Assessment Report on the Cambodian National Assembly Elections 2003', p. 25.

recent years has shown how socio-economic and political change since as early as 1970 has transformed and stripped customary practices of dispute resolution in rural areas of traditional ideals.[64] According to this view, dispute resolution practices at village level have been transformed over time to the point where they are now subject to the powerful influence of predatory political-economic networks that access and control the lion's share of wealth and resources generated after 1991.

The EU's assertion that there 'is a strong preference for informal/conciliation mechanisms for the settlement of disputes' and that conciliation works, ignores evidence that shows that powerful political-economic forces which subvert 'institutional/formal dispute mechanisms' elsewhere in the system are at play at the village and commune levels. Village chiefs and commune officials connected to or involved in local CPP-connected networks of wealth accumulation from land grabbing and other corrupt exploitation of natural resources use their positions to protect the interests of the networks from aggrieved, dispossessed and exploited individuals seeking redress. The SRP draws many of these individuals and victims of exploitation into its ranks, making them targets for political bias, harassment and violence at the hands of CPP loyalists within local authorities. Poor and powerless victims and witnesses of political violence and other crimes are reluctant to lodge complaints and challenge authorities connected to power and wealth for fear of reprisals.

According to the EU's figures, out of the 349 official complaints lodged during the campaign period, 143 'were resolved' at the CEC and a further 43 at the PEC, demonstrating the effectiveness and success of conciliation processes. These numbers seemed to confirm and reinforce the EU's culturally relativistic view that Cambodians prefer informal dispute resolution mechanisms. An alternative view of the efficacy of conciliation, put forward by a highly experienced monitor for the UN Human Rights Office and scholar of Cambodian politics, was grounded in his participatory observation of the reality in Kampong Cham province during the campaign. Like the EU, from this perspective, 'conciliation' was successful, but only to the extent it reinforced a

---

64. For a full discussion of conciliation in Cambodia, see Heder, 'Political Theatre in the 2003 Cambodian Elections'. See also Fabienne Luco, 'Between a Tiger and a Crocodile: Management of Local Conflicts in Cambodia: An Anthropological Approach to Traditional and New Practices'. Phnom Penh (UNESCO).

distinctly contemporary culture of impunity protecting CPP authorities and allowing 'widespread political violence, election law violations and intimidation of voters'.[65] It sent a clear message that opposition was in any form dangerous, and its consequences socially and economically dire, even fatal. In endorsing and 'applauding' the success of conciliation at the CEC level, the monitor concluded that the EU and UNDP were in effect 'directly and indirectly buttressing CPP power by taking appearances for reality and seeming to support or be duped by the CPP'.[66]

Party Politics and the Campaign

Commune election results in 2002 were another decisive blow to the political fortunes of F'pec. In the year or so after those polls, the party continued its downward spiral amidst continued factional infighting and deep divisions over Ranariddh's apparent acquiescence to Hun Sen. A weak and compliant coalition partner like Ranariddh was just what Hun Sen and the CPP needed to maintain dominance. The system however could not function without at least the appearance of a credible opposition if the benefits of international legitimacy were to continue unhindered. The SRP thus needed to be carefully managed and controlled, its participation and survival allowed, but restricting its capacity to mount an effective and credible challenge through the ballot box. Sam Rainsy's continual strident criticism of Hun Sen contrasted starkly with Ranariddh's relatively muted acceptance. Hun Sen's attitude to the SRP was illustrated when, in response to Rainsy's calls for his removal, he publicly warned Rainsy 'to be careful' as he 'didn't want to crush' him because he wanted to 'keep an opposition [in existence] to preserve representative democracy'.[67]

Keeping up the appearance of representative democracy was a high priority for the CPP while working to ensure any opposition was effectively neutralized by whatever means necessary. The SRP however had made considerable progress electorally in 2002 and it seemed likely to make more gains at F'pec's expense in 2003. It was also a priority therefore

---

65. Heder, 'Political Theatre in the 2003 Cambodian Elections', p. 169.

66. Ibid., p. 70.

67. Kuch Naren and Molly Ball. 'PM Warns Sam Rainsy To Tone Down Rhetoric', *The Cambodia Daily*, 31 March 2003.

for Hun Sen, and to a large extent Ranariddh, to publicly maintain the appearance of and commitment to the idea of a CPP–F'pec coalition.[68] Coalition politics was an indispensable tool in Hun Sen's strategies for exploiting and manipulating F'pec weaknesses. By contrast, while coalition politics had some benefits for his party, Ranariddh had to contend with discontented elements within the party – especially former resistance fighters – angry and resentful toward senior fellow party members who had not fought in the resistance, and yet enjoyed the full benefit of high office. In particular, the F'pec co-Minister of the Interior, You Hockry, was accused of abusing his position, corruption and nepotism. Attempts to have him removed from his post in mid-2002 ultimately failed after a National Assembly vote went in his favour.[69]

The You Hockry case encapsulated the general malaise within F'pec and underscored the power and control Hun Sen and the CPP had over the system. Indeed, for some political analysts, there was a real sense that many within F'pec had resigned themselves to the fact that the CPP could not be defeated electorally, and they would be better off playing a subservient and obedient role within the coalition.[70] Such was the level of cynicism that there were rumours substantiated by some F'pec party members that the CPP was helping to finance F'pec's electoral campaign.[71] In spite of this, others within the party felt that their interests would be better served elsewhere, triggering a series of high level defections from F'pec to the SRP and the notable resignation of the party's deputy secretary general, Kem Sokha, who would go on to play a prominent future role in national politics.[72] The influx of F'pec officials into the SRP was almost matched by the number of SRP officials, disgruntled with what they perceived as Sam Rainsy's undemocratic

68. Kim Chan and Lor Chandara. 'PM Faces Up To Criticism From F'pec', *The Cambodia Daily*, 5 December 2002.

69. Lor Chandara. 'Funcinpec You Hockry No Longer an Issue', *The Cambodia Daily*, 26 August 2002.

70. Heder, 'Political Theatre in the 2003 Cambodian Elections', p. 170.

71. Author's interview with an F'pec parliamentary candidate. Phnom Penh, June 2003.

72. Lor Chandara. 'Key F'pec Official to Leave Politics for NGO', *The Cambodia Daily*, 10 October 2002.

leadership style, joining the ranks of F'pec, as individuals weighed up their options as the campaign approached.

It was against this backdrop of self-interested elite political manoeuvrings that the three main parties prepared for the official 2003 campaign, starting June 26 and ending July 25. In the weeks before the campaign, senior F'pec officials, in an effort to distance themselves from Hun Sen, had become more critical of CPP performance. This triggered familiar patterns and themes as party leaders traded insults and recriminations, especially surrounding the events of the 1997 coup. Party leaders focused on tried and tested campaign styles. Again the CPP rhetoric relied on the role it played in the removal of the Khmer Rouge and its subsequent record in securing peace and stability for the development of infrastructure projects, schools and hospitals. F'pec typically drew on royalist credentials and highlighted the lack of substance and corrupt underpinnings of CPP's claims to development. Sam Rainsy's appeals to social justice and promises of improvements in working conditions for civil servants were marred by yet more toxic anti-Vietnamese rhetoric. Ranariddh too engaged in anti-Vietnamese sentiment with oblique references to immigration and territorial issues as they related to Vietnam.

Serious and realistic elaborations of how to achieve stated policy goals and promises were virtually absent from all party political platforms. Nevertheless, most observers did concur that the campaigning was an improvement on the past.[73] For the first time, for example, under the auspices of the NDI, televised debates took place between senior party members, and local NGOs organized similar events. Such positive improvements in campaigning were however overshadowed by a significant uptick in election violations, intimidation and extensive vote buying, and a 'massive increase' in the numbers of civil servants illegally engaged in campaign activities, seriously compromising the previously stated principle of neutrality.[74] While all parties engaged in ambiguous and euphemistic 'gift giving', the CPP with more resources and money was by far the more active and effective in offering incentives and inducements to secure votes.[75]

---

73. UNCOHCHR, 'The 2003 National Assembly Elections', December 2003, p. 4.

74. EUEOM, 'Final Report on the [2003] Elections', p. 24.

75. UNCOHCHR, 'The 2003 National Assembly Elections', p. 4.

Polling, Counting and Results

With the exception of minor incidents and violations, all national and international observers reported satisfactory and relatively trouble-free polling and counting processes.[76] According to organizations like COMFREL voter turnout was nonetheless disturbingly low when compared to previous elections. Based on their figures, only 87.25 per cent of a possible 6.09 million, or if the 4 per cent 'ghost voters' found by COMFREL on the voter lists are included, 6.34 million registered voters, cast ballots. Questions were asked about why more than a million eligible voters didn't vote, particularly as up to 400,000 were unable to register. Voter apathy, poor weather conditions and logistical problems are all plausible reasons to explain these anomalies. However, according to COMFREL, they can't be 'differentiated from sinister ones' such as violence, intimidation and manipulation of the voter lists and polling.[77]

Indeed, at first glance, the actual distribution of votes among the parties suggests the elections were reasonably competitive. The CPP received 47.3 per cent of the popular vote, which converted into 73 seats in the National Assembly. F'pec received 20.75 per cent of the popular vote and 26 seats. The SRP won more of the popular vote than F'pec, with 21.87 per cent, but because of the seat allocation system, received two seats less, with 24. The remaining votes were distributed among the twenty smaller parties that took part, but none of them won any seats. Factors like political violence, intimidation, partiality of election authorities, inaccurate voter lists, misuse of state resources and biased media access combined to create an environment where competition was undoubtedly restricted, undermined and compromised in favour of the CPP.

Under these circumstances, it was hardly surprising when the SRP and F'pec immediately rejected the results, precipitating another seemingly interminable political standoff that would last almost a year before a new government was finally formed in June 2004. On the day after state television announced incomplete results on July 29, Sam Rainsy and F'pec's Prince Sirivudh held a press conference publicly rejecting them, claiming them to be 'a ploy to have the doctored numbers

76. EUEOM, 'Final Report on the [2003] Elections', p. 28.
77. COMFREL, 'Assessment Report on the Cambodian National Assembly Elections 2003', p. 6.

rubber-stamped by the NEC'.[78] Not long after Rainsy and Ranariddh announced the formation of the 'Alliance of Democrats', refusing to form a coalition with Hun Sen as Prime Minister. On August 8 the NEC announced the official preliminary results, allowing the SRP and F'pec to register their complaints. On the same day, F'pec lodged a complaint with the Constitutional Council accusing the NEC of 'failing to implement its duties, of bias, incompetence and irresponsibility' in such a way that it contradicted the 'voters' will'.[79] In a separate complaint it accused the NEC of not 'having conducted the electoral process according to the Law and Regulations'. The SRP contested the results countrywide and demanded recounts in several areas, including a re-vote in the town of Poipet in Banteay Meanchey province, where over 45 per cent of registered voters failed to turn out.

All of the complaints submitted to the Constitutional Council by F'pec and the SRP were dismissed in a manner that COMFREL felt raised 'important and serious issues about the procedure and judgement'.[80] F'pec's complaint of NEC bias and incompetence was dismissed by the CC on the grounds that 'the case was not within its competence'. Given that the CC was the final arbiter in election disputes and complaints, the ruling was the clearest indication that it lacked the power and political will to conduct a proper investigation into complaints. After a final hearing on August 27, the SRP held a press conference where it described the CC's behaviour as farcical. At the same time, it stated that it would not be staging demonstrations as expected, opting instead to 'strengthen the alliance' with F'pec in the hope of removing Hun Sen through political pressure over time.[81]

Democratic Progress or Authoritarian Consolidation: Final Assessments

Unlike in 2002, the EUEOM in its final 2003 report avoided making reference to the elections marking 'progress in the consolidation of

---

78. Luke Reynolds and Yim Samean, 'Parties Band Together Against CPP results', *The Cambodia Daily*, 30 July 2003.

79. COMFREL, 'Assessment Report on the Cambodian National Assembly Elections 2003', p. 31.

80. Ibid.

81. EUEOM, 'Final Report on the [2003] Elections', p. 40.

democracy in Cambodia'. Instead it described the 2003 event as having been well conducted 'but there was still a long way to go to full democracy'.[82] Statements like this are fully in accord with some of the basic tenets of liberal democratic governance, which hold that it is a process for the long term. In one way or another, almost all of the principal international and national observer group assessments implicitly or explicitly reflected this reality. Three international observer groups, the US Long Term Observer Group (LTOG) managed by 'The Asia Foundation', the Asian-based EMO ANFREL and the EU deployed long-term observers in the months before the elections. LTOG deployed 15 observers in the provinces from May until August. ANFREL had 10 long-term observers trained by the Asia Foundation from May until July, and the EU deployed 37 observers in teams of two in eighteen provinces from June until the end of August.[83] The USAID-funded International Republican Institute (IRI) conducted three extensive pre-election assessment missions in January, April and June, as did the NDI.[84] All of these groups also deployed short-term observers to monitor polling and counting. UNDP and the UN Human Rights Office by virtue of their mandates monitored the process from start to finish. COMFREL, the largest of the Cambodian EMOs, had well-established and extensive networks at the national, provincial, district and commune levels. They had trained and deployed 1,800 long-term and 15,000 short-term observers covering almost every polling station.[85]

Final assessments produced by the various observers groups differed in style and emphasis, but all covered to greater or lesser degrees the problems and obstacles that compromised the overall integrity of the elections. As major donors and partners of the RGC, the EU and UNDP

---

82. Ibid., Executive Summary.

83. Tim Meisburger, 'Summary of Observations of the US Long term Observer Group (LTOG) During the 2003 Cambodian Elections', September 2003, p. 14.

84. International Republican Institute, 'Cambodia 2003 National Assembly Elections', available at http://www.iri.org/sites/default/files/Cambodia's%202003%20National%20Assembly%20Elections.pdf. Statement of the NDI pre-Election Delegation to Cambodia's 2003 National Assembly Elections. Phnom Penh, 5 June 2003, available at https://www.ndi.org/files/1594_kh_statement_060503.pdf.

85. COMFREL, 'Assessment Report on the Cambodian National Assembly Elections 2003', p. 39.

lauded procedural improvements and the NEC's overall performance. In stark contrast, the US LTOG recommended that 'responsibility for election adjudication should be removed from the NEC into the hands ... of an independent multi-party body'. In addition, it stated that the predominantly CPP make-up of the election committees crippled the complaints system and significantly decreased the overall credibility of the elections process.[86] IRI and NDI assessments concurred that despite improvements, the overall process and environment was critically flawed.[87]

COMFREL's final analysis differed significantly from other assessments in that it raised the issue of the 'split in international opinion' between those in the EU, Japan and Australia, among others, who felt the elections, despite the problems, were 'fair enough', marking progress in democratic development, and those like the US LTOG who felt the they were 'fundamentally flawed'. COMFREL concluded that the elections did not meet what they described as international standards for freedom and fairness.[88] Establishing whether or not the elections were free and fair, or just 'fair enough', missed the point. It is self-evident that political violence, intimidation, coercion, biased election authorities and abuse of state resources, among other election-related crimes and violations of the law, are neither free nor fair and don't represent democratic progress. The fact that these un-democratic practices had to greater or lesser degrees consistently been part of Cambodian elections since 1993 clearly showed that the democratic impulse alluded to in international assessments was being suppressed and contained. Far from marking democratic progress, the evidence showed that elections were used as instruments by the CPP to consolidate authoritarian power and control in ways that satisfied minimal acceptable criteria for international legitimacy, that is, political stability and flawed competitive elections.

It is misleading therefore to think that because significant numbers of the electorate voted for parties other than the CPP that the elections

---

86. Meisburger, 'Summary of Observations of the US Long term Observer Group', pp. 16–19.

87. IRI, 'Cambodia 2003 National Assembly Elections'; NDI, 'Pre-election Delegation to Cambodia's 2003 National Assembly Elections'.

88. COMFREL, 'Assessment Report on the Cambodian National Assembly Elections 2003', pp. 40–41.

were truly competitive and the outcome uncertain. The elections were competitive, but because of the identified problems were not competitive enough to allow the opposition a realistic chance of winning. It is a false compromise therefore to state that democratic progress is made when the assumed democratic tendencies are suppressed by authoritarian forces. However, in the case of the 2003 elections, an argument for moderation or choosing the middle ground may be desirable and expedient if it furthers the interests of those taking such a position. But in doing so, it serves to further constrain and delay democratic development. Indeed, in the context of a liberal democratic governance project, this in all likelihood is intentional until circumstances are such that vested political-economic interests are not threatened or destabilized. From its point of view, the EU was probably correct in stating that Cambodia 'has a long way to go to full democracy'. In the final analysis, the 2003 elections were the culmination of a ten years effort by the CPP to take control and manage elections, thus preventing a repeat of the 1993 results. One senior CPP official triumphantly summed up the situation just after the 2002 commune elections when he said that 'in 1993 we didn't know how to manage elections, now we know exactly what we are doing.'[89]

Post-Election End Game?

Manipulation and control of internationally supported elections is, however, only one part of the political drama, albeit a major one. It took just over eleven months of political elite manoeuvring, negotiation and intrigue before a new government was finally formed in July 2004. The SRP-F'pec 'Alliance of Democrats' (AD) refused to enter into government with the CPP until their demands were met. Negotiations brokered by Sihanouk towards the end of 2003 included the idea of a tripartite coalition, something to which Hun Sen initially agreed. AD demands for electoral, judicial and anti-corruption reforms as well as a shake-up of village-level administration and key senior government, military and police positions were seen as unrealistic. In essence, the reforms threatened to undermine the very foundations upon which Hun Sen's power and influence had been built and consolidated. As time wore on and the AD position became more entrenched, Hun Sen later backed

---

89. Interview with Author. Ministry of Information. April 2002. Phnom Penh.

away from the idea, fearing his marginalization or even neutralization within a coalition he could no longer manipulate and control.

In response, he reverted to the concept of a CPP–F'pec coalition without the direct involvement of the SRP. Matters were further complicated for Hun Sen when behind the scenes intimations that the Chea Sim faction was predisposed towards the tripartite framework and reform reignited old rumours of divisions within the CPP. [90] Faced with challenges from all sides, Hun Sen and his supporters worked hard to exploit weaknesses within the AD and manage dissent within his party. A turning point was reached in March 2004 when it emerged that a 'secret meeting' had taken place in Bangkok between Ranariddh, the Thai Defence Minister, Chaovalit Yongjaiut, and the Cambodian business tycoon Ly Yung Phat, who was acting on Hun Sen's behalf. Hun Sen and Ranariddh 'agreed by telephone to a 60-40 split of "commissions" on government business deals between CPP and F'pec'.[91] At a further meeting on March 15, Hun Sen and Ranariddh agreed on another CPP–F'pec coalition without consulting their parties but with the possibility of allocating F'pec posts to the SRP.

With Sihanouk's idea of a three-way coalition dead in the water, negotiations between Ranariddh and Hun Sen over the distribution of power within the new government trundled along into June amidst accusations of horse-trading and the buying of positions.[92] This was followed by a series of dramatic events when, at the end of June, Ranariddh and Hun Sen agreed on the composition of the government and a hugely controversial 'package vote' to install it. To accommodate competing demands from factions within both parties, the government bureaucracy was doubled in size, to include five deputy prime ministers and numerous new secretaries and under-secretaries of state. The 'package vote' demanded by Hun Sen was intended to remove any uncertainty that he and Ranariddh would retain their positions as Prime Minister and President of the National Assembly respectively. Under the arrangements at the time, the President and Vice-Presidents of the

---

90. See for example Steve Heder, 'Hun Sen's Consolidation: Death or Beginning of Reform', *Southeast Asian Affairs 2005*, pp. 113–30.

91. Ibid., p. 118.

92. Yun Samean and Lor Chandara, 'Hun Sen Says Some Are Trying to Buy Positions', *The Cambodia Daily*, 18 May 2004.

National Assembly were installed through a separate two - thirds vote majority of parliamentarians. They then put forward a nominee for the position of Prime Minister for approval by the King.

The drama intensified on July 6 when Sihanouk, frustrated and angry about the package vote, announced his intention to abdicate once the new assembly had been approved. In response to the uproar surrounding the illegality of the package procedure, an 'Additional Constitutional Law' was approved by the National Assembly on July 8 allowing it to proceed. Ranariddh's accommodation of Hun Sen's demands for a package vote was enough to convince many within F'pec and the SRP that the AD reform agenda had for all intents and purposes been dropped. Rumours immediately began to circulate that Hun Sen had bribed Ranariddh with fabulous sums of money and lavish gifts including an aircraft.[93]

In a further twist in the drama, Sihanouk, now overseas, refused to approve the new law as required by the constitution, leaving it instead to Chea Sim as President of the Senate and acting Head of State in the King's absence to act according to his 'conscience'. Chea Sim refused to do so. Hun Sen, suspecting a plot, met with senior CPP leaders and insisted that Chea Sim leave the country, which would allow the F'pec Vice-President of the Senate Nhek Bun Chhay to act as Head of State in his absence. On July 13, with Chea Sim showing reluctance to go overseas, Hun Sen's security forces surrounded his Phnom Penh residence, and he was told his life could be in danger.[94] He was then escorted to the airport and put on a plane for Bangkok ostensibly for medical treatment. Nhek Bun Chhay signed the bill into law. To manage the anger and dissent within the parties and to eliminate uncertainty, Hun Sen insisted that the assembly vote with a show of hands rather than the customary secret ballot. Two days later on July 15 the assembly approved the new deal; Hun Sen became Prime Minister with a new mandate, and Ranariddh the President of the National Assembly.

With Ranariddh's complicity, Hun Sen had once again skilfully out-manoeuvred opponents and effectively silenced his detractors outside and inside his party. Combined with Nhek Bun Chhay's role in ratifying

---

93. Yun Samean. 'Gov't Returns Plane Once Owned by Ranariddh', *The Cambodia Daily*, 12 July 2004. See also Heder, 'Hun Sen's Consolidation', p. 119.

94. Heder, 'Hun Sen's Consolidation', p. 120.

the constitutional law allowing the package vote to go through the Assembly, Ranariddh's acquiescence to Hun Sen marked the beginning of the end for F'pec as a credible force in Cambodian politics. Having boycotted the Assembly vote, the 24 SRP parliamentarians were left virtually without power and influence within the new assembly. Hun Sen's power and control appeared almost complete and unassailable. At the end of July, speaking about the outcome of events, Sihanouk said the country was "'overwhelmed" by a national division, an extremely serious political crisis which will in the days and months to come worsen more'.[95] Less than three months later he finally abdicated, but not before he succeeded in having his preferred successor, his son and Ranariddh's half-brother, Prince Sihamoni formally named as the new monarch.

At least on the surface, Sihanouk's pessimistic prognosis was outdone by impressive economic growth figures. CPP victories in the commune elections and the formation of the new government in 2004 had given a boost to foreign investor confidence. Cambodia's relationship with China was going from strength to strength as massive Chinese investment and aid began to have an impact. In spite of past government performance, western donors fully endorsed the new coalition arrangements and seemed content to continue with liberal governance and development projects as before. Below the surface, however, discontent with inequalities of wealth and increased landlessness was growing. Large Economic Land Concessions (ELC) sold to foreign investors and their Cambodian tycoon partners were leaving increasing numbers of rural dwellers dispossessed and angry. Protests and demonstrations by garment workers demanding better pay and conditions continued to be frequent events in Phnom Penh. Further local elections were scheduled for 2007 followed by the next round of parliamentary elections in 2008. After the 2002 and 2003 polls, it was doubtful that ordinary people's grievances would be heard in a meaningful way in future elections. Against the odds, civil groups and EMOs together with the SRP would nonetheless continue with the struggle to establish a freer and fairer electoral system.

---

95. Lor Chandara and Wendy Leung. 'King: Cambodia Democracy is in Trouble', *The Cambodia Daily*, 28 July 2004.

CHAPTER 8

Electoral Development 2004–08

*T*he coalition deal struck between Ranariddh and Hun Sen in 2004 marked the end of more than a decade of struggle for control and management of internationally supported elections. Hun Sen had again shown donors and political opponents his superior skills and determination in manipulating electoral politics before, during and after the vote. With F'pec playing another a weak and subordinate role within another weak and submissive coalition, and the SRP apparently isolated in the National Assembly, the possibility of truly competitive commune and parliamentary elections in 2007 and 2008 seemed remote. Hun Sen and CPP power were virtually absolute. Overwhelming victories in both those elections seemed to confirm the status quo. Against a backdrop of accelerating socio-economic change, political elite behaviour in the run up to the 2008 elections continued in familiar ways but produced some profound and far-reaching changes. Ranariddh's final capitulation to the might of Hun Sen finished F'pec as a credible political force.

Results from the 2007 commune and 2008 National Assembly elections reflected these political realities. In 2007, the CPP won 61 per cent of the commune vote compared with the 25 per cent won by the SRP. F'pec competed in the elections without Ranariddh, who was effectively removed from his position, resigning as president in 2006. Continuing its downward electoral spiral, F'pec won only 5 per cent of the vote. After leaving F'pec, Ranariddh created and led the Norodom Ranariddh Party (NRP), winning 8 per cent of the total vote in 2007. Only 30 out of the 1,621 commune chief positions were held by members of parties other than the CPP; 28 from the SRP and 2 from F'pec.[1] In the 2008 parliamentary elections, the CPP recorded its biggest ever win, securing 90 seats in the National Assembly. The SRP did not increase its share

---

1.   COMFREL, 'Final Assessment and Report on the 2007 Commune Council Elections', Phnom Penh, 2007, p. 5.

of the vote from 2003, but did increase its number of seats by 2, to a total of 26. F'pec plummeted further, winning only two seats, the same number as the NRP. Another newly formed political grouping, the Human Rights Party (HRP) led by former senior F'pec senator Kem Sokha, won three seats.[2] The two thirds majority electoral formula used in previous national elections was replaced with a '50 plus one system' via constitutional amendment in 2006. This change intended to reduce the number of parliamentary seats required by one party with a majority to form a government alone, thereby preventing lengthy and damaging post-election stand-offs.

Given these landslide victories it seemed that the power of authoritarian elections had been consolidated by the CPP. National and international observer reports recorded similar problems to those that had plagued previous elections.[3] There was a sense that Cambodian elections were becoming increasingly meaningless, subjected as they were to the power of Hun Sen and the CPP. Understanding and explaining outcomes, however, was not as straightforward as the results of the elections seemed to suggest. Preparations for the elections took place alongside accelerating socio-economic changes underway since the early 1990s. Between 2004 and 2008, Cambodia experienced a period of rapid and sustained economic growth that was transforming state–society relations in complex and uncertain ways. A large percentage of the population were under the age of twenty-five, with no personal experience or memories of the Khmer Rouge, and little or no memory of UNTAC. An increasingly aspirational and youthful population brought with it its own unique challenges in terms of employment, education and political representation.[4]

Renewed pressure on the government from established international donors for institutional reform in the wake of the formation of the new

2. COMFREL, 'Final Assessment and Report on the 2008 National Assembly Elections', Phnom Penh, 2008, p. 64.

3. COMFREL, 'Final Assessment and Report on the 2007 Commune Council Elections'. See also COMFREL, 'Final Assessment and Report on the 2008 National Assembly Elections', and EU Election Observer Mission (EUEOM), 'Final Report, National Assembly Elections, 27 July', Phnom Penh, 13 October 2008.

4. UNDP Country Team 'Situational Analysis of Youth in Cambodia', May, Phnom Penh, p. 13.

coalition was mitigated by increasing Chinese influence in Cambodian affairs. The Chinese had less to say about democratic governance within the kingdom than did the longer established western donors and their allies in ASEAN.[5] Donors through the UNDP nonetheless remained committed to the financial and technical support of the elections. Moreover, the abdication of Sihanouk and the coronation of his son Norodom Sihamoni as the new King, together with the probability of internationally backed tribunals to prosecute surviving members of the Khmer Rouge for war crimes and crimes against humanity, epitomized a general feeling that Cambodia was – for better or worse – moving into a new era.

The social and political effects of these changes were very much unpredictable and highly uncertain as the new coalition moved forward. That said, as events unfolded after July 2004, it became increasingly likely that the outcome of the elections in 2007 and 2008 would be a foregone conclusion. Regardless of the possible outcome, elections remained at the forefront of the struggle between the Hun Sen regime and its opponents for control over the future trajectory of the country's development. Civil society groups, EMOs and their international supporters remained steadfast in their efforts to improve the quality of the process at all stages of the electoral cycle. They were motivated in their belief that despite their authoritarian character elections would continue to play an indispensable role in future political development.

Economic Growth and Elections

It was within the contexts of Hun Sen's political supremacy and of accelerating socio-economic change that preparations for the next round of commune and national elections took place. Economically, it was a period of impressive rates of growth and increased wealth accumulation for the patronage networks of business tycoons, military, police, ministers and local officials revolving around Hun Sen and his party loyalists. Recent statistics show that between 1999 and 2008 the economy grew on average by 9.1 per cent per annum. As elsewhere, because of the global economic crisis, economic growth slowed to 0.1

---

5. See for example, M. Sullivan, 'China's aid to Cambodia', in C. Hughes and K. Un (eds), *Cambodia's Economic Transformation*, Copenhagen: NIAS Press, 2011, Chapter 3.

per cent in 2009, recovering to 5 per cent in 2010, and has been growing steadily since.[6] This growth has been driven principally by expansion in the garment, manufacturing and tourism sectors, and to a lesser extent in construction and agriculture. At the time, the political implications of rapid socio-economic change were difficult to gauge. As far as elections were concerned, much would depend upon perceptions among voters of the underlying distribution of political–economic power, and the behaviour of the political elite and associated patronage networks.

In this sense, the sources of economic growth, wealth accumulation and distribution of benefits were key factors. Impressive macro-economic growth could be attributed to a variety of factors, not least of which was the outcome of the military and political struggles from July 1997 onwards, culminating in the consolidation of Hun Sen power via the previous three elections. Stabilization of the general security situation after the dissolution of the Khmer Rouge in 1999 created conditions that attracted increasing numbers of foreign visitors and investors, mainly tourists and associated service industries and garment manufacturers. Such was the level of activity in these sectors that by the early 2000s Cambodia was said to be moving through the post-conflict phase in its development toward a period of economic transformation.[7] According to this analysis, relative political stability and security was manifest in an expansion of economic activity which was qualitatively different from the economy that had shored up and maintained post-conflict CPP patronage networks within the formal state structure in the 1990s.

As the political-economic situation evolved in the early 2000s, these existing patronage networks began adjusting to the new conditions. Political elite accommodation in the lead up to and after 1998 led to the reintegration of remaining factions of all armed forces, ostensibly under the centralized control of Hun Sen. This in turn impacted upon the ways in which the patronage networks made up of military personnel, state officials and entrepreneurs engaged in profiteering from state and natural rural resources, especially illegal logging. Since the 1980s, and

---

6. Saing Chan Hang, 'Binding Constraints on Economic Growth in Cambodia: A Growth Diagnostics Approach'. Cambodian Development Resource Institute (CDRI), Working Paper Series, No. 80, Phnom Penh, 2013, Executive Summary, vii.

7. Hughes and Un, *Cambodia's Economic Transformation*, Chapter 1.

into the 1990s, control of the immensely profitable trade in 'conflict resources' like timber had been highly decentralized. As political power began to accrue in the hands of Hun Sen and the CPP, and as the negative social and environmental impacts that illegal logging was having drew international attention, the situation began to change.

International organizations like Global Witness began to highlight social and environmental devastation caused by the illegal extraction of natural resources like timber, and placed the issues firmly in the international media spotlight.[8] Some estimates suggest that the value of timber exported from Cambodia from the signing of the peace accords to the late 1990s amounted to about USD 2.5 billion, of which only 5 per cent found its way into state coffers. Analysts refer to this as a period of 'anarchic logging', indicative of the lack of formalized central state control of 'peripheral' forested areas and associated illicit revenues.[9]

In response to international and donor pressure, in 1998 Hun Sen pledged to tackle the problem of decentralized and 'anarchic logging'. The subsequent introduction of a concession system to regulate logging activities ultimately failed to curb the excesses of concessionaires, leading to the suspension of the concessions and all logging in 2001.[10] In the same year, the government introduced an amended land law followed by a forestry law in 2002. This reinforced control of land for economic purposes including logging and the extraction of revenues from forests and protected conservation areas.

Rather than regulate and formalize the use of land and natural resources, the promulgation of land and forestry laws – thus centralizing government control of 'state public land' – created new opportunities for patronage networks to extract revenues, profits and rents for personal gain at the expense of the national coffers. Large-scale illegal logging has therefore continued up to present times, but under the tighter

---

8. See Global Witness Cambodia, http://www.globalwitness.org/campaigns/corruption/oil-gas-and-mining/cambodia.

9. See for example P. Le Billion and S. Springer, 'Between War and Peace: Violence and accommodation in the Cambodian logging sector', cited in S. Milne and S. Mahanty (eds), *Conservation and Development in Cambodia: Exploring frontiers of change in nature, state and society.* London: Routledge, 2015.

10. See for example S. Milne, K. Pak and M. Sullivan, 'Shackled to nature? The post-conflict state and its symbiotic relationship with natural resources', cited in Milne and Mahanty, *Conservation and Development in Cambodia.*

centralized control of the Hun Sen regime. Based on evidence gathered between 2004–07 and published in an explosive report entitled 'Family Trees', Global Witness revealed that the illegal logging was continuing and involved military personnel, the police and Forestry Administration officials. The report charged that the 'most powerful logging syndicate is led by relatives of Prime Minister Hun Sen and other senior officials'.[11] Furthermore, recent research suggests that the extraction of luxury rosewood in the early 2000s, to satisfy increased demand from places like China, netted windfall profits for elites and government officials with direct links to the Prime Minister that 'arguably match or exceed those of the 1990s'.[12]

Scandalous revelations concerning illegal logging in the early 2000s overshadowed the transformation of the Cambodian economy as political elites and patronage networks began to diversify their economic interests. Official moratoria stopping logging and the transport of logs in 2002 were accompanied by a significant rise in government-granted 'Economic Land Concessions' (ELCs), some of which were used to circumvent logging bans because they allow forested areas to be cleared for agribusiness purposes. Since the enactment of the 2001 land law, the granting and management of ELCs by the government have been a major source of rural and urban discontent, with ELCs at the center of an exponential rise in the number of land disputes and conflicts as concessionaires encroach upon or 'grab' land, negatively affecting livelihoods of rural and urban communities. Other types of concessions involving land for commercial uses such as industry, residential, tourism and mining have also been a source of serious and violent disputes and protests in recent years.

National and international human rights groups and civil organizations have recorded in detail the negative social and environmental impacts ELCs and land concessions have been having over the last two decades. Successive UN Secretary General special representatives and special rapporteurs in particular have produced in-depth reports

---

11. Global Witness, 'Cambodia's Family Trees: Illegal logging and the stripping of public assets by Cambodia's elite'. Washington D.C., June 2007.

12. See S. Milne, 'Cambodia's Unofficial Regime of Extraction: Illicit Logging in the Shadow of International Governance', *Critical Asian Studies*, Vol. 47, No. 2, 2015, pp. 200–18.

analysing the plight of affected communities and government responses. Problems encountered are familiar ones. There is a general lack of
accountability and transparency on behalf of government officials and
concessionaires when granting and managing concessions, many of
whom operate behind 'a veil of secrecy'.[13] Perfectly good existing laws are
not enforced, or when they are, it is to the advantage of the concessionaires. Affected communities are often denied their rights and forcibly
evicted from their land with inadequate or no compensation. Planned
relocation schemes are often poorly organized and inappropriate for
the needs of the affected communities. Protests and resistance by such
affected communities and individuals are frequently met with violence
involving local police or military connected with the companies and
concessionaires. Many of the larger concessionaires are members of the
Senate or have direct relations with senior ministry officials, rendering
protesters virtually powerless in the face of state backed power.

Socio-Economic Change: Who Benefits?

The question of who the beneficiaries of the ongoing socio-economic
transformation are is profoundly political in nature and bound up with
perceptions and interpretations of Cambodia's recent past. As one might
expect given recent history, the Hun Sen regime perceives and interprets
historical narratives in fundamentally different ways to its opponents and
detractors. The annual January 7 celebrations in Phnom Penh to mark
the current leadership's role in the removal of the Khmer Rouge from
power in 1979 are a potent expression of the CPP's claim to legitimate
authority. According to this narrative, it is the CPP under the leadership
of the 'strongman' Hun Sen that, in the interests of national survival, has
successfully fought off all challengers to ensure the necessary political
stability and security with which Cambodia could emerge from the past
and prosper. Despite these claims, national elections results prior to
2008 consistently produced more votes for opposition parties, strongly

---

13. Report of the Special Rapporteur on the Situation of Human Rights in Cambodia,
Surya, P. Subedi, 'A Human Rights Analysis of economic and other land con-
cessions in Cambodia'. September 2012, Summary p 3. See also previous UN
Human Rights Office Cambodia thematic reports focused on land concessions,
2004, 2007 at http://cambodia.ohchr.org/EN/PagesFiles/Reports/Thematic-
Reports.htm.

suggesting that this narrative has not been accepted wholesale by the electorate.

As compelling as the narrative might be to some, maintaining legitimate claims to authority remains a central concern for the CPP. Competing narratives that challenge CPP discourses persist. In its favour, the party's emergence as the most powerful political force means it has benefited enormously from the economic changes since the early 2000s. Aside from the evident and vast personal wealth accrued by individuals within the party and its patronage networks, the economic boom has to some extent reinforced dominant CPP historical narratives within the body-politic as general improvements began to be felt around the country. At the same time, the extent to which these improvements and benefits could be directly attributed to state-led development policies is highly questionable. Taking political credit for socio-economic improvements by virtue of control of the state is something the CPP has the monopoly on whether or not this reflects an actual reality.

Economic growth after political stabilization did bring about some socio-economic benefits for the general population in the period 2004–08. After almost a decade of limited developmental achievements and delays since the 1993 elections, due mostly to political infighting, there were signs of positive change. Most visible and much welcomed was the gradual improvement in physical infrastructure such as roads and transport links. After years of neglect, Cambodia's notoriously bad road system underwent an overhaul. Main roads in Phnom Penh and other provincial towns began to be upgraded and repaired. Outside of the capital, funding for major infrastructural projects began to flood into the country. Much of this came from foreign donors like the Asian Development Bank (ADB), Japan, Korea and increasingly China. In this regard, Cambodia benefits from membership of the Greater Mekong Sub-Region (GMS), an economic cooperation initiative established in 1992 between the mainland Southeast Asian countries of Cambodia, Laos, Thailand, Vietnam and Myanmar, and the south-western Chinese province of Yunnan and the Guangxi Zhuang autonomous region, supported by the ADB.

Economic activity within the GMS and infrastructural developments such as improved road and transport links opened up the country to regional and international markets. Benefits in terms of access to markets and employment opportunities, reduced journey times and easier movement of people, goods and services began to be felt relatively quickly. But because of the narrow base of economic growth and the worsening situation regarding management of ELCs and 'other' land concessions, the overall impact on income and consumption levels within the general population were yet to be felt. A 2004 UNDP study of macro-economic growth and policies on poverty levels stated that economic growth in the previous decade had 'not produced any significant poverty reduction' and that there were signs that in some areas it was getting worse.[14] Using the Human Development Index (HDI), the report noted that despite a decade of growth, Cambodia was ranked 130 out of 175 countries.[15] This included actual declines in per-capita consumption levels, 'fewer public health facilities, rising child mortality, poor education outcomes and rural underemployment'. Of particular concern was the rise in inequality between rural and urban areas. In fact, according to the report, most of the economic growth had been confined to 'urban enclaves', while 'rural growth had barely kept pace with the increase in population'.[16]

International Pressure to Reform?

Since foreign aid for reconstruction and development started to flow into the country in 1992–93 overall poverty reduction and reform efforts had fallen short of expectations. This situation prompted donors like the World Bank to take a more rigorous approach to the issues in its dealings with the Cambodian government. Previous donor approaches including the introduction of performance benchmarks intended to help push the government down the path of reform had by 2004 been largely ineffective. As the new coalition government took up its duties, and just before the December Consultative Group (CG) meeting to decide aid and assistance, the government unveiled its flagship reform package, the 'Rectangular Strategy for Growth, Employment, Equity and Efficiency'.

---

14. Melanie Beresford, Nguon Sokha, Rathin Roy, Sau Sisovanna and Ceema Namazie, 'The Macroeconomics of Poverty Reduction in Cambodia', United Nations Development Programme, March 2004.

15. Ibid., p. 30.

16. Ibid., p. 14.

In a speech in July, the prime minister said that he was 'convinced that Cambodia has no choice but to continue to seriously implement comprehensive and deepening reform programs'.[17] At the centre of the strategy was a commitment to good governance, seen as an essential prerequisite for economic growth and development. Focusing upon government commitments to reform and good governance, the World Bank issued a detailed analysis of the key governance and reform challenges facing the Cambodian government in a report entitled 'Cambodia at the Crossroads'.[18] Because of previous government failures to follow through on its commitments to reform in key areas, the authors of the report were unequivocal in their belief that it would take much more than the policies set out in the 'Rectangular Strategy' 'to transform governance in Cambodia so that it is supportive of and not destructive of the development process'.[19] The tone of the report was pessimistic. Future equitable growth and poverty reduction were according to the report at risk if the government did not reverse previous governance failures.[20]

The report, issued a month before the CG meeting, was viewed by some commentators as amounting to the strongest stance taken yet by donors on the government's repeated failings when it came to implementing reforms. For others, it was nothing other than a re-hashing of previous approaches, whereby donors pledge what the government asks for in return for promises that are not kept.[21] At the December meeting donors pledged approximately US$500 million in aid disbursements.[22] Despite the negative prognosis, Cambodia's economy managed to survive and even flourish. Growth peaked at over 13 per cent in 2005, and with the exception of 2009 continued to grow at impressive rates. High rates of growth, however, could not be attributed to the enactment and

---

17. Cambodia New Vision, 'Address by Samdech Hun Sen on the "Rectangular Strategy" for Growth, Employment, Equity and Efficiency'. Unofficial Translation from the Khmer, http://cnv.org.kh/en/?p=446, accessed 13 May 2014.

18. World Bank, 'Cambodia at the Crossroads: Strengthening Accountability to Reduce Poverty', Phnom Penh 2004.

19. Ibid., para 3, p. 1.

20. Ibid.

21. Liam Cochrane, 'Government takes scolding, $500 million from donors', *Phnom Penh Post*, 17 December 2004.

22. Ibid.

implementation of good governance reforms. All indicators continue to show today that Cambodia's weak governance structures and worsening corruption are among the biggest obstacles to sustainable and equitable development.[23] Subsequent World Bank reports produced in 2006 and 2007 showed that despite some improvements in poverty reduction and HDIs, inequitable growth was increasing unabated.[24]

UNDP 'Strengthening Democracy and Electoral Processes'

Practical applications of donor ideas related to institutional reform and good governance continued to be channelled through the UNDP. If the government was not prepared to follow through on commitments to reform, then donor programmes to strengthen democracy and electoral processes might achieve results. However, like the World Bank and other donors, the UNDP had very little to say about the political-economic power structures that subvert and weaken the same processes they want to strengthen. The UNDP and its partners nonetheless continued to provide technical and financial support to the NEC, but with a shift in emphasis away from short-term support for one-time electoral events to a longer-term approach. Based upon a request by the RGC in February 2005, the UNDP committed to a 3 year $6.5 million project to strengthen 'democracy and electoral processes in Cambodia'. This multi-donor project was intended to support the NEC in the preparation of 'free, fair, transparent and sustainable elections, improve electoral legal frameworks and promote the development of a culture of democracy and civic participation'. In addition, it was ready to coordinate donor assistance for the 2007 and 2008 elections should the RGC make a request for additional support for these events.[25]

---

23. World Bank, 'The Fight Against Corruption' (2013), available at http://web.world-bank.org/WBSITE/EXTERNAL/COUNTRIES/EASTASIAPACIFICEXT/CAMBODIAEXTN/0,,contentMDK:21053665~pagePK:141137~piPK:141127~theSitePK:293856,00.html, accessed 13 May 2014.

24. See for example, World Bank, 'Cambodia's Sustaining Rapid Economic Growth in a Challenging Environment'. Report No 49156-KH, January 2009. See also Hughes and Un, *Cambodia's Economic Transformation*, pp. 12–15.

25. Royal Government of Cambodia and United Nations Development Programme 'Strengthening Democracy and Electoral Processes in Cambodia'. January, 2006, http://loy9.com.kh/wp-content/uploads/2014/01/A-project-on-strengthening-democracy.pdf.

The strategic long-term goals of the project were therefore designed to be different from the support the UNDP had provided in the past. Reflecting on previous experience, it concluded that while elections were important, they were not sufficient for the 'development and sustainability' of democracy in Cambodia in the long-term. A longer-term approach therefore would focus on broader initiatives moving beyond 'event-specific' processes 'to consolidate the democratic base of the country' in the period in between elections. Accordingly, this would involve increased civic participation and the inculcation of a democratic culture, 'using an appropriate combination of technical and policy advice, consultative processes, educational activities and media capacity building'.[26] As a necessary but insufficient condition for these long-term strategic goals, good elections, from this perspective, require four elements including: 'an electoral law fully tuned to provide a free and fair' process, 'an electoral commission which is truly autonomous and fearless', an administrative structure that ensures the franchise can be exercized freely and without fear, and 'an electorate which is fully aware of its rights and responsibilities'.[27]

Such a normative and comprehensive appraisal of democracy-promotion in Cambodia came with an important caveat revealing the UNDP's experience of operating within the parameters of existing power structures. As a note of caution, the UNDP stated that support would be reviewed if changes 'rendered' the NEC 'less, rather than more independent'. It somewhat vaguely added that the same would be the case for other components of the project if the feasibility of each was affected by future political decisions.[28] After close involvement in all of Cambodia's elections since 1993, the UNDP was fully cognizant of the political obstacles preventing the realization of the lofty ideals outlined in the project statement. By alluding to potential political problems, it drew attention to the fact that the four components it was promoting were the very same areas that had been consistently compromised and manipulated by elements within the CPP during each of the elections the UNDP had helped organize since 1993.

---

26. Ibid., p. 7.

27. Ibid.

28. Ibid.

Socio-Political Developments and Elections

The political and social realities related to economic transformation within which the UNDP intended 'to promote the development of a democratic culture and civic participation' after 2004 placed formidable obstacles in the way of those goals. Much like the World Bank and its failures to fully promote a neo-liberal governance reform agenda, the UNDP was not prepared, at least publicly, to tackle the politically volatile question of the nature of the regime established by Hun Sen and the CPP after the 1998 elections.[29] To do so in a meaningful way would likely destabilize the status quo, thereby jeopardizing the interests of neo-liberal proponents and development professionals.

The lengthy standoff before the new coalition was formed in 2004 showed the destabilizing effects that authoritarian, controlled elections can have. The negative socio-political consequences of rapid economic growth, the concentration of wealth in the hands of the few, the widening gap between rich and poor, the growing numbers of dispossessed and the depletion of natural resources and environmental degradation represented serious challenges to the regime and its supporters come election time. In addition, more young people were eligible to vote in 2007 and 2008 than before. It was estimated that more than 300,000 school leavers per year were entering the markets looking for too few jobs.

Continuing flows of donor aid and foreign direct investments were creating visible changes. New and improved roads opening up previously inaccessible parts of the country, a boom in construction, the appearance of the first automated bank teller machines in 2005, the proliferation of English language schools and other institutes of learning, all combined to give an impression that, despite ongoing problems, things were improving. Furthermore, Cambodia's huge development aid industry and NGO sector were bringing young Cambodians into contact with individuals and ideas from all over the world. Foreign volunteering in the NGO sector and overseas student exchange programmes were becoming big business. Young Cambodians were being exposed to and sharing snapshots of lives and experiences of citizens from other countries in the region and beyond, particularly the US, Australia and France. Families who had fled Cambodia and settled in these places in the 1970s and 80s were returning in greater numbers with resources, knowledge and

29. See Hughes and Un, *Cambodia's Economic Transformation*, p. 13.

skills, taking full advantage of and creating new business opportunities. Concomitant improvements in access to telecommunications and the availability of the Internet were connecting more people with the out- side world, laying the foundations for an explosion in the use of mobile social networking technologies and media among Cambodian youth. All of these factors combined to create a feeling of vibrancy, mostly con- centrated in Phnom Penh, that seemed to temporarily crowd out some of the more immediate and pressing socio-economic problems.

Understanding Elections 2007–08

After the final outcome of the 2003 national elections, there seemed little doubt that in the absence of substantive reform, CPP power and control was unlikely to be seriously challenged through the ballot box in 2007 and 2008. Results from the commune and national assembly elections indicated that the CPP had simultaneously managed growing discontent, especially among those impacted by economic concessions, as well as benefited from the general perception that the situation was politically stable enough to bring about improvements. In the face of continued opposition those electoral victories were not however necessarily straightforward. Much would still depend upon the CPP's response to continued discontent and opposition from the SRP and civil society groups pushing for reform of the system within the context of continued international financial and technical support. Rejection of the 2008 results by opposition parties and criticisms of the process from both national and international observers again displayed the nature of the political and economic system, and the role played by elections in its maintenance and reproduction.

Among the various explanations of the CPP's landslide victories were the weakness and disunity of the opposition. Political elite conduct in the run up to the elections resulted in dramatic and far-reaching changes to opposition party politics. The targeting of the SRP by Hun Sen with the collusion of Ranariddh, followed by the implosion of F'pec and culminating in Ranariddh's departure, were among the most dramatic.[30] Attacks against the SRP by coalition partners were provoked by Sam Rainsy's public allegations that Hun Sen had been directly involved in

---

30. See for example Heder, 'Hun Sen's Consolidation: Death or Beginning of Reform', pp. 113–10.

the killing in January 2004 of the prominent and popular trade union activist Chea Vichea. Hun Sen responded by issuing a defamation suit against Rainsy, who in turn responded with a countersuit, accusing Hun Sen of involvement in the hand grenade attack on the SRP protest rally in March 1997. Relations between the leaders deteriorated further amidst allegations that senior SRP officials had been secretly involved in creating a covert militant rebel force. Cheam Channy, in charge of the SRP's 'Committee 14', responsible for gathering information on military and security issues, was targeted by CPP intelligence for allegedly creating a 'secret army'.[31]

Rainsy later accused Ranariddh of receiving bribes from Hun Sen to form the new coalition with the CPP, causing F'pec to issue a defamation suit against him. Political elite shenanigans continued with more allegations against Rainsy for serious misconduct. F'pec and CPP parliamentarians sought the lifting of his parliamentary immunity and his prosecution for allegedly lying to the King in a letter about planned anti-royalist protests that were to be staged upon Sihanouk's return to Phnom Penh and blamed on the SRP.[32] According to Rainsy's accusers, the letter was responsible for hastening the King's decision to abdicate, a decision that for political purposes neither Hun Sen nor Ranariddh wanted at the time.[33] Matters came to a head in February 2003 when the National Assembly voted behind closed doors to lift the parliamentary immunity of three SRP officials, including Sam Rainsy, on grounds of criminal defamation, and Cheam Channy for his involvement in the organization of a secret militant force. Cheam Channy was subsequently arrested and sentenced to seven years' imprisonment in August. Sam Rainsy was later tried and found guilty in absentia, receiving an eighteen month prison sentence on two counts of criminal defamation.[34]

---

31. Ibid., p. 122.

32. Luke Reynolds and Lor Chandara, 'Rainsy Leaves Country After King's Abdication', *The Cambodia Daily*, 9 October 2004.

33. Sihanouk was fearful that a 'puppet king', perhaps Ranariddh, would replace him or a fully-fledged republic would be created under the dictatorship of Hun Sen. See Heder, 'Hun Sen's Consolidation: Death or Beginning of Reform', p. 122.

34. Report of the Special Representative of the Secretary General for Human Rights in Cambodia, Yash Gai. E/CN/4/2006/110/add.1, 8 March 2006, para 44.

Events in 2005 were indicative of a general trend begun after the formation of the new government to co-opt or eliminate any opposition to the coalition arrangements within the main parties. Control over submissive but suitably rewarded coalition partners would reduce further the future competiveness of elections to the advantage of Hun Sen and the CPP. Acceptance of the political-economic realities of the regime's control over access to wealth and connections to CPP business networks made it easier for SRP and F'pec defectors to acquiesce. Under these conditions, elections and the government positions they promised could be readily bought and sold in advance of the polls, rendering them virtually meaningless in a competitive sense. Recalcitrant and persistent critics of the coalition like Sam Rainsy, Cheam Channy and others were thus subjected to spurious legal actions.

Irrespective of these attacks, by early 2006 political elite relationships had moved into a new phase. Working relations between Hun Sen and Sam Rainsy seemed to improve as existing cracks in the F'pec–CPP coalition and within F'pec itself widened. As part of an apparent rapprochement with Hun Sen, in February Rainsy was granted a royal pardon allowing him to return to Cambodia without fear of arrest and imprisonment.[35] Shortly after his return, Rainsy met with Hun Sen when both leaders agreed upon a SRP proposal to amend the constitution to change the electoral formula, allowing future governments to be formed using a 50 per cent plus one seat formula instead of the existing two thirds majority.[36] The move, ostensibly meant to prevent any more lengthy post-election standoffs and reduce the bloated ranks of the bureaucracy, was met with mixed reactions from some SRP and F'pec members who viewed the amendment as yet another capitulation to the power of Hun Sen.[37] Certainly for Hun Sen, who was becoming increasingly frustrated with the behaviour and competence of F'pec officials within the coalition, the prospect of ruling without his troubled partner

---

35. Cheam Channy also received a pardon.

36. Yun Samean and Samantha Melamed, 'CPP, Rainsy Want Electoral Rule Change', *The Cambodia Daily*, 14 February 2006.

37. Yun Samean and Whitney Kvsanger, 'Assembly Expands Use of "50-Plus-One" Formula', *The Cambodia Daily*, 16 March 2006.

had its advantages.[38] By contrast, the amendment would potentially threaten Ranariddh's already weakened position further, both within the coalition and his own party, which could work to the electoral advantage of the SRP. Ultimately there was enough support within the National Assembly to pass the amendment into law in March.[39]

The proposed amendment came at a time when relations between Ranariddh and Hun Sen were deteriorating. With the real possibility of a change in the electoral formula, Hun Sen intensified his verbal personal attacks against Ranariddh and his party, citing alleged corruption, nepotism and undue influence of F'pec 'mistresses' in political affairs. On the eve of the vote for the amendment, Hun Sen dismissed F'pec veterans, co-Minister of Defence Nhek Bun Chhay and co-Minister of Interior and Deputy Prime Minister Prince Sirivudh, setting in motion a series of events that would see the eventual removal of Ranariddh from his position as President of the party. Nhek Bun Chhay and Sirivudh represented opposing veteran military and royalist factions within the party, both of which were able to allocate F'pec positions within the coalition. Sirivudh was criticized by veterans within the party of abusing his post for personal gain at the expense of some party veterans.[40] The following day, Ranariddh, beset by dissent within his own party and accusations of misconduct in his personal life, resigned as President of the National Assembly. Ranariddh's misfortunes continued when in October 2006 he was ignominiously removed as the President of the party he had led since 1992, and given the title 'Historic President'. That title was later retracted by the party leadership when Ranariddh announced his intention to register his own political party. In March 2007 he received in absentia an 18 month prison sentence for fraud, after becoming embroiled in a property scandal involving the former F'pec party headquarters. He remained in self-imposed exile in Malaysia before returning to Cambodia in September 2008, after his conviction

---

38. Yun Samean, 'PM Attacks Funcinpec in Speech', *The Cambodia Daily*, 15 February 2006.

39. Yun Samean, '"50-Plus-One" Amendment is Approved', *The Cambodia Daily*, 3 March 2006.

40. Heder, 'Hun Sen's Consolidation: Death or Beginning of Reform', p. 121.

was quashed by royal amnesty.[41] Shortly after his return, he took the decision to leave politics altogether.[42]

CPP, Elections and Project Largesse

CPP attempts to marginalize, neutralize or destroy opposition in between election events through overt pseudo-legal means or covert exploitation of party weaknesses was nothing new. The key difference in the 2004–08 period was that these efforts had succeeded in breaking up post-1993 patterns of political elite behaviour, forcing the opposition to seek alternative modes of engagement with the regime. The performance of opposition parties in the 2007 and 2008 elections reflected this reality. For the first time since 1993, the combined percentage of votes in National Assembly elections for the NRP, F'pec and SRP, including the newly formed Human Rights Party (HRP), was just over 17 per cent less than that of the CPP, which won just over 58 per cent of the vote.

CPP electoral victories in 2007–08 must be considered within the broader context of the socio-political economic conditions within which the elections took place. Demonstrable effects of Hun Sen's treatment of Ranariddh and Sam Rainsy after 2004 sent powerful messages to ordinary Cambodian voters. But public displays of Hun Sen's superiority vis-à-vis his opponents in F'pec and the SRP had not prevented large numbers of voters from supporting parties other than the CPP in the past. Government complicity in covering up high profile murders of politicians like F'pec's Om Radsady in 2003 and the trade union activists Chea Vichea and Ros Sovannarith in 2004, or Hy Vuthy in 2007,[43] reverberated with chilling effect. This however did nothing to stop politicians like Rainsy or activists and civic organizations from criticizing government abuses and inaction. Arrests and detentions of outspoken critics and human rights activists in 2005 and 2006 highlighted

---

41. Post Staff, 'Ranariddh returns, vows loyalty to govt', *Phnom Penh Post*, 29 September 2008.

42. Cat Barton and Vong Sokheng (2008) 'Ranariddh quits politics', *Phnom Penh Post*, 3 October.

43. Eang Mengleng and James Welsh, 'Eight Years On, Assassination of Union Leader Remains Unsolved', *The Cambodia Daily*, January 2012. See also Dan Poynton and Sam Rith, 'Another widow for the union movement', *Phnom Penh Post*, 9 March 2007.

the CPP's fear of the effects of widespread criticism on the electorate's perceptions of the party's image. Notable cases included the arrests at the end of 2005 of Mam Sonando, owner of the popular Beehive Radio station, and Rong Chhum, president of the Teachers Association, in connection with the government's controversial border agreement with Vietnam, signed by Hun Sen.[44] These were followed by the arrests of Kem Sokha, the then President of the Cambodian Center for Human Rights (CCHR) and Yeng Virak, Director of the Community Legal Education Center (CLEC), on similar charges.

To ensure electoral success, the CPP had to rely on more than just opposition disunity and the stifling of freedom of expression. Mobilization and misappropriation of state resources in the service of the CPP had long been a key element in the party's electoral victories since 1993. In 2008, national and international observer groups noted that the CPP's dominant, vigorous and well-funded election campaign was supported through the use of state resources.[45] COMFREL in particular reported an overall increase in the use of state resources, such as media, and the active participation of state employees such as civil servants, state officials and the armed forces in campaigning for the CPP by comparison with previous elections. In the months before the official campaign period, CPP officials were constantly featured on national television inaugurating local infrastructural projects including irrigation schemes, roads and new schools.[46]

As the party with control over access to the lions' share of resources and money, the CPP has always had a decisive financial edge over opponents come election time. Displays of CPP wealth and largesse during a period of sustained economic growth were thus of particular importance for delivering votes during the 2007 and 2008 electoral cycles. By investing in local infrastructure, the party portrayed itself as

---

44. Human Rights Watch, Cambodia, 'Hun Sen Systematically Silences Critics', January 2005. Available at http://www.hrw.org/news/2006/01/03/cambodia-hun-sen-systematically-silences-critics. Accessed May 2014.

45. COMFREL, 'Final Assessment and Report on the 2008 National Assembly Elections', p 8. EUEOM, 'Final Report, [2008] National Assembly Elections', p. 26.

46. EUEOM, 'Final Report, [2008] National Assembly Elections', p 24. See also D. Craig and K. Pak, 'Party Financing of Local Investment Projects: Elite and Mass Patronage', in Hughes and Un, *Cambodia's Economic Transformation*. p. 219.

the only one capable of delivering 'development' to local communities. Using state media, and backed by the activities of 'party working groups' (PWG) operating at every level of the administration, from the centre to the village, the CPP was engaged in providing funds for the construction of local roads, canals irrigation projects and schools. Observations made by researchers during the 2008 election campaign noted Hun Sen's daily appearances on television reading out lists of requests for local construction projects followed by the proclamation, 'Choun tam samnaumpo', literally translated as, 'Granted according to your request'. [47]

The granting of requests sent to the prime minister and the bestowal of local projects would be facilitated by the PWG, which would secure funds for the projects from a variety of sources within CPP patronage networks and among international donors. The PWG comprised government officials from all levels of the administration, from ministers and district governors to commune and village chiefs, all of whom were linked in one way or another to the networks and international sources of aid. In this way, lines between the party and state became indistinguishable. While funding for the projects may have come from different contributors, either CPP-affiliated tycoons and local entrepreneurs who paid their dues, or international NGOs, the projects 'gave face' to prominent CPP members who were identified as providing the sources of funding for the projects. The system was thus highly politicized with the express purpose of delivering votes. [48]

While these types of activities may have contributed to CPP electoral success in 2007 and 2008, they might not have played such a decisive role as some researchers suggest. Despite spectacular displays of wealth and largesse, CPP support for local infrastructure projects was limited and very rarely if ever extended beyond the actual construction of roads, canals, irrigation systems or schools. Outside of the electoral cycles there appeared to be no support for operation and maintenance, underscoring the highly selective and politicized nature of the 'giving'. It was also recognized that there were 'considerable horizontal imbalances' in areas where the CPP had less political support among the population.[49] This could have also contributed to the problem of rising inequality, as

---

47. Craig and Pak, 'Party Financing of Local Investment Projects', p. 219.

48. Ibid., p. 220.

49. Ibid., p. 236.

some areas, for political reasons, were marginalized or excluded. In addition, other anthropological research suggests that rural Cambodians were neither 'ignorant of nor mystified by the reasons' for poverty or changes in the local economy and fully understood the idea of 'political gifts'.[50] From this perspective, Cambodians were aware that the wealth of the city was based upon the poverty of the countryside.[51] Thus, the distribution of largesse in the form of local infrastructure alone and not in investment in public services was recognized as displays of political power and wealth, not necessarily state-led development.

National and International Perspectives

Impressive pre-election displays of wealth and political power backed by frequent violent suppression of criticism and dissent were effective tools in laying the groundwork for the elections proper. These alone however were insufficient to ensure the desired outcomes, which required continued careful management of the various stages of the election process. In this regard, final assessments of the 2007 and 2008 elections produced by national and international observer groups revealed a familiar litany of problems and obstacles preventing political parties and voters from participating on a level playing field. Aside from the obvious differences between the election of local councillors and members of the National Assembly, the problems and issues encountered in 2007 and 2008 were more or less the same. Indeed, in spite of the identification and recognition of these problems in 2007, very little if any progress had been made by the time of the National Assembly election the following year.

By 2008, as the same kinds of electoral issues kept resurfacing, national and international assessments became more sophisticated and predictable. In general, and almost without exception, various observer groups stated that both elections marked some kind of 'progress', democratic and technical, but failed to reach unspecified international standards of freedom and fairness. As in 2002 and 2003, the tendency was to measure progress by the reduction in serious violence and killings, and by technically well-administered polling and counting phases.

---

50. E.W. Davis, 'Imagined Parasites: Flows of Monies and Spirits' in Hughes and Un, *Cambodia's Economic Transformation*, p. 327.
51. Ibid.

Nonetheless, unacceptable levels of political intimidation, violence and threats directed at political party activists together with serious administrative shortcomings persisted. National and international analysis of the extent and impact of these problems depended upon the perceptions and interests of the particular organizations involved in producing reports.

After more than a decade of monitoring, observing, lobbying and advocacy, EMOs like COMFREL and NICFEC had established themselves as credible and professional organizations with extensive networks covering all areas of Cambodia. COMFREL in particular, as a self-styled representative of civil society in all matters electoral, invested heavily in the idea that elections were but one part, albeit a central one, in a broader democratic process of civic participation in decisions that affect the everyday lives of ordinary Cambodians. With financial and technical backing from a wide range of international donor organizations, they, much like the SRP, survived in order to add legitimacy to a political system increasingly dominated by one party. As such, they had to tread a fine line between legitimate criticism of flawed elections and presenting a radical challenge to the dominance of the CPP. By characterizing both the 2007 and 2008 elections as steps in 'strengthening democratic governance', while at the same time forensically analysing non-democratic aspects of the elections process, they expressed a belief in the value of elections as instruments for bringing about positive social and political change.

From this perspective, elections provided opportunities, despite formidable constraints, to indirectly challenge the domination of the CPP in ways that had to be tolerated to ensure the legitimacy of the system. However, based upon the findings of EMO assessments in 2007 and 2008, progress over the previous decade had been minimal, and in some areas, such as the illegal use of state resources in service of the CPP, had worsened. With some technical variance, the key problem areas as identified by the EMOs were typically the same. Aside from violence, intimidation and coercion at any level, the integrity and performance of the electoral authorities at all levels remained top of the list of problems. Partisan electoral authorities had according to COMFREL 'emboldened hard line party [CPP] activists to use coercive tactics against voters'.[52] At the same time, administrative restrictions meant many voters were not

---

52. COMFREL, 'Final Assessment and Report on the 2008 National Assembly Elections', p. 6.

fully informed about their rights, preventing them from participating in the process. Other voters, according to the findings, faced obstructions when they arrived at polling stations. As in previous elections, despite modest procedural improvements, the NEC was reluctant or failed to 'acknowledge or resolve elections violations in an expeditious and fair manner'.[53] Similarly, regardless of improvements in access, the CPP still had the lions' share of media access, especially before the official campaign period.

Amendments to the LEMNA in June 2006 increased the number of NEC members from 5 to 9 but did little to improve its image. Observer groups cynically noted that by allowing the SRP and F'pec to put forward two nominees, any previous 'pretence' of NEC neutrality was gone.[54] SRP and F'pec involvement in the reconstitution of the committee did not alter the fact that it remained under the control of the CPP-dominated MoI. Decisions were taken by a majority vote and the majority of members continued to be affiliated with the CPP.

Of particular concern to domestic observer groups was the continued low turnout of voters by comparison to other elections. The numbers of actual voters in the 2007 local elections were down by as much as 20 per cent when compared with 2002. Out of the 8.1 million registered voters in 2008, just over 75 per cent cast ballots. Although more people than ever before voted, this was a lower percentage turnout of registered voters than any of the previous three National Assembly elections. After 15 years of similar electoral outcomes voter apathy was no doubt a contributing factor. Because of the continuing trend in low turnouts since the 2002 local elections, serious questions were being asked by EMOs and political parties about the accuracy and quality of voter lists and the improper use of other related documents such as identity forms, Voter Information Notices (VIN) and Form 1018. With the possibility of almost 2 million registered voters not voting, EMOs and international groups felt that voter registration and voter lists were being manipulated to deny large numbers of people the right to vote.[55]

---

53. Ibid.

54. COMFREL, 'Final Assessment and Report on the 2007 Commune Council Elections', p. 11.

55. COMFREL, 'Survey Report on Voter Lists and Registration', Phnom Penh, July 2009, p. 5.

Indeed, discrepancies and irregularities with the voter lists used for the 2008 elections, involving the removal and addition of ineligible and newly eligible voter names, were cited as one of the reasons by the SRP and HRP for the rejection of the election results. They claimed that 'countless' numbers of likely opposition supporter names had been 'extracted' from the lists. In addition, they argued that Form 1018, intended for eligible voters without any official identification documents, was issued by CPP-controlled authorities to illegitimate voters to artificially increase the numbers of votes for the CPP. Voter registration audits (VRA) conducted by COMFREL, NICFEC, the Center for Advanced Study and the NDI found that 57,000 voter names had in fact been incorrectly removed from the lists.[56] Furthermore, the NEC was unable to provide precise information about the forms other than the total number issued. A survey of the voter lists conducted by COMFREL in 2009 found that as many as 440,000 1018 forms had been used, which differed from the NEC's figure supplied to the EUEOM of 324, 819.[57]

It was not possible to fully substantiate the extent to which deletions from the voter lists and the widespread use of 1018 forms were used to deliberately disenfranchise opposition supporters and increase CPP voter numbers. In its final assessment, the EUOM observers confirmed fraudulent use of the forms. In incidents reported by the EU, observers noted that details recorded on the forms did not match those on the voter ID lists.[58] Individuals who were interviewed told observers that persons issuing the forms told them to vote for the CPP.[59] The fact that the commune clerks, and village and commune chiefs, many of whom were CPP leaders, were responsible for the maintenance of the voter lists and the issuing of Form 1018 supports claims that the system had been manipulated to the advantage of the CPP.

EMOs and opposition political parties also reported widespread political discrimination and disenfranchisement of voters due to problems with the distribution of the VINs by local CPP officials, particularly village chiefs. In spite of concerns from previous elections, the NEC con-

---

56. COMFREL, 'Final Assessment and Report on the 2008 National Assembly Elections', p. 33.

57. Ibid., p. 8.

58. EUEOM, 'Final Report, [2008] National Assembly Elections', p. 18.

59. Ibid., p. 19.

tinued to entrust village chiefs with the distribution of the notices.[60] The VIN provides individual voters with important information including the date of the election, the polling station where they are registered and a serial number on the voter list. COMFREL's 2009 survey estimated that as many as 440,000 eligible voters were obstructed from voting.[61] Many voters could not find their names on voter lists despite having voted in previous elections, nor could others find their polling station because they had not received a VIN, thus preventing them from voting. Despite NEC statements that 85 per cent of all VINs had been distributed, observer groups including the EU reported significant differences between provinces, with the figure being as low as 60 per cent in Phnom Penh, where the SRP had strong support, and over 90 per cent in other places.[62]

Almost all national and international assessments agreed that voter registration and the use of VINs and 1018 forms were open to manipulation and abuse by local CPP-aligned officials. On other central issues like media access, campaign financing, the security environment, implementation of election laws and codes of conduct and complaints and appeals procedures, both the EU and EMOs felt they fell well short of acceptable standards for the conduct of free and fair elections. Indeed, the EUEOM concluded that the Cambodian state had breached its responsibility for ensuring that violations of rights and freedoms as they related to the elections process were adequately remedied.[63]

After more than fifteen years of national and international observation and assessment of Cambodian elections, identifying the problems was no longer the key issue. Technical improvements in election administration, vaunted by the UNDP since 1998 in the context of its ongoing partnership with the NEC, had not had any impact on the underlying political obstacles preventing a level playing field for parties opposed to the CPP and the electorate. UNDP assessments, while acknowledging continued problems with the NEC, failed to focus on the root political causes of those problems. This was hardly surprising given that control over key aspects of the election apparatus, like the election authorities

---

60. EUEOM, 'Final Report, [2008] National Assembly Elections', p. 1.

61. COMFREL, 'Survey Report on Voter Lists and Registration', p. 8.

62. EUEOM, 'Final Report, [2008] National Assembly Elections', p. 17.

63. Ibid., p. 3.

and mobilization of state resources, was essential for the maintenance of CPP power. Thus, technical and legal improvements were not going to make a real difference to electoral outcomes unless there was the political will to ensure they were implemented in practice. As long as elections continued to pose a threat to CPP power and control, that was unlikely to happen.

In the final analysis, the 2007 and 2008 elections not only reaffirmed but entrenched further CPP control of the process. After the formation of the new coalition in 2004, Hun Sen, by artifice and pseudo-legal means, successfully exploited weaknesses within the main opposition parties. Sam Rainsy's self-imposed exile to avoid incarceration on dubious legal charges and Ranariddh's ultimate humiliation had a profound impact on electoral opposition to the CPP. Well in advance of the elections, F'pec's submission to the wealth and power of its coalition partner sent unambiguous messages to the electorate. Sam Rainsy's absence from the country and eventual pardon in 2006, combined with a steady stream of defections from SRP and F'pec, reinforced ideas about CPP omnipotence and the opposition's impotence.

Accelerating social change and impressive economic growth could be used to support CPP propaganda which claimed that they were party with the wherewithal to sustain growth and political stability. Damaging social and environmental effects of rapid economic transformation, particularly rising inequality, was accompanied by government warnings about the consequences if the status quo was destabilized. Unsolved and deeply flawed official investigations into ritual-like murders of senior politicians and labour union activists on the streets of Phnom Penh served as reminders of the potential lethal consequences of challenging the established order. Protracted bans on demonstrations and the arbitrary arrest and detention of human rights and other civic activists on the flimsiest of legal grounds demonstrated the ruling party's hyper-sensitivity to criticism of government policies.

The virtual destruction of F'pec and the marginalization of the SRP, together with the suppression of dissent and government criticism more generally, would not necessarily guarantee future electoral victories. Maintaining legitimacy and support in the face of rising inequality and shifting social dynamics and demographics remained a significant challenge for the CPP. Political advantages could be accrued from sustained macro-economic growth, but the manner in which wealth was concentrated, generated and distributed among a small group of predatory political–economic elites was a problem from an electoral perspective. Land disputes over concessions involving government officials and CPP-affiliated business tycoons backed by state security forces were creating anger and discontent among growing numbers of dispossessed and alienated country-dwellers. In the towns and cities there were not enough jobs or access to quality educational opportunities for a new generation of restive and aspirational young voters. Outside the NGO sector, employment was often poorly paid in the civil service, construction, tourism and garment sectors. Garment sector workers in particular – made up of mostly SRP supporters – continued to protest and press for better pay and conditions.

Countering the electoral challenges posed by these groups required the CPP to take control of an official historical narrative that placed the party at the forefront of positive developments since the early 2000s. Portraying themselves as saviours from the horrors of the past and guarantors of peace, stability and development, the party sought to deflect opposing interpretations that saw them as the biggest obstacles in the way of sustainable and equitable development. Mollification of foreign donor demands for reforms that threatened to undermine the system upon which CPP power rested was a central aspect of that narrative. Significant political capital could be gained from continuing inflows of foreign aid despite unfulfilled government commitments to enact key reforms. At the same time, a strengthening of relations between Cambodia and China yielded considerable 'no political strings attached' aid and investment, mitigating the longer-established western donor calls for reform.

Continued international technical and financial support for elections, however, was an essential legitimizing aspect of government work with donors. The UNDP remained the principal conduit for international electoral assistance. Under the broader rubric of 'democratic governance', the UNDP partnership with the Ministry of Interior-controlled NEC worked unsuccessfully to improve the image of the committee as an independent and credible institution through the improvement of technical and legal standards. Political obstacles created and maintained by senior CPP leaders prevented those standards from being fully implemented in practice, perpetuating the reputation of the NEC as a partisan tool of the ruling party. Cosmetic changes to the membership of the committee, supposedly in an attempt to assuage detractors in 2006, did very little to boost confidence in the capacity of the committee to operate independently from the political constraints imposed by the CPP leadership.

Like other politically sensitive areas, under the prevailing authoritarian structures fundamental reform of the electoral system was not possible without significant changes within the CPP itself. On the surface, results in 2007 and 2008 belied the potential threat that elections continued to pose to the party's top leadership, having experienced defeat in the 1993 UNTAC elections. Since then, the party had redoubled its efforts to ensure that such an outcome never occurred again. To do that, with witting and unwitting international aid, the party had come to rely upon the manipulation and authoritarian control of the key levers of the electoral machinery.

This is not to say that internationally supported 'authoritarian elections' are irrelevant beyond the one-party dominance of the state. On the contrary, during the electoral cycle, the whole of the 'political and social system is on display'.[64] Mobilization of conspicuous wealth and state resources through party working-groups to deliver votes in the countryside for the CPP exposed the façade of infrastructural projects that lacked long-term sustainable investment and the provision of adequate public services. Failure by authorities to properly investigate serious-election related crimes, including murder, reflected the general, chronic culture of impunity for perpetrators of political violence. The killings of the SRP-affiliated newspaper journalist Khim Sambo and his son, days before the 2008 elections, brought the total number of murders of journalists to twelve since 1993. An overall reduction in election-related murders and violence had not led to the eradication of widespread, localized intimidation, coercion and harassment of voters and opposition party activists by local CPP authorities.

The reduction in serious incidents of violence accompanied by the disenfranchisement of hundreds of thousands of voters through administrative misconduct marked a new phase in the struggle between the authorities, opposition political parties and EMOs over the form and

---

64. N.D. Palmer, *Elections and Political Development*, p. 1.

conduct of electoral processes. From the point of view of regime legitimacy, less high profile electoral violence drew approval from international donors and observers. At the same time, it added another dimension to the fight by EMOs and relevant civil groups to pin down further the actions and behaviour of the electoral authorities. Thus, EMOs and civil groups continued to play an important if constrained role alongside the SRP and HRP in challenging the iniquities of the state through a struggle for greater transparency and accountability through elections.

CPP electoral victories in 2007 and 2008 exhibited a self-assuredness and belief in the power of Hun Sen and the party to sustain their pre-eminent position at the apex of the Cambodian state for years to come. That belief received a timely political boost three weeks before the 2008 polls after UNESCO listed the 11th-century Preah Vihear Temple situated on the north-west Thai–Cambodian border as a world heritage site. Disputes between Thailand and Cambodia over ownership of the temple and the surrounding land had persisted since the early 20th century, and was a politically volatile issue in both countries. In 1962, the temple was officially recognized as belonging to Cambodia, but disputes over ownership of the surrounding land continued. The Cambodian government's successful submission to UNESCO was an immense source of national pride for Cambodians. A subsequent tense stand-off between Thailand and Cambodia included a build-up of troops on both sides of the border before the elections. Politically, this episode gave the CPP an electoral advantage over its opponents in countering opposition claims that they were incapable of defending Cambodia's national sovereignty and independence.[65]

Aside from the conduct of the 2007 and 2008 polls, nationalist sentiment suggested that the struggle by opposition parties and civil groups for transparent and accountable electoral processes in 2012 and 2013 would continue. It had taken Hun Sen and the CPP a decade and a half to master control of internationally supported elections. It was unlikely therefore that they would release their authoritarian grip and implement any significant electoral reforms in time for the next cycle. Outcomes of future elections thus depended on the extent to which opposition

---

65. K. Un, 'Cambodia's 2008 election: end of opposition?' *Open Democracy*, 5 August 2008. Available at http://www.opendemocracy.net/article/cambodia-s-2008-elections-the-end-of-opposition. Accessed June 2014.

parties could re-energize and organize to mount a serious and credible challenge to the CPP. As far as the CPP was concerned, much would depend on the way in which it continued to manage and control increasing inequality and discontent among the general population. In any event, Cambodian elections, despite or perhaps because of their authoritarian nature, still had a central role to play in future political dramas.

CHAPTER 9

The 2013 Elections – Voter Backlash

O n 28 July 2013, Cambodians turned out to vote in national elections for the fifth time since the historic UNTAC polls in 1993. For over twenty years, the CPP had worked hard to ensure that the loss to F'pec in 1993 was not repeated in subsequent polls. During this time CPP strategies, including violence, intimidation, judicial harassment and control of state resources were used to manipulate and dominate electoral politics. By the end of the first commune elections in 2002, followed by national elections a year later in 2003, their position seemed unassailable. This seems to have been confirmed after an expected landslide victory in 2008. The loss of 22 National Assembly seats in the 28 July 2013 election thus sent shockwaves throughout the CPP, and took many analysts and long-time commentators of Cambodian politics by complete surprise. A loss on that scale was especially surprising after the CPP had again won the vast majority of seats on the 1,633 commune councils in local elections the year before.

Under the unified banner of the Cambodian National Rescue Party (CNRP), formed just before the 2013 elections, Sam Rainsy's SRP and Kem Sokha's HRP combined to win 55 seats. None of the six other competing parties including F'pec won any. In terms of the popular vote, only 4 per cent or just over 289,000 votes separated the CNRP from the CPP. At a press conference shortly after the polls, CNRP President Sam Rainsy and deputy Kem Sokha rejected the results, claiming massive irregularities with voter lists and the possible disenfranchisement of as many as 1.3 million voters. They proposed the formation of a joint committee comprising the CNRP, CPP, NEC, UN and relevant national and international NGOs to fully investigate the irregularities.[1] CPP officials immediately dismissed

---

1. Meas Sokchea and Cheeang Sokha, 'Election Results Rejected', *Phnom Penh Post*, 30 July 2013.

the idea, setting in motion a boycott of the National Assembly by CNRP elect members that continued for over a year.

While few could deny the surprising nature of the results, discontent and with resentment of the manner in which the CPP governed Cambodia had always been present among large sections of the population. What was truly surprising, given the authoritarian nature of Cambodian elections since UNTAC, was that discontent and resentment were unmistakably manifest during polling in 2013. By comparison with 2008 the 2013 election result was a clear indication of a definitive shift within the electorate and the body politic more generally, the political implications of which were highly uncertain. And yet, as surprising as the CNRP gains were, the CPP still had a clear majority to form a new government alone. Furthermore, the irregularities and problems cited by the CNRP in the days after the elections, later supported by findings from EMOs and international organizations, were nothing new. The post-election behaviour of CNRP leaders and their unwillingness to join a government with the CPP was also to be expected.

Post-Election Drama

In the period immediately after the elections it looked like the CNRP had the CPP on the back foot, politically. Mass peaceful protests were organized by the CNRP leadership calling for fresh elections. Parts of central Phnom Penh were locked down by police and security forces causing traffic chaos inside and outside the city. A heavy military presence added to the tension. As the protests continued tensions escalated. On the evening of September 15, police opened fire on a crowd of protesters and commuters attempting to make their way out of city through heavy traffic. One young man was shot in the head and several others were treated for bullet wounds.[2] Less than month later a street vendor was shot and killed and more injured as police opened fire during a garment workers strike.[3]

---

2. Cambodian League for the Promotion and Defense of Human Rights (LICADHO), statement: 'Indiscriminate Police Brutality and Death amid Mass Post-Election Protest Condemned by Civil Society', Phnom Penh, 16 September 2013, http://www.licadho-cambodia.org/pressrelease.php?perm=323, accessed June 2015.

3. LICADHO, statement: 'On the International Day to End Impunity, LICADHO Publishes Data on 10 Fatal Shootings by the Cambodian Police and Military',

By mid-December protesters had ensconced themselves in an area of the city known as 'Freedom Park', where they erected temporary shelters and platforms to voice their demands. Against the backdrop of fraught negotiations between the CPP and CNRP, protests continued into the new year. CNRP leaders voiced support for striking garment workers demanding a minimum wage of US$160 per month. In late December labour union representatives rejected a Ministry of Labour (MOL) plan to incrementally increase wages reaching the garment workers request for US$160 by 2018. Not satisfied, garment workers staged their own protests calling for the increase to take effect immediately. On 29 December many disgruntled workers joined together with CNRP supporters in the largest march of the post-election period. Sensing an opportunity to pressure the government further the CNRP prepared to hold another march in early January, calling on garment workers, civil servants and teachers to join.[4]

Before the march could take place the government and security forces seized the initiative. Beginning on 2 January, military police and security forces mounted a crackdown and violently broke up the protests. The following day four people were shot dead and many more injured as security forces continued to disperse protesters. In response, CNRP leaders announced their intention not to return to the negotiating table scheduled for that day. On 4 January a collection of police, military police and civilians moved into Freedom Park, violently removed protesters and tore down the shelters and platforms. Shortly afterwards the Ministry of Interior issued a ban on all street protests and marches. Freedom Park was cordoned off for several months.[5]

Having reasserted authority the government and the CPP were in a stronger position vis à vis the CNRP leadership at the negotiating table. The momentum gained since the end of the elections by the CNRP had effectively been lost. From a weakened position, Sam Rainsy and Kem Sokha dropped demands for an independent investigation, opt-

---

Phnom Penh, 23 November 2013, http://www.licadho-cambodia.org/pressrelease.php?perm=329, accessed June 2015.

4. LICADHO, 'When Freedom Meets Oppression: Timeline of Recent Events', Phnom Penh, 9 February 2014, http://www.licadho-cambodia.org/articles/20140209/137/index.html, accessed June 2015.

5. Ibid.

ing instead for promises of electoral and institutional reform. On this basis the deadlock between the two parties ended in July 2014 almost a full year after the elections. Smiling for cameras on the steps of the Cambodian Senate Sam Rainsy and Hun Sen shook hands after having agreed to work together and develop 'a culture of dialogue' to tackle key national issues. The 55 CNRP parliamentarians-elect took their seats in the National Assembly and a joint CPP-CNRP commission was formed to examine electoral reform.

By early March 2015 some electoral reforms had been enacted but not to the satisfaction of a group of civil society groups and election monitoring organizations calling themselves the Election Reform Alliance (ERA).[6] Changes to the constitutional status and restructuring of the NEC were cautiously welcomed, but there were still doubts about how it would perform in the run up to the 2017 and 2018 elections.[7] Amendments to an existing Law on the Election of Members to the National Assembly (LEMNA) by contrast were severely criticized by the ERA.[8] Civil society leaders were particularly alarmed by provisions which they argued restricted the freedoms of expression and movement of non-governmental organizations and associations working in the field of elections.[9] Article 83 of the new law permitted civil servants, local authorities, national police, armed forces and court officials to take part in campaign activities in support of a political party or candidate outside of normal working hours or when they not performing official duties. CSOs argued that the new provision contradicted article 82 of the previous LEMNA and article 15 of the Law on Political Parties, which places limitations on the political activities of the armed forces, the police and court officials. The involvement of security forces and local authorities in election-related violence and intimidation of voters and opposition

---

6. The Election Reform Alliance (ERA) was formed before the 2013 Elections and is made up of approximately 25 prominent civil society organizations. See for example https://eracambodia.wordpress.com/about/, accessed December 2015.

7. COMFREL, 'Democracy, Elections and Reform in Cambodia. 2014 Annual Report', March 2015.

8. Personal Interviews with NEC members and leaders of civil society member organizations of the ERA, September 2015, Phnom Penh.

9. COMFREL and ERA, 'Table Assessment of Changes to the LEMNA'. Internal document, English version. Phnom Penh, January 2016.

party members has been well documented. The failure of court officials to administer justice in the vast majority of cases involving members of the security services and local officials in election-related crimes has also been a recurrent problem in previous elections.[10]

The Election Reform Alliance's concerns about the limitations and restrictions placed upon them and political parties by the amendments were well founded. By July 2015 the reform process and the culture of dialogue was in tatters. After what turned out to be nothing more than a lull, in July 2015 the CPP reverted to previous strategies intended to marginalize, intimidate, harass and weaken political opponents. CNRP activists were targeted for arrest and given hefty prison sentences after being charged with insurrection during the 2014 protests.[11] The following month a Sam Rainsy Party senator, Hong Sok Hour, was arrested and detained, contravening his senatorial immunity, after the prime minister accused him of treason. He was charged with incitement and forgery after posting on Facebook documents related to a controversial and supposedly fake 1979 Cambodian–Vietnam border treaty.[12]

The targeting of CNRP members continued into the latter half of the year. In a shocking and flagrant display of violence two CNRP members of parliament were dragged from their vehicles in front of the National Assembly building and beaten, one severely, by military personnel from Hun Sen's personal body guard unit. The incident took place after a demonstration by CPP supporters calling for the removal of CNRP vice-president Kem Sokha from his position as vice-president of the National Assembly. Sokha was later removed from this post. In November and December, a number of arrest warrants related to old

---

10. See for example previous election reports from The Office of the High Commissioner for Human Rights, OHCHR Cambodia, http://cambodia.ohchr.org/EN/PagesFiles/Reports/Thematic-Reports.htm, accessed January 2016.

11. Meas Sokchea, 'CNRP activists sentenced for "insurrection"', *Phnom Penh Post*, Tue, 21 July 2015

http://www.phnompenhpost.com/national/cnrp-activists-sentenced-insurrection, accessed January 2016

12. Taing Vida. 'Sok Hour defence balks at evidence demands', *Phnom Penh Post*, Fri, 27 November 2015

http://www.phnompenhpost.com/national/sok-hour-defence-balks-evidence-demands, accessed January 2016

and new charges were issued against CNRP president Sam Rainsy.[13] To avoid arrest Rainsy fled the country before the warrants could be served and remained in self-imposed exile.

The suppression of political opposition happened in the midst of general discussions about possible outcomes in the 2018 elections. Civil society groups, like ERA for example, were considering the political implications of a CNRP or CPP defeat at the 2018 polls.[14] Speculation about the possibility of a peaceful transfer of power in the event of a CNRP victory was rife. References to a 'Cambodian Spring' and a 'Colour Revolution' helped to fuel speculation about future instability and civil unrest. As in the past, Hun Sen lost no time in reverting to threats of civil war, claiming that CNRP policies would alienate entrenched business interests and senior elements in the military and be hostile to Vietnam.[15] While Hun Sen's threats of war and violent repression of political opposition was nothing new, the timing of the events in 2015 was a good indication of the threat the CPP felt future elections posed to the status quo.

Given these events, understanding and explaining how politically significant the 2013 election results were is not straightforward. Their significance over time would depend on how the CPP understood and responded to what was an obvious rejection of the party's dominance, and the extent to which the CNRP could remain united and capitalize on the gains made in preparations for the 2017 and 2018 polls. Understanding the events and issues in the five years leading up to the 2013 elections provides an essential context to help explain the results and the aftermath.

---

13. Chhay Channyda and Taing Vida, 'Rainsy Stripped of Law Maker Status', *Phnom Penh Post*, 16 November 2015, http://www.phnompenhpost.com/national/rainsy-stripped-lawmaker-status, accessed February 2016. Mech Dara, 'Yet another warrant out for Rainsy's arrest', *Phnom Penh Post*, 6 January 2016, http://www.phnompenhpost.com/national/yet-another-warrant-out-rainsys-arrest, accessed February 2016.

14. Personal interviews and discussions with ERA members, September 2015, Phnom Penh. See also COMFREL, 'Democracy, Elections and Reform in Cambodia. 2015 Annual Report', March 2016, pp. 6–7.

15. Kang Sothear and Alex Willemyns, 'PM says CNRP's Land Plans Will Stoke War', *The Cambodia Daily*, 23 September 2015. See also, Alex Willemyns. ' Hun Sen Pondering Defeat, War on Mind', *The Cambodia Daily*, 26 October 2015.

Post-2008, Business as Usual?

Attempts by the SRP, HRP, NRP and F'pec to join forces to reject the election results in 2008 and prevent the formation of a new government were short-lived. Complaints submitted to the NEC by the opposition parties and passed on to the Constitutional Council for final adjudication were not upheld. Soon after, F'pec and the NRP decided to drop the pretence of a boycott and participate in the inauguration ceremony for the new legislature in September. Facing possible loss of seats due to dubious constitutional interpretations, the SRP and HRP took a similar decision, ended the boycott and joined the National Assembly. On 24 September, a new government even bigger than the bloated previous administration was formed via the controversial package vote used to end the deadlock in 2004. Unlike then, however, without having to consider a coalition partner, and with only 29 opposition party seats, the CPP effectively controlled key positions on all parliamentary commissions.

The absence of a protracted post-election standoff was indicative of a general resignation felt among the opposition to the realities of the political system. By the same token, the system could not legitimately function without the semblance of a credible opposition. Having apparently learnt from past experience, the SRP and HRP sensed an opportunity, and instead considered the possibility of a merger in preparation for the 2013 polls. Some among them felt they would win in 2013 if they could unite and remain united.[16] From the initial floating of the idea in late 2008, it would take almost another four years before a formal merger happened and the SRP and HRP became the Cambodian National Rescue Party (CNRP) in July 2012.

In the meantime, the trajectories of political and socio-economic developments after the 2008 polls followed familiar paths. In November 2009 the National Assembly voted to lift Sam Rainsy's parliamentary immunity, allowing the courts to prosecute him on charges of causing racial discrimination and destroying demarcation posts on the Cambodia–Vietnam border in the south-western province of Svay Rieng. In January 2010 Rainsy was convicted *in absentia* along with two villagers, fined

---

16. Yang Samean, 'SRP, HRP Brokering New Alliance in Assembly', *The Cambodia Daily*, 30 September 2008.

and sentenced to two years in prison.[17] Further related charges were brought against him later in the year, resulting in an additional 10-year prison sentence for allegedly falsifying public documentation, with SRP officials claiming that Vietnamese border markers had been placed well within Cambodian territory. To avoid serving his sentences, Rainsy once again remained outside Cambodia in self-imposed exile for almost four years.

Rainsy's provocative actions on the Cambodian Vietnamese border in 2009 and subsequent prison sentences led to further harassment and intimidation of the opposition by the CPP. Following previous patterns, Rainsy remained in exile until enough international and internal pressure was brought to bear, forcing Hun Sen to act and agree to a royal pardon. The pardon, which came into effect just two weeks before elections, quashed his prison sentence and allowed him to return to Cambodia to participate in the elections, but prevented him from voting or running as a candidate.[18]

Rainsy's Return July 2013

NEC-imposed restrictions on Sam Rainsy's right to vote and stand as a candidate due to his criminal convictions at the time of registration were temporarily overshadowed by the tumultuous reception he received when he returned to the country a little over a week before the elections. Probably not since the return of Sihanouk in 1991 had so many Cambodians turned out to greet a political leader returning from overseas. Tens of thousands of people lined the route from the airport as he made his way towards Phnom Penh's 'Freedom Park', where he and CNRP leaders addressed the large crowd. The crowds that greeted the CNRP leadership wanted to see real change and genuine improvements in living standards, working conditions and an end to the suppression of basic political and civil rights and freedoms.

The huge numbers of people who turned out far exceeded expectations and took Sam Rainsy and the CNRP leadership by surprise, especially in view of the fact that the CPP had secured yet another

---

17. Meas Sokchea and Sebastian Strangio, 'Sam Rainsy sentenced in absentia', *Phnom Penh Post*, 28 January 2010.

18. Denise Hruby and Huch Naren, 'Sam Rainsy Granted Royal Pardon by King', *The Cambodia Daily*, 13 July 2013.

overwhelming victory in the commune elections the year before. Based on those results, and with Rainsy then still in self-imposed exile, some CNRP politicians had been doubtful about the party's chances in 2013.[19] However, after seeing the enthusiastic crowds, there was a sense among them that a clear and present momentum for change could be harnessed in time for the elections. While some CNRP leaders felt they could win, for others the sense of surprise at the huge numbers of people showing up to see Sam Rainsy's return seemed to suggest that many voters were in reality expressing discontent with the system of governance more generally rather than support for the CNRP *per se*. That is to say, if many voters believed, as some analysts had suggested, that the CNRP could not realistically deliver on their promises if they won the elections, they felt nonetheless they had nothing to lose by voting for them.[20] In short: a protest against the CPP rather than an unequivocal belief in the capacity of the CNRP to govern effectively.

In terms of the actual results in 2013, what was remarkable was that in just over a year since the commune polls, the SRP–HRP merger produced an increase of over 1.1 million votes for the CNRP. The CNRP significantly increased its share of the vote in all provinces and municipalities when compared to the commune elections. By contrast, the CPP, with the exception of the north-east province of Ratanakiri, lost votes in every province and municipality, dropping from 3.5 and 3.6 million in the previous commune and 2008 elections respectively to 3.2 million in 2013. Taking into account overall increases in the numbers of voters from 2008 to 2012, the CPP lost over 396,000 votes in the period between elections; over 635,000 more ballots were counted in 2013 than in 2008, most of which probably went to the CNRP. Because of the proportional electoral system, the CPP nevertheless retained an overall majority of seats in 14 provinces. But, as in the case of Kandal province, the difference between the CNRP gaining one more seat over the CPP was as little as 166 votes.[21] Crunching the numbers when the differences in some instances were so small was vitally important for the CNRP

---

19. Personal interviews with CNRP parliamentarians, Phnom Penh, June 2014.

20. Personal interviews with civil society organization leaders, Phnom Penh, June 2014.

21. COMFREL, 'Democracy, Elections and Reform in Cambodia. 2013 Annual Report', March 2014, p. 77–78.

leadership in claiming victory amidst allegations of more manipulation and fraud.

Socio-economic Developments

Aside from the increases in the numbers of actual voters, the mechanics of the seat allocation system and the allegations of irregularities, a cursory glance of the results shows that, for the first time since F'pec's majority win in 1993, the CPP came close to losing in 2013. A deeper analysis of the socio-economic circumstances surrounding the elections may help to better explain the outcome. The World Bank's 2013 Cambodia poverty assessment report entitled 'Where have all the poor gone?' for example offers insights in that regard.[22] The Bank's own pithy answer to the question was 'Not very far!' Using its own figures for the 2004–11 period, the report showed that 'household consumption had increased by 40 per cent, and inequality in consumption actually decreased from 2007, resulting in overall poverty reduction from 52.2 to 20.5 per cent'.[23] However, the report warned that the majority of those lifted over the poverty line remained highly vulnerable, where even the smallest change in circumstances, for example the loss of 1,192 Cambodian riel per capita per day, about $US 30, would have doubled the poverty rate in 2011.[24] Furthermore, while inequality using the Gini Index showed that inequality had decreased since 2007, the actual gap between rich and poor in absolute terms had widened by 2011.[25]

Decreasing levels of poverty as measured by the World Bank and the RGC were made possible because the 'values' upon which they were based were so low in the first place. To illustrate the point, according to the World Bank, from 2000 to 2010 Cambodia recorded 'the best improvement in the region' in terms of the UN HDI, but still had the lowest ranking in the region, and in 2012 was positioned globally at 138 out of 187 countries.[26] Further, as the Bank's report makes clear, 'pover-

---

22. World Bank, 'A Country Study ACS4545. Where Have All the Poor Gone? Cambodia Poverty Assessment 2013', November 2013.

23. Ibid., p. XII.

24. Ibid., p. 18.

25. Ibid., p. XVI.

26. Ibid., p. 12. See also UNDP in Cambodia, http://www.kh.undp.org/content/cambodia/en/home.html. Accessed June 2104.

ty reduction was far from complete'. This was reflected in the 'sluggish pace of poverty reduction in 2001' compared with the 2007 and 2009 periods when most of the reductions occurred. Thus, the recent pace of poverty reduction has, according to the report, been difficult to maintain, with estimates showing that the annualized rate of reduction is only one percentage point compared with 15.2 per cent for 2007 and 2009.[27]

A significant part of the problem identified by the World Bank is that poor people in Cambodia today are different from the poor of the 1990s. From this viewpoint, the top priority in the 1990s was providing enough food for families. Today, as the report states, the nation's poor, 90 per cent of whom live in rural areas, have higher expectations and aspirations. In addition to basic needs like food and shelter, their priorities include material goods like motor scooters, modern technological gadgets such as laptop computers and smart phones as well as education and healthcare for themselves and their children.[28] Like poverty reduction, the World Bank report also highlights notable improvements in per capita Gross National Income and access to education and health in the 2004–11 period. But again improvements are coming from pre-existing low levels.

Continued average economic growth rates of seven per cent per annum have pushed per-capita Gross National Income from US$400 in 2004 to US$1,000 in 2013, just below what international development organizations consider to be middle-income status. Based on the report's findings, access to consumer and durable goods like TVs, motorbikes and mobile phones have increased significantly. Rising basic living costs over the same period however means that many ordinary Cambodians have little disposal income for luxury items. In terms of education, literacy rates over the period reviewed have improved. More specific figures show that despite general improvements by 2011, only '29 per cent of adults 25 years and older had finished primary school'. Problems at the primary level have knock-on effects on secondary education; as many as 40 per cent of students start primary school 2 years late and finish at age fifteen instead of twelve. This has negative consequences for secondary enrolment and retention rates, which in turn compounds the broader problem of the high numbers of students who, from about the age of 13,

27. World Bank, 'A Country Study ACS4545', p. 47.
28. Ibid., p. 47.

drop out of the education system altogether.[29] The reasons for this are mainly economic. Teachers are poorly paid and the general standard of education is generally very poor. Increasingly, people who can afford it are turning to the private sector for their educational needs.

A similar story exists in the area of healthcare. Access to health services, maternal mortality and immunization rates against common infectious diseases like measles, diphtheria, whooping cough, tetanus (DPT) and Bacillius Calmette-Guérin (BCG) have all improved in the last decade. Nonetheless, according to World Bank assessments, all of Cambodia's mortality rates are higher than average when compared to the developing countries of East Asia and the Pacific, and only sixty-five per cent of the poorest people are fully immunized.[30] When it comes to accessing healthcare, the World Bank reported that the majority of poor people have shunned public health services and turned to a private sector of small, unregulated clinics or small pharmacies and 'drugs shops' for treatment and curative care. Statistics show that the percentage of poor people seeking healthcare in the public sector increased from 2004 to 2009, but then decreased from 26 per cent in 2009 to only 16 per cent in 2011.[31] Furthermore, the numbers of people using provincial and district hospitals dropped 'by half from 2007 to 2011 from only 1.4 per cent to 0.6 per cent respectively'.[32]

An evident shift towards the private sector for basic health and education is indicative of a general feeling among Cambodians of the poor quality provided by the state. Beyond some 'Scholarship' and 'Health Equity' programmes, funded mainly from international sources to help the poor, the government does not according to the World Bank have 'any major social protection programs'.[33] The implementation of a 2011 National Social Protection Strategy (NSPS) introduced by the government to address the problem of providing social protection for all Cambodians has been implemented slowly, and according to the World Bank report, there were 'no new initiatives in 2013'.[34]

---

29. Ibid., p. XIX.
30. Ibid., p. 74.
31. Ibid., p. 75.
32. Ibid.
33. Ibid., p. XX, see also p. 78 for external funding of Health Equity programmes.
34. Ibid.

Taking into consideration incremental improvements reported by the World Bank, socio-economic challenges for the majority of ordinary Cambodian voters in the period from 2008 up to the 2013 elections were quantitatively and qualitatively different from the problems faced in the 1990s. After a temporary dip in 2009, inequitable economic growth continued, accompanied by an even greater demand for land and natural resources from domestic and foreign investors. Soaring land prices and rises in the cost of living created new social and political problems. Land conflicts and evictions to make way for new rural and urban developments increased in number alongside protests and demonstrations by factory workers and civil servants demanding improved pay and conditions. In 2014, the Cambodian human rights organization LICADHO estimated that just over half a million people had been negatively affected by state-related land conflicts since 2000.[35] According to the organization, over 2.1 million hectares of land had been given over to private entities through the Economic Land Concession system since 1993.[36] In many incidents, government security forces and military personnel worked on behalf of private companies to violently suppress any protests.

High-profile cases of such conflicts have gained widespread international attention. For example, a 99-year lease was awarded to Shukaku Incorporated in 2007 to develop Boeung Kak Lake, a large natural feature in the centre of Phnom Penh, and the surrounding area. Aside from serious implications for flooding in the city, the development threatened to displace as many as 4,000 families and turned into a long-standing dispute between those who were forcibly evicted and the government. Shukaku is owned by a Vice President of the Cambodian Chamber of Commerce and CPP Senator Lao Meng Khin, whose wife is the owner of the development company Pheapimex that controls other controversial land concessions involved in disputes around the country.[37] The legal status of

---

35. LICADHO, 'The Great Cambodian Giveaway: Visualizing Land Concessions over Time', available at http://www.licadho-cambodia.org/concession_timelapse/, accessed June 2014.

36. Ibid.

37. LICADHO, Statement Joint Organizations, 'Open Letter regarding forced eviction of Boueng Kak Lake residents to Mr. Kep Chuktema, Governor of the Municipality of Phnom Penh', 2008, http://www.licadho-cambodia.org/pressrelease.php?perm=196, accessed June 2014.

the land was altered by a sub-decree in 2008 from state public land to state private land, allowing for the contested 99-year lease to be granted. In May 2012, residents from the Boeung Kak community were arrested during a peaceful protest. Community activist Yorm Bopha, who continued to advocate on behalf of the arrested residents, was herself jailed in December on trumped-up charges unrelated to the land dispute.[38]

The Boeung Kak Lake case was just one of a number that highlighted the arbitrary arrests and targeting of activists and human rights workers after 2008. Between 2010 and 2012, groups like LICADHO reported disturbing trends involving threats and attacks targeting community representatives involved in land disputes, factory workers, union leaders, NGO staff and journalists. Individuals from these groups were subjected to violence, intimidation, harassment, arrest, imprisonment and murder.[39] Mam Sonando, a long-time government critic and owner of the independent Beehive Radio station, was arrested and charged with 'insurrection' in what was clearly a politically motivated case.[40] After international condemnation of the sentences, the charge as later changed and he was released four months after US President Obama's historic visit to Cambodia in November 2012, when he referred to the case in talks with Hun Sen.[41] Earlier that year, the prominent and outspoken environmental activist Chut Wutty was shot and killed by a military policeman working as a security guard for a private company suspected of illegal logging in the Cardamom Mountains, in the country's south-west. The circumstances surrounding his murder were never properly investigated, raising more questions about who was ultimately responsible.[42]

Chut Wutty's murder drew worldwide condemnation and underlined the persistent, broader problem of impunity for state officials

---

38. LICADHO, 'Briefing Update: The Yorm Bopha Case', http://www.licadho-cambodia.org/reports/files/177LICADHOBriefBopha2013-English.pdf, accessed June 2014.

39. LICADHO, 'Attacks and Threats Against Human Rights Defenders in Cambodia 2010-2012'. December 2012, p. 1.

40. Ibid.

41. Radio Free Asia, 'Journalist's Case Raised by Obama', 27 November 2012, at http://www.rfa.org/english/news/cambodia/journalist-11272012165221.html. Accessed July 2014.

42. May Titthara and David Boyle, 'Environmental Activist Chut Wutty Shot Dead', *Phnom Penh Post*, 26 April 2012.

and security and military personnel who were connected to private business interests and involved in killings and violence against activists and civilians. Between May 2011 and November 2012, organizations like LICADHO recorded eight instances where security and military forces opened fire against civilians during peaceful protests, strikes and demonstrations. In March, during a garment-factory worker protest in Bavet town, Governor Chhouk Bandith fired shots into a crowd, critically injuring a young woman and injuring two more. Despite being sacked from his post and receiving a lenient sentence for his actions, he was not arrested and detained after his conviction, and as of February 2014 remained at large.[43] In another incident in May, Heng Chanta, a 14-year-old girl, was killed by authorities during a security forces operation in an area embroiled in a land dispute; no action was taken against the perpetrators.[44]

When considering socio-economic data and the political ramifications of the 'epidemic' rise in land conflicts since 2008, the meaning of the 2013 election comes more clearly into view. As the elections approached, both national and international actors engaged in the process responded in different ways, reflecting the meanings they attached to land issues. Clearly concerned by political problems caused by land disputes, the CPP moved to assert control over the situation in an effort to assuage international and national critics. In 2011, in response to the Boeung Kak Lake debacle, the World Bank suspended all new projects in Cambodia.[45] The government had previously cancelled financing for a World Bank-supported Land Mapping and Administration Project (LMAP) in 2009 after a review by the bank led to disagreements over social and environmental concerns driven by the increase in land disputes.[46]

43. May Titthara and Stuart White, 'A year after trial, still free', *Phnom Penh Post*, 27 February 2014.

44. LICADHO, 'Attacks and Threats Against Human Rights Defenders in Cambodia 2010-2012', p. 1.

45. Reuters, 'World Bank stops funding for Cambodia over Evictions', 9 August 2011, Phnom Penh.

46. Statement from the World Bank on Termination by Royal Government of Cambodia of the Land Management and Administration Project, 6 September 2009, at http://web.worldbank.org/WBSITE/EXTERNAL/COUNTRIES/ EASTASIAPACIFICEXT/CAMBODIAEXTN/0,,contentMDK:22303344~menu

As resistance to ELCs intensified in rural and urban areas and international attention to the problems spread, in May 2012 Hun Sen issued 'Order 01BB', more commonly referred to as Directive 01. This was followed shortly afterwards in June by a national land measuring and titling exercise, employing teams of youth volunteers known collectively as the 'Heroic Samdech Techo Volunteer Youth'. Order 01BB was intended to temporarily suspend all new ELCs and implement a 'leopard skin' policy, ostensibly to mitigate the adverse social and political effects of the land disputes, and prevent ELCs from encroaching upon inhabited family and community lands.[47] Under the land titling scheme, a group of young volunteers bearing the 'quasi-royal title' Samdech Techo, adopted by Hun Sen himself, were to measure and demarcate land, after which hundreds of thousands of land titles were to be handed out country-wide.[48]

While the order was initially welcomed by civil groups, a glaring 'loophole' excluded concessions that had been agreed upon in principle before the announcement, meaning that despite the moratorium, new ELCs would nonetheless be granted after May. Moreover, the land titling campaign excluded disputed areas where people who could potentially be evicted from their land needed titles most. To be sure, many people benefited from the titling scheme, but the exclusion of others in areas under dispute, due to the Directive 01 loophole, suggested that the motivation was to control and contain the land problem. In this regard, some analysts have suggested that the militaristic tone of the 'leopard skin' metaphor was akin to a 'counter-insurgency' policy designed to squeeze out and defeat political opponents by seizing control of small pockets of unclaimed land.[49] Retention of tight control, especially in rural areas, was a priority concern for the CPP. Politically, the ongoing unrest and resistance to land grabs and ELCs presented opportunities

PK:293861~pagePK:1497618~piPK:217854~theSitePK:293856,00.html, accessed July 2014., accessed July 2014.

47. ADHOC, 'A Turning Point? Land, Housing and Natural Resources Rights in Cambodia in 2012', February 2013, p. 34.

48. Ibid. See also Human Rights Watch, 'Cambodia: Land Titling Campaign open to Abuse', 12 June 2012, http://www.hrw.org/news/2013/06/12/cambodia-land-titling-campaign-open-abuse, accessed July 2014.

49. Human Rights Watch, 'Cambodia: Land Titling Campaign open to Abuse'.

for CPP opponents to exploit before the elections. Thus, Directive 001 and the titling campaign could be seen as an attempt by Hun Sen and the CPP to appease critics while at the same time tighten its political and security grip on an increasingly unpredictable situation ahead of the elections.

Electoral Reform?

Under these conditions, the possibility of thoroughgoing reform of the electoral system, which had been continually called for by civil groups and some international actors in the previous decade, was more remote than ever. In meetings with the NEC in February 2013, EMOs, civil groups and political party representatives did manage to secure some agreement on procedural and regulatory processes from the NEC, but most of the substantive suggestions concerning the recruitment of election officials, disclosure of political party campaign finances, control of Identification Certificates for Elections (ICE), and neutrality of NGOs were not accepted.[50] Because of past problems, much of the attention of EMOs, civil groups and the NDI before the election was focused on voter registration lists. After revision of the lists, over 9.67 million voters had been registered by December 2012. Two separate independent voter registration audits (VRA) were subsequently conducted by EMOs and the NDI. Both audits found serious shortcomings and irregularities, including missing names, misspelled or deleted names, names used by someone else, over-registration and 'ghost voters'. A NDI, NICFEC and Center for Advanced Study (CAS) survey found that 11 per cent of respondents who believed they were registered for the elections could not be found on the lists.[51] In its own separate survey, COMFREL estimated that a possible 1.25 million people had been disenfranchised.[52] Over one million people did not receive VINs, and as in previous elections, those who were issued VINs were subjected to political intimidation by

---

50. COMFREL, 'Democracy, Elections and Reform in Cambodia. 2013 Annual Report', pp. 42–45.

51. National Democratic Institute (NDI), Report of the Voter Registration Audit (VRA) in Cambodia, 2013.

52. COMFREL, 'Democracy, Elections and Reform in Cambodia. 2013 Annual Report', p. 10.

local CPP-affiliated authorities. In addition, according to COMFREL over 300,000 multiple names appeared on the lists.[53]

International technical and financial engagement with both the 2012 and 2013 elections was minimal. For the first time since 1993, Cambodians were fully responsible for organizing the elections without international assistance. Apart from its regular programming, the UNDP after 2009 was not directly involved with the NEC in preparing the polls.[54] After sending observer missions to assess the previous two national elections, the EU did not participate in 2013. Virtually none of the major recommendations made by previous EU missions related to election reforms had been adopted by the government.[55]

An apparent withdrawal of the usual international actors like the UNDP and EU from the election preparations was accompanied by critical reports from the UN Special Rapporteur for Human Rights in Cambodia. With a specific focus on elections issues, his July 2012 report to the Human Rights Council of the UN General Assembly urged the government to enact election reforms in time for the 2013 polls. Stated in the context of the twentieth anniversary of the Paris Peace Accords in 2011, he expressed concern over 'capacity gaps that persist in the elections process'.[56] Acknowledging the benefits of the recommendations that Cambodia had received from multilateral and bilateral agencies to reform the elections process, he regretted that most of them had not been implemented.[57] In sum, the report reaffirmed that there were 'major flaws in the administration of elections in Cambodia and urgent and longer-term reforms are needed to give Cambodians confidence in the electoral process and in the workings of the National Election Committee'.[58]

---

53. Ibid.

54. Personal communication with UNDP official, Phnom Penh, July 2014.

55. Simon Lewis and Phorn Bopha, 'Rainsy Tells Election Observers to Stay Away', *The Cambodia Daily*, 26 February 2013.

56. United Nations General Assembly, Human Rights Council, Report of the Special Rapporteur on the Situation of Human Rights in Cambodia, Surya, P. Subedi, A/HRC/21/63, 16 July 2012.

57. Ibid., summary.

58. Ibid.

No Reform, Elections as Usual?

Precisely because of past experiences, there was no reason to believe that the recommendations for electoral reform set out at the end of the Special Rapporteur's July 2012 report would be fully implemented before the 2013 elections. On the contrary, since 1993, authoritarian control of elections had been a *sine qua non* in Hun Sen's strategy for maintaining and reproducing political and economic power. Electoral reform, like other aspects of the governance reform agenda, threatened that power. It was no surprise therefore that one of the central obstacles to successful negotiation in the post-election standoff in 2013 was a complete overhaul of the elections administration. While the results were unexpected, the elections were conducted along familiar lines, revealing and reinforcing CPP dominance in key areas of the process.

On the positive side, a shift away from the use of deadly violence continued. The number of recorded cases of serious, violent incidents before and during the election campaign was the lowest since 1993. No killings of political party members or activists were reported.[59] National observer groups nonetheless described a generally threatening and intimidating atmosphere directed at opposition party members, activists and voters. Death threats directed at CNRP party members and voters, and arbitrary arrests and detentions for those perceived as non-CPP supporters were persistent features of the elections process.[60] In some areas of the country, analysts described what amounted to an absence or rejection of fear on a scale larger than previously seen during elections.[61] Although the general level of fear associated with elections had been difficult to measure, these observations went some way in helping to explain the results. Probably driven by other factors such as disillusionment and an overall refusal to tolerate existing political economic arrangements, voters seemed to be less fearful in their willingness to express political views inside and outside of the ballot box. This was a

---

59. COMFREL, 'Democracy, Elections and Reform in Cambodia. 2013 Annual Report', p. 15.

60. LICADHO, 'Year 2013 in Review: Cambodian Elections', 18 March 2014. Available online at http://www.licadho-cambodia.org/articles/20140318/139/index.html. Accessed July 2014.

61. Interviews with civil society group leaders, June 2014, Phnom Penh.

significant departure from previous elections, especially in the face of continued repression of dissent.

Both the CPP and CNRP attempted to instil fear and insecurity in the minds of the electorate using familiar psychological and emotional memes. In the months before the elections, Hun Sen frequently resorted to blatant threats of withdrawal or cutting of CPP funding and charitable contributions for infrastructural development projects like schools, bridges, irrigation projects and pagodas if the CNRP won the election.[62] Indirectly referring to the activities of the party working groups (PWG), including CPP-affiliated business tycoons and other wealthy individuals, the prime minister made clear distinctions between the use of privately sourced CPP budgets as opposed to official national budgets for socio-economic development. Beyond the construction and renovation of major roads, in the five years since the last election there was a lack of substantive investments in the delivery of public goods and services such as education and health, possibly signalling that the provision of 'off budget' CPP aid and development projects through patronage networks might actually be politically counterproductive. In addition, Hun Sen's frequent referral in the CPP-dominated media to the threat of civil war in the event of a CNRP electoral victory seemed to have lost any potency or relevance it may have once had for those who turned out to vote.[63] In a similar fashion, the CNRP reverted to anti-Vietnamese rhetoric in an attempt to malign Hun Sen and the CPP. By continuing to link contemporary Cambodian-Vietnamese border issues and Cambodia's historical relationship with the Vietnamese to Hun Sen and the CPP, the CNRP risked stoking dangerous racist sentiments.[64]

Regurgitation of well-worn base political rhetoric on both sides illustrated a continued lack of imagination with regard to engaging the electorate in meaningful ways. Instead, familiar efforts to undermine and weaken political opponents before the elections took precedence over any notion of debate among the political elite. Two months before the elections in June, the National Assembly's Permanent Committee, com-

---

62. Neou Vannarin, 'Hun Sen Says CPP Largess Will End if Election Is Lost', *The Cambodia Daily*, 7 March 2013.

63. Colin Meyn, 'Will Hun Sen's Threat of War Translate into Votes?' *The Cambodia Daily*, 27 June 2013.

64. LICADHO, 'Year 2013 in Review: Cambodian Elections'.

prising solely CPP members, expelled all 29 opposition party members from the assembly after they merged to form the CNRP. This move was justified on the basis that parliamentarians cannot be members of two parties at the same time, triggering distracting legal and constitutional debates. Attracting formal statements of protest from international donors, the move was nothing more than a demonstration of Hun Sen and the CPP's capacity to chasten the opposition and grandstand its authority.[65] In a separate and at times farcical pre-election episode, the government mounted a smear campaign against CNRP Vice-President Kem Sokha, which involved wild accusations of Khmer Rouge crime denial, parental neglect and paedophilia. The campaign embarrassingly backfired when, in an effort to publicly display his magnanimity, Hun Sen technically broke the law when he admitted to preventing Kem Sokha's arrest before he engaged in an alleged sexual encounter with an underage girl. Hun Sen later admitted to 'deliberately breaking the law' to avoid being accused by his detractors of interfering in the personal life of an opposition politician.[66]

Such political theatrics at election time was hardly new. However, Hun Sen and the CPP were well aware of the potential electoral threat posed by the unification of the SRP and HRP. Politically, from this perspective, the situation was serious. After a year of increasing social unrest and resistance to CPP-power elite behaviour, the party had to maximize every available advantage. Post-election assessments clearly showed the extent to which the CPP took that threat seriously and capitalized on its capacity to control key aspects of the election process.

National and international observer groups reported a familiar list of problems preventing opposition parties from competing on a level playing field. Aside from the major controversies surrounding voter registration irregularities, voter lists and the misuse of related documentation like the VINs and identification certificates, the CPP retained tight control of media access, both TV and radio. Misuse of state resources and employees to the advantage of the CPP was also widely reported. Despite attempts by EMOs and civil groups to regulate the amount of

65. Colin Meyn and Phorn Bopha, 'US Rebukes Government's Expulsion of the Opposition', *The Cambodia Daily*, 10 June 2013.

66. Neou Vannarin and Zsombor Peter, 'Hun Sen Defends His Decision to Break the Law', *The Cambodia Daily*, 20 June 2013.

money political parties spent on campaigns before the elections, no such rules and regulations governing party financing existed. Comfrel estimated that, even excluding money spent on mass propaganda, vote buying and gift-giving, the CPP spent USD 15 million on its campaign, 'five times more than the CNRP who spent five million.'[67]

A lack of trust in the electoral authorities from the NEC down to the PECs and CECs persisted. In addition, observers noted an actual increase in the number of complaints during the campaign period, recording more incidents than the total number received in the 2003 and 2008 elections combined. Investigation and resolution of complaints by the NEC and CECs in the immediate post-election period was not carried out to the satisfaction of opposition parties, reinforcing the chronic lack of trust in the electoral authority's ability to act impartially. Problems continued with the electoral authority's inability to fully implement and enforce the electoral legal framework and various codes of conduct, as well as regulations and procedures for administering the key phases of the process from voter registration, to the campaign, polling, counting and post-election dispute resolution.

Irrespective of the persistence of these familiar problems, observers and analysts noted a discernable shift in attitude among the electorate. There appeared to be a general feeling among opposition supporters and perhaps among traditional CPP voters that change in the status quo through the ballot box could be possible. National observer groups noted a greater awareness among people of their political and civil rights and participation, particularly among sizable numbers of young Cambodian voters. Unlike in past elections, there seemed to be a willingness among voters to express their political views freely, without fear of reprisal from CPP-affiliated authorities.

This confidence and lack of fear could be attributed to a number of factors including the momentum gathered after Sam Rainsy's return just before the elections. Whether or not people believed the CNRP was capable of replacing the CPP in government, it appeared that opposition party unity had animated and galvanized existing anti-government sentiment in ways not seen since the 1993 elections. This momentum continued into the campaign period during CNRP-organized forums,

---

67. Ibid. Personal interviews with civil society organization leaders and CNRP parliamentarians, June 2014.

which succeeded in attracting large numbers of people who were confident enough to participate despite the possibility of retaliation from local authorities. In the years since the 2008 elections, government failure to adequately meet socio-economic expectations of large segments of the population, alongside growing unrest and discontent with government complicity in the excesses of a small economic elite, left voters feeling that they had nothing to lose by voting for the CNRP. [68]

Another possible factor was that many within the ranks of the CPP-affiliated patronage networks were also expressing dissatisfaction with existing political economic arrangements. Immediately after the elections, rumours began to circulate that a significant percentage of poorly paid soldiers – including Hun Sen's personal bodyguard unit – and civil servants once loyal to the CPP had registered discontent by voting for the CNRP. [69] Civil servants' pay increases had always featured in the election campaign rhetoric of both the CPP and the opposition in past elections. However, in 2013 the CNRP presented a simple seven-point platform promising to pay civil sector employees a minimum $250 per month and garment workers $150, as well as providing a social security system and free access to health and education. [70] Part of the funding for the pay increases according to the CNRP would be generated by increased taxes on casinos and ELCs. [71] The CPP responded by arguing that low-level civil servants' salaries had been steadily increasing over time. To prove the point, in August, before the official election results were announced, the government increased 90,000 civil servants' salaries by about 40 per cent, from just over US$60 per month to around US$86, still far below what the CNRP claimed they would do if elected. [72]

The timing of the government's civil servants' pay increase before the announcement of the official election results was indicative of the

---

68. Personal interview with adviser to senior CPP official, Phnom Penh, May 2014.

69. Hul Reaksmey, 'Low-Paid Civil Servants to Get Pay Boost', *The Cambodia Daily*, 8 August 2013. Personal interviews with civil society leaders, Phnom Penh, June 2014.

70. Ben Woods and Eang Mengleng, 'CNRP Proposes Minimum Wage, Law for Garment State Workers', *The Cambodia Daily*, 1 March 2013.

71. Ibid.

72. Vong Sokheng and Shane Worrall, 'Civil servants to see raise', *Phnom Penh Post*, 8 August 2013.

nervousness among many CPP officials. Tried and tested methods of manipulation and control used to secure convincing electoral victories had proved to be considerably less effective than in the past. Even discounting the widely reported irregularities and abuses – especially with voter lists and associated voter forms – the differences in votes between the two principal antagonists brought to the surface the collective dramas that had been under way since the end of the 1993 elections. Not since 1997 had the CPP faced such a formidable electoral challenge. The evolution of the post-1998 political-economic system put in place by Hun Sen and his supporters and underpinned by elections had by 2013 begun to decay. As in 1993, forces ultimately responsible for heralding change came from within the body politic. How the architects of the system respond to the discernible shift within the electorate before the next scheduled elections in 2018 remains to be seen.

If post-election events are any indication of the future political trajectory, then further instability and violent social unrest before the next elections are highly likely if the government continues in its failure to address key reforms in a meaningful way. Because authoritarian elections are the principal mechanism by which power is maintained, the reforms challenging CPP control and influence over the process before 2018 are unlikely to be fully implemented in practice. Yet as the results in 2013 clearly showed, despite its best efforts to control the process, the party was unable to exert as much influence to determine the results as it had in the past. Nevertheless, a thorough overhaul of the existing electoral system demanded by opposition parties and concerned civil groups may not be the catalyst for further social and political change. The government's refusal to do so in ways that will satisfy these demands will determine political developments for good or ill. Post-election violent suppression of demonstrations and protests followed by more severe restrictions on freedoms of assembly and expression are the earliest indication of future political instability.

Continuity and Change: Future Elections in Cambodia

It was no coincidence that the national elections of 2013 ended in more or less the same way as they did in 1993, 1998, 2003 and 2008: in dispute over irregularities and allegations of fraud. With the exception of 2008, all other elections ended after lengthy and often violent political standoffs between the opposition and the CPP. Given the nature of Cambodia's elections, this was hardly surprising. Over the preceding two decades, internationally supported elections in Cambodia have been the central mechanism through which Hun Sen and the CPP have legitimized, maintained and reproduced its authoritarian grip on political-economic power. At the same time, elections have been the principal instrument through which political and civil opposition have persistently struggled to challenge Hun Sen's system of governance. The 2013 elections represented a dramatic change in the dynamics of that struggle, as an increasing number of voters formally registered discontent with the manner in which Hun Sen and the CPP governed Cambodia.

Events after the July 2014 rapprochement between Hun Sen and Sam Rainsy thus indicated that the CPP needed to re-evaluate its approach to the opposition. Unlike in the past, the CNRP continued to present a unified stance in its demands for an internationally backed inquiry and possible early elections. However, international intervention in the form of an independent committee to investigate credible allegations of serious electoral irregularities was unlikely. International donors, especially the EU, were well aware of the politically destabilizing effects of elections in Cambodia. For similar reasons an early election was never a realistic consideration outside CNRP circles. The preparedness of security and armed forces to use live ammunition against protesters in 2013 and 2014 was proof enough to show the CPP's intent not to tolerate a concerted political challenge. And yet it had to control the damage done to the party's image and credibility by the 2013 elections.

By accommodating CNRP demands for electoral reform the CPP could achieve a number of objectives. First, by initially forcing the CNRP to back away from demands for an internationally backed investigation the CNRP ran the risk of losing political momentum and discrediting itself among many of its supporters demanding real change. Second, a commitment to a reform process limited further criticism of the government and the party among some international observers and some voters. And third, another lengthy period of reform negotiations would allow the party leadership CPP the time needed to develop and consolidate its electoral strategy for the commune elections in 2017, followed by key parliamentary elections the following year. By the end of 2015 all indications suggested that to greater or lesser degrees the CPP had achieved all of these objectives.

Facing criticism for what some grassroots supporters viewed as a virtual capitulation to the CPP in July 2014, the CNRP was on the back foot politically. According to election monitoring organizations like COMFREL, the much vaunted election reforms pushed for by the CNRP leadership fell short of expectations. Amendments to the laws on the election of members of the National Assembly and commune councils were judged by civil society groups to be more restrictive than the previous law.[73] The constitutional status of the newly restructured NEC was greeted with cautious optimism. Nevertheless, doubts lingered about the committee's capacity to stay out of reach of CPP interference. The reappointment of the previous NEC secretary general Tep Nytha in January 2016 did nothing to assuage the doubters.[74] A new computerized voter registration system using voters, biometric data adopted by the NEC was, however, seen as a positive step towards reducing electoral fraud and administrative errors.[75]

Renewed repression of CNRP activists and leadership in July 2015 exposed the extent to which Hun Sen and the CPP were not genuinely committed to thoroughgoing electoral reform. Provoked by CNRP political rhetoric in early 2015 and active CNRP engagement in disputed Cambodian-Vietnamese border areas, the CPP leadership reacted swiftly and authoritatively.[76] The arrest and jailing of CNRP activists and a Sam Rainsy Party senator before the removal of the party's vice president from his position in the National Assembly were clear warnings that an emboldened aspirational political opposition would still not be tolerated. The lifting of Sam Rainsy's parliamentary immunity and his removal from parliament came days after he asserted that the opposition

---

73. COMFREL, 'Democracy, Elections and Reform. Annual Report 2015'. March 2016, pp. 48–50.

74. Kuch Naren, 'Tep Nytha Reappointed to NEC Post', *The Cambodia Daily*, 16 January 2016.

75. COMFREL, 'Democracy, Elections and Reform. Annual Report 2015', p. 50.

76. Meas Sokchea, 'We're no Funcinpec', *Phnom Penh Post*, 21 April 2015; Alex Willemyns and Mech Dara, 'CNRP to Order Lawmakers Silent on VN Border Issue', *The Cambodia Daily*, 14 September 2015.

ʒue of Democracy (NLD) party's historic victory in the
tions in early November were a portent of things to come
...ʋodia's 2018 elections.[77]

The issues of electoral reform and the suppression of political opposition together illustrates the importance of elections for the CPP in
maintaining the status quo. To some extent this helps explain the repet-
itive nature of Cambodian electoral competition. However, the 2013
election results tipped the balance of electoral power back in favour of
the CNRP. CPP reaction to the results thus followed more or less typical
patterns but with some differences. As early as February 2015, Hun Sen
had begun the process of shoring up his power by placing more loyal
senior military and police officials on the CPP Central Committee. Hun
Sen's second son, two-star General Hun Manith, became head of the
armed forces intelligence department. His eldest son, Lt. General Hun
Manet, is head of Cambodia's counter-terrorism unit.[78] In an effort to
undermine CNRP support bases at home and abroad, Hun Sen's sons
have been instrumental in attempts to reach out to the youth and the
Cambodia diaspora. His youngest son, Hun Many, a CPP parliamentarian and the leader of the CPP-affiliated Union of Youth Federations, has
engaged with youth groups, especially through Facebook, and has for a
number of years been tasked with presenting a more acceptable face of
the CPP.[79] Hun Manet has been engaged in similar activities overseas.[80]

The activities of Hun Sen's sons are part of a broader CPP strategy to
control younger voter behaviour and restrict the impact that information
technology and social media have on the political landscape, especially
during election cycles. In the 2013 election campaign the CNRP capitalized on the rapid spread of information via mobile phone devices and
social networking sites like Facebook among its support base, many of
whom are young voters. In December, during a university graduation

77. Alice Cuddy and Meas Sokchea, 'Myanmar opposition victory resonates in
    Cambodia', *Phnom Penh Post*, 11 November 2015.

78. Radio Free Asia, 'Hun Sen's Cambodia Names Son Head of Military's Intelligence
    Department', 22 October 2015, http://www.rfa.org/english/news/cambodia/
    appointment-10222015170944.html. Accessed January 2016.

79. Kevin Ponniah, 'Hun Many opens up to criticism', *Phnom Penh Post*, 11 June 2014.

80. Mech Dara and Shaun Turton, 'CNRP reacts Manet's recruitment drive', *Phnom
    Penh Post*, 19 January 2016.

ceremony, Hun Sen warned Facebook users that authorities could easily trace individuals who post insulting or critical comments about him or government policy.[81] His comments came after a university student was arrested and subsequently sentenced to 18 months in prison for a Facebook post daring people to join him in a colour revolution.[82] In August 2015, the Ministry of Education issued a directive reminding students and teachers that political activities of any kind will not be tolerated in universities and institutions of higher learning. Institutions violating the ban could face closure and staff and students removal from their positions. [83] By contrast, it is well known that high ranking CPP use events like university student graduation ceremonies as political platforms. [84]

International Factors

Internationally, the lack of engagement in the election - preparations in 2013 was indicative of the fact that technically all of the necessary legal and procedural mechanisms were to greater or lesser degrees in place. What was missing was the political will necessary to create an even, competitive playing field. After almost 20 years of manipulated elections there was a growing tendency among some former diplomats to rail against a lack of direct public criticism by donors to the Hun Sen regime. In an almost contrite fashion, in February 2014, former Australian Foreign Minister Gareth Evans, one of the chief architects of the Cambodian international peace process in the 1980s, publicly acknowledged that diplomats in the 1990s had been duped by Hun Sen's regime's commitments to democracy and human rights.[85] In an unprecedented and widely disseminated newspaper opinion piece he stated that

---

81. Pech Sotheary, 'Hun Sen warns Facebook users that he's watching', *Phnom Penh Post*, 29 December 2015.

82. Ouch Sony and Taylor O'Connell, 'Student Gets 18 Months for Call for "Color Revolution"', *The Cambodia Daily*, 16 March 2016.

83. Mech Dara, 'Ministry Warns of Punishment For Political Activity in Schools', *The Cambodia Daily*, 12 August 2015.

84. Khuonn Karim. 'Hun Sen Sells "Win-Win Policy" to Students', *The Cambodia Daily*, 16 June 2015.

85. Alex Willemyns. 'Gareth Evans Calls For Sanctions on Government', *The Cambodia Daily*, 28 February 2014.

'for far too long Hun Sen and his colleagues have been getting away with violence, corruption, and media and electoral manipulation without serious internal or external challenge'. He added that 'the Cambodian government has been getting away with murder' and that that the accusation that 'as many as twenty of Hun Sen's close associates have each amassed as much as $1billion dollars through misappropriation of state assets' was plausible.[86]

Irrespective of these allegations, international donors, in particular the EU and Japan, viewed the CPP-CNRP agreement in July 2014 as an opportunity to resume support for elections in 2017 and 2018.[87] In 2015, they committed to support the new voter registration process, civil society engagement and voter education. The EU also announced its intention to recommence an election observer mission. Other donors, such as NDI and the Australian government, have pledged support in the areas of voter registration lists and the new national ID card system, respectively.[88] EU support and presumably other donor support are based on technical and political assumptions that the reform process and the culture of dialogue remain on track. The EU stated that it reserved the right to withdraw financing if it became 'clear that the 2017–18 elections will take place in an environment that is not effective democratic competition'.[89]

Events in the second half of 2015 put the EU's right to withdraw financing to the test. Physical assaults and judicial harassment were part of a deliberate attempt by elements within the CPP to intimidate and weaken the CNRP in the long run up to the elections. While these actions were routinely condemned by international donors, funding for electoral reform continued virtually uninterrupted. However, the European Parliament did pass a resolution condemning the targeting of CNRP members and called for the charges against Sam Rainsy and other officials to be revoked and the prosecution of the individuals responsible for the beating of the two CNRP MPs. Some of the EU parliamentarians

---

86. Ibid.

87. European Union. Annex 2 'Action Document for the Support to the electoral reform in Cambodia' https://ec.europa.eu/europeaid/sites/devco/files/aap-cambodia-annex2-20151214_en.pdf. Accessed January 2016.

88. Ibid.

89. Ibid., p. 12.

who took part in the vote speculated that EU aid to Cambodia could be under threat if concerns about democracy and human rights are not addressed by the RGC.[90]

In the final analysis, the 2013 election results reflected some of the significant socio-economic and political changes under way in Cambodia. Whether or not they represented a rejection of CPP governance or support for the CNRP was unclear. What was clear was that large numbers of Cambodian voters – especially among the youth – are desirous of change that would have a meaningful and positive impact upon their lives and livelihoods. Government performance in the five years after the previous elections in 2008 had not been satisfactory enough to maintain the CPP's complete dominance of electoral politics. Added to this was a noticeable reduction in fear in openly expressing political views and a greater awareness of voters' rights and responsibilities. Looked at from these perspectives the 2013 elections did bring to the surface a positive shift in consciousness among the electorate.

How significant a shift this turns out to be remains to be seen. Sam Rainsy's pardon and rapturous return from exile in July 2013 without doubt was instrumental in the CNRP's electoral success and indicative of a change in mood among voters. Familiar post-election events, however, suggested that any notion of a rupture within the political elite was premature. To be sure, the results for the CPP were a wake-up call. Party insiders were genuinely shocked by the extent of the losses.[91] By engaging with the opposition on electoral reform the CPP successfully deflected further criticism from both national and international sources. When the reforms came they left a lot to be desired in the eyes of civil groups like the Electoral Reform Alliance. Indeed, the amendments to the election laws were generally regarded by civil groups as restrictive. A newly restructured NEC and voter registration system were positive steps forward but because of past experiences doubts about the committee's ability to provide a level playing field for elections lingered.

Use of lethal force to suppress demonstrations clearly showed the government's unwillingness to tolerate continued dissent. Attempts to

---

90. Alex Willemyns, 'Aid threatened as EU calls for Rainsy's return', *Phnom Penh Post*, 27 November 2015.

91. Personal interview with CPP party member involved in the government's formal response to allegations of electoral fraud, Phnom Penh, June 2015.

weaken and marginalize opposition were nothing new, but the timing of the suppression of the CNRP leadership came as something of a surprise. The electoral threat facing the CPP was as great as it had ever been, necessitating a determined and early response. Control of the situation had to be as absolute as possible within the limitations of electoral competition. Elections for the CPP remained necessary but troublesome instruments for governance. CNRP efforts to capitalize on the momentum gained during the elections amounted to very little, even alienating its leadership from some of its grassroots supporters. After the signing of the July 2014 agreement the CPP moved quickly to prevent the CNRP from making any political capital from the deal.

Not long after an arrest warrant was issued in November Sam Rainsy promised to return to Cambodia to face arrest and possible imprisonment. His failure to make good on his promise alienated him further among CNRP supporters. Claiming he wanted to avoid any violence that his return might provoke, Rainsy said he preferred instead to seek a diplomatic solution that would enable him to return to Cambodia without the threat of arrest.[92] Several days later the European Parliament in Strasbourg passed a resolution in support of Rainsy's return; he remained overseas. How politically significant the EU resolution will be in deciding his fate ahead of the elections in 2017 and 2018 is not clear. What is clear is that the 2013 election results demonstrated the power of Cambodian elections to challenge the entrenched power of the CPP. More importantly, for the future of Cambodian political development they also raised crucial questions related to a possible CPP electoral defeat in 2018. Thus, the thorny question of a transfer of power in the event of a CPP defeat continues to dominate public discourse as both sides prepare for the 2017 and 2018 elections.

---

92. Mech Dara and Alex Willemyns, 'Sam Rainsy Seeking Deal Before Return', *The Cambodia Daily*, 19 November 2015.

Conclusion

*I*n 1991 the Paris Peace Accords set Cambodia's political development on a new and unpredictable political trajectory. As the centrepiece of the UNTAC operation, internationally financed and managed elections were designed to put the country on a path of peace, prosperity and democratization. In a post-Cold War era of political transition in former communist one-party states, it was generally accepted in international Western donor circles that competitive multi-party democratic elections were the best mechanism by which to achieve these objectives. In many cases, outcomes of elections to formalize transition in these states and end protracted civil wars in the early 1990s turned out to be much less democratic than some Western liberal democratic ideologues had hoped. Cambodia's experience between 1992–93 was held up as an ideal example of what can happen when Western liberal democratic values and mores are imposed from the outside. Multi-party elections were seen as an essential first step in the process of democratic acculturation in countries that had little or no prior experience of democracy. Others argued that elections should only be held after the rule of law and democratic institutions had been firmly established and consolidated. Thus, a period of liberal governance was necessary, preferably utilizing international development expertise to expunge 'illiberality' and pave the way for 'free and fair' elections at a later date.

Ideology and policy prescriptions often have a difficult time coming to practical terms with internal and external social, political and economic realities in any given setting. Sterile debates in the 1990s about what democratic elements ought to be in place before credible elections could be held temporarily diverted attention away from more prosaic issues of national and international political-economic interests and control. Proponents of transitional and post-conflict elections compellingly argued, for example, that before and during the process, the whole of the political and social system is on display, enabling observers to see what is there and what isn't in a democratic sense. This implies that, in situations where aid and international assistance is provided in support of elections, donors and development professionals can assess and target programmes in the democratization process. More often than not, in fact, focus was directed at what was lacking in the host country without giving too much consideration to the motivations and interests of the observers and interveners. As the 1990s steadily wore on, it became apparent that international aid and assistance may have actually been a part of the problem, as stated international commitments to items like free and fair elections, democracy and human rights were not matched by results on the ground.

Often, donor recourse to realpolitik was buttressed by subjective historical interpretations, along with unexamined and misinformed cultural explanations to account for the ineffectiveness of aid in tackling the problems it was purported to help solve. Diplomatic rhetoric surrounding commitments to universal ideals whilst pursuing national, regional and international interests in less than ideal ways was of course nothing new. However, by the end of the 1990s, if not before, glaring inconsistencies and contradictions of post-Cold War Western liberal idealism were obvious to those closely following events in places like Cambodia. The notion of an 'international community' – at least in Cambodia in the 1990s – comprised a fragmented, disparate, often discordant group of actors pursing different interests and agendas. To be sure, many professed interest in the idea of democracy and human rights, but differed in attitude and method as to how such ideals things could be realised. Ideologically, within the international community engaged in supporting Cambodian elections and providing assistance more generally, there existed a mix of both democratic and authoritarian tendencies that have had profound impacts in shaping outcomes.

Simply put, in considering the above interpretation, Cambodian elections since 1993 have meant different things to different people. For the majority of Cambodians traumatized by civil war, the UNTAC elections represented peace and the hope of a better life to come. For others, interested in democratization and human rights, elections meant opportunities to organize themselves in pursuit of those goals with international funding and support. Having had elections foisted upon them by outside forces, the CPP leaders had little choice but to embrace them in ways that would ensure their political survival. As unpopular incumbents, open political competition alongside an opposition in internationally organized elections was a considerable threat, and defeat had to be avoided at all costs. In contrast, the elections were seen by the Khmer Rouge as providing opportunities as well as obvious threats to their survival as a political and military force. In reality, their decision not to participate but to continue to attempt to manipulate the political process from afar ultimately led to their final demise. From the outset, F'pec and other Sihanouk-era forces had the most to gain. Elections under international control meant that they stood a good chance of realizing their retrospective claims to at least some state control.

Internationally and regionally, the UNTAC elections meant different things. Political and economic stability through international disengagement from the Cambodian imbroglio was uppermost in the minds of international powers. An elected government with which to do business was an essential pre-requisite for further geopolitical engagement, investment, trade and aid. From this perspective, according to decision makers at UN HQ in New York, successful elections had to take place at all costs within the allotted time frame and budget. In this sense, it was a temporal, pragmatic event with little thought for future democratic development beyond the formation of a new coalition government. Taken together, the meaning attached to the elections determined the behaviour and conduct of all national and international groups. While the elections served a purpose in producing a new formal governance structure, the circumstances under which it was formed and the distribution of power within it had dramatic consequences for the preparation, conduct and outcome of future elections.

In acquiescing to demands for an equal share of power, Ranariddh, Sihanouk and the UN effectively gave the CPP and ultimately Hun Sen the necessary leverage to regain what had been lost through the polls. Under this new political system, future control over elections success would be a central component in Hun Sen's and the CPP's strategies to reconsolidate overall control of the Cambodian state. Due to international constraints and support, complete control over elections was not possible. Instead the careful manipulation of events and processes before, during and after the polls to secure victory and a concomitant semblance of national and international legitimacy was required. Matters were made more difficult by an emergent civil society pushing for a greater say in the affairs of government, especially with regard to the organization and conduct of elections, as well as an increasingly popular and dissident opposition, some of which rallied around Sam Rainsy. Furthermore, substantial international technical and financial assistance was needed to build a new election infrastructure virtually from scratch, contributing to increased tensions between all groups.

For almost three years, between early 1996 and the end of 1998, national politics was consumed by machinations and manoeuvrings related to preparations for elections. With political and economic stakes as high as they were, conflict and confrontation was inevitable. Senior UN representatives engaged in the preparations were well aware of Hun Sen's strategy to eliminate any opposition even before the March 1997 atrocity and the brief but bloody coup several months later. Having presided over the rout and murder of opponents, the path was clear for the CPP to exercise enough control, with international technical and financial assistance, to engineer a favourable outcome in the 1998 elections. As crooked as those elections were, they served the interests of international donors frustrated by the constant political infighting which had obstructed the path to full political economic re-engagement in Cambodia.

In spite of the manner in which Hun Sen and his loyalists cleared the political ground in 1997, an opposition of sorts was essential to keep the system credible enough to satisfy the interests of foreign donors. The 1998 election results showed that amidst widespread intimidation and violence perpetrated by local officials, the police, the military and the security forces, there was still considerable voter resistance to the dominance of the CPP. Electoral performance by the opposition parties was all the more impressive given the level of damage inflicted on their organizational capacities in the aftermath. Moreover, the 1998 elections provided further opportunities for EMOs and other relevant civil groups engaged in the election process to evolve, providing a third, ostensibly neutral strand outside of party politics. With these elements in place, future CPP election victories could not be guaranteed without continued manipulation and authoritarian control. When the dust finally settled after opposition-led, post-election protests and street violence, the struggle switched to a reform of the elections process, especially the controversial NEC, hastily assembled only months before the elections.

From an international perspective, the lead up to the 1998 elections exposed manifest differences in approach among the various actors and agencies, especially within the UN system. International condemnation of the 1997 coup and the extrajudicial killings of senior F'pec personnel did not translate into concrete action against Hun Sen or perpetrators within the CPP. On the contrary, Hun Sen was rewarded by international donors with continued technical and financial assistance for elections, only having to concede on the issue of the return of Ranariddh and other opposition leaders to participate in them. Divisions among the high level diplomatic group and the UN Office for Human Rights deepened as election-related abuses and killings continued throughout 1997 and 1998. Although ultimately unsuccessful, attempts by elements within the Phnom Penh diplomatic community to curtail and suppress the dissemination of human rights reports, they typified the tacit international donor support for elections, whatever the costs.

Belief among some international diplomats in the sincerity of the new government's commitment to the reform of the system after the 1998 elections proved to be misplaced. Reform in key areas like the judiciary, law enforcement and elections threatened the very base upon which the CPP and Hun Sen's power and control were built. Very little substantive progress was made. As a central plank in the donor driven agenda, decentralization and deconcentration reforms were enacted, but came via flawed local elections in 2002. While some international donors applauded the creation of commune councils, overwhelming CPP victories in these elections reinforced its power, especially in rural areas. Repeated patterns of intimidation, violence and killings involving state officials, security and military forces against opposition party members and activists and voters, coupled with the misuse of state resources, especially the media, were used to secure overwhelming electoral success for the CPP. Although international observer groups acknowledged that problems existed, confirming reports of abuses from EMOs and national and international human rights organizations, donors were not prepared to impose sanctions upon the government, preferring instead to make recommendations for them to put their house in order before the next National Assembly elections the following year.

By the end of the 2002 it was clear to most analysts and observers of Cambodian politics that the CPP was not prepared to relinquish any control of the elections administration beyond piecemeal changes to the NEC membership in order to appease national and international critics. Extensive EMO lobbying and advocacy campaigns focused on voter education and electoral reform were partially successful in reaching out to more voters, but had very little impact on the reform of the elections administration. Hun Sen's authoritarian grip on elections was further facilitated by events outside of Cambodia. The events of September 2001 in New York, followed by the Bali Bombing in 2002, bolstered the position of 'strongmen' like Hun Sen and his notorious police chief Hok Lundy, as Cambodia became an ally in the so-called 'War on Terror'. Abuses perpetrated by US military personnel at the prisons Abu Ghraib in Iraq and Guantanamo Bay in Cuba added to renewed accusations of Western double standards. Notions of democracy and 'free and fair' elections were becoming increasingly difficult for Western leaders to sustain as the neo-conservative-led, neo-imperial agenda was rolled out in Afghanistan and Iraq.

Meanwhile, back in places like Cambodia, regional security issues and political threats against the state were used as justification for controlling opposition forces and dissenting voices, often through targeted killings, violence and other extrajudicial means. At the same time, donor technical and financial support for elections in partnership with the NEC continued. A technical and legal approach led by the UNDP sought to minimize or depoliticize sensitive issues, for example NEC reforms. Cosmetic changes to the membership of the committee before the 2003 polls did little to instil confidence in the impartiality and independence of the NEC among opposition parties and civil society organizations. International and national observers commended the NEC on some technical improvements and an overall reduction in violence, but could not avoid the fact that the same problems remained regarding the conduct of elections, regardless of previous recommendations made to the government.

Voting patterns in the National Assembly elections in 2003 continued to show strong support for opposition parties, which would likely grow if elections were conducted on a level playing field free from excessive CPP control. It was on this basis that the opposition-led 'Alliance of

Democrats' embarked upon the longest post-election political standoff yet against the CPP. When the government was finally formed in June 2004, its composition reflected Hun Sen's wiliness in manoeuvring and manipulating the political elite both inside and outside his own party. Ranariddh's and F'pec's capitulation to Hun Sen amidst embarrassing accusations of bribery and betrayal precipitated the discrediting of the opposition more generally among voters. By the summer of 2004, any lingering doubts about Hun Sen's pre-eminence at the top of the hierarchy had been finally dispelled.

From the 2003 elections up to and including 2008, the CPP benefited politically and economically from impressive macro-economic growth and relative political stability. After ten years of slow progress hampered by political infighting, visible signs of change began to manifest themselves around the country. Asian Development Bank and Chinese investment in roads, bridges and other large infrastructure and communications projects were opening up the country. Increased numbers of tourists, foreign investments, a construction boom and better than expected performance in the garment sector were at the forefront of socio-economic change. Norodom Sihanouk's abdication and his replacement by his son Norodom Sihamoni symbolized the profound changes that were underway in Cambodia. Politically, once back in government alongside the CPP, Hun Sen was able to exploit F'pec's weaknesses, ultimately humiliating Ranariddh into bowing out of politics altogether. Attempts by Hun Sen to eliminate or marginalize Sam Rainsy and other opposition and human rights activists and journalists through threats, arrests, detention on trumped-up charges and intimidation were also partially successful. Rainsy's self-imposed exile to avoid arrest in 2005 on dubious charges of defamation and incitement, followed by Ranariddh's political demise, sent strong signals to voters of a fragmented and weak opposition. The creation of the Human Rights Party (HRP) by the former senior F'pec official Kem Sokha did provide a third alternative to SRP and F'pec, but not in time to make any real difference in either the 2007 local elections or the National Assembly elections the year after.

Despite strong criticism by the World Bank in late 2004 about lack of progress with agreed-upon reforms, the Cambodian government nonetheless received the aid pledges it had asked for even though it had failed to fulfil its commitments. The downturn in economic growth projected by the World Bank in its 2004 assessment did not materialize. Hun Sen and CPP-affiliated patronage networks continued to amass more wealth from illegal logging and economic land concessions. Proceeds and patronage were used to fund CPP victories in the 2007 local and 2008 National Assembly elections. In 2008 in particular, victory was made possible through the extensive use of state resources and personnel, and administrative malfeasance and incompetence, all funded through CPP patronage networks and reinforced by constant coverage on state and private media in the months before the elections.

Irrespective of a reduction in high profile electoral violence and killings of opposition party activists and members, fear, intimidation and coercion of large sections of the electorate remained a persistent feature of the elections landscape in 2003 and 2008. A reduction in state-backed violence beginning in 2002 and 2003 was accompanied by an increase in bureaucratic and administrative problems associated with the manipulation of voter lists and voter identification documents by CPP-affiliated local authorities, especially village and commune chiefs. Opposition parties, supported by the findings of national observer groups, argued that well over a million voters in both the 2003 and 2008 elections had been disenfranchised due to administrative incompetence and the political manipulation of election-related documents. The apparent incapacity and unwillingness of electoral authorities to investigate and act against violations of electoral laws and NEC rules, regulations and codes of conduct fuelled post-election disputes. The outright rejection of almost all opposition complaints by the NEC, upheld by the Constitutional Council in all elections, did nothing to instil confidence in the integrity and impartiality of the system.

By the end of the 2008 process, international donors engaged in Cambodia's elections had little choice but to accept that no matter how technically and legally sound the system was, there was no political will to ensure it functioned in an independent and impartial manner. Indeed, long-term international observer groups like the EU could do nothing more than make similar recommendations to those that the UN and other donors had been making for nearly a decade. They were fully aware that the CPP was so entwined with formal and informal structures of state that the government was incapable of implementing recommendations, because to do so would undermine the type of elections its continued power relied upon.

At this juncture it appeared that Cambodian elections had become nothing more than instruments for legitimizing Hun Sen's and the CPP's authoritarian political–economic control of the Cambodian population and territory. And yet, elections since 1993 had to be competitive enough to allow opposition parties to participate in without directly challenging the ability of the CPP to manipulate outcomes in its favour. The capacity to do this rested on a variety of strategies, not least of which was to convince voters of the righteousness of the CPP's superiority, backed up by the use of necessary force, fear and intimidation alongside the promise of a share in the material benefits of its hollow brand of development. Coupled with persistent attempts to eliminate and marginalize or otherwise discredit opponents and control key aspects of the electoral administration, this strategy had, up to and including the 2008 elections, proved to be reasonably successful. Endorsement of the flawed system through continued technical and financial assistance and JIOG and EU observation missions provided an international legitimizing dimension to the strategy.

By the time of Sam Rainsy's arrival back in Cambodia after yet another period of self-imposed exile followed by a politically endorsed royal pardon in July 2013, it seemed this strategy was wearing thin. The huge crowd gathered at the airport to greet Rainsy took CNRP leaders and many others completely by surprise, indicating a possible shift in mood among growing numbers of Cambodian voters. Prior to this, resistance to CPP governance remained isolated in pockets, visible in isolated but numerous land disputes and labour demonstrations. While the SRP and HRP had made very modest gains in the 2012 commune elections, the CPP continued to display political command and control in rural areas. Any hint of the beginning of a possible mass organization of existing discontent had been ruthlessly nipped in the bud by military police and security forces. Usual targets included legitimate dissenting voices critical of the illegal excesses of state action, accused under the typically false pretexts of terrorism and insurrection.

Past fears among voters about the political, military and economic consequences of an outright CPP defeat through the ballot box was legitimate. However, the 2013 election results indicated that this fear was dissipating sufficiently enough to reduce the numbers of people voting for the CPP. Calls for change at CNRP rallies and forums reflected the accelerating socio-economic developments experienced during the five years since the end of the 2008 elections. The disproportionate distribution of benefits accrued from the vast accumulation of wealth by an increasingly smaller group of predatory elites centred around Hun Sen was a growing source of discontent, especially among an aspirational, restive, largely excluded but technologically savvy younger generation who used social media like Facebook and mobile devices to good effect. Anger and resistance to the CPP's chronic political-economic cronyism, manifested in land disputes and labour demonstrations before and after the elections, clearly showed that many more Cambodians were no longer prepared to tolerate the trampling of civil and political rights without registering their discontent.

The conduct of the elections and the responses of the political elite to another protracted post-election drama were salutary reminders of the entrenched power of Hun Sen and the CPP. Not only did problems with electoral processes and administration persist, but, according to national and international observer reports, efforts by the CPP to maintain its distance from the CNRP through control of the usual channels intensified with impunity. Moreover, the noticeable lack of international engagement before, during and immediately after the elections was indicative of a general willingness on behalf of donors to leave the government to its own devices irrespective of the problems and continue to conduct business more or less as usual. After almost two decades of technical and financial support for Cambodian elections, those donors interested in seeing electoral transparency and accountability had, for all intents and purposes, failed.

The CNRP's failure to secure its post-election demands for an independent, internationally supported investigation was hardly surprising. International donors engaged with electoral politics in Cambodia had worked hard in the previous two decades to ensure peace and political stability at the expense of free and fair elections. And yet the 2013 results clearly showed that elections in Cambodia were competitive enough to inflict serious losses on the CPP. Responses to those losses by the CPP followed similar patterns. A commitment to electoral reforms that could be manipulated at a future date, followed by the violent and legal suppression of opposition to the CPP, operated from the same political play-book used for almost two decades. The timing of the suppression and the legal cases against senior CNRP leaders, including Sam Rainsy, however, revealed the extent to which the CPP feared defeat at the 2017 and 2018 polls.

Sensing a possible shift among the political elite and the electorate in light of the 2013 results, international donors like the EU and Japan were prepared to re-engage and support the election reform process. The EU resolution calling for charges against Sam Rainsy to be dropped, allowing him to return to Cambodia without facing arrest, did not interfere with continued EU financial and technical donor support for the 2017–18 elections. Donors like the EU are fully aware of the political risks associated with electoral support. Re-engagement with Cambodia's elections after the July 2014 agreement must be therefore be treated with a certain amount of caution. How donors will respond to if the integrity of the election reform process is compromised by the CPP is uncertain.

Future electoral outcomes will be determined to a great extent by the capacity of the CNRP to remain united in the face of inevitable attempts by Hun Sen and the CPP to eliminate them before the 2017 commune and 2018 National Assembly elections. Whatever happens, Cambodia's elections will continue to be key multi-dimensional sites of contestation between those forces maintaining power and control to preserve and perpetuate self-interested agendas, and those striving to usurp them. Elections in Cambodia hold out the possibility of positive social and political change. In the meantime, if the current regime continues to hold sway, the already accelerating negative social, political and environmental costs inherited by the next generation of Cambodians could well be irreversible.

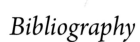

Bibliography

Adams, Brad, 'Cambodia: July 1997: Shock and Aftermath'. Available online at http://www.hrw.org/news/2007/07/27/cambodia-july-1997-shock-and-aftermath. Accessed May 2013.

ADHOC, 'A Turning Point? Land, Housing and Natural Resources Rights in Cambodia in 2012', Phnom Penh, February 2013.

Agreement on a Comprehensive Political Settlement of the Cambodian Conflict. Part 1. Article 6. October 1991. Paris.

Ayres, D. 'Decentralisation: A Review of Literature'. Commune Council Support Project. August, Phnom Penh, 2001.

Barber, Jason, 'Negotiations falter as heat goes on Ta Mok', Phnom Penh Post, April 1997.

Barber, Jason and Huw Watkin, 'Hun Sen left seat-less at the UN', Phnom Penh Post, 10 October 1997.

Barton, Cat and Vong Sokheng, 'Ranariddh quits politics', Phnom Penh Post, 3 October 2008.

Beetham, David. Democracy and Human Rights. Cambridge: Polity Press, 2000.

Beresford, Melanie, Nguon Sokha, Rathin Roy, Sau Sisovanna and Ceema Namazie. 'The Macroeconomics of Poverty Reduction in Cambodia'. United Nations Development Programme. March, 2004.

Biddulph, R. 'Decentralisation and Commune Council Reforms: Immediate Opportunities for Cambodian NGOs'. Oxfam GB in Cambodia. December. Phnom Penh, 2000.

Bou Saroeun, 'Calls for Land Reform', Phnom Penh Post, 4-17 February 2000.

Bush, George H. W. State of the Union Address, 29 January 1991. Available online at http://www2.hn.psu.edu/faculty/jmanis/poldocs/uspressu/SUaddressGHWBush.pdf, accessed November 2014.

Cambodia New Vision, 'Address by Samdech Hun Sen on the "Rectangular Strategy" for Growth, Employment, Equity and Efficiency'. Unofficial Translation from the Khmer. Available online at http://cnv.org.kh/en/?p=446. Accessed 13 May 2014.

Chan Sophal et al. 'Cambodia: Challenges and Options of Regional Economic Integration'. Conference Papers. Cambodia Development Resource Institute (CDRI), pp. 10–21. Phnom Penh, October 1998.

Chaumeau, Christine, 'King returns, gives nod to Ung Huot', Phnom Penh Post, 12 September 1997.

Clark, Elizabeth Spiro. 'Why Elections Matter', *The Washington Quarterly*, Summer, 23.3, 2000, pp. 27–40.

Cochrane, Liam. 'Government takes scolding, $500 million from donors', *Phnom Penh Post*, 17 December 2004.

COMFREL (Committee for Free and Fair Elections), 'Final Report, the 1998 National Assembly Elections in Cambodia'. Phnom Penh, February 1998.

————, 'Annual Narrative Report for the year 2000: Activities, Achievement and Impact'. Phnom Penh, 2000.

————, 'Report of the Commune Council Elections (February 03, 2002)', Phnom Penh, March 2002.

————, 'Statement on Election Reforms in Cambodia', 8 July 2002.

————, 'Assessment Report on the Cambodian National Assembly Elections 2003'. Available online at http://www.comfrel.org/eng/components/com my-publications/files/79153401 Result Report 2003 NA Election Report COMFREL 2003 En Fina.pdf. Accessed June 2013.

————, 'Final Assessment and Report on the 2007 Commune Council Elections', Phnom Penh, 2007.

————, 'Final Assessment and Report on the 2008 National Assembly Elections', Phnom Penh, 2008.

————, 'Survey Report on Voter Lists and Registration'. Phnom Penh, July 2009.

————, 'Democracy, Elections and Reform in Cambodia. 2013 Annual Report', March 2014.

————, 'Democracy, Elections and Reform in Cambodia. 2014 Annual Report', March 2015.

————, 'Democracy, Elections and Reform in Cambodia. 2015 Annual Report', March 2016.

COMFREL and ERA, 'Table Assessment of Changes to the LEMNA'. Internal document, English version. Phnom Penh, January 2016.

COMFREL and NICFEC. 'Pre Election Assessment Joint Statement, 25 July'. Phnom Penh, 2003.

COMFREL, NICFEC, Cambodian Human Rights Action Committee (CHRAC), and Star Kampuchea, 'Joint Statement of Concerns over the Selecting Procedures of the National Election Committee Members for the 2003 National Assembly Elections', Phnom Penh, 10 October 2002.

Congressional Research Service Report for Congress. The Navy Department Library. 'Terrorism in Southeast Asia'. Updated 18 November 2003. Available online at http://www.history.navy.mil/library/online/terror-ism%20in%20southeast%20asia.htm. Accessed June 2013.

Coren, Michael, 'Elections Hok Lundy reads the riot act', *Phnom Penh Post*, 28 February 2003.

Craig, D., and K. Pak, 'Party Financing of Local Investment Projects: Elite and Mass Patronage', in C. Hughes and K. Un (eds), *Cambodia's Economic Transformation*. Copenhagen: NIAS Press, 2011.

Courtes, Marie-Christine, 'Between a hammer and an anvil', *Phnom Penh Post*, 27 March 1998.

Cranenburgh, O.V., 'International Policies to Promote African Democratization', in Jean Grugel (ed.), *Democracy without Borders: Transnationalization and Conditionality in New Democracies*. Cambridge: Polity Press, 1999.

Crossette, Barbara, 'Cambodian leaders in exile seek international monitoring of new elections', *New York Times*, 28 September 1997.

Cuddy, Alice and Meas Sokchea, 'Myanmar opposition victory resonates in Cambodia', *Phnom Penh Post*, 11 November 2015.

Dahl, Robert. *'Democracy and Its Critics'*. New Haven: Yale University Press, 1989.

'Diplomats Hand Over Election Guidelines', *The Cambodia Daily*, 27 November 1997.

Dassa, Ira, Keith Schultz, Evan Gottesman, and Brad Adams, 'Murder of a man with no enemies', *Phnom Penh Post*, 28 February 2003.

Davis, E.W., 'Imagined Parasites: Flows of Monies and Spirits', in C. Hughes and K. Un (eds), *Cambodia's Economic Transformation*. Copenhagen: NIAS Press 2011.

Doyle, Kevin, 'Stalking Terrorism Will Test Inter-ASEAN Trust', *The Cambodia Daily*, 12 November 2002.

Doyle, Kevin and Sambath Thet, 'Funcinpec Predicts Commune Election Win', *The Cambodia Daily*, 21 March 2000.

Doyle, M.W., *UN Peacekeeping in Cambodia: UNTAC's Civil Mandate*. Boulder: Lynne Rienner, 1995.

Eang Mengleng and James Welsh, 'Eight Years On, Assassination of Union Leader Remains Unsolved', *The Cambodia Daily*, January 2012.

Edwards, Penny. 'Imagining the other in Cambodian Nationalist Discourse Before and During the UNTAC Period', in S. Heder and J. Ledgerwood (eds), *Propaganda, Politics and Violence in Cambodia: Democratic Transition under United Nations Peace-keeping*. Armonk, New York: M.E. Sharpe, 1996.

Elstra/OSS Core group meeting, 2 December 1995.

Embassy of Japan, 'Statement of the Japanese Election Observation Mission on Commune Council Elections in the Kingdom of Cambodia February 3rd, 2002'. Phnom Penh, 5 February 2002.

EUEOM (EU Election Observer Mission Cambodia), 'Final Report on the Commune Elections', 2002.

———, 'Cambodia Commune Council Election 3 February 2002'. Available online at http://www.ecoi.net/file_upload/625_tmpphpwkuMbS.pdf. Accessed May 2013.

———, 'Final Report on the Elections of the Members of the National Assembly, 27 July 2003', 2003.

———, 'Final Report, National Assembly Elections, 27 July'. Phnom Penh, 13 October 2008. Available online at http://www.ecoi.net/file_up-load/625_tmpphpwkuMbS.pdf. Accessed June 2013.

European Union, 'Financing Agreement between The European Community and The Royal Government of Cambodia. Title: Support to the Democratic Electoral Process in Cambodia. Project Number: ALA 97/0513', October 1997.

————— , 'Special Representative's report on Elections in Cambodia', 26 July 1998.

————— , 'Action Document for the Support to the electoral reform in Cambodia', Annex 2, https://ec.europa.eu/europeaid/sites/devco/files/aap-cambodia-annex2-20151214_en.pdf. Accessed January 2016.

Findlay, T. *The Legacy and Lessons of UNTAC*, SIPRI Report, No 9. Oxford: Oxford University Press, 1995.

Fontaine, Chris, 'Election Watchdogs gear up', *Phnom Penh Post*, No. 15, July 1996.

Frieson, K., 'The Politics of Getting out the Vote in Cambodia', in S. Heder and J. Ledgerwood (eds), *Propaganda, Politics and Violence in Cambodia: Democratic Transition under United Nations Peace-keeping*. Armonk, New York: M.E. Sharpe, 1994.

————— , 'The Cambodian Elections of 1993: A Case of Power to the People?', in R.H. Taylor (ed.), *The Politics of Elections in Southeast Asia*. Washington, D.C.: Woodrow Wilson Center Press and Cambridge University Press, 1996.

Global Witness, 'Cambodia's Family Trees: Illegal logging and the stripping of public assets by Cambodia's elite'. Washington D.C., June 2007.

Global Witness Cambodia. Available online at http://www.globalwitness.org/campaigns/corruption/oil-gas-and-mining/cambodia. Accessed July 2013.

Gottesman, Evan, *Cambodia After the Khmer Rouge: Inside the Politics of Nation Building*. Chiang Mai: Silkworm Books, 2003.

Grainger, Mathew. 'UN blasts CPP's domination of state-run media', *Phnom Penh Post*, 3 July 1998.

————— , 'International observers' report "too political"', *Phnom Penh Post*, 17 July 1998.

————— , 'Critics say JIOG statement jumps the gun', *Phnom Penh Post*, 31 July 1998.

————— , 'Lessons from the 1998 national election', *Phnom Penh Post*, 1 February 2002.

Hayes, Michael, 'After Pol-Pot: the politics of survival', *Phnom Penh Post*, June 1997.

————— , 'Hun Sen moves as KR talks completed', *Phnom Penh Post*, July 1997.

————— , 'The CFF attack: schools of thought', *Phnom Penh Post*, 8–21 December 2000.

Heder, Steve, 'Cambodian Elections in Historical Perspective', in John, Vijghen (ed.), *People and the 1998 National Elections in Cambodia: Their Voices, Roles and Impact on Democracy*. Phnom Penh: Experts for Community Research, No. 44, 2002.

————, 'Hun Sen and Genocide Trials in Cambodia', in J. Ledgerwood (ed.), *Cambodia Emerges from the Past: Eight Essays*. Southeast Asia Publications. Center for Southeast Asian Studies. Northern Illinois University, 2002.

———— , 'Political Theatre in Cambodia: State, Democracy, Conciliation'. Unpublished conference paper. Phnom Penh, October 2004.

———— , 'Hun Sen's Consolidation: Death or Beginning of Reform'. *Southeast Asian Affairs 2005*, Singapore: ISEAS, pp. 113–30.

———— , 'Political Theatre in the 2003 Cambodian Elections: State Democracy and Conciliation in Historical Perspective', in Julia C. Strauss and Donal Cruise O'Brien (eds), *Staging Politics: Power and Performance in Asia and Africa*. London: I.B. Taurus, 2007.

Hruby, Denise and Huch Naren, 'Sam Rainsy Granted Royal Pardon by King', *The Cambodia Daily*, 13 July 2013.

Hughes, Caroline, 'Strategies and Impact of Election Observer Coalitions in Cambodia'. Phnom Penh: Experts for Community Research (ECR), Report No. 38, 2000. With assistance from Chhor Bonnaroath.

———— , 'Political Parties in the Campaign', in John L. Vijghen (ed.) *People and the 1998 Elections in Cambodia: Their Voices, Roles and Impact on Democracy*. Phnom Penh: Experts for Community Research (ECR), January 2002.

———— , *The Political Economy of Cambodia's Transition*. London: RoutledgeCurzon, 2003.

Hughes, Caroline and Tim Conway, 'Understanding pro-poor political change: the policy process'. London: Overseas Development Institute (ODI), 2003.

Hughes, Caroline and Kheang Un (eds), *Cambodia's Economic Transformation*, Copenhagen: NIAS Press, 2011.

Hughes, Caroline, with Real Sopheap, 'Nature and Causes of Conflict Escalation in the 1998 Election'. Phnom Penh: Cambodia Centre for Conflict Resolution under the auspices of the Cambodia Development Resource Institute, 2000.

Hul Reaksmey 'Low-Paid Civil Servants to Get Pay Boost', *The Cambodia Daily*, 8 August 2013.

Human Rights Watch, 'Cambodia's Commune Council Elections: A Human Rights Watch Backgrounder', January 2002.

———— , 'The Run-Up to Cambodia's 2003 National Assembly Election: Political Expression and Freedom of Assembly Under Assault'. A briefing paper, June 2003.

———— , 'Cambodia: Hun Sen Systematically Silences Critics', January 2005. Available online at http://www.hrw.org/news/2006/01/03/cambo-dia-hun-sen-systematically-silences-critics. Accessed May 2014.

———— , 'Cambodia: 15 Years on , No Justice in Grenade Attack. Available at http://www.hrw.org/news/2012/03/29/cambodia-15-years-no-justice-grenade-attack Accessed May 2014.

———— , '"Tell Them I Want to Kill Them": Two Decades of Impunity in Hun Sen's Cambodia, 2012'. Available online at http://www.hrw.org/sites/default/files/reports/cambodia1112webwcover_1.pdf. Accessed June 2014.

——— , 'Cambodia: Land Titling Campaign open to Abuse, June 12, 2012'. Available online at http://www.hrw.org/news/2013/06/12/cambodia-land-titling-campaign-open-abuse. Accessed July 2014.

Human Rights Watch Report. '*Cambodia at War*', 1 March 1995. Available at http://www.refworld.org/cgi-in/texis/vtx/rwmain?page=publisher&-publisher=HRW&type=&coi=KHM&docid=3ae6a7dd8&skip. Accessed April 2013.

International Republican Institute (IRI). 'Preliminary Statement on Cambodia's February 3, 2002 Commune Council Elections', 4 February 2002.

——— , 'Cambodia 2003 National Assembly Elections'. Available at http://www.iri.org/sites/default/files/Cambodia's%202003%20National%20Assembly%20Elections.pdf. Accessed June 2013.

'Inter-Parliamentary Union Delegation to observe the election in Cambodia', report. Available online at http://www.ipu.org/elcn-e/rptcamb.htm#Treatment. Accessed March 2013.

Jenner, Raoul M. 'Cambodian Chronicles (II): The Very First Steps Towards a Very Fragile Peace'. Far Eastern Research Center, Belgium, 1992.

——— , 'Cambodian Chronicles: non-paper'. Far Eastern Research Center, Belgium, 1993.

——— , 'Let the Khmers decide on democracy', *The Nation*, Bangkok, 10 June 1993.

Joint International Observer Group (JIOG), 'Press Release', 27 July 1998.

Jordans, Jay, 'Persecution of Cambodia's Ethnic Vietnamese During and Since the UNTAC Period', in S. Heder and J. Ledgerwood (eds), *Propaganda, Politics and Violence in Cambodia: Democratic Transition under United Nations Peacekeeping*. New York: M.E. Sharpe, 1996.

Kay Kimsong, 'Opposition Demonstrators: NEC Controlled by the CPP', *The Cambodia Daily*, 25 February 2002.

Khmer Institute for Democracy, 'Fair Trial Principles', 2006. Available online at http://www.khmerrough.com/pdf/FairTrialPrinciples160606.pdf Accessed April 2013.

Khuonn Karim. 'Hun Sen Sells "Win-Win Policy" to Students', *The Cambodia Daily*, 16 June 2015.

Khuy Sokheoun, Catherine Philp, Ham Samnang, Deutsche Presse-Agentur and Agence France-Presse, 'Murder Fuels Fears of Political Violence', *The Cambodia Daily*, 6 March 1998.

Kihara, David. 'Rights Officials See Flaws in Terror Pledge', *The Cambodia Daily*, November 13, 2002.

Kim Chan and Lor Chandara, 'PM Faces Up To Criticism From F'pec', *The Cambodia Daily*, 5 December 2002.

Kimsan Chantara and Jeff Hodson, 'Supreme Council of Magistracy Convenes', *The Cambodia Daily*, 4 December 1997.

Kimsan Chantara and Jeff Smith. 'B-40 Rocks Siem Reap Motorcade', *The Cambodia Daily*, 25 September 1998.

Kuch Naren, 'CNRP Officials Imprisoned on Insurrection Charges', *The Cambodia Daily*, 17 July 2014.

———, 'Tep Nytha Reappointed to NEC Post', *The Cambodia Daily*, 16 January 2016.

Kuch Naren and Molly Ball. 'PM Warns Sam Rainsy To Tone Down Rhetoric', *The Cambodia Daily*, 31 March 2013.

Kumar, Krisna, (ed.) *Postconflict Elections, Democratization and International Assistance*. Boulder, Colorado: Lynne Rienner, 1998.

Kumar, Rajesh, 'UN agency condemned for lobbying tactics', *Phnom Penh Post*, Issue 11/4, 15–28 February 2002.

Kyne, Phelim, 'Commune elections back to the future', *Phnom Penh Post*, Issue 8/16, 6–19 August 1999.

Law on Administration of Communes (English). NS/RKM/030/05. Chapter two. Article 9.

Le Billion, P. and S. Springer, 'Between War and Peace: Violence and accommodation in the Cambodian logging sector', cited in S. Milne and S. Mahanty (eds), *Conservation and Development in Cambodia: Exploring frontiers of change in nature, state and society*. London: Routledge, 2015

Ledgerwood, J. and J. L. Vijghen, 'Decision-Making in Rural Khmer Villages', in J. Ledgerwood (ed.), *Cambodia Emerges from the Past: Eight Essays*. Southeast Asian Publications, Center for Southeast Asian Studies, Northern Illinois University, 2002.

Lenaghan, Nick, 'Hardliners Split as PMs Quarrel', *Phnom Penh Post*, June 1997.

———, 'Asean says "No" – foreign aid put on ice', *Phnom Penh Post*, July 1997.

Lewis, Simon and Phorn Bopha, 'Rainsy Tells Election Observers to Stay Away', *The Cambodia Daily*, 26 February 2013.

LICADHO (Cambodian League for the Promotion and Defense of Human Rights), 'Statement Joint Organisations, Open Letter regarding forced eviction of Boueng Kak Lake residents to Mr. Kep Chuktema, Governor of the Municipality of Phnom Penh, 2008'. Available online at http://www.licadho-cambodia.org/pressrelease.php?perm=196. Accessed June 2014.

———, 'The Great Cambodian Giveaway: Visualizing Land Concessions over Time', September 2012. Available online http://www.licadho-cambodia.org/concession_timelapse/. Accessed June 2014.

———, 'Attacks and Threats Against Human Rights Defenders in Cambodia 2010–2012'. December 2012.

———, 'Briefing Update: The Yorm Bopha Case'. Available online at http://www.licadho-cambodia.org/reports/files/177LICADHOBriefBopha2013-English.pdf. Accessed June 2014.

———, 'Year 2013 in Review: A shrinking space for assembly and expression in Cambodia', 19 March 2014.

————, 'Year 2013 in Review: Cambodian Elections', 18 March 2014. Available online at http://www.licadho-cambodia.org/articles/20140318/139/index.html. Accessed July 2014.

Lizée, Pierre. "The Evolution of Great Power Involvement in Cambodia", in D. Werfel and B. Burton, *Southeast Asia in the New World Order*. New York: St Martins Press, 1996.

Lor Chandara, 'CPP, Funcinpec Ink Accord', *The Cambodia Daily*, 25 May 2001.

————, 'Funcinpec You Hockry No Longer an Issue', *The Cambodia Daily*, 26 August 2002.

————, 'Key F'pec Official to Leave Politics for NGO', *The Cambodia Daily*, 10 October 2002.

Lor Chandara and Kevin Doyle, 'Ranariddh Drops Demand on Riot Explanation', *The Cambodia Daily*, 14 February 2003.

Lor Chandara and Stew Magnuson. 'Protesters Dig In at "Democracy Square"', *The Cambodia Daily*, 27 August 1998.

Luco, Fabienne, 'Between a Tiger and a Crocodile: Management of Local Conflicts in Cambodia. An Anthropological Approach to Traditional and New Practices'. Phnom Penh, UNESCO, 2002.

McPhillips, Jody, 'Sam Rainsy Says He Will Accept Results if Observers Do', *The Cambodia Daily*, 5 February 2002.

Magistad, Mary Kay, 'Court builds Ranariddh's case', *Phnom Penh Post*, October 1997.

Magnuson, Stew and Pin Sisavann. 'Rainsy, Interior Trade Accusations', *The Cambodia Daily*, 22 August 1998.

Marcher, Anette. 'Rights groups face prosecution'. Human Rights Watch 2000 Cambodia Report, 1 September 2000. Available online at http://www.hrw.org/wr2k1/asia/cambodia.html. Accessed June 2013.

Meas Sokchea, 'We're no Funcinpec', *Phnom Penh Post*, 21 April 2015.

Meas Sockchea and Daniel Pye, 'CNRP's Sunday "tsunami"', *Phnom Penh Post*, 22 December 2013.

Meas Sokchea, Cheeang Sokha and Shane Worrell, 'Election Results Rejected', *Phnom Penh Post*, 30 July 2013.

Meas Sokchea and Sebastian Strangio, 'Sam Rainsy sentenced in absentia', *Phnom Penh Post*, 28 January 2010.

Mech Dara, 'Ministry Warns of Punishment For Political Activity in Schools', *The Cambodia Daily*, 12 August 2015.

Mech Dara and Shaun Turton, 'CNRP reacts Manet's recruitment drive', *Phnom Penh Post*, 19 January 2016.

Mech Dara and Alex Willemyns, 'Sam Rainsy Seeking Deal Before Return', *The Cambodia Daily*, 19 November 2015.

Meisburger, Tim, 'Summary of Observations of the US Long term Observer Group (LTOG) During the 2003 Cambodian Elections', September 2003. Document in Author's possession.

'Memorandum of Understanding between the United Nations and the Royal Government of Cambodia on the International Electoral Observers'. Copy of the text, 14 April 1998. Document in Author's possession

Meyn, Colin, 'Will Hun Sen's Threat of War Translate into Votes?', *The Cambodia Daily*, 27 June 2013.

Meyn, Colin and Phorn Bopha, 'US Rebukes Government's Expulsion of the Opposition', *The Cambodia Daily*, 10 June 2013.

Milne, S., 'Cambodia's Unofficial Regime of Extraction: Illicit Logging in the Shadow of International Governance', *Critical Asian Studies*, Vol. 47, No 2, 2015, pp. 200–28.

Milne, S. and S. Mahanty (eds), *Conservation and Development in Cambodia: Exploring frontiers of change in nature, state and society*. London: Routledge, 2015

Milne, S., K. Pak and M. Sullivan, 'Shackled to nature? The post-conflict state and its symbiotic relationship with natural resources', in S. Milne and S. Mahanty (eds), *Conservation and Development in Cambodia: Exploring frontiers of change in nature, state and society*. London: Routledge, 2015.

Moorthy, Elizabeth, 'Robinson content with "full and frank discussion', *Phnom Penh Post*, 30 January 1998.

Moorthy, Elizabeth and Jason Barber, 'Exiles vow no return yet', *Phnom Penh Post*, August 1997.

Myers, Bill, 'Two Large Election Donors Stay Out Of Debate', *The Cambodia Daily*, 16 August 2002.

National Democratic Institute for International Affairs (NDI), 'The July 26, 1998 Cambodian National Assembly Elections', Phnom Penh, 1998.

———, 'The 2002 Cambodian Commune Council Elections', Phnom Penh, 20 March 2002.

———, 'Pre-election Delegation to Cambodia's 2003 National Assembly Elections', Phnom Penh, 5 June 2003. Available online at. https://www.ndi.org/files/1594_kh_statement_060503.pdf. Accessed June 2013.

———, 'Report of the Voter Registration Audit (VRA) in Cambodia', Phnom Penh, 2013.

Neou, Kassie, with Jeffrey C. Gallup, 'Conducting Cambodia's Elections'. *Journal of Democracy*, Vol. 10, No. 2, April 1999, pp. 153–64.

Neou Vannarin, 'Hun Sen Says CPP Largess Will End if Election Is Lost', *The Cambodia Daily*, 7 March 2013.

Neou Vannarin and Peter Zsombor, 'Hun Sen Defends His Decision to Break the Law', *The Cambodia Daily*, 20 June 2013.

Ouch Sony and Taylor O'Connell, 'Student Gets 18 Months for Call for "Color Revolution"', *The Cambodia Daily*, 16 March 2016.

Pape, Eric, 'I believe we will be killed one by one', *Phnom Penh Post*, 27 March 1998.

———, 'Will voters agree to bite the bullet'? *Phnom Penh Post*, 22 May 1998

————, 'CPP master plan for poll victory', *Phnom Penh Post*, 5 June 1998.

————, 'Hun Sen, King combine to convene council', *Phnom Penh Post*, 7/12, 19 June–2 July 1998.

Palmer, N.D., *Elections and Political Development: The South Asia Experience.* London: C. Hurst, 1975.

Pech Sotheary, 'Hun Sen warns Facebook users that he's watching', *Phnom Penh Post*, 29 December 2015.

Peou, Sorpong, 'Diplomatic pragmatism: ASEAN's response to the Julky 1997 coup', 1998. Available online at http://www.c-r.org/accord-article/diplomatic-pragmatism-aseans-response-july-1997-coup. Accessed June 2013.

————, *Intervention and Change in Cambodia? Towards Democracy?* Chiang Mai: Silkworm Books and Singapore: Institute of Southeast Asian Studies, 2000.

Pin Sisovann and Matt Reed, 'Assembly Allows Opposition to Join NEC', *The Cambodia Daily*, 28 July 2001.

Ponniah, Kevin, 'Hun Many opens up to criticism', *Phnom Penh Post*, 11 June 2014.

Post Staff, 'Hun Sen: Exhorting the Party', *Phnom Penh Post*, July 1996.

————, 'A Hint of Hope for Elections', *Phnom Penh Post*, April 1997.

————, 'Funcinpec Renegade backed by Hun Sen', *Phnom Penh Post*, April 1997.

————, 'Elections Debate: What's the alternative?' *Phnom Penh Post*, 12 September 1997.

————, 'Kevin's views labelled "regrettable"', *Phnom Penh Post*, October 1997.

————, 'Buying your way into democracy – NEC bribes alleged', *Phnom Penh Post*, 2 January 1998.

————, 'UN rights envoy appeals for end to VN bashing', *Phnom Penh Post*, 17 July 1998.

————, 'Hun Sen gives new cabinet its tasks', *Phnom Penh Post*, Issue 7/27, 11–24 December 1998.

————, 'Inside Funcinpec: Cracks Apparent', *Phnom Penh Post*, 30 April 1999.

————, 'Striking workers shot', *Phnom Penh Post*, June 23-July 6, 2000.

————, 'Mobs go berserk in anti-Thai frenzy Thai embassy torched; businesses gutted', *Phnom Penh Post*, 31 January 2003.

————, 'Hambali was here', *Phnom Penh Post*, 29 August 2003.

————, 'Ranariddh returns, vows loyalty to govt', *Phnom Penh Post*, 29 September 2008.

Post Staff and Reuters, 'Asean backs off as Hun Sen digs in', *Phnom Penh Post*, July 1997.

————, 'King dangles abdication card', *Phnom Penh Post*, 29 August 1997.

Poynton, Dan and Sam Rith, 'Another widow for the union movement', *Phnom Penh Post*, 9 March 2007.

Radio Free Asia, 'Journalist's Case Raised by Obama', 27 November 2012.

Available online at http://www.rfa.org/english/news/cambodia/journal-ist-11272012165221.html. Accessed July

———— , 'Hun Sen's Cambodia Names Son Head of Military's Intelligence Department', 22 October 2015. Available online at http://www.rfa.org/english/news/cambodia/appointment-10222015170944.html. Accessed January 2016.

Reuters, 'World Bank stops funding for Cambodia over evictions', Phnom Penh, 9 August 2011.

Reynolds, Luke and Lor Chandara, 'Rainsy Leaves Country After King's Abdication', *The Cambodia Daily*, 9 October 2004.

Reynolds, Luke and Yim Samean, 'Parties Band Together Against CPP results', *The Cambodia Daily*, 30 July 2003.

Rizzi, Claudia and Nick Lenaghan, 'F'pec "remembers the resistance" in congress date', *Phnom Penh Post*, January 1996.

Roberts, David W., *Political Transition in Cambodia 1991–99: Power, Elitism and Democracy*. Richmond: Curzon Press, 2001.

Roome, P., 'Assistance to the Ministry of Interior on Basic Legislation for Decentralised Commune Councils with the support of United Nations Capital Development Fund'. Project CMB/97/C01, December 1998.

Royal Government of Cambodia and United Nations Development Programme, 'Strengthening Democracy and Electoral Processes in Cambodia'. January 2006. Available online at http://loy9.com.kh/wp-content/uploads/2014/01/A-project-on-strengthening-democracy.pdf. Accessed July 2013.

Saito, Mhari, 'Commune Election Law Sent Back for Changes', *The Cambodia Daily*, 24 November 1998.

Sam Rainsy Party Statement, 'Linders One Percent Solution'. Phnom Penh, 4 August 1998.

Samreth Sopha and Elizabeth Moorthy, 'Funcinpec relies on royalty, anti-VN rhetoric', *Phnom Penh Post*, 17 July 1998.

Saing Chan Hang. 'Binding Constraints on Economic Growth in Cambodia: A Growth Diagnostics Approach'. Cambodian Development Resource Institute (CDRI), Working Paper Series, No. 80, Phnom Penh, 2013.

Saing Soenthrith, '200 Garment Workers Protest Low Wages Forced Overtime', *The Cambodia Daily*, 13 May 1998.

Saing Soenthrith and Kay Kimsong, 'Region Needs To Fight Terrorism, Sar Kheng Says', *The Cambodia Daily*, 29 May 2002.

Saing Soenthrith and Teth Sambath, 'Senior Advisor to Ranariddh Shot, Killed', *The Cambodia Daily*, 19 February 2003.

Samnang Ham, 'Date of Commune Elections Moved to Feb 3', *The Cambodia Daily*, 23 March 2001.

Schumpeter, J.A., *Capitalism, Socialism, and Democracy*. London: Unwin University Books, 1952.

Schedler, Andreas, (ed.), *Electoral Authoritarianism: The Dynamics of Unfree Competition.* Boulder: Lynne Rienner, 2006.

Scroggins, Hurley, 'Moves to get Pol Pot in the dock', *Phnom Penh Post,* June 1997.

Slocombe, Margaret, *The People's Republic of Kampuchea 1979–1989.* Chiang Mai: Silkworm Books, 2003.

Smith, Jeff, 'EU Say Wait on Final Verdict for Credible Poll', *The Cambodia Daily,* 30 July 1998.

Sok Pov, 'Factional Fighting Jolts the Northwest', *Phnom Penh Post,* March 1997.

Stephens, Sarah, 'Government agrees to quarterly aid review meetings', *Phnom Penh Post,* 5–18 March 1999.

———, 'UN rep causes upset at CG meet', *Phnom Penh Post,* 25 June–8 July 1999.

Sullivan, M., 'China's aid to Cambodia', in C. Hughes and K. Un (eds), *Cambodia's Economic Transformation.* Copenhagen: NIAS Press, 2011.

Taylor, Robert H. (ed.). *The Politics of Elections in Southeast Asia.* Washington D.C.: Woodrow Wilson Center Press and Cambridge University Press, 1996.

Thayer, Nate, 'Last Act: Sihanouk's Plan to Retake the Reins of Power', *Far Eastern Economic Review,* 23 June 1994.

———, 'Secret talks led to final purge', *Phnom Penh Post,* August 1997.

Thet Sambath, 'Funcinpec Divided over Possible Return of '97 Renegades', *The Cambodia Daily,* 8 March 2000.

———, 'Security Stepped Up Ahead of Voter Registration Period', *The Cambodia Daily,* 10 December 2002.

The Cambodia Daily and News Services, 'Hun Sen Holds Surprise Meeting With King', *The Cambodia Daily,* 9 June 1998.

Titthara, May and David Boyle, 'Environmental Activist Chut Wutty Shot Dead', *Phnom Penh Post,* 26 April 2012.

Titthara, May and Stuart White, 'A year after trial, still free', *Phnom Penh Post,* 27 February 2014.

Un, K. 'Cambodia's 2008 election: end of opposition?' *Open Democracy,* 5 August 2008. Available online at http://www.opendemocracy.net/article/cambodia-s-2008-elections-the-end-of-opposition. Accessed June 2014.

UNCOHCHR (United Nations Cambodia Office of the High Commissioner for Human Rights), Copy of the speech delivered by H.E. Sar Kheng, Acting Co-Prime Minister, Deputy Prime Minister, and Co-Minister of Interior in the closing ceremony of the seminar on 'Election Systems and Preparations', 25 October 1995.

———, Legal Assistance Unit Memorandum 'Election Seminar and Related Events', 1 November 1995.

————, Note for the File: Harassment and Intimidation of Members of the FUNCINPEC Party, 27 June 1996.

————, Legal Assistance Unit. Confidential Memorandum. Briefing note on the Preparation of Elections in Cambodia. 23 February. Phnom Penh, 1997.

————, United Nations Cambodia Office for Human Rights. Memorandum. Election Donor Meeting at UNDP, 5 June 1997.

————, 'Media and the Elections: Updated Statistics'. 23 July 1998.

————, Report of the Special Representative of the Secretary General for Human Rights in Cambodia, Mr. Peter Leuprecht. E/CN.4/2001/103, 24 January 2001.

————, 'The 2003 National Assembly Elections', December 2003.

UNDP (United Nations Development Programme). Note to the File. Elections Coordination Meeting of the 2nd April 1997. UNDP Service Center, Phnom Penh, 10 April 1997.

————, Copy of minutes of UNDP 5th and 6th Elections Coordination Meetings, 11 May 1997.

————, Election Coordination Meeting. Note to the File. UNDP Service Centre, Phnom Penh, 26 June.1997.

————, Note to the File on the Occasion of the adhoc Elections Coordination Meeting for Donors, 22 August 1997.

————, Note to the file. 9th Elections Coordinating Meeting. UNDP Service Centre, 30 December 1997

————, 9th Election Coordination Meeting. UNDP Service Center, 6 February 1998.

————, Note to the file. 12th Election Coordination Meeting. UNDP Service Center, Phnom Penh, 20 March 1998.

————, 'Report on the Elections of the Commune Councils', Cambodia, March 2002.

————, 'Report on the Elections of the Commune Councils'. Phnom Penh, March 2002.

————, 'Cambodia Annual Report 2003', Phnom Penh, 2003.

UNDP in Cambodia. Available online at http://www.kh.undp.org/content/cambodia/en/home.html. Accessed June 2014.

UNDP Country Team. Situational Analysis of Youth in Cambodia. Phnom Penh, May 2009.

UNDP Open trust fund, 'Report to Donors on their contribution to the 1998 Cambodia Elections through the 28 December', Phnom Penh, 1998.

UNEAS (United Nations Electoral Assistance Secretariat), First meeting of the Joint International Observer Group (JIOG), Phnom Penh, 1 June 1998.

————, Weekly Report 23–29 June. Phnom Penh, 30 June 1998.

———— , Joint International Observer Group (JIOG) Press Release. Phnom Penh, 27 July 1998.

UNOHCHRC (Cambodian Office of the United Nations Centre for Human Rights), Memorandum to the Royal Cambodian Government. Evidence of Summary Executions, Torture and Missing Persons Since 2–7 July 1997, 21 August 1997.

———— , The Human Rights situation in Cambodia: Note on apparent instances of politically motivated violence and intimidation, prepared by the Cambodian Office of the High Commissioner for Human Rights, May 20–June 15, 1998.

———— , Cambodia Office of the High Commissioner for Human Rights. Fortnightly report, June 1–June 18, 1998.

———— , Monitoring of Intimidation and Violence, Report 10–17 July, 1998.

———— , 'Commune Councils Elections 2002'.

———— , Report of UN Secretary General's Special Representative for Human Rights in Cambodia. A/57/230. 27 September 2002.

UNOSGRC (Office of the UN Secretary-General's Representative in Cambodia). 0311. Monthly Report for April. From Paris to Takhmau by FAX. CPY 049. 1996.

———— , 0311. CPY 049. Secretary General's Special Representative. Monthly Report for April 1996.

———— , United Nations Secretary General's Special Representative reports 0311, CPY 049 April 1996, and 0397 CPY 064, May 1996.

———— , Secretary General's Special Representative Monthly Report for May 1996. 'Ranariddh Responds'. 31 May 1996. UNOSGRC0397. CPY 064. 1996.

———— , Preparations for the Elections. Cryptofax CPY 102. Phnom Penh, 4 September 1996.

———— , OO125. Crypto Fax CPY025. Minutes of meetings held during Mr. Vendrell's visit to Cambodia 23 February–26 February 1997, Part I. Phnom Penh, 4 March 1997.

———— , Weekly Report 102 covering the period from 19 to 25 August 1996. UNOSGRC0645. CPY 097. 1996.

———— , Report of the Secretary-General of Human Rights in Cambodia. A/52/489. 17 October 1998. Copy of letter from Hun Sen and Ung Huot to United Nations Secretary General, Kofi Annan. Phnom Penh, 13 April 1998.

———— , Comments on the Phnom Penh Response 13 April to SG's letter re UN Co-ordination of Observers'. Thomas Hammarberg. Phnom Penh, 15 April 1998.

———— , Copy of letter from The Special Representative of the United Nations Secretary General for Human Rights, Thomas Hammarberg to the United Nations Department of Political Affairs Assistant Secretary General, Alvaro de Soto, 15 April 1998.

———, Meeting of the Informal Group of Ambassadors on Cambodian Elections. UNOSGPRC 0701. CPY 21227, May 1998.

———, Office of the Secretary General's Personal Representative Cambodia report: UN Assessment Meeting. 5 June 1998. UNOSGPRC 0750. CPY 222.

———, Secretary General's Personal Representative, Lakhan Mehrotra. Report: Friends of Cambodia – 20 June. CPY 240. 22 June 1998.

———, 'Special Representative of the United Nations Secretary-General for Human Rights in Cambodia appeals calls for a new review of the media situation', 25 June 1998.

———, Special Representative of the Secretary General for Human Rights in Cambodia. 'Commune Councils Elections 2002. Media and Freedom of Expression', 2002.

United Nations, Report of the Secretary-General on the Implementation of Security Council Resolution 792 (1992). S/25289, Electoral Matters, paragraph 33, 13 February 1993.

———, Fourth progress report of the Secretary-General, 3 May 1993.

———, Secretary General Representative in Cambodia. Monthly Assessment Report for the month of March 1995. UNSGRC1051.

———, UN General Assembly Document A/50/332. III. Electoral Assistance, August 1995. Available at http://www.un.org/Depts/dpa/ead/ea_content/ea_types_of_assist.htm. Accessed April 2013.

———, HQS New York. Outgoing Code Cable CYP 029 P2/9. To: B. Widyono, SGRC, Phnom Penh. From: M. Goulding United Nations. Date: 26 June. Number 1809. Subject Vendrell's Report. 1996.

———, Report on Francesc Vendrell, Director of the United Nations Department of Political Affairs, Asia and the Pacific Division visit to Cambodia: 10–13 June 1996. Outgoing Code Cable 1809. United Nations, HQS, New York. 26 June 1996.

———, Correspondence between UNDPA and UNSGRC. 'Response to RGC's request for technical electoral assistance', CYP-32. 11 April 1998.

———, Secretary General's Special representative: Monthly Report for January 1997. UNOSGRC 0069. CPY 014.

———, Report of the Secretary-General. Situation of Human Rights in Cambodia. A/52/489. 17 October 1997. 39–56. 41.

———, Secretary General's Special Representative for Human Rights. Text of correspondence from Thomas Hammarburg to UN Secretary General's Special Personal Representative Lakhan Mehrotra. Comments on the Phnom Penh Response 13 April to SG's letter re UN co-ordination of observers. 15 April 1998.

———, USG/DPA New York. Subject: Meeting of the Informal Group of Ambassadors on Cambodian Elections. 27 May 1998.

———, UNOSGPRC 0750.Cryptofax.CPY 222. From Lakhan Mehrotra

UNOSGPRC to Kieran Prendergast USG/DPA New York. Subject: UN Assessment meeting. 5 June 1998.

———, UNOSGPRC 0701. Cryptofax. CPY212. From Lakhan Mehrotra UNSGPRC to Sir Kieran ———, Outgoing cable to Mehrotra, SGPRC, Phnom Penh from Prendergast, United Nations, New York. Briefing to the Security Council. 1447. CYP 102. 14 July 1998.

———, Special Representative of the United Nations Secretary-General for Human Rights in Cambodia Monitoring of Intimidation and Violence, Report 10–17 July 1998.

———, Situation of human rights in Cambodia. Report of the Secretary-General. A/53/400, 17 September 1998, 42–67.

———, Letter dated 22 October from His Excellency Mr. Ung Huot and His Excellency Samdech Hun Sen addressed to the UN Secretary-General, document S/1997/998, Annex I, 1998.

———, Situation of Human Rights in Cambodia. Report of the Special Representative of the Secretary-General for Human Rights in Cambodia, Mr Thomas Hammarberg. E/CN.4/1999/101, 26 February 1999.

———, Report of the Special Representative of the Secretary General for Human Rights in Cambodia, Yash Gai. E/CN/4/2006/110/add.1, 8 March 2006.

———, General Assembly, Human Rights Council Report of the Special Rapporteur on the Situation of Human Rights in Cambodia, A/HRC/21/63. 16 July 2012.

———, Cambodia-UNTAC. Available at http://www.un.org/en/peacekeeping/missions/past/untacbackgr2.html#three . Accessed April 2013.

———, Report of the Special Rapporteur on the Situation of Human Rights in Cambodia, Surya, P. Subedi. A Human Rights Analysis of economic and other land concessions in Cambodia. September 2012.

US Department of State. Report to the Congress on the Anti-Thai Riots in Cambodia on January 29, 2003, 14 May 2003. Available online at. http://2001-2009.state.gov/p/eap/rls/rpt/20565.htm. Accessed June 2013.

UNTAC (United Nations Transitional Authority in Cambodia), 1157. Preparations for Elections and Reporting. Crypto Fax to: Akashi, UNTAC, Phnom Penh. From Annan, United Nations New York, Number. Subject: CYP 189, March 1992

———, Information/Education Division. *Digest and Analysis of the Cambodian News Media: Party of Democratic Kampuchea*, 23 April 1992.

———, Information/Education Division. *State of Cambodia News Broadcast Media*. 22–29 July. CPP Extraordinary Party Congress 27–29 July, Full Digest, 1992.

———, Control Team Report. Secret Memorandum, Cabinet of the Council of Ministers (COM), No. 1909, 17 October 1992, Prey Veng Appendix, Phnom Penh, 1992.

————— , Statement by Mr. Akashi, Special Representative of the Secretary-General for Cambodia. Establishment of a Neutral Political Environment, 19 November 1992.

————— , Information/Education Division. Field Trip Report: Phnom Penh, 7–12 January 1993.

————— , Information/Education Division. Analysis Reports 1/930 Criticisms of UNTAC by Hun Sen, Chakrapong, Sihanouk. January 1993.

————— , Information/Education Division. Analysis Report. Assessment of Popular Support for Political Parties, 8 January 1993.

————— , Information/Education Division. Summary of Press Conference by the Special Representative of the Secretary-General for Cambodia, Mr Yasushi Akashi. Phnom Penh, 11 January 1993.

————— , Information/Education Division. Digest and Analysis of SoC Print Media. Full Report, 6–23 February. 1993.

————— , Electoral Component. Civic Education Training and Material, 19 February 1993.

————— , Preparations for Elections and Reporting. Crypto Fax to: Akashi, Phnom Penh, from Annan,

————— , Free Choice Electoral Component Newsletter. Civic Education Sweeps Cambodia's Provinces . Issue No. 16, March 1993.

————— , Information/Education Division. Report on Political Intimidation in Battambang. 19 March 1993.

————— , Control Team: Transcript of Meeting between Hun Sen and SRSG Akashi. Monday 22 March, Council of Ministers. Phnom Penh, 25 March 1993.

————— , Information/Education Division. Information Control Report. Interview with Norodom Ranariddh on FUNCINPEC Radio, 26 March 1993.

————— , Free Choice Electoral Component Newsletter. Interview with Tim Carney (Director of UNTAC Education and Information Division). Issue No.16, 26 March 1993.

————— , UN Secretary Generals' Address to the Staff of UNTAC. Phnom Penh, 8 April 1993.

————— , The Control Team. 'Deputy Special Representative of the Secretary General. Profile. 16 April 1993.

————— , Information/Education Division. Analysis Report. Defection of FUNCINPEC/ANKI Figures to SoC/CPP 24 April. 1993.

————— , UN Special Representative Yasushi Akashi's letter of response to Chea Sim, President Cambodia People's Party. Phnom Penh, 9 June 1993.

————— , Information/Education Division. Notable Reports in the Cambodian Media. 23 May to 5 June 1993. Analysis/Assessment Unit. 18 June 1993.

————— , Austin, R.H.F. UNTAC Interoffice Memorandum. CPP Electoral Complaints. Phnom Penh, 21 June 1993.

————— , 'Report of the Special Representative's Electoral Advisory Committee.

Phnom Penh, 23 September 1993.

Vachon, Michelle, 'Donor Meeting Looks at Wide Range of Reforms', *The Cambodia Daily*, 16 January 2002.

Vong Sokheng and Shane Worrall, 'Civil servants to see raise', *Phnom Penh Post*, 8 August 2013.

Watkin, Huw, 'Experts recommend local elections be postponed', *Phnom Penh Post*, 6–19 September 1996.

——— , 'Tony Kevin: Captives, Cables and Non-Coups', *Phnom Penh Post*, October 1997.

Willemyns, Alex, 'Gareth Evans Calls For Sanctions on Government', *The Cambodia Daily*, 28 February 2014.

——— , 'Aid threatened as EU calls for Rainsy's return', *Phnom Penh Post*, 27 November 2015.

Willemyns, Alex and Mech Dara, 'CNRP to Order Lawmakers Silent on VN Border Issue', *The Cambodia Daily*, 14 September 2015.

Widyono, Benny, *Dancing in Shadows: Sihanouk, The Khmer Rouge, and The United Nations in Cambodia*. Lanham: Rowman & Littlefield, 2008.

Woods, Ben and Eang Mengleng, 'CNRP Proposes Minimum Wage, Law for Garment State Workers', *The Cambodia Daily*, 1 March 2013.

Woodsome, Kate, 'Coalition of Unions Cancels Planned Strike', *The Cambodia Daily*, 12 February 2003.

World Bank, 'Cambodia at the Crossroads: Strengthening Accountability to Reduce Poverty'. Phnom Penh, 2004.

——— , 'Cambodia's Sustaining Rapid Economic Growth in a Challenging Environment'. Report No 49156-KH, January 2009.

——— , 'Statement on Termination by Royal Government of Cambodia of the Land Management and Administration Project', 6 September 2009. Available online at http://web.worldbank.org/WBSITE/EXTERNAL/ COUNTRIES/EASTASIAPACIFICEXT/CAMBODIAEXTN/0, ,contentMDK:22303344~menuPK:293861~pagePK:1497618~piP-K:217854~theSitePK:293856,00.html. Accessed July 2014.

——— , 'A Country Study ACS4545. Where Have All the Poor Gone? Cambodia Poverty Assessment', November 2013.

——— , 'The Fight Against Corruption'. Available online at Accessed 13 May 2014.

Yun Samean, 'Comfrel Unveils Plan for Reforming NEC', *The Cambodia Daily*, 14 August 2002.

——— , 'Beehive Radio Founder Mulls Reviving His Dormant Party', *The Cambodia Daily*, 26 November 2002.

——— , 'Gov't Returns Plane Once Owned by Ranariddh', *The Cambodia Daily*, 12 July 2004.

——— , 'PM Attacks Funcinpec in Speech', *The Cambodia Daily*, 15 February 2006.

———— , '50-Plus-One' Amendment is Approved', *The Cambodia Daily*, 3 March 2006.

———— , 'SRP, HRP Brokering New Alliance in Assembly', *The Cambodia Daily*, 30 September 2009.

Yun Samean and Lor Chandara, 'Hun Sen Says Some Are Trying to Buy Positions'. *The Cambodia Daily*, 18 May 2004.

Yun Samean and Whitney Kvsanger, 'Assembly Expands Use of "50-Plus-One" Formula', *The Cambodia Daily*, 16 March 2006.

Yun Samean and Samantha Melamed, 'CPP, Rainsy Want Electoral Rule Change', *The Cambodia Daily*, 14 February 2006.

Index

bold=extended discussion or other significant mention;
n=footnote